NYERERE AND AFRICA:

END OF AN ERA

Biography of
Julius Kambarage Nyerere (1922-1999)
President of Tanzania

GODFREY MWAKIKAGILE

D1714098

Protea Publishing

Nyerere And Africa: End Of An Era. Biography of Julius
Kambarage Nyerere (1922-1999) President of Tanzania
Godfrey Mwakikagile

First Edition Worldwide

ISBN 1-931768-74-9   soft cover

ISBN 1-931768-75-7   hardcover

Protea Publishing. USA

email: kaolink@msn.com

web site: www.proteapublishing.com

CONTENTS

ACKNOWLEDGMENTS

I AM deeply grateful to many individuals and institutions who have served as a source of some of the material I have used to write this book. While the analysis is mine, and a lot of the information I have used is also mine since I am the primary source because of my first-hand knowledge of Tanzania and Africa as a whole; I must also acknowledge that my work would not have been completed without the secondary sources I have cited to fortify my thesis.

Space does not permit me to name all those whose works have provided documentary evidence to support my analysis. They include writers and publishers, professors and academic institutions, politicians and journalists, as well as ordinary people without whom leaders are nothing. I must, however, make special mention of the following:

Colin Legum of *Africa Contemporary Record*; Professor Ali A. Mazrui, director of the Institute of Global Cultural Studies at the State University of New York, Binghamton, and former chairman of the political science department and dean of the faculty of arts and social sciences at Makerere University, Kampala, Uganda, and director of the Center for Afro-American and African Studies at the University of Michigan, among other positions; Hackman Owusu-Agyemang, Ghanaian member of parliament, later minister of foreign affairs under President John Kufuor; Professor Adam Hochschild, University of California, Berkeley; Professor Ronald Aminzade, sociology department, University of Minnesota; Professor Haroub Othman, Institute of Development Studies, University of Dar es Salaam, Tanzania; Ann Talbot of the International Committee of the Fourth Internationale, London; Jorge Castaneda, author of *Companero: The Life and Death of Che Guevara*; Gamal Nkrumah, columnist and editorial writer, *Al-Ahram*, Cairo, Egypt; Samir Amin, economist, author, and director of Forum du Tiers Monde, Dakar, Senegal; Ikaweba Bunting of the Mwalimu Nyerere Foundation, Dar es Salaam, Tanzania; Sam G. Amoo, a specialist in conflict resolution, United

Nations Development Programme (UNDP), New York; David Martin, news and deputy managing editor, the *Standard* Tanzania; the South Centre, Geneva, Switzerland, and many other individuals and institutions.

Their special contribution is evident throughout the book. But I am equally indebted to the rest. That I have not named them here does not, in any way, diminish their contribution to the successful completion of my work. They have been given full attribution in this study I undertook fully aware of its immense scope. I would not have been able to complete it without the vital information I obtained from secondary sources and which I used in my analysis.

And to the people of Tanganyika, later Tanzania, who gave Julius Nyerere to Africa and to the world, special acknowledgment must be made to them for making his leadership possible. Without them, Africa - let alone the rest of the world - would probably not even have heard of Nyerere, except as a distinguished academic as he probably would have been, had he continued to teach instead of becoming a politician. They provided the stage on which he demonstrated his qualities as a leader of international stature, one of the few titans Africa - indeed the world - has produced in a span of centuries.

Equally important to the execution of this project is my publisher, without whom this book may not have been published when it was. But, like the rest of my works, it will have to be judged on its own merit by those who read it. They include members of the general public for whom it is also intended besides those in the academic community.

Although this work is partly biographical, that is not the main focus of my study. My emphasis is on Nyerere's policies in a Pan-African context and on his leadership in Tanzania and Africa as a whole. That is why I chose the title, *Nyerere and Africa: End of an Era*, the first and in fact the only one I came up with. I was satisfied with it right away and thought that it was comprehensive enough to cover every subject I have addressed in the book. But my publisher felt that it would also be appropriate to highlight the biographical aspect of my work - in fact an entire chapter is devoted to that - and added the subtitle, *Biography of Julius Kambarage Nyerere (1922 - 1999) President of Tanzania.*

Even if I wanted to, I would not have been able to handle the immense task of writing Nyerere's biography in a comprehensive way. That is a project which, to my knowledge, was undertaken by a team of three renowned and highly capable Tanzanians who had access to all the vital sources of information, including President Nyerere himself, needed to write such a book: former ambassador Ferdinand Ruhinda, editor of the *Daily News* in the seventies after I left the paper, and campaign manager for President Benjamin Mkapa, my former editor at the *Daily News* who helped me to go to school in the United States; Professor Haroub Othman; and Professor Ahmed Mohiddin. They were working on it when Nyerere died.

Although my publisher added the sub-title, I have had full control over the entire content of my work and even the main title itself. I have also edited and typed the entire book myself without my publisher's involvement or any other help. Therefore I am fully responsible for everything found in this humble analysis.

But, while I accept full responsibility for the mistakes, which may be found in my work in terms of facts and analysis, I must also acknowledge that writing this kind of book is a collective enterprise, not a singular effort by the author alone. We are mere mortals, with frailties, and are able to see far only because we stand on the shoulders of others. And the more we scan the horizon, the more we realize how little we know.

INTRODUCTION

JULIUS NYERERE was one of the most influential leaders in the twentieth century, and his death in October 1999 marked the end of a political career that spanned almost half a century. It also marked the end of an era of the African founding fathers who led their countries to independence in the sixties.

This work looks at some of the major policy initiatives and achievements by Nyerere, a leader whose humility and dedication led millions of ordinary people in Tanzania and elsewhere to identify with him, and pay him the highest tribute by simply saying, "He was one of us." There is probably no higher tribute, simple yet profound, to a man who earned great respect around the world, from the most humble to the most exalted, including his enemies. A towering intellectual, and a paragon of virtue, he had profound insight and highly analytical skills and knew exactly what he wanted to do for Tanzania and for Africa as a whole. Yet he was not without fault, and admitted his mistakes, unlike most leaders who see that as a sign of weakness and not an attribute of leadership.

The book is also a telescopic survey of the major events that have taken place across the continent during the post-colonial period. Included are events in which President Nyerere played a critical role, influencing the course of African history. It is also a study of the modern African state under the one-party system and how its foundation was laid in the sixties, Africa's decade of euphoria marking the end of colonial rule.

My role in this undertaking is not one of an entirely disinterested observer. I was born and brought up in Tanganyika, now Tanzania. I also lived and grew up under Nyerere. Yet, because of that, I bring to this study a perspective many people who could have undertaken the same project, don't have, if they were not born and reared in Tanzania and did not live under Nyerere. But in spite of this, my analysis of the events in Tanzania, and elsewhere across the continent in which Nyerere played a major and sometimes the most prominent role, is not in any way distorted by bias, compromising scholarship. And as a former news reporter in Tanzania when Nyerere was president, I was in a position to evaluate events objectively in the same way I have in this work; true to my conviction, shared by others, that dispassionate analysis should be the guiding principle in scholarly pursuits and other works for the sake of truth.

The analytical context I have used from a Pan-African perspective to address some of the major themes in this work underscores one fundamental reality about Africa: the continent is littered with non-viable political entities we call independent countries; most of them failed states or on the verge of collapse. Therefore the call for regional integration, even for continental unification though a remote possibility, is not a mere academic exercise but a matter of sheer survival. The state is still the basic unit in the international system, and may not be entirely replaced. But many of its functions are being assumed by regional bodies at the macro-national level, and even on a continental scale as in Europe where they have a functional Pan-European entity, the European Union (EU), with a common currency, a common parliament and other integrated institutions.

Africa has simply failed to unite, with tragic consequences, as was clearly demonstrated in the Congo and in Rhodesia in the sixties when a united response - in the practical sense, with troops under a Pan-African high command as urged by Kwame Nkrumah and Julius Nyerere - could have made a difference. Rwanda was another tragic failure, as was Somalia, Sierra Leone, Liberia, Mozambique, the Congo again, and many others. Through the decades, the Organization of African Unity (OAU) - replaced by the African Union (AU) in June 2001 but which was not formally launched until July 2002 - was no more than a prestigious debating club for Africa's tin-pot dictators. Nyerere dismissed it in the seventies as nothing but "a trade union of tyrants." And he worked relentlessly throughout his political career to achieve African unity, culminating in the unification of Tanganyika and Zanzibar in 1964; a union he engineered, and the only one of independent states that has ever been formed on the continent.

While I have ended this study with a chapter from a personal perspective, reflecting on Tanzania and on the leadership of Julius Nyerere, I have done so only to the extent that my reflections help further illuminate the themes I have addressed in a book that may not do justice to one of the towering figures in history. As Professor Ali Mazrui described Nyerere: "In global terms, he was one of the giants of the 20th century.... He did bestride this narrow world like an African colossus."[1]

CHAPTER ONE:

ONE-PARTY SYSTEM AND NATIONAL UNITY: CONSOLIDATION OF THE NATION-STATE

SOON AFTER INDEPENDENCE, African countries faced the formidable task of nation-building, an undertaking which in most cases proved to be more difficult than the struggle for independence itself; except in a few countries where Africans had to resort to armed struggle to win their freedom.

But the Mau Mau phenomenon, if we may collectively call all the liberation wars, was not continental in scope, although it had the potential to develop into one if the colonial authorities continued to ignore the demands of Africans. In the majority of cases, the colonial rulers transferred power to the nationalist leaders on peaceful terms; not because they wanted to, but because that was better than the alternative. The prospect for mass insurrection in the colonies was real, and the colonial powers knew they would not have been able to contain it forever, as was clearly demonstrated in Angola, Mozambique, Guinea-Bissau, Zimbabwe, Namibia, and finally South Africa itself, the bastion of white minority rule on the continent.

But nation-building, which meant - and still means - economic development and modernization more than anything else, could not be done in countries which were not quite nations yet, although they identified themselves as such. It is true that Africans in the colonies fought for independence as one people. But that does not mean that they really considered themselves as one. As the premier of Northern Nigeria, Sir Ahmadu Bello, said during the Nigerian civil war (1967 - 1970), which threatened to split the country along ethnic lines:

> Politicians always delight in talking loosely about the unity of Nigeria. Sixty years ago there was no country called Nigeria. What is now Nigeria consisted of a number of large and small communities all of which were different in their outlooks and beliefs. The advent of British and Western

education has not materially altered the situation and these many and varied communities have not knit themselves into a complete unit.[1]

It is a sentiment that was echoed by the Northern Nigerian delegation to the Ad Hoc Conference on the Nigerian Constitution in Lagos in September 1966:

We have pretended for too long that there are no differences between the people of Nigeria. The hard fact which we must honestly accept as of permanent importance in the Nigerian experiment especially for the future is that we are different peoples brought together by recent accidents of history. To pretend otherwise will be folly.[2]

But it was not just the Northern Nigerians who felt this way. The leaders of all the three massive regions, which then constituted the Federation of Nigeria -formed in 1946 -, expressed the same sentiment, only in varying degrees. In the midst of the civil war itself, the Biafran leader Colonel Odumegwu Ojukwu made an impassioned plea before the Organization of African Unity (OAU) in Addis Ababa, Ethiopia, on August 5, 1968, for recognition of his secessionist region as an independent state on grounds of incompatibility:

The former Federation encompassed peoples of such vast political, economic, religious and cultural differences as could hardly ever have co-existed peacefully as one independent political entity.[3]

And as far back as 1947, the leader of Western Nigeria, Chief Obafemi Awolowo, stated in his book *Path to Nigerian Freedom*: "Nigeria is not a nation. It is a mere geographical expression. There are no Nigerians."[4] And in the 1950s, the decade preceding independence, Northern Nigerians talked seriously about pulling out of the federation and establishing their own independent state, as did Awolowo in 1953 when the British Colonial Secretary Oliver Lyttelton ruled that Lagos shall remain federal territory as capital of the federation. Awolowo wanted Lagos to be incorporated into the Western Region under his jurisdiction, since it was located in Western Nigeria, his tribal homeland of the Yoruba. When the British colonial secretary ruled against that at the constitutional talks on the future of Nigeria attended by all Nigerian leaders in London in August 1953,

Awolowo stormed out of the conference and threatened to pull the Western Region out of the federation. Only Eastern Nigeria did not threaten to secede. Ironically, it was also the first to secede, but only after it was compelled to do so by the massacres of tens of thousands of its people - 30,000 to 50,000 - in Northern Nigeria in 1966, and by the unwillingness of the northern and the federal authorities to intervene and stop the pogroms.

But such secessionist sentiments were not peculiar to Nigeria. The history of the former Belgian Congo during the turbulent sixties is well known when Katanga Province, led by Moise Tshombe, seceded only 11 days after Congo won independence on June 30, 1960. South Kasai Province, home of the Baluba tribe, also seceded in December 1961 under the leadership of Albert Kalonji who declared himself king of Kasai. And the remaining four provinces also tried to establish themselves as independent states in the early sixties.

In Ghana, the Ashanti were resolutely opposed to a unitary state established by Dr. Kwame Nkrumah, and made unsuccessful attempts to have a federal constitution, which would have enabled them to retain their independence through extensive devolution of power short of sovereign status. For centuries before the advent of colonial rule, Ashanti, also known as Asante, had existed as an independent nation ruled by the Asantehene (king). It was also one of the most powerful kingdoms in pre-colonial Africa before it was finally conquered by the British in one of the bloodiest wars in colonial history.

Uganda was also seriously threatened by the attempted secession of the Buganda kingdom. Like Ashanti, Buganda was also an independent nation before the imposition of colonial rule, and was ruled by a king known as kabaka in the local Kiganda language. Even after independence, the kingdom considered itself to be a separate nation. On May 20, 1966 almost four years after independence, the kingdom's parliament known as Lukiiko demanded Uganda's expulsion from Buganda by May 30 because it did not fully recognize the national government's jurisdiction over the kingdom. And it did not relent until Ugandan Prime Minister Milton Obote, in a swift military move, took over Kabaka Edward Frederick Mutesa's palace. The kabaka went into self-imposed exile in Britain where he continued to rail against

Ugandan authority over his kingdom. Other kingdoms in Uganda - Toro, Bunyoro, Ankole, and the princedom of Busoga - were also opposed to the national government. They considered themselves to be autonomous entities with their own political systems and institutions independent of central authority, as had been the case before the conquest of Africa and imposition of colonial rule by Europeans.

Zambia also had to contend with secessionist threats, especially by Barotse Province also known as Barotseland, ruled by its own king. Other provinces and different tribes were also embroiled in ethnoregional rivalries. But the greatest threat to national integrity came from Barotseland. However, they all posed great danger to national unity and, for a short period in February 1968, President Kenneth Kaunda resigned as head of state. As he put it, he was "upset by a terrible provincial and tribal approach to our national problems."[5]

It was true elsewhere across the continent, and such ethnoregional loyalties caused a lot of problems for the young nations, which had just won independence as "one people," yet had to contend with tribalism - hence secession in a number of cases - as the biggest threat to national unity. Compounding the problem was the fact that, contrary to what many people had expected, independence did not bring immediate relief to millions of Africans trapped in poverty and suffering from disease and ignorance; even decades after the end of colonial rule, millions across the continent have yet to enjoy the fruits of independence.

Such rising expectations only fueled resentment against central authority, as Africans grappled with the problems of nation-building with only scant resources in countries which are the poorest of the poor in the world. And they could not expect to survive as nations if they were structured along tribal lines. Therefore, even before nation-building could be seriously considered, every African country had to contend with another formidable task: forging a sense of common identity and loyalty to the nation composed of different tribes, many of which were suspicious and jealous of each other or one another, and sometimes outright hostile towards each other. So, tribes "had to go." They could no longer exist as autonomous entities for one simple reason. Tribalism is incompatible with nationalism, and nation-building is impossible without nationhood. And you can't have nationhood without a genuine feeling of common citizenship and identity which goes beyond saluting the same flag and traveling on the same passport.

Therefore, right from the beginning, consolidation of the nation-state - institutions of authority over national territory - went hand-in-hand with nation-building. One could not be given priority over the other, and the state could not be consolidated without containing or neutralizing tribalism. Tribalism was, and still is, a constant threat to the existence of African countries, almost all of which were artificially created during the partition of Africa by the European powers about 115 years ago at the Berlin Conference which lasted from November 1884 - February 1885. With the exception of the Arab countries in North Africa, and Somalia which is almost entirely composed of ethnic Somalis except for a small number of people from Bantu tribes in Kenya, Tanzania and Mozambique who were taken there as slaves by the Arabs during the slave trade, none of the countries on the continent are ethnically homogeneous entities. Even Botswana is not entirely Tswana, although it is about 98 percent. Nor is Swaziland entirely Swazi, although it is in overwhelming numbers in black Africa's last kingdom.

After the partition of Africa, the countries created were no more than a collection - not even an amalgamation - of different, often antagonistic, tribes just lumped together by the colonial powers to satisfy their imperial ambitions. The colonial boundaries were arbitrarily drawn without the slightest concern for the interests and well-being of Africans. All the tribes, not just some, saw themselves as independent entities or nations - even if held captive by other tribes - and would secede anytime if they got the chance to do so. Besides their skin color and hair texture, they saw themselves as different from each other, and the nation-state a mere imposition by alien intruders from Europe, thus making the task of nation-building a very complicated one. As Obafemi Awolowo said, the people who are called Nigerians - a collection of more than 250 different ethnic groups - are as different from each other as the people of different European countries are.[6]

But African countries have survived as political entities, despite the odds against them through the decades since independence. Therefore, just holding them together, preventing them from falling apart, is a great achievement even though they have survived as weak nations. But Africa would have been even weaker, much weaker, had the countries broken up along tribal lines, with each tribe ruling itself as was the case in pre-colonial times, except for conquered tribes which were ruled by others.

Yet African countries are not given credit for that. Keeping the tribes together is an enormous task even today. And maintaining the countries as functional units, where members of different tribes and races work together and even identify themselves as one people, is an even greater achievement, considering the fact that the disruptive forces inherent in such complex multi-ethnic societies are beyond the capacity of the state to contain them without using a skillful combination of persuasive and coercive power. There is no army that can stop all the tribes in a country from tearing it apart if they decide to go their own way. Only a few can be destructive enough, wreaking havoc nationwide.

Therefore in fairness, if African leaders are considered to be a failure in many areas, which they are, frankly speaking, they should at least be given credit for keeping their countries united and, in some cases, for creating a sense of common identity among different tribes within their national boundaries. As Julius Nyerere said many years after he stepped down as president of Tanzania, his greatest failure was that although he managed to unite Tanganyika and Zanzibar to create Tanzania in 1964, he was never able to persuade the leaders of neighboring countries to form a larger federation, a move he believed would have made the region a powerhouse:

> I felt that these little countries in Africa were really too small, they would not be viable - the Tanganyikas, the Rwandas, the Burundis, the Kenyas. My ambition in East Africa was really never to build a Tanganyika. I wanted an East African federation. So what did I do in succeeding? My success is building a nation out of this collection of tribes.[7]

He also went on to say: "A new leadership is developing in Africa.... The military phase is out. I think the single-party phase is out."[8]

A few years after independence, the one-party state was introduced in most African countries and justified by the leaders on the grounds that it was the most effective apparatus for mobilizing different tribes under one leadership to achieve national unity. And it proved to be a potent weapon, although in more than one way, including suffocation of legitimate dissent in most cases. But, in spite of its shortcomings, the one-party system did eliminate one danger which threatened practically all African countries during the early years of independence when peoples of different tribes did not identify with each other as one people: formation of political parties along ethnic and regional lines in the name of democracy under a multi-party system, despite constitutional bans against formation of such parties There would always have been ways to circumvent that, including formation of ethnoregional alliances to the exclusion of others.

That would have been the end of African countries. Besides Nkrumah, Nyerere was probably the most articulate exponent of the one-party state on the continent, and its most successful practitioner for two decades; Tanzania became a *de jure* one-party state in 1965, and Nyerere stepped down from the presidency in 1985, although he continued to be chairman of the ruling party (Chama Cha Mapinduzi - CCM - Party of the Revolution) until 1990, two years before multi-party politics was introduced with his full support. As he said in an interview not long before he died:

> I really think that I ran the most successful single-party system on the continent. You might not even call it a party. It was a single, huge nationalist movement.... I don't believe that our country would be where it is now if we had a multiplicity of parties, which would have become tribal and caused us a lot of problems. But when you govern for such a long time, unless you are gods, you become corrupt and bureaucratic.... So I started calling for a multiparty system.[9]

Few would say it would have better for African countries to have split up along tribal lines, plunging them into chaos and civil wars, than to have peace and unity under one-party rule that guaranteed their survival as nations even if that meant curtailed freedom, suffocating dissent. There was not one African country that was safe then, or is safe today, from the danger of tribalism. And that includes those composed of small tribes, such as Tanzania whose 126 tribes - except one or two - are too small, weak and poor to survive as viable entities even if they wanted to secede. But if tribalism is widespread, even small tribes can be just as disruptive. Aware of the danger of tribalism, President Nyerere addressed the subject in his annual radio broadcast to the nation on the seventh independence anniversary on December 9, 1968. He spoke in Kiswahili, the national language:

> I have begun to hear whispers about tribalism. Just after independence, we got complaints that people were being appointed to government positions on the basis of tribalism, and we immediately appointed a commission to look into the allegations. The commission proved without any doubt that there was no tribalism in the allocation of jobs in government.
>
> But just recently, I began to hear this complaint again. I did not treat it lightly. We called some of these people who were saying there is tribalism, and told them to give their evidence either to me or to Chief Mang'enya (the ombudsman). We promised to investigate immediately. But they have not given us one shred of evidence....
>
> Tanzanians who had the opportunity for higher education during colonial rule were mostly Wahaya, Wachaga, and Wanyakyusa. And because most of the education was provided by missionaries, most of these people are also Christians. And when we replace Europeans who hold responsible jobs, and give those jobs to Tanzanians, the people who get them come mostly from these three tribes. Therefore, if you ask me why Wahaya, Wachaga, and Wanyakyusa have most of the jobs, which require higher education, the answer is very obvious. They are the ones who got higher education during colonial times. I would say, look at the positions in politics, where a person is not asked about his educational qualifications. Look at Parliament, the National Executive, the Central Committee of TANU (ruling party), and at the Cabinet. How many Wanyakyusa, Wahaya, or Wachaga are members? You will find that perhaps there aren't any, or there is one or two....
>
> It is the job of the government to help, even favour, the more backward parts of the country, especially regarding education. We are doing this and will continue to do so. But if a Mchaga, a Mhaya or a Mnyakyusa young man were denied a job because of his tribe - when he is capable and there is no other Tanzanian with the necessary qualifications - then we would be practicing a very stupid and very evil kind of tribalism which led to the establishment of Biafra.[10]

It would have been very easy for such people, who were complaining about tribalism yet could not prove it was a factor in the allocation of jobs as President Nyerere said, to form their own political parties on tribal and ethnoregional basis - and even forge alliances with other "victimized" tribes - under the multiparty system and ignite tribal conflict; a potential catastrophe the one-party system, which embraced and accommodated all the tribes under the same political tent, was able to contain and neutralize in many African countries, especially in the early years of independence when the countries were in their formative stage trying to forge a true sense of national identity among the different ethnic groups.

This should not, in any way, be misconstrued as a defense of dictatorship but an objective appraisal of the functional utility of the one-party system and the positive role it played in saving African countries from splitting along tribal lines. And that entailed curtailment of freedom in many cases; a sad necessity, not in all but in some cases, when it was critical to avert the catastrophe of national disintegration. In most cases, it was sheer abuse of power, with many leaders invoking the specter of national disintegration to perpetuate themselves in office. But that does not mean that the positive role played by the one-party system as a unifying force during those critical years should be ignored; a positive contribution even some African leaders don't want to acknowledge simply because they are so much opposed to one-party rule, although for good reasons, mostly abuse of power. As Nicephore Soglo, former president of Benin, stated after losing the election in 1996:

> The West African country of Benin held elections in March (1996). I lost the presidency....
>
> While former President Mathieu Kerekou has returned to power, there is a difference now. Twenty-four years ago, he came to power by the barrel of the gun. This year it was by way of the ballot box....
>
> Many claim that Africa is different, that it is not ready for democracy. Ethnic tensions are pointed to as poisoning democracy. We have ethnic tensions in Benin. We have managed them. Sadly, many African leaders of the early independence years used these same arguments to justify their repressive rule.[11]

Yet Benin itself, then known as Dahomey, was almost torn apart by ethnic strife during the early years of independence, something Soglo conveniently overlooks. It is a subject I have also addressed in one of my books, *Military Coups in West Africa since the Sixties.*[12]

Would a multiparty system, with several parties formed on ethnic and regional basis, as was the case in Dahomey in the sixties, have served the country better? Or would it have made things worse, exacerbating ethnoregional rivalries and hostilities? It is true that Nicephore Soglo conceded ethnic tensions still exist in Dahomey today, as they do in other African countries. And Benin has survived under those tensions in a democratic environment of multiparty politics. But that is today.

African countries are stronger today as political entities than they were during their early years of independence, although all are still vulnerable to ethnic conflicts; but not as vulnerable as they were when they emerged from colonial rule. They were very young then, newly born. They did not have strong governments. They did not command full allegiance from different tribes, which regarded central authority as an alien institution imposed on them to destroy their tribal and traditional values and leadership. And all their political institutions, inherited from the departing colonial masters, were not restructured to reflect African realities and accommodate or harmonize conflicting ethnoregional interests. They were not firmly established and could have collapsed any time from the slightest push by tribalists if these tribal chauvinists had the opportunity to form opposition parties to promote their agenda. And being tribalists and regionalists, they naturally would have appealed to tribal sentiments to achieve their goals, which would be at variance with national aspirations.

The situation is different today across Africa. African countries are more mature. They have survived an entire generation since independence. And they don't need one-party rule as they did before, except - and that's may be - in some cases such as Rwanda and Burundi where the one-party system embracing both the Hutu and the Tutsi may be the only way to guarantee justice and equality for all. The Tutsi will never win an election against the Hutu majority under a multiparty system. Political parties in both countries have always been structured along ethnic lines, excluding the Hutu majority from power, except in Rwanda from 1962 to 1994 when the Hutu were in control. Both Rwanda and Burundi have historically been dominated by the Tutsi for about 400 years since they came from the northeastern part of Africa and conquered the Hutu. The one-party system may also be a temporary safeguard against national disintegration when a country faces total collapse, requiring the need for a united or coalition government under strong leadership.

Although it is true that African countries today are ready for multiparty democracy, Soglo's contention that such a system would have been appropriate for Africa even in the sixties after independence does not correspond to reality even in his own country. How could it have contained tribalism and ethnoregional rivalries in Dahomey, as Benin was then called, during those early years of independence?

Dahomey won independence on August 1, 1960, under the leadership of Hubert Maga, a northerner. His main support came from the north because the country was plagued by ethnic rivalries, especially between northerners and southerners. Because of such ethnoregional rivalries, President Maga did not have clear mandate to rule the country, since he hardly had any support in the south. And as expected, southerners also had their own leaders who enjoyed little support in the north, President Maga's ethnoregional stronghold. Justin Ahomadegbe had solid support in the south, while another leader, Migan Apithy, commanded allegiance in the central part of the country and in some parts of the south. Such divisions made it virtually impossible for the national leaders to govern effectively. In October 1963, President Hubert Maga was overthrown in a military coup led by Colonel Christophe Soglo, a southerner.

But the coup did not end ethnic and regional rivalries. Democracy was tried but thwarted by ethnic rivals. When Dahomey tried to hold elections in 1970 after the results of the 1968 electoral contest were annulled, northern and southern politicians were so bitterly divided that the elections were cancelled. It would, of course, be an oversimplification to blame all of Dahomey's problems on ethnic rivalries. Economic problems and social unrest across the country caused by a number of factors also played a significant role and made it difficult for the government to exercise effective control. They were one of the main reasons why President Hubert Maga's government was overthrown. But all these problems were exacerbated by ethnic rivalries, which have always plagued African countries since independence, even in times of economic prosperity and political stability rarely enjoyed on this troubled continent.

Contending that the multiparty system would have served African countries better than the one-party system in the early years of independence when they were most vulnerable to ethnic and regional rivalries, is to ignore the destructive nature of ethnonationalism; the most potent force in the world even today, as much as it has been throughout history. It is also to ignore the potential for disruption unscrupulous politicians always exploit in multiparty politics, a term synonymous with multi-tribal politics in the African context. Because of its tolerance of dissent, the multiparty system enables - even if it does not legally allow - almost anybody, including tribalists and regionalists and other disruptive elements, in the name of democracy to form political parties with a hidden partisan agenda while professing national unity. And Africa has already suffered and continues to suffer from some of the worst excesses of this ethno-nationalist impulse.

In the sixties, ethnic hatred of the Igbos in Nigeria exploded with such unconstrained fury that it almost destroyed Africa's largest nation at a cost of more than one million lives, mostly Igbo. It also exploded in Rwanda where almost one million Tutsis were slaughtered in only three months, and in neighboring Burundi where hundreds of thousands of Hutus were massacred by the Tutsi in the 1990s alone. And the massacres continued as the Tutsis refused to share power with the Hutu on meaningful basis. Where was the multiparty system to avert such catastrophe? Instead, it fanned flames in all three countries.

When Nigeria exploded during the sixties, it was a multiparty state. But all the parties were regionally entrenched with a strong ethnic bias. Even the National Convention of Nigerian Citizens (NCNC) - until 1960 known as the National Council of Nigeria and the Cameroons - which was led by Dr. Nnamdi Azikiwe and had supporters in all three regions of Nigeria, was strongest in the Eastern Region dominated by the Igbos. The Action Group led by Chief Obafemi Awolowo enjoyed overwhelming support among the Yorubas who dominate the Western Region. And the Northern People's Congress (NPC) led by Sir Ahmadu Bello, the Sardauna of Sokoto, was firmly entrenched in the Northern Region dominated by the Hausa-Fulani; Bello was Fulani.

Would a one-party state, under a single party of national unity, have helped Nigeria in its turbulent times through the years? No one knows, given its size and complexity as a multi-polity of more than 250 ethnic groups and religious differences especially between the predominantly Muslim north and Christian as well as animist south. But one thing is certain, however controversial it may be. Militocracy - or military rule also known as stratocracy - as a kind of "one-party state," at least kept the country united, through coercion, and prevented the genocidal rampage that took place during the sixties and which was triggered by tribalism. This is not to justify military rule - soldiers do not have the mandate to rule, should stay in the barracks, and obey the rule of law under democratically elected leaders - but simply to point out that an ethnically diverse population with a history of tribal conflict needs strong leadership under one central government capable of accommodating all groups on equal basis.

The alternative is national disintegration, or a weak federal system - or confederation - under which different ethnic groups become autonomous entities with the right to secede. A weak federal system is better than total disintegration of African countries into hundreds of independent ethnostates. But most countries across the continent chose one-party and authoritarian rule to contain tribalism and maintain national unity. And it worked.

Even today, when most African countries are trying to experiment with multiparty politics, a case can still be made for one-party rule. If the multiparty system is going to enable people to form political parties on ethnic or regional basis and even form alliances to prevent members of some ethnic groups from winning public office, then one-party rule is justified to maintain national unity and guarantee equality for all. Or let some people go, if they are excluded from power by their fellow countrymen. They have the right to establish their own independent state and rule themselves, as the Igbos did in the late sixties.

It is true that one-party rule has been a tragedy in most African countries for decades. But when you have ethnoregional rivalries accentuated by multiparty politics, one-party rule may be a better alternative. It may be the only way members of all tribes and all regions can compete for office on equal basis because the single party is open to everybody, as was the case in Tanzania under President Julius Nyerere. In fact, Tanzania's ruling party was more than just a political party. It was a national movement.

In defense of multiparty politics, an argument can be made that the constitution prohibits formation of tribal or regionally entrenched parties. And it can. But in practice, how effective is it? Tribal and regional parties - or parties with a hidden agenda to promote tribal and regional interests - have ways of legally qualifying for the ballot under the constitution by merging with other ethnoregional parties to win national mandate. They may seem to be nationally representative. But they will continue to be tribalist if their purpose of forming a coalition is to exclude members of some regions or tribes from winning elections. And such alliances have been formed in the past, although in the case of Azikiwe's NCNC, its decision to form an alliance with the Northern People's Congress at independence in 1960 was not in pursuit of a tribal agenda.

Dr. Azikiwe's NCNC and the Northern People's Congress (NPC) led by Sir Abubakar Tafawa Balewa but dominated by Sir Ahmadu Bello, formed an alliance which excluded Awolowo's Action Group from the first African federal government formed at independence in October 1960. It would, of course, be wrong to characterize the alliance as tribalist deliberately intended to exclude Yorubas from power. It was a marriage of convenience for political expediency. Azikiwe's party, the NCNC, was not ethnic but national in character. It was the only party, which had members in all three regions and even won seats in the Northern and Western Regional Assemblies, the regional strongholds of the Hausa-Fulani and the Yoruba, respectively.

Therefore Azikiwe's move was a tactical alliance with a party - the Northern People's Congress - which had the largest number of representatives in the federal legislature, although it represented only one region: Northern Nigeria. It was also the most tribalistic, and most conservative, of all the Nigerian political parties dominated by northern Muslim traditional rulers who brooked no dissent. Even the Action Group, led by Awolowo, an uncompromising Yoruba bigot who died in 1986 at the age of 76, had some members in the Eastern Region, although not many. But in spite of its virulently ethnoregional bias, the Northern People's Congress emerged as Nigeria's ruling party, since it dominated the federal legislature because of the structural imbalance of the federation favoring the north.

The British colonial rulers formed a structurally flawed federation of three massive regions - instead of several - dominated by the country's three largest ethnic groups. The smaller ones were left out of the equation and never became a factor in determining the future of the country. They were frozen out of power. The Northern Region had the largest population, officially, although the other two regions disputed the census figures. The census was deeply flawed.

But because of the numerical preponderance enjoyed by the north, based on those census figures, the region also produced the largest number of representatives in the national legislature. An entire half of the members of the Nigerian parliament were northerners who, by simple majority rule, were legally entitled under the constitution to form the federal government. And that meant a national government dominated by the Northern People's Congress whose dominant figure was the Sardauna of Sokoto, Sir Ahmadu Bello. The federal prime minister, Tafawa Balewa, also a northerner and titular head of the Northern People's Congress and the Nigerian Federal Government, was no more than a puppet manipulated at will by the Northern Premier Ahmadu Bello.

Nigeria emerged from colonial rule with a federal constitution, which theoretically guaranteed justice and equality for all. But its future looked bleak because of the lopsided nature of the federation favoring the north at the expense of the other regions, and excluding minority groups from the center. And it had catastrophic consequences, plunging the country into civil war only a few years later, a conflict that almost destroyed the nation.

The flawed structure of the federation continued to be a source of many problems and instability even after the federation was restructured several times; it now has 37 states, the last added by democratically elected President Olusegun Obasanjo, a southerner. And because of historical inequalities in the allocation of power, northerners dominated the federation for almost 40 years since independence. Most of the rulers were soldiers from Northern Nigeria. Tribalism and regional biases continue to be some of the major problems Nigeria faces, and northern military rulers only made the situation much worse. As Professor Crawford Young stated in his article, "The Impossible Necessity of Nigeria: A Struggle for Nationhood," in *Foreign Affairs:*

During most of Nigeria's 27 years (almost 30 years until May 1999 when Olusegun Obasanjo took over as elected president) of military rule, the senior autocrat has been from the north. The two civilian prime ministers (one was actually a president, Shehu Shagari, 1979 - 83) - from 1960 to 1966, and 1979 to 1983 - (the only civilian rulers the country had since independence in 1960 before Obasanjo, a former military head of state, was elected as a civilian president in 1999) were both Hausa-Fulani, the politically and demographically dominant ethnic category in the north. Even though Generals Yakubu Gowon (1966 - 1975), Ibrahim Babangida (1983 - 1993), and Sani Abacha (1993 - 1998) are not themselves Hausa-Fulani, (they are all northerners and) Nigerians view them as integral parts of what Wole Soyinka terms 'a self-perpetuating clique from the yet feudally oriented part of the country.'[13]

Soyinka goes on to denounce this ruling clique in his book, *The Open Sore of A Continent: A Personal Narrative of the Nigerian Crisis:*

(It is an) infinitesimal but well-positioned minority.... In denouncing the activities of this minority, described variously as the Sokoto Caliphate, the Northern Elite, the Kaduna Mafia, the Hausa-Fulani oligarchy, the Sardauna Legacy, the Dan Fodio Jihadists, et cetera, what is largely lost in the passion and outrage is that they do constitute a minority - a dangerous, conspiratorial, and reactionary clique, but a minority just the same. Their tentacles reach deep, however, and their fanaticism is the secular face of religious fundamentalism.[14]

And when Sani Abacha, a demented Kanuri - not Hausa-Fulani - from Kano, annulled the results of the June 1993 presidential election won by Moshood Abiola, a Yoruba from the southwest but who was able to garner impressive support in the eastern and northern parts of Nigeria as well, in addition to overwhelming backing in his native Yorubaland in the west, he only confirmed fears among many Nigerians that he was determined to perpetuate northern domination of the federation and pushed the country to the brink of disaster. The country almost split along ethnic lines, and would probably have, had he not suddenly died of a heart attack in July 1998, reportedly after being poisoned by a prostitute. The results of the June 1993 elections had actually been annulled by his predecessor, Ibrahim Babangida, but Abacha sealed the annulment instead of reversing it after he seized power and imprisoned Abiola when he claimed office the following June as the legitimate president of Nigeria. Abacha had the chance to rectify the situation. But he chose not to, and made the annulment final. And as Soyinka said about this betrayal and denial of the people's mandate: "(It was) the most treasonable act of larceny of all time: It violently robbed the Nigerian people of their nationhood."[15]

Soyinka is not alone in doubting that Nigeria will continue to exist as a single political entity. Many other Nigerians share the same sentiment. They include a significant number of Yorubas, Igbos, Ogonis, Ijaws and others in the Niger Delta who have been marginalized, especially under northern military rulers who dominated the federation for decades. Even the three titans of the Nigerian independence movement - Nnamdi Azikiwe, Obafemi Awolowo, and Ahmadu Bello - did, at different times, question the viability of the structurally flawed federation, and even the wisdom of preserving Nigeria as one country. Ethnic rivalry and mistrust was, and still is, the fundamental problem threatening the existence of Nigeria.

Soyinka, like many Nigerians and other Africans including this writer, still would like to see Nigeria remain united, but admits: "I...frankly could not advance an invulnerable reason for my preference for a solution that did not involve disintegration."[16]

Even more tragic for Africa is the fact that Nigeria is not the only country facing this bleak prospect. The Democratic Republic of Congo, the giant nation that has become the bleeding heart of Africa right in the middle of the continent, has been virtually partitioned into fiefdoms dominated by rebel groups in the east and by an inept and powerless central government that exercises virtually no control over the remaining parts of the country, since 1998 when the insurgents launched a rebellion - ignited by Rwanda and Uganda, with Burundi's involvement - to overthrow President Laurent Kabila. The rebellion continued after his son Joseph Kabila took over, following his assassination in January 2001. This former Belgian colony, which lost at least 10 million people under the brutal imperial rule of King Leopold II, has been the scene of carnage for more than a century. Between August 1998, when the rebellion started, and June 2001, about 3 million people died in eastern Congo as a result of the war. And the carnage continued. The Congo should never have been one country. And as Professor Crawford Young wrote about another giant African nation: "Nigeria has little cultural logic; its peoples would never have chosen to live together."[17]

Most of the tribes in other African countries would not have chosen to live together either. Before the advent of colonial rule, each had its own leaders. And had it not been for the European colonial rulers who partitioned Africa and lumped different tribes together, they would have continued to live the same way as independent micro-nations or ethnostates. The secessionist attempts by all three regions in Nigeria dominated by three main ethnic groups is instructive in this context.

Yet, in Nigeria like everywhere else across the continent, attempts were made by African leaders to transcend tribalism and regionalism for the sake of national unity. When Dr. Nnamdi Azikiwe formed an alliance with Federal Prime Minister Tafawa Balewa, a northerner, it was with the hope that although Nigerians "would never have chosen to live together," they could at least try to contain or even submerge their tribal and regional differences in order to live together. Therefore this alliance was different from many others in one fundamental respect: It was not formed to promote tribal interests or deliberately exclude Yorubas from power but to save Nigeria as a collective entity, with the predominantly Yoruba party, the Action Group, forming the official opposition.

However, there have been other alliances in Nigeria and other African countries that have been formed deliberately to promote tribal interests and exclude members of some ethnic groups from holding public office; for example the Igbo in Nigeria. Tribal and regional parties forming such alliances in order to technically qualify as "national parties" under the constitution which expressly forbids formation of such parties are not complying with the constitution - they are circumventing and subverting the constitution. And if there is no other way members of excluded groups can be protected and qualify for office, then - short of secession - the one-party system is totally justified under those circumstances, since it is capable of accommodating members of all tribes and regions on equal footing. It is in this context that the one-party system should be viewed as a very effective weapon against tribalism in African countries. And that was especially the case when they were just new nations trying to establish themselves shortly after independence.

Even as late as the 1990s and beyond, many people in

Tanzania questioned the functional utility of the multiparty system because of the divisions and the violence it caused in what had been one of the most peaceful and stable countries in Africa for decades when it was under one-party rule. Tanzania was a one-party state for almost 30 years under the leadership of President Julius Nyerere. And not once in those years was the country hit by violence caused by political factions pursuing partisan interests as happened after the introduction of multiparty democracy which has even provided an opportunity for many tribalists to form tribal associations; a phenomenon unheard of under Nyerere. Even students at the University of Dar es Salaam, who are supposed to be liberal-minded, have formed tribal organizations. As one student from Tanga complained in an interview with one of Tanzania's leading newspapers, *The Guardian,* on July 20, 2002, the situation on campus was so bad that even a sick student could not count on getting help from a roommate who was not a member of the same tribe. Help had to come from his or her fellow tribesmen and their organization. And that is tragic, posing great danger to national unity that was carefully nurtured by the nation's founding father Mwalimu Julius Nyerere for almost half a century.

If Tanzania is to remain a strong, stable, and united nation, then tribal associations should be banned, and should not enjoy legal protection from the government in the name of pluralism. People of different tribes should belong to the same civic organizations, which may be called the Tanzania Brotherhood Associations, in place of tribal associations. Otherwise Tanzania may be headed toward catastrophe, with prospects for tribal conflict and national disintegration being a distinct possibility.

That is the main reason why, in a national survey conducted before the introduction of multiparty politics in the early 1990s, the majority of Tanzanians who participated in it were resolutely opposed to the adoption of the multiparty system. They feared it would divide the country and threaten national stability and were vindicated a few years later when violence erupted following the general election in 2000 which resulted in a number of deaths, prompting President Benjamin Mkapa to publicly wonder if the people were not wiser than the leaders when they rejected the multiparty system in the early nineties. But the multiparty system was introduced, anyway, against prevailing national sentiment and in defiance of the people's will. Yet the people, popularly known as *wananchi* in Kiswahili meaning citizens or owners of the country, were vindicated by subsequent events, including the irresponsible conduct of some opposition parties such as the Democratic Party under the leadership of a fiery fundamentalist minister, Christopher Mtikila, inciting violence and preaching racial and religious intolerance.

The people of Tanzania should have voted in a referendum to determine their wish, although the national survey conducted in the early 1990s was comprehensive enough as a statistical tool to gauge collective national sentiment toward divisive politics legitimized by multiparty democracy. And they should have been allowed to continue living under a one-party state if that is what the majority wanted. The electoral mandate won by the ruling Chama Cha Mapinduzi (CCM) - Party of the Revolution or Revolutionary Party - which virtually constitutes a *de facto* one-party state, seems to indicate that. It is the same party that has ruled Tanzania since independence: Tanganyika African National Union (TANU) on the mainland, and Afro-Shirazi Party (ASP) on the isles, until the two parties merged in 1977 to form CCM, as urged by Nyerere.

But there is really no need for one-party rule in any African country, except in extreme cases when nations are in danger of collapsing because of ethnic conflicts or violence between political parties pursuing partisan interests at the expense of national unity and stability. That is an emergency involving national survival and cannot be dismissed lightly. Even Western multiparty democracies submerge their differences in times of national crisis. Therefore African countries should be not be expected to act differently when their survival is at stake. And when opposition parties are so weak, unable to win national mandate because of rivalry and lack of direction within the opposition camp, they lose the rationale for their existence and even resort to subversive tactics to win power. They also do everything they can to weaken or frustrate the government in order to make it look bad before the electorate from whom it won the mandate to rule. And incumbents also invoke this to stifle legitimate dissent, and justify repressive rule and a return to the status quo ante in order to re-institute one-party rule, mostly *de facto*, in this era of multiparty democracy.

There are, of course, exceptions to this common trend toward multiparty democracy sweeping across the continent. Rwanda and Burundi are prime examples. The Hutu and the Tutsi in both countries may be beyond the point where they could have genuinely tried to resolve and submerge their differences in an amicable way, if they ever took that route. Even one-party rule intended to forge national unity and guarantee peace and security for all, is not going to work in these two countries. The hostility between the Hutu and the Tutsi runs so deep, and has been going on for so long, that partition of Rwanda and Burundi along ethnic lines seems to be the only solution to this problem. And it is impossible for slaves and masters to live together as equals. The Tutsi have been holding the Hutu in feudal subjugation for 400 years, and still dominate both countries today, in spite of the fact that they are a small minority who comprise about 14 percent of Burundi's population, and only about 9 percent of Rwanda's; while the Hutu constitute a formidable 90 percent of Rwanda's population, and 85 percent of Burundi's, with the Twa (pygmies) making up 1 percent of the population in each of the two countries. Ultimately, numbers will determine the fate of these twin states, with dire consequences for the Tutsi minority if they continue to subjugate the Hutu majority.

However, the solution of partition suggested here in the case of Rwanda and Burundi is not appropriate in all contexts where African countries are torn by ethnic conflicts, as many of them have been since independence in the sixties. Nor does it mean that the solution is viable today, as ethnic strife continues to threaten the integrity of African nations. Like secession, partition should only be the ultimate solution, as a last resort, if nothing else works; for example in the case of Sudan where the Arabs in the north want to perpetually dominate an enslave blacks in the south and forcibly convert them to Islam in order to transform the country into a fundamentalist theocratic state based on a radical interpretation of the Koran. Had such a solution been implemented in the past, it would have split up African countries along tribal and regional lines, creating non-viable mini-ethnostates. It was avoided because of the one-party system and the coercive power of the state, which helped forge national unity on the anvil of uniformity. And such uniformity was possible only under the one-party system because of its monolithic nature, contrasted with the multiparty system, which many politicians and their supporters unscrupulously exploit to pursue ethnoregional interests at the expense of national unity. Therefore, in spite of its shortcomings, and there are many, there is no question that the one-party system saved African countries from falling apart and, indeed, saved Africa.

There is also no question that the multiparty system is good and, in most cases, is even better than one-party rule. But having a multiparty system just for the sake of it, even when it is going to tear the country apart along tribal and regional lines with members of different parties appealing to ethnoregional loyalties, is not very good statesmanship. In countries threatened by ethnic rivalries, as almost all African countries are including Tanzania where - despite its excellent reputation for peace and harmony - some opposition parties thrive on ethnoregional loyalties, it is utterly naive, or rank dishonesty, to discount that. And it has been vindicated by history: the former Belgian Congo, although at the instigation of Western powers and financial interests, exploiting local rivalries; Nigeria, because of the massacre of the Igbos which forced them to secede; Uganda, Ghana, and even Zambia, are some of the countries which were seriously threatened by ethnic conflicts and rivalries in the sixties, although - especially in the case of Nigeria and may be even the Congo - the one-party system would probably not have prevented the horrendous tragedies that befell these two giant nations and almost destroyed them in the turbulent sixties.

It was with those problems in mind that most African countries adopted the one-party system soon after independence; knowing full well that if they did not submerge the tribe, the tribe would destroy the nation. The rationale was extended even to the individual level. The primacy of the community, hence the nation, was invoked over the interests of the individual; admittedly, with dire consequences in many cases. But this approach had a perfectly rational basis. Forging a national ethos that would fuse the people of different tribes into an organic whole, and not just as a collection of antagonistic groups, entailed placing the interests of the community above those of the individual including his freedom. It was not done for political expediency but for national survival; an imperative underscored by President Sekou Toure when he said:

> We have chosen the freedom, the right, the power, the sovereignty of the people, and not of the individual. Before this people you should have no individual personality. Our personality becomes part of the personality of the nation.[18]

And anyone who was not ready to submerge his personality and freedom in the supra-entity called the nation in the interests of the people was considered to be more than just a dissenter - he was a "traitor"; although he himself, like everybody else, was one of the people constituting "We the people," without whom there would be no people. And that was one of the most tragic aspects of the one-party state, its benefits notwithstanding. Thus, the ethic of individual freedom became anathema to the nationalist ideologies of the young African countries whose existence and survival was predicated on the inculcation of the primacy of a collective ethos throughout the populace. In a very tragic way, individual freedom was considered to be as dangerous to national integrity as tribalism was. As Sekou Toure put it:

> Tribal, ethnic, and religious (as well as political) differences...have caused so much difficulty to the country and people.... We are for a united people, a unitary state at the service of an indivisible nation.[19]

Therefore, it is critical to understand the context in which such nationalist sentiments were articulated across the continent, before one passes judgment, condemning African leaders as dictators just lusting for power. Most of them were, and still are. But inculcation of the ideal of collective will and spirit, as opposed to individual liberty, was critical to the very survival of African countries during the early years of independence. These were countries which did not really even "exist" as countries, except on the map and as a mere collection of tribes, many of them hostile toward each other and haphazardly put together by the colonial rulers, with little in common in terms of loyalty to higher authority, each having its own princes, chiefs, and other traditional rulers. It was a Herculean task to build a nation out of such an amorphous whole. Even some ardent critics of Africa in Western countries concede that much. As Robert Greenberger wrote about Tanzania -

a country the size of Texas, Oklahoma and West Virginia combined, or bigger than Nigeria in terms of area, and made up of more than 120 tribes - in *The Wall Street Journal*:

> Nyerere was a skilled nation builder. He fused Tanzania's 120 tribes into a cohesive state, preventing tribal conflicts like those plaguing so much of Africa.[20]

Jomo Kenyatta, the Grand Old Man (called Mzee in Kiswahili) of the African independence movement, accomplished the same feat in Kenya, although to a smaller degree, compared to Nyerere. So did Nkrumah in Ghana, Sekou Toure in Guinea, Obote in Uganda, Kaunda in Zambia, and other African leaders elsewhere on the continent, but in varying degrees of success.

Yet, there was also abuse of power in most countries across the continent under the one-party state and military rule during those years of national consolidation, and all the way through the decades since independence. That is what makes the multiparty system so appealing in all African countries today, including Tanzania, which was very peaceful and stable, and relatively free, under President Nyerere's one-party state for almost 30 years. Curtailment, and in most cases total denial, of individual freedom was not always necessary to maintain national unity and stability in the fledgling states. Most African leaders invoked the specter of national disintegration just to perpetuate themselves in office and suffocate dissent, as they still do today. Yet, without putting a premium on national interest, and inculcating the ideals of a collective national spirit, a common identity, and commitment to national unity even at the expense of individual freedom in some cases, there probably would be no African countries, as we know them today. We would have hundreds of "nations": micro-states, none of them viable, structured along tribal lines, making it impossible for Africa to survive let alone develop. Therefore, the emphasis on national survival was justified. But it did not justify dictatorship, although it justified curtailment of freedom in some cases.

The invocation of slogans such as "national survival," "national unity," "One Zambia, One Nation," "Harambee! - Let's Pull Together," "Uhuru na Umoja - Freedom and Unity," "the people, not the individual, come first," and many others, has always been an integral part of the indoctrination process for which African countries are despised in the West as a diversionary tactic to justify dictatorship. And in many cases such criticism by Westerners and others is justified. But let us also be brutally frank: We all practice indoctrination. Western countries do, communist countries do. So do all the rest, including Africa.

Inculcation of individual and national values is indoctrination. Even glorification of a nation's practices and beliefs, values and traditions, ideals and ideology, is a form of indoctrination. When Americans are taught that capitalism is better than socialism or communism, that is indoctrination, even if it is true; which it is. When they are taught that America, the first republic since Rome, was founded on the twin ideals of liberty and equality, that is indoctrination, even if it is not true; which it isn't. America was founded on slavery, and thrived on slavery. Millions of Americans were not taught - and are still not taught - in school and when growing up that African slaves and their descendants helped build America more than anybody else, especially in its early years, and without being paid. As Malcolm X said, African slaves worked "from can't see in the morning to can't see in the evening without being paid a dime. Yet we built this country...and we aren't American yet. As long you and I have been here, we aren't American yet." African slaves built America's foundation without which the country would not have survived and thrived as a nation. And it would not be what it is today, as the richest nation in history, had it not been for the forced labor extracted from African slaves and their descendants. They made America rich. Yet they were never paid one cent for it.

But a number of black American conservatives contend otherwise. One is Dr. Thomas Sowell, an economics professor and a prolific author, who argues in his book, *Race and Culture*,[21] that there is no conclusive evidence showing that America derived net economic benefits from slavery. He and a number of other blacks, especially conservatives, are opposed to reparations for slavery for various reasons. They are mostly middle-class and upper class blacks who are detached from their own people in a desperate attempt to be accepted by and integrated into white America. Yet, they are not accepted by whites as equals. Alienated from their own people, and rejected by white America, they are caught in a predicament similar to the situation many educated Africans were trapped in during colonial times. Western education "de-Africanized" them, mentally. Yet it did not elevate them to the same status enjoyed by their colonial masters and other whites; a subject I have addressed in one of my books, *Africa and the West*.[22] It is also a subject - in the American context - black nationalist scholar, Professor Harold Cruse, has tackled in his magnum opus, *The Crisis of the Negro Intellectual*.[23] And as he said about slavery and the myths being propagated to distort American history, in another book, *Rebellion or Revolution?*

America lies to itself that it was always, from the beginning, a democratic nation when its very constitution sanctioned and upheld chattel slavery. Moreover, America conveniently forgets that the first capitalist 'free enterprise' banks and stock markets in the land were made possible by accumulated capital accrued from the unpaid labor of Negro slaves. But it would be too much to expect contemporary America to go back over its own history and reassess all these racial facts.[24]

America does not want to face that because it still has a serious racial problem - although it is no longer a racist society in the legal sense - and wants to continue propagating the myth that African slaves and their descendants did not significantly, if at all, contribute to the economic growth of the United States. This myth is an integral part of America's racist ideology, and it is indoctrination. Yet, all this indoctrination, which started as soon as Africans were taken to America in chains, has not always worked. Even slaves knew better; they had to, they were the ones doing all the work on the plantations without pay. As Bailey Wyat, a former slave and although illiterate, put it poignantly in broken English when arguing for redistribution of land to former slaves not long after the Emancipation Proclamation:

We has a right to the land where we are located. For why? I tell you. Our wives, our children, our husbands has been sold over and over again to purchase the land.... And then didn't we clear the land, and raise the crops? And then didn't them large cities in the North grow up on the cotton, on the sugars, on the rice that we made? ...I say they has grown rich and my people is poor.[25]

When America denies that, to insulate itself from reality

and its ugly past, it is practicing indoctrination that is no better than the kind practiced by many African leaders and their people when they blame American imperialism for all their problems. Nor is it wrong for Americans to say capitalism is better than communism, just as it is not wrong for Africans to say Pan-Africanism is better than nationalism, and nationalism better than tribalism. Indoctrination serves a purpose, good or bad. Hitler preached a racist ideology. It was even taught to the young. And it was indoctrination at its worst, with dire consequences at a cost of more than 6 million lives of people who belonged to the "wrong race," mostly Jews. But it could have served a good purpose under a different kind of leadership, with a different ideology, unlike that of Nazi Germany.

In Africa, indoctrination has also served a purpose. And it has served Africa well in many areas when it corresponds to reality. And that included justifying centralization of power "in the name of the people" during the early years of independence under one-party rule. That is because a strong central government was vital and critical to national unity and survival, in pursuit of economic development by mobilizing resources at the national level under one leadership. That was also the case in the United States when Alexander Hamilton argued that a strong central government was necessary for the young nation. It is doubtful that America would have survived without it. This was clearly demonstrated when the states constituting the union adopted a federal constitution at the Philadelphia convention in 1787 to replace the Articles of Confederation in order to establish a strong central government.

In addition to instituting a unitary state, most African countries also adopted a common or similar ideology to develop their economies and consolidate national unity. The approach most took towards development was socialism, and its concomitant, centralization of power, as the most effective mechanism for rapid mobilization of resources at the national level; and as a weapon against tribalism and regionalism. As Professor Ali Mazrui states in his book *Towards A Pax-Africana*:

A former Labour Party Colonial Secretary, Arthur Creech Jones, once remarked that he did not consider it the duty of that office to impose socialism on the colonies. In the case of Africa it has now turned out such an imposition was not necessary. No ideology commands respect so widely in Africa as the ideology of 'socialism' - though, as in Europe, it is socialism of different shades. In Guinea and Mali a Marxist framework of reasoning is evident. In Ghana Leninism was wedded to notions of traditional collectivism. In Tanzania the concept of *Ujamaa*, derived from the sense of community of tribal life, is being radicalized into an assertion of modern socialism. In Kenya there is a dilemma between establishing socialism and Africanizing the capitalism that already exists. In Nigeria, Senegal and Uganda some kind of allegiance is being paid to the ideal of social justice in situations with a multi-party background. There are places, of course, where no school of socialism is propagated at all. But outside the Ivory Coast there is little defiant rejection of the idea of 'socialism' in former colonial Africa.

Yet the kind of socialism, which Arthur Creech Jones would have propagated, was a socialism operating in the context of a multi-party system of politics. What is more common in Africa, however, is a socialism wedded to a one-party structure of government.[26]

Dr. Mazrui's book was first published in 1967, the same year Tanzania adopted its famous Arusha Declaration in February, outlining the country's socialist policies. It was a period - throughout the sixties - when interest in socialism among African leaders was at its peak, with most countries across the continent having adopted the socialist ideology in one form or another within that decade of euphoria, which also marked the end of colonial rule. By 1968, most African countries had won independence.

But their war against tribalism, ignorance, disease, and poverty had just begun. And African countries saw socialism as the best solution to these problems, with central planning being one of its most attractive features. And it is easy to understand why. When all tribes and regions are brought together under one leadership, there is no room for division along ethnoregional lines. If power is too decentralized, it can help strengthen tribal and regional institutions to the detriment of national unity. That is the argument African countries used to justify concentration of power at the center. And they made a rational choice under the circumstances when they instituted the unitary state during those years when African countries were so fragile, and national unity virtually non-existent.

And their belief in socialism as the best means to achieve rapid economic development was not without foundation. There was the example of the Soviet Union, with all its faults; yet persuasive enough that development could indeed be achieved in a relatively short time - as opposed to the centuries it took the West to develop - if decision-making on the allocation of the nation's resources, which include people, was centralized. Even some of those who criticized African leaders for taking the socialist path felt that the leaders were vindicated in their belief because of the rapid industrialization the Soviet Union was able to achieve within 40 years under socialism; although the foundations of the future great nation had been largely built by Peter the Great in the preceding years.

There was another equally compelling argument why African leaders chose socialism over capitalism: equitable distribution of wealth to achieve social justice. They saw capitalism as a predatory system for survival of "the fittest" under which people sought to accumulate wealth without the slightest concern for the poor and for the well-being of others. "I got mine, you get yours. Each to his own," is the underlying logic of capitalism. Although it is true that capitalism capitalizes on greed, there is no question that it provides incentives to production more than socialism does, much as some of us may hate its predatory instincts. But that is part of its nature. If you like its virtues, be prepared to accept its vices.

By contrast, socialism emphasizes sharing. Therefore, with its redistributive ethic, it was seen as morally superior to capitalism which nurtures and nourishes predatory instincts in man; pursuit of profit being incompatible with social justice, since people exploit others to accumulate wealth. In short, capitalism is based on inequality, and is therefore the very antithesis not only of social justice but human equality.

But probably the biggest attraction to socialism among African leaders was that - as the only ones who "knew what was best" for the people and the nation - it enabled them to control all the nation's resources in order to plan and direct economic development; something that is impossible under capitalism where economic development of the whole country is mostly left to the invisible hand of the free market. But under socialism, they were not only able to choose development targets and allocate resources to achieve national goals; they even used coercive means to achieve these goals. All this was seen as necessary to achieve economic development. As Dr. Kwame Nkrumah put it:

> The economic independence that should follow and maintain political independence demands every effort from the people, a total mobilization of brain and manpower resources. What other countries have taken three hundred years to achieve, a once dependent territory must try to accomplish in a generation if it is to survive....
>
> Capitalism is too complicated a system for a newly independent nation. Hence, the need for a socialistic society. But even a system based on social justice and a democratic constitution may need backing up, during the period following independence, by emergency measures of a totalitarian kind. Without discipline, true freedom cannot survive.[27]

Most African leaders did not explicitly say they were going to employ "measures of a totalitarian kind," as Nkrumah bluntly stated. But they ruled that way, and still do. And besides saying "capitalism is too complicated a system for a newly independent nation," Nkrumah - like most African leaders - also believed that the capitalist system would only perpetuate exploitation of their countries by the metropolitan powers. Capitalism was not only identified with colonialism; it was organically linked to their former colonial masters who were determined to continue exploiting Africa; capitalism, by nature, being an exploitative system and an integral part of colonialism and imperialism as the history of Africa clearly demonstrated since slavery and colonization. If it was adopted by the newly independent nations as the best path towards economic development, local capitalists would continue to work with foreign capitalist interests to exploit the people. Even African leaders such as Tom Mboya found much that was desirable in socialism. As he stated:

> It might be argued that African socialism stands in a class by itself. This is not true. The basic tenets of socialism are universal and we are either socialists by these basic principles or not at all.... I strongly believe that in the field of economic relations we can be guided by the traditional presence of socialist ideas and attitudes in the African mental make-up.[28]

Yet, Mboya was not a socialist, at least not in the same way Nyerere, Nkrumah, and Sekout Toure were, in terms of policy formulation and implementation. If Mboya was a socialist, then Nyerere was a capitalist. They were poles apart. And his socialism must have been shelved when he was a cabinet member in Kenya's capitalist government under Kenyatta where he held key ministerial posts including economic planning.

But articulation of his feelings on the relevance of socialism to Africa shows the kind of strong appeal the socialist ideology had across a broad spectrum of African leaders during the sixties and through the decades. Today, of course, with the collapse of the Soviet Union and its satellites, it is a discredited ideology. But that does not diminish the significant role it played in the establishment and consolidation of the African nation-state through the years under the one-party system, which has also been replaced by the multiparty system in most African countries, although only in theory. Most are *de facto* one-party states.

But there is also no question that both socialism and the one-party system had a negative impact on African countries in terms of diminished freedom and retarded economic growth. There were some notable achievements in the economic arena, but not as significant as they would have been had African governments adopted a free-market approach even with limited state intervention in the economy. However, when looked at in the context of the sixties when most African countries won independence, and even in the seventies when they were still struggling to consolidate their nation-states as much as they are still struggling to do so today, the negative impact of both socialism and the one-party system should be weighed against the fact that the African nation-state was established against overwhelming odds and would probably not exist today had African leaders taken a different path.

In Africa, unlike in Europe, nationalism preceded the establishment of the nation-state. The leaders who campaigned for independence had to appeal to nationalist sentiments of non-existent nations in order to create a sense of collective identity among different and antagonistic ethnic groups, which constituted the colonies. And it was a formidable task. Convincing members of different tribes that they were the same people - as Tanganyikans and not just Sukumas, Nyakyusas, Zanakis, Digos, Chaggas, Ngonis, Gogos, Makondes, Nyamwezis, Yaos, Hayas, Pares, Hehes, Benas, Makuas or Kingas; Ghanaians and not just Ewes, Fantis, Ashantis, Gonjas, Dagombas, Nanumbas, or Konkombas;

Kenyans and not just Kikuyus, Kambas, Luos, Luhyas, Samburus, Masais, Pokots, Merus, or Somalis - required strong central authority at the national level under a unitary state with no room for divisive politics and partisanship so typical of the multi-party system. And the one-party system as well as socialism, both with an instinct for mass mobilization under one strong leadership at the national level, provided just the kind of institutional tools and mechanisms which enabled Africans to establish, build, and consolidate the nations which exist today across the continent, however fragile they may be.

This is not gloss over the negative impact of socialism and one-party rule on African countries. Both had tragic consequences. They stifled individual initiative, lowered productivity, and curtailed freedom. But they also taught and enforced discipline, similar to army discipline, to maintain national unity which would have been impossible without mass regimentation in societies fragmented along ethnic lines. Therefore, the positive contribution of socialism and one-party rule must also be acknowledged, at least in the African context where, instead of the 53 countries we have today, we probably would have hundreds, equal to the number of tribes and racial groups on the continent.

If that is what multi-party "democracy" is going to do, weaken or split up countries, then it is recipe for disaster. African countries should therefore not rule out a return to the status quo ante if circumstances dictate, and temporarily re-institute one-party rule - but not socialism, there is no need for it - before returning to multi-party democracy. But the decision to form such government of national unity must be by popular consent approved in a referendum. Otherwise, when faced with the prospect of national disintegration and bloodshed as a result of ethnic conflicts, let the people learn the hard way; if they want their countries to dissolve in anarchy under the multiparty system, which thrives on divisive politics in the name of democracy even when national survival is at stake.

African nationalists of all ideological stripes have always been very much aware of the danger our countries face because of their pluralistic nature as multi-ethnic societies or multi-national states. As Dr. Nnamdi Azikiwe, who was no admirer of the one-party system, said when he warned against the Pakistanization -

balkanization - of Nigeria:

It is essential that ill will be not created in order to encourage a Pakistan in this country. The North and South are one, whether we wish it or not. The forces of history have made it so.[29]

Preservation of national integrity is better than the ghastly alternative of total disintegration, which can also be averted by extensive devolution of power to the regions and districts, but while retaining strong central authority. One-party rule, with all its faults, has been able to maintain national unity across much of Africa. Only time will tell whether or not its antithesis, the multiparty system, will be able to do the same. And it can, if it effectively contains tribalism and regional loyalties, as the one-party system has done, by establishing parties that are truly national in character cutting across regional and ethnic lines. Unfortunately, few tribes in Africa have demonstrated the capacity to transcend ethnoregional loyalties for the sake of national unity. The perennial ethnic rivialries, which continue to threaten the very existence of African countries, is a rueful reminder of that.

Probably the best solution to this seemingly intractable problem is for African countries to limit the number of political parties - preferably to three - to broaden the base of support cutting across ethnic lines. Members of different tribes will then have to learn to live together, and work together, as members and supporters of those few parties in order to build strong African nations without promoting tribal and regional interests at the expense of their fellow citizens. As Mrs. Charity Ngilu, the first woman to be a serious contender for Kenya's presidency, lamented after the 1997 general elections which the incumbent Daniel Arap Moi won because the opposition was hopelessly divided along tribal lines and failed to rally behind a single candidate:

Honourable Mwai Kibaki got most votes in 1997 from the Kikuyu, Honourable Raila Odinga from the Luo, Honourable Kijana Wamalwa from the Luhya and I myself from the Kamba. President Moi got most of his votes from the Rift Valley. Is this the Kenya we want?[30]

Is this the Africa we want for the sake of multi-party politics?

The adoption of the multiparty system should not blind us to reality. And the reality in this context is that ethnic politics, and manipulation and exploitation of tribal loyalties in the quest for national office, is a dominant feature of the African political landscape. And it is going to remain that way for a long, long time in most countries across the continent. How to address this problem is going to be one of the main challenges Africa will have to face in the twentieth-first century, which South African President Thabo Mbeki has declared to be the century of the African Renaissance.

CHAPTER TWO:

MILESTONES:
AFRICA SINCE THE SIXTIES

AFRICA has come a long way since the sixties, and still has a long way to go. The tortuous journey has been marked by important milestones, which can help us look at Africa in its proper historical context, as we recall some of the major events that have taken place on the continent since independence.

The year 1960 occupies a special place in the annals of the continent probably more than any other in one fundamental respect: It was the year when an unprecedented number of African countries won independence, a feat that was never duplicated in any of the following years. A total of 17 countries won independence in 1960. The United Nations called it Africa's Year. The attainment of sovereign status by so many African countries in a single year ushered in a new era for the continent whose most celebrated decade was the euphoric sixties.

But 1960 was also a tragic year for Africa. It was a year marred by the Congo crisis, an unprecedented catastrophe at the dawn of Africa's post-colonial era. The Congo tragedy was engineered and fueled by Western powers. Communist countries stepped in at the invitation of the nationalist forces in their desperate attempt to oust a puppet regime backed by the United States and spearheaded by the CIA. It was also supported by Belgium, the former colonial power, apartheid South Africa, France and other Western powers and financial interests. It was a coalition of forces, and a concerted effort, determined to perpetuate domination and exploitation of Africa and dismember the Congo in pursuit of Western interests.

The crisis erupted right in the middle of Africa, earning the Congo the unenviable distinction as the bleeding heart of Africa. More than 100,000 people, mostly Congolese, perished in the early sixties alone in this conflict which also had ideological dimensions involving super-power rivalry between the United States and the

Soviet as well as the People's Republic of China. Among the casualties was Congo's first and popular prime minister, Patrice Lumumba. Compounding the tragedy was Africa's inability to do anything to end the conflict right on its own soil. As Julius Nyerere said about the Congo crisis in a speech in August 1961 about three months before he led Tanganyika to independence:

> I am an advocate of African unity. I believe firmly that, just as unity was necessary for the achievement of independence in Tanganyika or any other nation, unity is equally necessary to consolidate and maintain the independence which we are now achieving in different parts of Africa.
>
> I believe that, left to ourselves, we can achieve unity on the African continent. But I don't believe we are going to be left to ourselves! I believe that the phase through which we are emerging successfully is the phase of the first scramble for Africa - and Africa's reaction to it. We are now entering a new phase. It is the phase of the second scramble for Africa....
>
> I used the phrase 'the second scramble for Africa.' It may sound farfetched, in the context of the Africa of the 1960's....But anybody who thinks this is farfetched has been completely blind to what is happening on the African continent....
>
> There were obvious weaknesses in the Congo situation, but those weaknesses were deliberately used in a scramble for the control of the Congo....So I believe that the second scramble for Africa has begun in real earnest. And it is going to be a much more dangerous scramble than the first one.[1]

The assassination of Lumumba, like the Congo tragedy itself as a whole, was an important milestone in the history of Africa. Much is known about the CIA's and Belgium's involvement in Lumumba's assassination, which American President Dwight Eisenhower wanted carried out as soon as possible. A team of CIA agents worked on a covert operation which involved more than one assassination scheme including poisoning and shooting the Congolese leader with a high-powered telescopic rifle. Even the CIA station chief in the Congo, Laurence Devlin conceded that much after Lumumba was killed. He also confirmed this in an interview as late as 1996 from Princeton, New Jersey, where he lived. So did Dr. Sidney Gottlieb, a CIA doctor, who went to Congo in September 1960 with a poison kit to kill Lumumba. Many people have written about the subject, which I have also addressed in one of my books, *Africa after Independence: Realities of Nationhood,*[2] in a chapter exclusively devoted to the Congo crisis. And as John Reader states in his book, *Africa: A Biography of the Continent*:

> An agent (of the CIA) was dispatched to Leopoldville. An initial assassination plan required someone to apply a dose of poison to Lumumba's toothbrush; alternatively, a high-powered rifle with telescopic scope and silencer was proposed....
>
> In a radio broadcast on 5 September (1960), President Kasavubu, urged by American diplomats, Belgian political advisers, and Congolese supporters, announced that he had dismissed Lumumba as prime minister. When the news reached Lumumba, he in turn rushed to the radio station and announced that he had dismissed Kasavubu as president. Confusion ensued. Some parts of the Congo declared their support for Lumumba, others for Kasavubu and Ileo (the new prime minister), and parliament voted to annul both decisions.
>
> With arrests and counter-arrests by the contending parties threatening yet another round of violent disturbance, the impasse was resolved on the evening of September 14 when the twenty-nine-year-old army chief of staff, Colonel Joseph Mobutu, announced that he was taking power in the name of the army.... Then, in a move that warmed the hearts of the CIA agents who had been indoctrinating him for weeks, Mobutu ordered the Soviet and Czechoslovak embassies to get out of the Congo within forty-eight hours....
>
> Though deposed by Mobutu on 14 September 1960, after just seventy-six days in office, Lumumba continued to live at the prime minister's residence in Leopoldville, guarded by an inner ring of UN troops in the garden to prevent his arrest and surrounded by an outer ring of Mobutu's troops on the perimeter to prevent his escape. Hence the difficulty of obtaining access to his toothbrush that the CIA agents had experienced.[3]

But his days were numbered, and he fell right into the hands of his enemies, the most powerful of whom were the Belgians and the Americans helped by their Congolese henchmen, including Mobutu:

> Meanwhile, Lumumba's supporters regrouped in Stanleyville. At the end of November Lumumba decided to join them - a fatal move. He was arrested en route and handed over to Mobutu's army.
>
> Lumumba was consigned to a military prison, but his supporters continued to have an unsettling effect on the country at large.... Kasavubu and his (American and Belgian) advisers decided that he should be sent to Elisabethville, the Katangan capital, where the errant Tshombe was in charge.
>
> On 17 January 1961, Lumumba and two colleagues (Maurice Mpolo and Joseph Okito) were flown to Katanga, where a Swedish warrant officer with the United Nations forces witnessed their arrival:
>
> 'The first to leave the aeroplane was a smartly dressed African. He was followed by three other Africans, blindfolded and with their hands tied behind

their backs. The first of the prisoners to alight had a small beard [Lumumba]. As they came down the stairs, some of the *gendarmes* ran to them, pushed them, kicked them and brutally struck them with rifle butts; one of the prisoners fell to the ground. After about one minute the three prisoners were placed in a jeep which drove off....'

Neither Lumumba nor his colleagues were ever seen again. It is believed they were taken to a farmhouse on the outskirts of Elisabethville, where they died at the hands of Katangese officials and Belgian mercenaries.[4]

It was also said that Lumumba was killed in the presence of Tshombe himself. And there was ample evidence showing that the United States and Belgium had conspired to eliminate Lumumba; further confirmed by intelligence and diplomatic messages coming from each other's capital. One was a cable from the American ambassador in Brussels, on July 19, 1960, advising Washington that Lumumba had "maneuvered himself into a position of opposition to West, resistance to United Nations and increasing dependence on Soviet Union and on Congolese supporters who are pursuing Soviet ends.... Only prudent, therefore, to plan on basis that Lumumba government threatens our vital interests in Congo and Africa generally. A principle (sic) objective of political and diplomatic action must therefore be to destroy Lumumba government as now constituted, but at the same time we must find or develop another horse to back which would be acceptable in rest of Africa and defensible against Soviet political attack."[5]

That horse turned out to be Mobutu, one of the most loyal servants of the West who started working for the CIA even before he became head of the Congolese army. At the time of his appointment as head of the army, he was Lumumba's private secretary, and already on the CIA payroll. And both the Americans and the Belgians - as well as others including the French, and the apartheid regime of South Africa - supported Mobutu. Therefore, they were all responsible for what happened in the Congo; the Americans and the Belgians being the most culpable.

The West did not want any truly independent nationalist to lead any African country. They wanted puppets they could manipulate at will. And Lumumba was not one of those stooges. On independence day, June 30, 1960, Lumumba gave a fiery response to Belgian King Baudouin's patronizing speech which even Joseph Kasavubu, a conservative leader and friend of the

West, found to be offensive and demeaning. Lumumba's speech was not well received in the West. Western governments saw Lumumba as a threat to their economic, political and strategic interests in the Congo and the entire continent. A true nationalist and Pan-Africanist, he believed that political independence was meaningless without economic independence. Therefore Africa had to cease being an economic colony of Europe or a plantation for the metropolitan powers. Yet, Western powers - especially Belgium, the United States and France - had invested heavily in the Congo to exploit its vast amount of minerals and other resources. And Lumumba, because of his independent and pro-African policies, was a direct threat to this hegemonic control of the Congolese economy by the West. As Professor Adam Hochschild of the University of California-Berkeley says about the CIA's involvement in Lumumba's assassination in his book, *King Leopold's Ghost: A Story of Greed, Terror, and Heroism in Colonial Africa*:

An inspired orator whose voice was rapidly carrying beyond his country's borders, Lumumba was a mercurial and charismatic figure. His message, Western governments feared, was contagious. Moreover, he could not be bought. Anathema to American and European capital, he became a leader whose days were numbered. Less than two months after being named the Congo's first democratically chosen prime minister, a U.S. National Security Council subcommittee on covert operations, which included CIA chief Allen Dulles, authorized his assassination. Richard Bissell, CIA operations chief at the time, later said, 'The President [Dwight D. Eisenhower]...regarded Lumumba as I did and a lot of other people did: a mad dog...and he wanted the problem dealt with.'

Alternatives for dealing with 'the problem' were considered, among them poison - a supply of which was sent to the CIA station chief (Laurence Devlin) in Leopoldville - a high-powered rifle, free-lance hit men. But it proved hard to get close enough to Lumumba to use these, so, instead, the CIA supported anti-Lumumba elements within the factionalized Congo government, confident that before long they would do the job. They did. After being arrested and suffering a series of beatings, the prime minister was secretly shot in Elizabethville in January 1961. A CIA agent ended up driving around the city with Lumumba's body in his car's trunk, trying to find a place to dispose of it...

The key figure in the Congolese forces that arranged Lumumba's murder was a young man named Joseph Desire Mobutu, then chief of staff of the army and a former NCO in the old colonial *Force Publique*. Early on, the Western powers had spotted Mobutu as someone who would look out for their interests. He had received cash payments from the local CIA man and Western military attaches while Lumumba's murder was being planned.[6]

Hochschild was in the Congo during that time, and had first-hand knowledge of some of the events that went on and which had to do with Lumumba's assassination:

> I had been writing about human rights for years, and once, in the course of half a dozen trips to Africa, I had been to the Congo.
> That visit was in 1961. In a Leopoldville apartment, I heard the CIA man, who had too much to drink, describe with satisfaction exactly how and where the newly independent country's first prime minister, Patrice Lumumba, had been killed a few months earlier. He assumed that any American, even a visiting student like me, would share his relief at the assassination of a man the United States government considered a dangerous leftist troublemaker.[7]

The CIA and the Belgian government not only worked together to assassinate Lumumba; they plotted to get rid of him in the most gruesome manner. New revelations about the assassination by some of the people who were directly involved in it only add to our understanding of the sinister plot as one of the most diabolical deeds in the history of post-colonial Africa, conceived by some of Africa's worst enemies. Some of these revelations come from a Belgian sociologist, Ludo de Witte, who quotes some of the killers in his book, *The Assassination of Lumumba*,[8] published in 1999. And they were right on target, although it took them some time to get to Lumumba. But the objective was clear. As CIA Director Allen Dulles wrote: "In high quarters here, it is the clear-cut conclusion that if [Lumumba] continues to hold high office, the inevitable result will [have] disastrous consequences...for the interests of the free world generally. Consequently, we conclude that his removal must be an urgent and prime objective."[9] De Witte explains in detail the prominent role the Belgian government played in Lumumba's assassination. According to *U.S. News & World Report*:

> De Witte reveals a telegram from Belgium's African-affairs minister, Harold d'Aspremont Lynden, essentially ordering that Lumumba be sent to Katanga. Anyone who knew the place knew that was a death sentence.
> When Lumumba arrived in Katanga, on 17 January (1961), accompanied by several Belgians, he was bleeding from a severe beating. Later that evening, Lumumba was killed by a firing squad commanded by a Belgian officer. A week earlier, he had written to his wife, 'I prefer to die with my head

unbowed, my faith unshakable, and with a profound trust in the destiny of my country.' Lumumba was 35.

The next step was to destroy the evidence. Four days later, Belgian Police Commissioner Gerard Soete and his brother cut up the body with a hacksaw and dissolved it in sulfuric acid. In an interview on Belgian television last year (1999), Soete displayed a bullet and two teeth he claimed to have saved from Lumumba's body....

A Belgian official who helped engineer Lumumba's transfer to Katanga told de Witte that he kept CIA station chief Laurence Devlin (in Leopoldville) fully informed of the plan. 'The Americans were informed of the transfer because they actively discussed this thing for weeks,' says de Witte. But Devlin, now retired, denies any previous knowledge of the trnasfer.[10]

Other sources give similar and sometimes almost identical accounts of the assassination, thus corroborating each other. According to one such source: "A U.N. investigating commission found that Lumumba had been killed by a Belgian mercenary in the presence of Tshombe."[11] The Belgian mercenary was said to be a CIA agent, and other American agents were also probably at the scene, in addition to the Belgians and their Congolese henchmen.

Lumumba went down in history as one of the most admired political martyrs in modern times. To many people, especially in Congo and other parts of the continent, he was and still is one of the most revered political figures in the history of post-colonial Africa, together - even if not necessarily in the same league - with leaders such as Julius Nyerere, Kwame Nkrumah, and Nelson Mandela. The Congo crisis was one of the biggest tragedies that befell Africa during the sixties. And its domino effect and devastating impact is still being felt today, as the Congo lies in ruins. It is, indeed, the bleeding heart of Africa.

The assassination of Lumumba ushered in a new era of political assassinations and military coups in sub-Saharan Africa. On January 13, 1963, almost exactly two years after Lumumba was brutally murdered, another prominent African leader, President Sylvanus Olympio of Togo, was assassinated in a military coup led by a 25-year-old sergeant, Etienne Eyadema, who became one of Africa's longest-ruling and most brutal dictators re-named Gnassingbe Eyadema. He was shot at the gates of the American embassy in Togo's capital, Lome. It was the first military coup in black Africa.

Although Lumumba was ousted earlier in 1960 when

another soldier, Mobutu, seized power, his ouster was not a typical military takeover - like the one in Togo in 1963 - but part of larger conspiracy by Western powers to dominate and break up the Congo; Mobutu seized power only later in November 1965 in a typical military coup. It was Western powers who engineered and backed up the secession of mineral-rich Katanga Province in July 1960 - only 11 days after Congo won independence on June 30 under the leadership of Prime Minister Lumumba - plunging the country into chaos and full-scale civil war. And they continued to support Katanga's secessionist leader Moise Tshombe until 1963 when his forces were defeated by UN peacekeeping troops sent to Congo at the request of Lumumba and other African leaders to keep the country united. Tshombe died in Algeria in June 1969 where he was held in captivity after his plane was forced to land, en route to Congo, to cause more mischief. He was 49. He was traveling from Spain. And he did everything he could to break up the Congo. Had the Congo disintegrated, it would have set a dangerous precedent for the rest of Africa, encouraging secession in other parts of the continent.

Tragically, another dangerous precedent was gaining prominence on the continent in the form of military coup when Eyadema assassinated President Olympio and seized power in Togo. Olympio's assassination drew swift condemnation from other African leaders. The government of Tanganyika under Julius Nyerere sent an urgent message to the UN Secretary-General, questioning the dubious credentials of Togo's new leadership:

> After the brutal murder of President Olympio, the problem of recognition of a successor government has arisen. We urge no recognition of a successor government until satisfied first that the government did not take part in Olympio's murder or second that there is a popularly elected government.[12]

At the founding of the Organization of African Unity (OAU) in May 1963 in Addis Ababa, Ethiopia, attended by African heads of state and government, the seat that would have been occupied by the late Togolese President Sylvanus Olympio was conspicuously empty in the conference hall, known as Africa Hall; sending a chilling message to the assembled leaders and future ones on how vulnerable their governments were to subversion by a mere handful of soldiers. But it was also a warning to aspiring coup makers that coups and assassinations would not be tolerated on the continent.

The new Togolese president was Nicholas Grunitzky, Olympio's brother-in-law and opposition leader who had been living in exile in neighboring Dahomey, re-named Benin. He was invited by Eyadema to return to Togo and assume leadership; only to be ousted by Eyadema himself four years later on January 13, 1967, on the fourth anniversary of Olympio's assassination.

Unfortunately, the stern warning by African leaders at the OAU summit in May 1963 to soldiers intent on overthrowing governments, fell on deaf ears. And military coups became a continental phenomenon and a ritual of African politics for almost 40 years from the sixties to the nineties. A total of 32 independent African countries were represented at the summit and signed the OAU Charter establishing the Organization of African Unity. They were: Algeria, Burundi, Cameroon, Central African Republic, Chad, Congo-Brazzaville, Congo-Leopoldville, Dahomey, Ethiopia, Gabon, Ghana, Guinea, Ivory Coast, Liberia, Libya, Madagascar, Mali, Mauritania, Morocco, Niger, Nigeria, Rwanda, Senegal, Sierra Leone, Somalia, Sudan, Tanganyika, Togo, Tunisia, Uganda, United Arab Republic (Egypt), and Upper Volta (now Burkina Faso).

Of the 32 countries, 26 had experienced military coups by the end of the 1990s, most of them more than once and sometimes within the same year. For example, three governments were overthrown in Sierra Leone within a month, in April 1968, and two in Nigeria in January and July 1966. Only Cameroon, Gabon, Morocco, Senegal, Tanganyika (renamed Tanzania after uniting with Zanzibar in 1964), and Egypt, among the OAU founders, escaped this scourge between the sixties and the nineties. But they all had, at one time or another, been targeted by soldiers trying to seize power. And Egypt had already experienced two military coups before then: one in 1952, and another in 1954. And it was the only country represented at the 1963 OAU summit that had been under military rule.

Almost exactly a year after the assassination of President Olympio on January 13, 1963, the armies of the three East African countries of Tanganyika, Kenya, and Uganda, mutinied in January

1964. The mutiny started in Tanganyika on January 20, and spread to Kenya next, and then to Uganda in only a matter of days. President Nyerere asked Britain for help to suppress the mutiny in Tanganyika. So did President Jomo Kenyatta in Kenya, and Prime Minister Milton Obote in Uganda. All three countries were former British colonies. But British troops did not stay long in Tanganyika. Uncomfortable with the presence of foreign troops on African soil, and in an independent country on top of that, Nyerere called for an emergency session of the Organization of African Unity (OAU) in Addis Ababa, Ethiopia, to ask for help from fellow Africans to replace British soldiers as soon as possible. Soon thereafter, Nigeria under President Nnamdi Azikiwe sent troops to Tanganyika to replace the British. Kenya and Uganda continued to rely on British assistance until the situation return to normal.

The army mutinies in the three East African countries helped inspire military coups on the continent when soldiers in other countries saw how they could use guns to extract concessions from civilian governments and even overthrow them at will. And they were some of the earliest manifestations of the intrusive power of the military in African politics as a continental phenomenon, and of what was yet to come in an even more violent way: coups and assassinations spanning four decades.

The 1964 military crisis in the three East African countries occurred around the same time two major political developments took place in what came to be known as Tanzania. On January 12, 1964, the Zanzibar revolution ended the political dominance of the Arabs when the Arab government was overthrown in one of the bloodiest conflicts in post-colonial Africa. Hundreds of people, probably no fewer than 2,000, were killed. Only about a month before on December 10, 1963, Zanzibar won independence from Britain. But the Arab leaders to whom power was transferred by the departing colonial masters excluded blacks from the government. Not long after the revolution, Tanganyika united with Zanzibar on April 26, 1964. The Union of Tanganyika and Zanzibar was renamed the United Republic of Tanzania on October 29 the same year.

However, some people in the region and elsewhere expressed strong reservations about the union, fearing that it was communist-inspired and would become a launching pad for communist penetration of Africa. Apprehensive of the situation, Ronald Ngala, leader of the Opposition - and the federalist Kenya African Democratic Union (KADU) - in the Kenyan parliament, had the following to say:

> I hope...that the overseas influence infiltrated into Zanzibar will not spread to Tanganyika in any malicious way.[13]

He made the comment on the same day Tanganyika united with Zanzibar, and mentioned "communist" influence on the former island nation because the Zanzibar revolution had been supported by some communists, including Fidel Castro, and some of the Zanzibari revolutionaries were communist or communist-oriented. But Ronald Ngala's fear of communist penetration of Tanzania, shared by others including the eccentric president of Malawi, Dr. Hastings Kamuzu Banda, proved to be unfounded. Through the years, Tanzania remained non-aligned - maintaining strong ties with both East and West - under President Nyerere and his successors, Ali Hassan Mwinyi (1985 - 1995); and Benjamin Mkapa who became president in 1995 not long after the collapse of communism except in a few countries such as China, Cuba, and North Korea where it remained a state ideology, even if not a functional one in all aspects. The union of Tanganyika and Zanzibar was the first between independent states on the entire continent, and the only one that has survived for decades.

Consummation of the union between Tanganyika and Zanzibar was a step towards African unity and consolidation of African independence. But only about a year-and-a-half later, Africa suffered a reversal in its quest for freedom. In November 1965, the same year and month General Joseph Mobutu overthrew President Joseph Kasavubu, the white minority government of the Rhodesian Front party led by Ian Smith in the British colony of Rhodesia declared independence illegally, totally excluding the black majority from power. The unilateral declaration of independence, which came to be known as UDI, was in outright defiance of the wishes and aspirations of not only the black majority in the colony but of the entire continent except the other white minority regimes in South Africa, South West Africa

(Namibia) which was ruled by apartheid South Africa, and in the Portuguese colonies of Angola, Mozambique and Portuguese Guinea (Guinea-Bissau), and in other colonial territories. Rhodesia was on the way to becoming another state like South Africa and a bastion of white power on the continent.

Since Rhodesia was a British colony, African leaders urged Britain to intervene and end Smith's rebellion. But Britain did nothing, prompting most African governments to break diplomatic relations with London, in protest. Yet the British government conceded it had jurisdiction over Rhodesia and the constitutional mandate to intervene in the rebellious colony, but still used twisted logic to justify non-intervention. It was neither impressive logic nor clever semantics, and triggered the following response from President Nyerere:

> What has Britain done since 11 November (when Rhodesia declared independence)? On that date Mr. Wilson (the British prime minister) used some strong words: he said 'it is an illegal act, ineffective in law; an act of rebellion against the crown and against the constitution as by law established.' But he then went on to instruct the civil servants of Southern Rhodesia to 'stay at their posts but not to assist in any illegal acts.' He was unable to explain how they could do that when they were serving an illegal government.
>
> As regards the use of force Mr. Wilson repeated his stock phrase despite the changed circumstances. Britain would not use force to impose a constitutional settlement, he said, but he went on to say that the British Government 'would give full consideration to any appeal from the Governor (of Rhodesia) for help to restore law and order.' Mr. Wilson refrained from explaining how the law could be more broken than it had been by the usurpation of power, that is to say, by treason. He refrained later from explaining how the Governor was to transmit his appeal once the telephone had been taken from him as well as all the furniture of his office, his staff and his transport.[14]

African countries continued to uphold what came to be known as the NIBMAR principle: No Independence Before Majority Rule. But rebel Prime Minister Ian Smith saw the future of Rhodesia from an entirely different perspective. He vowed, at different times, there shall be no majority rule in Rhodesia "not in my lifetime; not in one hundred years; not even in a thousand years." History proved him wrong within his own lifetime.

As the world entered the 21st century, Ian Smith was still living on his farm, but as an ordinary citizen this time, in a country he once ruled defiantly with a tight grip on the black majority. He was now living under his nemesis, Robert Mugabe, a black president, a man he once kept in prison for more than 10 years. Mugabe's crime was simple, yet profound in its implications for white minority rule. He was imprisoned for demanding independence on the basis of majority rule: one man, one vote, regardless of race, gender, class, religion, or national origin. He won, and Rhodesia became Zimbabwe. It was a crowning achievement after a long, bitter struggle, and one of the bloodiest in British colonial history. But, back in 1965, no one foresaw that realization of this goal would be many years away.

It was also in the same year that Africa witnessed another military coup. The coup was the second military takeover on the continent, after the first one in Togo only about two years earlier, and from which Africa had not yet recovered. On November 24, 1965, General Joseph Mobutu overthrew the government of President Joseph Kasavubu in Congo-Leopoldville, coincidentally only 13 days after the white minority regime of Ian Smith illegally declared independence for Rhodesia. Among the casualties was Evariste Kimba, appointed prime minister by President Kasavubu in October 1965 to replace Moise Tshombe who was invited in 1964 to return from exile to become Congo's premier as fighting intensified in Katanga Province. Kimba was hanged by Mobutu, as were other opponents - real and imagined - soon after the coup.

As Africa was still grappling with the Rhodesian crisis, and with the Congo, which was still in turmoil, two major developments of political and historical significance for the continent took place in 1966. On January 15, 1966, Nigeria, Africa's most populous country, was rocked by its first military coup in which Federal Prime Minister Sir Abubakar Tafawa Balewa, and two regional premiers and other top government officials, were assassinated. The coup was led by a group of young army officers from Eastern Nigeria, and it triggered a violent reaction against easterners living in Northern Nigeria after the Northern Premier Sir Ahmadu Bello, Federal Prime Minister Balewa, also a northerner, and a large number of northern military officers were killed. The other premier who was killed was Chief Samuel Ladoke Akintola of Western Nigeria. Tens of thousands of Eastern Nigerians were massacred in retaliation, pogroms which largely contributed to the secession of the Eastern Region and subsequent civil war in the following year, as did Nigeria's second military coup only a few months later in July 1966 in which the head of the federal military government, Johnson Aguiyi Ironsi, an easterner, was assassinated.

Another major political event in Africa in 1966 was the military coup in Ghana, only about a month after the first coup in Nigeria, which may have helped inspire it. On February 24, 1966, Dr. Kwame Nkrumah was overthrown while in Peking on his way to Hanoi at the invitation of Ho Chin Mihn to help end the Vietnam War. The coup was masterminded by the CIA. Black American ambassador to Ghana, Franklin Williams who was Nkrumah's schoolmate at Lincoln University, a historically black college in Pennsylvania, played a critical role in facilitating the coup. The coup makers were reportedly given at least $6 million by the CIA through the American embassy in Ghana to oust Nkrumah; his ouster partly inspired by his increasingly dictatorial rule, and by a deteriorating economy drained by expensive projects and failed socialist policies.

Dr. Nkrumah's downfall was significant in a number of respects. Not only was he one of Africa's most controversial presidents because of his daring and policy initiatives; he was also one of the most influential. Nkrumah was the first leader in sub-Saharan Africa to lead his country to independence on March 6, 1957. He was the most ardent proponent of immediate continental unification. He was the first black African head of state to institute a one-party state and adopt socialism. He was one of the strongest supporters of African independence and liberation movements. He articulated an ideology and concepts, which stimulated debate and had profound impact on the course of political events on the continent. And he remains, unto this day, the most influential African leader besides Julius Nyerere and Nelson Mandela; with Mandela's influence mainly as a moral authority, and not a political theorist like Nkrumah and Nyerere. In a poll conducted by the BBC in 2002, the majority of Africans who participated in the survey voted for Nkrumah as the most influential African leader in the twentieth century.

While many people in Ghana were debating the legacy of Dr. Nkrumah and adjusting to new life under military rule for the first time in their lives, Nigeria was hurtling towards disaster, inexorably propelled by the spiraling wave of violence as a result of the two military coups in 1966. The hour of reckoning came on May 30, 1967, when the leaders of Eastern Nigeria declared independence and renamed the secessionist region, the Republic of Biafra, "land of the rising sun." Secession of Eastern Nigeria from the rest of the federation was the biggest threat the country had faced since independence in 1960, and it had serious implications for the entire continent.

Nigeria was seen as an anchor of stability on a continent of weak states, and, because of its sheer size and enormous wealth mostly from oil, had the potential to become one of the most powerful countries in the developing world. Should it collapse, its weaker neighbors would inevitably be sucked into the vortex and suffer tremendously from the spill-over effects of the implosion. This dreadful prospect seemed to be a distinct possibility when, not long after Eastern Nigeria declared independence, hostilities broke out between the two sides in July 1967, plunging the country into civil war. From then on, until 1970, the Nigerian conflict became the dominant story dominating headlines across the continent.

The secessionist forces capitulated to federal might on January 12, 1970, and the war officially ended three days later, on January 15, when the Biafrans finally surrendered. More than one million people, mostly Igbo, perished in the conflict. Most of them died from starvation, which the military federal government used deliberately and effectively as a weapon against the Biafrans. Chief Obafemi Awolowo, vice-chairman of the Executive Council, hence vice-president of Nigeria under General Yakubu Gowon, unequivocally stated that starvation was a legitimate instrument of war against the secessionists to force them to surrender. Other estimates, including those of the BBC and other news organizations and relief agencies, put the death toll at 2 million. It was, until then, the deadliest conflict in modern African history, and one of the biggest humanitarian disasters the world had ever seen, evoking memories of the Jewish holocaust in Nazi Germany when 6 million Jews were exterminated.

The conflict in the Middle East also had direct bearing on Africa. When the third Arab-Israeli war broke out in June 1967, just one month before the Nigerian civil war erupted, almost all the

Arab countries in North Africa became directly involved in the conflict. Egypt, the leader of the Arab world and the most powerful Arab nation, played the most dominant role, sending to the front the largest number of troops among all Arab countries comprising North Africa and the Middle East; in fact, most Arabs in the world live in Africa, not in the Middle East, and Arab countries in Africa constitute the largest percentage of Arab land in the world.

In addition to Egypt, two other North African countries, Algeria and Libya, also sent troops. And most African countries supported the Arab cause, especially at the Organization of African Unity (OAU), the United Nations and in other international forums. It was also during this period that one of the most dominant political figures in the Arab world and on the African continent, President Gamal Abdel Nasser, died. He died of a heart attack on September 28, 1970. He was 52.

The year 1971 witnessed the emergence of a new political phenomenon on the African continent: Idi Amin. Ignorant and arrogant with only a standard two education - Americans call it second grade; flamboyant and comical, he earned himself a place in history for his atrocities and buffoonery few would envy. An eccentric and bizarre character, he admired Hitler and tried to emulate him. He even wanted to build a monument to the Fuhrer, in his likeness, in Uganda's capital Kampala. Yet he did not have a policy of systematic ethnic cleansing involving extermination, although he initially targeted members of the Langi and Acholi ethnic groups whom he thought were loyal to deposed President Milton Obote who was a Langi. They constituted a disproportionately large number of enlisted men and officers in the Ugandan army whom Amin swiftly replaced with men loyal to him. And through the years, he also targeted assorted groups, including real and perceived enemies, across the spectrum, and praised Hitler as a true nationalist for persecuting and exterminating Jews. He even expelled almost all Asians from Uganda in 1972, including Ugandan citizens of Asian - mostly Indian and Pakistani - origin, and gave them only three weeks to leave the country. About 70,000 left Uganda.

I remember the expulsions well. I was on the same flight, East African Airways (EAA), with some of the expelled Asians in November 1972 on the way to Britain, and got the chance to talk with an elderly Indian sitting next to me. He was one of those kicked out of Uganda by the burly dictator and talked about this forced exodus, about which I had known when I was a reporter at the *Daily News* in Dar es Salaam, Tanzania. The flight originated from Dar es Salaam, Tanzania's capital, where I caught the plane on my way to the United States for the first time as a student. Our first stop was Nairobi, Kenya; next, Kampala, Uganda, where the expelled Asians boarded the plane on their way to Britain and whatever other countries would take them in. Stripped of their possessions including financial assets, they landed in Britain, and in other countries such as Canada and the United States, destitute. Most of them ended up in Britain, Uganda's former colonial ruler. Almost all the passengers on the flight I was on from Uganda were Asians expelled by Idi Amin, as were those on subsequent flights, booked full.

President Julius Nyerere of Tanzania publicly condemned Idi Amin for expelling the Asians and called him a racist. Two other African leaders, President Kenneth Kaunda of Zambia and President Samora Machel of Mozambique, also criticized Amin for his brutalities and eccentric behavior in general. But it was Nyerere who was most explicit in his condemnation of Amin, and strongly criticized other African leaders for their silence and tolerance - and even admiration - of the Ugandan despot and for practicing tyranny in their own countries. He reminded them that had Idi Amin been white, and had the apartheid regime of South Africa gone on a genocidal rampage, slaughtering blacks across the country, these same leaders would have been furious. There would have been an outcry across the continent, calling for severe sanctions and even military action against the white murderers. But because Amin was black, other African leaders simply looked the other way, as they did when other atrocities were being committed across the continent by fellow Africans. Black leadership had become a license to kill fellow blacks.

Idi Amin was one of the most brutal tyrants Africa has ever produced. And he was probably the most notorious, grabbing international headlines every few days - sometimes everyday - for his antics and brutality. He went on a genocidal rampage, killing an estimated 500,000 - 8000,000 people during his eight-year blood-soaked reign of terror in a relentless campaign viciously prosecuted across ethnic lines by his henchmen. Everybody including his wives, was fair game, as he sought to eliminate all his enemies, real and imagined. And he himself participated in many of those killings, personally delivering the final blow. He also reportedly bragged about eating the flesh of his opponents.

After he was chased out of Uganda eight years later in April 1979 by Tanzanian troops and Ugandan exiles, he left the country in tatters; a monument to the incalculable damage he inflicted on that beautiful land and on his fellow countrymen during his brutal reign, drenched in blood on a scale unparalleled in the history of post-colonial Africa.

Other brutal dictators who earned notoriety in the seventies included President Masie Nguema of Equatorial Guinea. During his 11-year reign, from 1968 - 1969, he terrorized the entire country and left it in ruins. About one-third of the population, at least 100,000 people, fled into exile, and an estimated 40,000 were tortured and killed. His nephew, 33-year-old Colonel Teodoro Obiang Nguema overthrew him in August 1979. President Nguema tried to escape but was captured, tried for genocide and witchcraft, and executed with six aides in September 1979.

Another brutal tyrant with a knack for grabbing headlines like Idi Amin was President Jean-Bedel Bokassa of the Central African Republic. In January 1966, Colonel Bokassa overthrew President David Dacko, his cousin. He dissolved the national legislature, abolished the constitution, and banned political parties. Suspected political opponents were routinely arrested and summarily executed or tortured indefinitely. He was also said to practice cannibalism like Idi Amin, his friend.

In December 1976, Bokassa crowned himself Africa's first socialist emperor at a sports stadium in the capital Bangui in a ceremony that cost $20 million and drained the coffers of his impoverished nation. His official title was Emperor Bokassa I. His brutality knew no bounds. When school boys demonstrated against a government decree ordering them to buy uniforms from a shop partly owned by one of Bokassa's three wives, the notorious dictator ordered them arrested. About 100 of them were brutally murdered in April 1979. Bokassa himself personally killed 39 of the students.

The seventies also witnessed a series of other tragedies on

the African continent. In 1972, a campaign of ethnic cleansing in Burundi by the Tutsi military rulers claimed more than 200,000 Hutu lives within three months; a genocide which presaged what was to happen 22 years later in neighboring Rwanda, which has roughly the same ethnic ratio and composition and whose holocaust claimed even more lives than the massacres in Burundi. At least five times as many lives were lost in Rwanda, but of Tutsis this time, and at a rate five times faster than Hitler killed the Jews.

In 1974, one of Africa's most influential and revered leaders, Emperor Haile Selassie of Ethiopia, was deposed in a military coup. He died in 1975 in captivity, reportedly smothered with a wet pillow, and was buried in an unmarked grave, symbolically intended to shunt him into oblivion. Nyerere intervened and tried to save his life but did not succeed in convincing the military rulers to free the deposed emperor and spare his life. One of the reasons for his ouster was his unwillingness or refusal to admit that tens of thousands of his people were starving - he was ashamed, as an emperor. Also known as the Lion of Judah, and King of Kings, Haile Selassie was said to be a descendant of King Solomon and the Queen of Sheba, and the 250th king in that line of succession, although some dispute this claim to royal lineage.

But the military regime, which ended the monarchy, turned out to be ruthless on a scale unheard of during Emperor Haile Selassie's reign. In June 1974, Ethiopian troops overthrew the government and declared "war on feudalism." At least 200 former cabinet members and advisers to the emperor were arrested. Haile Selassie himself was deposed in September 1974, ending his 58-year reign as Africa's only emperor and one of the most respected leaders on the continent. The military junta officially abolished the Ethiopian monarchy in March 1975. After a protracted power struggle, Lieutenant-Colonel Mengistu Haile Mariam emerged as Ethiopia's ruler. A dictator, he went on to institute a reign of terror that claimed more than 5,000 lives in 1977 - 78. Nine assassination attempts on Mengistu were reported by his government in 1978, leading to the execution of many members of the ruling military junta. In 1981, Amnesty International estimated that 10,000 to 40,000 political prisoners remained in Ethiopian jails and prisons. Many were tortured and killed.

The famine in Ethiopia went on to claim more than one million lives through the seventies and early eighties. In 1982 - 85, Ethiopia had one of the worst droughts in its history. More than 9 million people faced starvation. A major international relief effort mobilized more than $700 million in government and private aid for the famine victims who received thousands of tons of grain and other supplies including medicine. Famine in other African countries such as Niger, Mali, Chad, and Upper Volta (renamed Burkina Faso in 1984), also claimed hundreds of thousands of lives during the same period.

Civil wars also dominated headlines in Africa during this period. In 1975, the Portuguese colonies of Angola and Mozambique won independence after 500 years of colonial rule; Portuguese Guinea, also the oldest colony, won hers as Guinea-Bissau in 1974, becoming the first Portuguese colony on the continent to emerge from colonial rule. But immediately after that, Angola was plunged into full-scale civil war - it actually never stopped between the three contending parties, the MPLA (Popular Movement for the Liberation of Angola), UNITA (Union for the Total Independence of Angola), and FNLA (National Front for the Liberation of Angola), which had been fighting for control of Angola while at the same fighting against the Portuguese. The FNLA withered in the late seventies, not long after Angola won independence, but UNITA continued to fight against the ruling MPLA through the decades and into the twentieth-first century. By the end of 2000, the war had cost more than one million lives and devastated the country. It ended in April 2002 after rebel leader Dr. Jonas Savimbi was killed by government soldiers in February the same year.

While the war in Angola was raging in the seventies, another major conflict erupted between Ethiopia and Somalia in 1977 after Somalia invaded its neighbor to reclaim the Ogaden Region - which is predominantly ethnic Somali - Ethiopia annexed in the 1890s. The two countries continued to fight intermittently through the years until 1988 when Somalia surrendered. The Somali army was devastated back in 1978 after eight months of intense warfare, but was still able to sustain a protracted conflict between the two countries through its surrogates, Somali guerrillas in the Ogaden, until 1988 when Somalia conceded defeat and signed a peace agreement with Ethiopia, virtually on the victor's terms.

It was also during the same period that Tanzania and Uganda went to war after Idi Amin invaded Tanzania in October 1978 and annexed 710 square miles of its territory in the northwest Kagera Region. He also had other territorial ambitions to seize and annex a corridor of Tanzanian territory and what then was the country's second largest city, Tanga on the east coast, ostensibly to have an outlet to the sea. But his imperial ambitions didn't get very far. Tanzania drove out the invaders and, together with an army of Ugandan exiles, marched all the way to Kampala, forcing Amin to flee the country in April 1979. He sought refuge in Libya, welcomed by another mercurial leader, Muammar al-Qaddafi who earlier sent troops and weapons to Uganda to help Amin fight Tanzania. The war, which lasted for six months and finally ended Amin's brutal dictatorship, inflicted a heavy blow on Tanzania and cost the poverty-stricken nation more than $500 million.

Africa entered a new decade, the 1980s, with some good news. In April 1980, white minority rule in Rhodesia came to an end after a 15-year guerrilla war of independence in which tens of thousands of people were killed. The country was renamed Zimbabwe. But the euphoria of independence was marred by the massacre of more than 20,000 people by government troops in the early 1980s in the opposition stronghold of Matebeland in southwestern Zimbabwe; a brutal campaign that exacerbated tensions between the country's two major ethnic groups, the Shona who constitute about 80 percent of the population and dominate the government, and the Ndebele who make up about 20 percent and once ruled the Shona before the advent of colonial rule.

But more than any other country in Africa, Sudan has suffered the longest from the scourge of war. Its war began in 1955, just before the country won independence from Britain and Egypt in 1956, and cost more than 500,000 lives by 1972 when the Arab-dominated government in the north reached a cease-fire agreement with the black insurgents in the south who had been fighting against Arab domination and for autonomy. The war re-ignited in 1983 and claimed more than two million lives by 1999 in that 15-year period alone. With about three million dead since 1955, it was the bloodiest conflict in African post-colonial history up to the end of the twentieth-century and beyond, and came to be known as the world's longest, bloodiest, and most forgotten war. In July 2002, the two sides signed the Machakos Agreement - in the town of Machakos, Kenya, under the auspices of Kenyan President Daniel arap Moi - and agreed to share power; allow the south to enjoy extensive autonomy; and hold an internationally supervised referendum after six years - in 2008 - to enable the people of the south decide if they wanted to remain part of Sudan or secede and establish their own independent nation. Whether or not the agreement will be implemented, given the duplicitous nature of the Khartoum regime, is an entirely different matter.

The mid-eighties saw the eruption of another major civil war in Africa, besides the conflict in Sudan that was already going on. In 1986, a rebel group called RENAMO (Portuguese acronym for Mozambique National Resistance) started waging a sustained military campaign against the FRELIMO government of Mozambique; FRELIMO is an acronym for Front for the Liberation of Mozambique, an organization that waged guerrilla war and ended Portuguese colonial rule in the country. The conflict between RENAMO and FRELIMO started earlier, before 1986, but escalated in the mid-eighties. RENAMO was created with the help of the Rhodesian security forces and supported by apartheid South Africa, the United States, and right-wing organizations in the West. Other countries, including Saudi Arabia, also supported RENAMO. The war went on for 16 years. When it ended in 1992, more than one million people had been killed, and at least five million ended up as refugees, mostly in Tanzania and Malawi. It was one of the most brutal wars in modern African history, characterized by gruesome mutilation, chopping off limbs, ears and lips like in Sierra Leone.

Chad was also embroiled in civil war in the 1980s. Civil conflict in Chad began in the sixties between Arabs in the north, who are mostly Muslim, and blacks in the south who are predominantly Christian. In the seventies and eighties, outside powers were involved in the conflict and switched sides, supporting one side and then the other, whenever it suited their interests. The United States and France were allies against Libya and her clients throughout the conflict. Tens of thousands of people died in the war in the seventies and eighties alone. The government of Hissene Habre, a northerner, killed more than 40,000 people and tortured more than 100,000 in southern Chad, his opponents' stronghold. The conflict was political as much as it was racial, as has been the case since the sixties when Arabs in the north, a minority in the country, tried to secede or establish an autonomous state with the help of Libya after they failed to dominate the country following the end of French colonial rule in 1960.

Famine also continued to ravage Africa in the 1980s, and many countries in a belt stretching across the north-central part of the continent from Mali to Ethiopia faced massive starvation. They were helpless and could only count on international relief efforts to alleviate their plight. Hundreds of thousands of people died. Drought was responsible for most of the famine, and also wiped out livestock. But mismanagement, corruption, wrong policies and inept leadership also played a major role in exacerbating the situation.

The collapse of communism in the late 1980s and early 1990s ushered in a new era round the globe. Just as the sixties saw most African countries become one-party states and socialist or socialist-oriented, the early nineties witnessed a reversal of that when almost all the countries embraced multiparty democracy and capitalism, once considered their nemesis in the quest for unity and development. After the end of communism, free-market policies were adopted in countries - including Russia and former Soviet satellites - which had pursued socialist policies for decades even before African countries won independence. And multiparty democracy found ready acceptance where it had been reviled by leaders as a tool of the capitalist West to divide and dominate weaker countries. African countries shared this view after they attained sovereign status. And when change came, showing that communism had failed, Africa was no exception from this reconfiguration of the political landscape. In the early 1990s, a wave of democratization swept across the continent, which had been dominated by one-party states since the sixties, and socialism was renounced as a state ideology even by countries, which had been the strongest exponents of this politico-economic philosophy.

The early nineties also witnessed the beginning of the end of apartheid in South Africa, the bastion of white supremacy on the continent. In February 1990, South Africa's most prominent political prisoner, Nelson Mandela, was released from prison after being incarcerated for more than 27 years. The apartheid regime finally collapsed in May 1994 when Mandela became president after the first multiracial democratic elections in the country's history. However, the transition to the new dispensation had also been marred by political and ethnic violence in the early nineties, which cost more than 10,000 lives within three years before the April 1994 elections, which were a spectacular success.

But in spite of the good news about the end of apartheid, whose demise was celebrated across the continent, 1994 was also a tragic year for Africa. It was the year when at least one million people, mostly Tutsi, were massacred by the Hutu in Rwanda within three months, at a rate five times faster than Hitler killed the Jews. The massacres took place - from April to July 1994 - around the same time South Africa was emerging from her nightmare of apartheid. It was a strange coincidence, "the best of times, and the worst of times," in the words of Charles Dickens. As Wole Soyinka stated in one of his articles, "The Blood-soaked Quilt of Africa," in May 1994: "Rwanda is our nightmare, South Africa is our dream." Tragically, the nightmare has not yet ended, not only in Rwanda but in many parts of Africa.

The bloodshed in Rwanda was only one of the tragedies that befell Africa during the nineties. It was a decade of wars, and AIDS, and other calamities. Besides having the largest number of AIDS victims and casualties, Africa also had the largest number of civil wars in the 1990s, more than in any other period since independence in the sixties. At least 25 countries were torn by civil conflicts: Algeria, Sierra Leone, Liberia, Guinea-Bissau, Sudan, Somalia, Ethiopia, Uganda, Rwanda, Burundi, Congo-Kinshasa, Congo-Brazzaville, Angola, Mozambique, Kenya, Chad, the Central African Republic, Cote d'Ivoire (Ivory Coast), Nigeria, Mali, Senegal, Niger, the Comoros, Lesotho, and South Africa during the transition from apartheid to democracy.

Some of the bloodiest conflicts that erupted in the nineties took place in Liberia and Sierra Leone. The war in Liberia started in December 1989, and in Sierra Leone in 1991. Both countries were totally destroyed. About 200,000 were killed in Sierra Leone, more than 100,000 maimed, and tens of thousands were uprooted from their homes and ended up as refugees in neighboring countries. In Liberia, also more than 200,000 were killed, more than 800,000 ended up as refugees, and about 6 to 8 percent of the total population perished in the seven-year conflict. In Sierra Leone, the rebels of the Revolutionary United Front (RUF) earned international notoriety because of their gruesome tactics, chopping off limbs, ears and lips, gouging out eyes, chopping off buttocks, and other brutalities inflicted on innocent civilians including the elderly, women, and babies only a few weeks old. They all met the same fate, sometimes with both arms and legs chopped off.

As the century came to an end, the wars were still raging in both countries. The war in Sierra Leone formally ended in January 2002, but there was no guarantee peace would be maintained after British troops, which ended the war, left the country. UN peacekeeping troops, the largest force ever deployed anywhere in UN's history, also helped restore peace but were not as effective as British combat troops. In Liberia, the war formally ended in 1996, but low-intensity warfare - and sometimes pitched battles in sporadic fighting in different parts of the country - continued through the years in an attempt by rebel groups to overthrow President Charles Taylor; a brutal warlord and dictator who intimidated his fellow countrymen into voting for him in 1997, with the implied threat that he would plunge Liberia back into war if he did not win the presidency. A thug even in office, he continued to use brutal tactics against real and perceived enemies, torturing and killing them. The brutalities helped fuel the war against his regime. In February 2002, he came perilously close to being overthrown when one of the rebel groups advanced towards the capital, Monrovia, and was within striking range - only about 20 miles - when government forces fought back. The conflict escalated into full-scale war in different parts of the country, forcing tens of thousands of refugees to flee and seek shelter elsewhere within Liberia and in the Ivory Coast and other neighboring countries.

The 1990s were tragic in another respect. These were also the years when Somalia died as a nation, pulverized from within, the only African country to "disappear" from the map; and the only country in the world that had no government and remained stateless from 1991 - when it first collapsed - well into the 21st century. It was also during this period that another nation, Eritrea, was born out of Ethiopia in May 1993. Ethiopia became the first African country to break up peacefully, and Eritrea the first to be born out of another since the advent of colonial rule and in the post-colonial era, although it once was an Italian colony and was forcibly incorporated into Ethiopia in 1952 by the United Nations as a condition for its "independence." Ethiopia ended up absorbing it, turning it into one of its provinces and a virtual colony. It was, for all practical purposes, the last "colony" on the continent, colonized within the "mother country," Ethiopia, and ended that status as Africa, with all her problems, staggered towards the beginning of another century, with hope and despair.

Some of the deadliest conflicts hardly made headlines outside Africa. In Congo-Brazzaville, a four-month civil war from June 5 - October 15, 1997, devastated the capital, Brazzaville. Entire parts of the city were reduced to rubble, and more than 10,000 people were killed in the capital alone when government troops of President Pascal Lissouba fought a militia group, the Cobra, supporting former miltary dictator Denis Sassuou-Nguesso. Lissouba, a former professor, won the presidency in a democratic election in 1992 but fled to Burkina Faso where he was granted asylum after he lost the war in 1997. Sporadic fighting continued in different parts of the country in the following years, with the Ninja rebels and other forces loyal to former President Lissouba and to the former Brazzaville mayor Bernard Kolelas who once served as prime minister under Lissouba, trying to oust President Denis Sassou-Nguesso.

And in 1998, another major civil war erupted in Guinea-Bissau between government troops loyal to President Joao Bernardo Vieira and rebel soldiers led by former army chief Ansumane Mane. The rebels seized most of the country and much of the capital, Bissau, and finally toppled the president in May 1999. Tens of thousands of people fled their homes, creating a major refugee crisis in one of the world's smallest and poorest countries. General Ansumane Mane was eventually killed by government troops in November 2000 for allegedly trying to launch a coup d'etat.

The last two years of the decade (1998 - 1999) also witnessed the bloodiest conflict on the continent since World War

II when Ethiopia and Eritrea went to war over a barren piece of land. The war involved tanks, fully mechanized battalions, combat jets and other modern weapons, but was mostly fought as trench warfare like World War I. The war cost more than 100,000 lives in a combined total of only a few weeks of intense fighting, sometimes claiming as many as 5,000 - 10,000 lives within a few days. Although the war was fought intermittently, it drained the economies of both countries, some of the poorest in the world. Both countries spent hundreds of millions of dollars, buying expensive and highly sophisticated weapons, while their people - especially in Ethiopia - were starving.

The 1990s were also a period when the AIDS epidemic wreaked havoc across the African continent, more than anywhere else, and continued to do so, well into the 21st century, with no cure in sight. The statistics were appalling, and AIDS became an acronym for Africa Is Dying Slowly. Since the beginning of the epidemic in the early 1980s, more than 20 million people in sub-Sharan Africa had died of AIDS by the end of 2000; more than twice the number of those who died in World War I. For example in Zimbabwe, at least 5,000 were dying per day. And about half of all 15-year-olds infected with the HIV virus that causes AIDS will eventually die of the disease, even if infection rates drop substantially through a combination of therapies - which are light years away for poverty-stricken Africa - and education on AIDS prevention.

Thus, even with the combined casualties from all the African wars since the 1950s and 1960s, including liberation wars against colonial regimes, the death-toll in those conflicts comes nowhere close to the number of people who died of AIDS in Africa by the end of the 1990s; a casualty rate that is bound to grow exponentially through the years, short of divine intervention or some miracle cure to stop the pandemic.

There was also another dimension to some of the African conflicts during this period. There were secessionist threats which led to skirmishes between the insurgents and government troops on the independence-prone island of Bioko in Equatorial Guinea in 1998, and in Caprivi Strip in Namibia in 1999 and beyond. However, they were not major threats. But there were other secessionist attempts on the continent that were far more deadly and escalated into full-scale war on the separatist islands of Anjouan and Moheli in the Comoros in September 1997, while the conflict in Casamance Province in Senegal had been going on as a full-scale guerrilla war since 1983 when secessionist forces in the region resorted to violence to achieve their goal.

There were other appalling statistics in the 1990s on this embattled continent. The civil war in the Democratic Republic of Congo, formerly Zaire, which drew armies from at least nine African countries, cost almost 2 million lives in Eastern Congo alone, between August 1998 when the latest round of fighting started and May 2000. By June 2001, more than 2.5 million people had died, and no fewer than 3 million by mid-2002 in the same region. The countries involved were the Congo itself, Zimbabwe, Angola, Namibia, Rwanda, Uganda, Burundi, Chad, and Sudan. Rwanda, Uganda and Burundi supported the rebels trying to overthrow the government, while the rest backed up the Congolese army in its war against the insurgents; there were about 20 rebel groups involved in the war, with conflicting interests. The intervention by foreign armies from other African countries internationalized the conflict that some people called "Africa's First World War"; a hyperbolic statement whose outlandish nature did not help to place the conflict in its proper historical context. Although it was an inflated statement, there was no question that the war was a major conflict with serious implications for the stability of the continent. And it was still going on as Africa entered the 21st century, as did most wars on the continent. Africa had declared war on itself.

Even in a continent used to wars, the casualty list is staggering. Millions of Africans have died in these conflicts: Angola, more than 1 million; Mozambique, more than 1 million; Congo, formerly Zaire, more than 3 million; Rwanda, about 1 million killed within 100 days; Burundi, between 250,000 - 500,000 killed within 5 years since the mid-1990s; Somalia, more than 500,000 dead in the 1990s; Ethiopia, tens of thousands dead; Eritrea, also tens of thousands dead in a senseless war with Ethiopia over some tiny, barren piece of land, two bald-headed men fighting over a comb; Sudan, more than 3 million dead since 1983; Sierra Leone, more than 200,000 dead, and more than 100,000 left limbless, their limbs, and even buttocks, ears and lips,

chopped off by rebels in an 11-year civil war from 19ᶜ
Liberia, more than 200,000 dead, about 6 - 8 percent oɪ ᴜ.
population, equivalent to 16.2 million - 20.6 million Americaɴᴜ
dead in a civil war within the same period. And this is not an
exhaustive list of the number of people killed in wars in this
mangled continent.

Some of the least known wars have also been some of the
deadliest. Uganda has, relatively speaking, a reputation for stability
in a region torn by conflict; although not like neighboring Tanzania
which is far more peaceful and stable than all the countries in East
Africa. Yet, for years, it had to contend with several rebel groups
since the eighties when President Yoweri Museveni assumed
power in 1986 after waging a successful guerrilla campaign against
the government. One of the bloodiest conflicts was in northern
Uganda where rebels of the Lord's Resistance Army backed by
Sudan killed tens of thousands of people and abducted just as
many, mostly children, forcing them to join the rebel army and
work as sex slaves and porters, in addition to playing combat role.
The rebel group continued to wage war as late as 2002, and
remained the deadliest among all the insurgents in Uganda
including those waging a sporadic guerrilla campaign in the
western part of the country.

In neighboring Kenya, more than 10,000 people were killed
within three weeks in a tribal war between the Pokot and Turkana
tribesmen in the northern part of the country in 1998. Earlier in
1992, ethnic cleansing in the Rift Valley Province, home of
President Daniel arap Moi and his fellow Kalenjin tribesmen,
claimed hundreds of Kikuyu lives, at least 1,300, and forced
300,000 others to flee for their lives, while their property was
ransacked and destroyed by the Kalenjins. Other tribal conflicts,
including those during the 1997 general elections in the Coast
Province and again in the Rift Valley Province, claimed more lives
in different parts of the country through the years.

In Nigeria, communal and ethnic violence threatened to
tear apart Africa's biggest nation and continued to do so well into
the 21st century. Within only three years since the inauguration of
President Olusegun Obasanjo in May 1999, the violence claimed
more than 10,000 lives in different parts of the country. The
conflicts were exacerbated by the introduction of Islamic law,

know as *sharia* (in Kiswahili, a language which is about 25 - 30 percent Arabic, *sheria* - not *sharia* - means law), in the predominantly Muslim states in the north, triggering clashes between Muslims and Christians originally from the south. Besides the religious dimension, the conflict was also ethnic. The Christians from the south, living in Northern Nigeria, are mostly Igbo and members of other ethnic groups, while the Muslims in the north are mostly members of the Hausa and Fulani ethnic groups which are so close to each other - ethnically, culturally, and religiously - that they are simply and collectively known as Hausa-Fulani; with the Fulani mainly constituting the ruling class. The conflicts in Nigeria, especially in the oil-rich Niger Delta, were also ignited and fueled by government neglect, prompting some people to call for secession.

The end of the 1990s were also marked by another tragedy. Famine threatened the lives of millions of people in East Africa. About 18 million people faced starvation in Ethiopia; 13 million in Kenya faced the same dreadful prospect, prompting one elderly Kenyan photographed and quoted by *The Washington Post* to say, "It's only you white people who can save us," a searing indictment against African governments in general for their inability and unwillingness to help their people. And 13 million people in Tanzania, about 40 percent of the population, were threatened by famine during the same period. Hardest hit were the countries in southern Africa that faced massive starvation at the dawn of the new century, especially in 2001 - 2002.   Malawi, Zambia, Zimbabwe, Angola, Botswana, Mozambique, Swaziland, Lesotho, Namibia, and even South Africa, all faced famine, only in varying degrees. Malawi, Angola, and Zimbabwe whose crisis was aggravated by the seizure of white-owned farms by President Robert Mugabe's government, were the hardest hit, and an international relief effort was launched to help alleviate the plight of millions of people in the region.

But there was also a glimmer of hope, at least for future generations, when the defunct East African Community (EAC), which collapsed in 1977, was revived in 2001 and became functional in 2002 in pursuit of stronger regional integration including federation. The member states are Kenya, Uganda, and Tanzania which may one day establish the East African federation that has been an elusive dream since 1963 when Julius Nyerere, Jomo Kenyatta and Milton Obote tried to unite the three countries. The prospects for regional integration also gave some hope to the people of West Africa when the countries in the region decided in 2000 to institute a common currency known as the Eco by 2004. It was an ambitious project whose fulfillment would depend on the commitment of the member states - Economic Community of West African States (ECOWAS) - to the ideal of regional integration.

The goal towards integration on a continental scale assumed another dimension in June 2001 when the Organization of African Unity (OAU) founded in May 1963 was replaced by the African Union (AU) to facilitate the establishment of a common market, a common currency - the Afro? - and other institutions including a continental parliament. The OAU officially came to an end at an annual summit of the African heads of state and government in Lusaka, Zambia, in June 2001 under the chairmanship of Zambian President Frederick Chiluba. It was skillfully led for an unprecedented three consecutive five-year terms by Dr. Salim Ahmed Salim of Tanzania who served as OAU secretary-general from 1986 to 2001. The African Union (AU) was formally launched in Durban, South Africa, in July 2002 under the chairmanship of South African President Thabo Mbeki.

And the Southern African Development Community (SADC) composed of 14 countries in East and Southern Africa, and the strongest economic bloc on the continent because of South Africa's membership, the continent's powerhouse, continued to grow and took further steps to achieve full economic integration in the region. Measures proposed include establishment of a common market, a common currency, and a regional parliament. On a continent dominated by bad news, the trend towards regional integration was some of the best news to come out of Africa as the 20th century came to an end.

But there was more bad news. Africa suffered another tragic loss at the end of the 1990s that was also an important milestone in the history of Africa. Tanzania's first president, Julius Nyerere, died on October 14, 1999. He was 77. Nyerere was one of the most prominent African leaders in the 20th century who spearheaded the independence movement across the continent. He was also one of the most articulate and ardent spokesmen for the

Third World. His death marked the end of an era in the history of post-colonial Africa, and the dawn of a new one in terms of ideological orientation and leadership. Nyerere was one of the last of the most prominent African leaders who led their countries to independence in the fifties and sixties. They included Kwame Nkrumah, Jomo Kenyatta, Nnamdi Azikiwe, Patrice Lumumba, Ahmed Sekou Toure, and Modibo Keita. He outlived them all, except Kenneth Kaunda, Milton Obote, Leopold Sedar Senghor, and Ahmed Ben Bella. His belief in socialism remained unshaken, and he died with his reputation for integrity intact.

Nyerere will be remembered for generations as one of the founding fathers of independent Africa and a staunch advocate of Pan-Africanism whose ideology and philosophy was embraced by those in the diaspora as well, comparable in stature to another uncompromising Pan-Africanist, Dr. Kwame Nkrumah. As one South African journalist wrote about Nyerere's role in the liberation of the countries in southern Africa from white minority rule: "All these countries are now free, with their liberation sprung from Dar es Salaam."[15] Another one stated: "From Dr. Nyerere's commitment flowed the liberation first of Mozambique, Angola, Guinea-Bissau and Cape Verde in the early '70s, followed by Zimbabwe in 1980, Namibia in 1990 and eventually South Africa."[16] And as Nyerere himself said about some of his achievements: "We took over a country with 85 per cent of its adults illiterate. The British ruled us for 43 years. When they left, there were two trained engineers and 12 doctors. When I stepped down, there was 91 per cent literacy and nearly every child was in school. We trained thousands of engineers, doctors and teachers."[17]

The death of Julius Nyerere evoked strong feelings from many people in different parts of the world, most of it positive. Some of the most memorable tribute came from Ghanaian Member of parliament, Hackman Owusu-Agyemang, who was also minority spokesman for foreign affairs, later minister of foreign affairs under President John Kufuor:

> Dr. Nyerere even in death at the state-owned St. Thomas Hospital in London, symbolized the humility and modesty that had come to be associated with his life-style.... That he retired from politics with nothing more than a second-hand tractor and a bicycle showed that as President he neither dipped his hands into state coffers nor private pockets. Nor were his hands covered with

anyone's blood....

His Ujamaa community-based farming collective which was conceived with due acknowledgement of the African communal way of life, in spite of its failure as a concept, demonstrated his sensitivity to the plight of his people and his desire to provide the needed leadership.... Dr. Nyerere indeed personified selflessness, sincerity and sensitivity.

An avowed fighter against colonialism and apartheid, Mwalimu who played a pioneering role in the O.A.U. will forever be remembered as an African leader with his name engraved in gold.

By his retirement from the Presidency of Tanzania in 1985, Dr. Nyerere lived up to his title as Mwalimu since he not only taught but demonstrated the virtue in bowing out even when the applaud is loud....

As we mourn the loss of this gem and giant of a statesman, we take consolation in the fact that death, coming at this time, has been the crown of a historic, rich and fulfilling life for Mwalimu Julius Nyerere.... The death of Dr. Julius Nyerere has robbed Africa of a leading light, whose exploits as a politician and statesman filled the hearts of Africans with joy and inspiration.

We...recall with nostalgia the passion and zeal with which a young Dr. Julius Nyerere together with our own Dr. Kwame Nkrumah and other African nationalists, prosecuted the anti-colonist and independence struggle to liberate Africa from foreign domination. That today, the last vestige of colonialism has been routed in Africa, is to a large extent, due to the untiring efforts of Dr. Nyerere and his co-fighters in the African liberation struggle.[18]

Tragically, he died when Africa, mired in conflict, needed him most. As he himself said not long before he died: "Africa is in a mess."

But in spite of all the tragedies the continent has endured through the years, there was also some good news out of Africa at the end of the 1990s, although not much. And it inspired many people across the continent. Africa's giant nation, Nigeria, finally returned to democracy in May 1999 after 15 years of uninterrupted brutal military dictatorship.

Where Nigeria is headed, and what the future has in store for the rest of Africa, was never meant for us to know. But we know one thing. We have come a long way since the sixties. And we still have a long way to go. We will keep on going, even if we don't get there. We have no other choice. And that is Africa's only choice.

CHAPTER THREE:

JULIUS NYERERE:
EARLY YEARS

HE WAS of peasant origin, but from a ruling family. He was the son of a chief of the Zanaki tribe, one of the smallest in Tanzania and in Africa with a total population of about 40,000. An excellent student, he was also known for his extraordinary brilliance and as an original thinker throughout his life and came to be acknowledged as a philosopher-king. Yet he also won accolades for his humility and simplicity and as one of the most humble leaders the world has ever produced. He was Julius Nyerere.

Julius Nyerere was born on April 13, 1922, in the village of Butiama near the town of Musoma in Mara Region on the southeastern shores of Lake Victoria in northern Tanganyika, now Tanzania. Only about a year before he was born, the British had assumed control of the former Germany colony, known as German East Africa, after Germany was defeated in World War I by the Allied forces. The colony was renamed Tanganyika.

The history of Tanganyika would have been entirely different had the Americans assumed control of the territory under the League of Nations mandate. In October 1920, British Prime Minister Lloyd George of the Liberal Party asked President Woodrow Wilson to take over and administer the former German colony as an American territory. But America's isolationist stance during that period precluded any possibility of such foreign involvement. Had Tanganyika become an American colony, it is possible the United States would have tried to annex it or keep it permanently as one of its overseas possessions, as successive American governments became increasingly involved in foreign ventures. And the struggle for independence, as well as the career of Nyerere, would have taken an entirely different turn.

Like any other typical African, Julius Nyerere grew up working on the farm and taking care of livestock. His future took an unexpected turn when he started attending school at Mwisenge

Primary School in Musoma. He was 12. It is said that the decision to send him to school was made after he demonstrated superb skills and great ability playing *bao*, an African game that requires superior strategic thinking and mathematical calculations. He always excelled at the game, beating older and more experienced opponents. As Arthur Wille, a Catholic priest who knew Nyerere for many years long before he became a national leader and worked as a missionary in Nyerere's home area and was taught the Kizanaki language by Nyerere, stated:

> At tea in the afternoons, Nyerere would frequently talk about himself. One day he told how he got the opportunity to go to school. His elder brother Wanzagi had not been given this opportunity. His father, Chief Nyerere, had a good friend, also a chief of the Ikizu tribe, Mohamedi Makongoro. They frequently enjoyed an African game called 'Soro' in Kizanaki or 'Bao' in Swahili. To play this game well requires a lot of intelligence. The game is played on a long board that has four rows of holes in it. Pebbles or seeds are moved along these holes in order to land them in such a position that you will confiscate your opponent's pebbles until they are finished. To do this, one has to figure many moves ahead and keep track in one's mind every position that you will end up in. When Julius' father would be busy, Julius himself would play this game with Chief Makongoro. Frequently, he would beat him. One day, Makongoro told Julius' father that he should send his son into school at Mwisenge that the British had started for the education of the sons of the chiefs. It was because of this prompting by Chief Makongoro that Julius was sent to primary school in Mwisenge.[1]

In 1934, he joined Mwisenge Primary School, a turning point in his life that coincided with that of another future African leader. It was around the same time that Kwame Nkrumah, who was Nyerere's senior by 13 years, left the Gold Coast - later renamed Ghana - for the United States to attend Lincoln University, a historically black college in Pennsylvania. He left in 1935. It was also in the same year, 1935, as Nkrumah states in his autobiography, *Ghana: The Autobiography of Kwame Nkrumah*,[2] that Nigeria's future president Nnamdi Azikiwe returned to Africa after attending school in the United States, while Nkrumah was on his way to Lincoln University. Julius Nyerere was then in standard two, what Americans call the second grade, in primary school.

Nyerere was at Mwisenge Primary School from 1934 to 1936. His Roman Catholic teachers quickly noticed him as an extraordinarily intelligent student. He also demonstrated remarkable ability in learning languages and quickly learned Kiswahili and English. In 1936, he excelled in the final examinations and earned academic distinction by topping the list of all the students throughout Tanganyika who took the examination to qualify for further education at Tabora St. Mary's Secondary School in western Tanganyika, an elite school run by Catholics. The school was patterned after private schools in Britain and had an excellent reputation for rigorous intellectual discipline, maintaining high academic standards. Nyerere proved to be a perfect match for this, and was again easily noticed by his teachers as he stood out among other students, excelling in class and in extracurricular activities. He completed his secondary school education at Tabora in 1943 with distinction.

It had been nine years since he started school, and one long journey from a rural peasant life to one at the centers of learning. And he was destined for higher goals. After leaving Tabora, he went to Makerere University College where he studied from 1943 to 1945. Even during those formative years in his life at Makerere, when he was barely out of his teens, he demonstrated a level of maturity beyond his age and deep concern for justice and equality, although he had not by then become a political activist as he himself conceded. It was when he was at Makerere that he formed the Tanganyika African Welfare Association. He was 21. As he explained years later:

> At Makerere in 1943, I started something called the Tanganyika African Welfare Association. Its main purpose was not political or anti-colonial. We wanted to improve the lives of Africans. But inside us something was happening.
>
> I wrote an essay in 1944 called the Freedom of Women. I must be honest and say I was influenced by John Stuart Mill, who had written about the subjugation of women. My father had 22 wives and I knew how hard they had to work and what they went through as women. Here in this essay I was moving towards the idea of freedom theoretically. But I was still in the mindset of improving the lives and welfare of Africans: I went to Tabora to start teaching.[3]

He taught at Tabora St. Mary's Secondary School, his alma mater, from 1946 - 1949. It was also when he was in his last year at Tabora that Nyerere went to Edinburgh University in Scotland for his master's degree.

The year 1949 was also another turning point in the life of Kwame Nkrumah and in the history of the Gold Coast. While Nyerere was at Edinburgh University where he enrolled in October 1949, Nkrumah was leading the struggle for independence in the Gold Coast. He returned to the Gold Coast from Britain in December 1947 after an absence of 12 years, mostly spent in the United States. When he was in Britain attending the London School of Economics, which became an incubator of many future African nationalists, Nkrumah was one of the main organizers of the Fifth Pan-African Congress held in Manchester in 1945 and which was attended by luminaries and future African leaders such as Nnamdi Azikiwe, Jomo Kenyatta and others. Kenyatta who was then living in Britian campaigning for Kenya's independence, a campaign he started in Kenya in 1928, was also one of the principal organizers of the Fifth Pan-African Congress and, together with Nkrumah, served as secretary. Nyerere was not one of the participants as some have written. He was at Makerere, and then at Tabora, in 1945, and did not go to Britain until 1949, for the first time, when he enrolled at Edinburgh University. But he did participate in and officially opened the Sixth Pan-African Congress held in Nkrumah Hall at the University of Dar es Salaam in Tanzania in 1974 in his capacity as conference host and president of the United Republic of Tanzania. It was the first such conference ever held on African soil, and none has been convened ever since.

In June 1949, about four months before Julius Nyerere entered Edinburgh University, Nkrumah announced at a rally in Accra the formation of the Convention People's Party (CPP) which was to lead the Gold Coast to independence as Ghana eight years later in March 1957. At Edinburgh, Nyerere followed closely the political developments in the Gold Coast and was very much impressed by Nkrumah. As he recalled years later not long before he died:

> The significance of India's independence movement was that it shook the British Empire. When Gandhi succeeded, I think it made the British lose the will to cling to empire. But it was events in Ghana in 1949 that fundamentally changed my attitude. When Kwame Nkrumah was released from prison, this produced a transformation. I was in Britain and, oh, you could see it in the

Ghanaians! They became different human beings, different from all the rest of us! This thing of freedom began growing inside all of us. First India in 1947, then Ghana in 1949. Ghana became independent eight years later. Under the influence of these events, while at university in Britain, I made up my mind to be a full-time political activist when I went back home. I intended to work for three years and launch into politics. But it happened sooner than I planned.[4]

Nyerere was at Edinburgh for three years and returned to Tanganyika in 1952 after earning a master's degree in history and economics. He was 30. He got a job as a history teacher at Pugu St. Francis Secondary School near Dar es Salaam, the capital of Tanganyika. He was the first Tanganyikan to earn a master's degree, and the first with such a degree to teach at a secondary school in the country. Unlike Tabora St. Mary's Secondary School whose highest educational level or class was standard 12, what Americans call grade 12, Pugu was a high school up to standard 14. It was also the first national secondary school established by Roman Catholics in Tanganyika, that later came to be known as St. Francis College, Pugu; and an elite Catholic School that admitted some of the best students from all parts of the country.

The colonial government was not pleased when Nyerere got a teaching position at Pugu. The British wanted him to teach at one of the government secondary schools, not at a mission school. Nyerere's decision to teach at a Catholic secondary school cost him financially. The colonial government downgraded his salary scale and offered him a salary for a teacher with a bachelor's degree, although he had a master's. The colonial authorities contended that this was an unprecedented case. No Tanganyikan in government service had ever received a salary for a master's degree. Therefore, although Nyerere had a master's degree and was the first Tanganyikan to earn such academic credentials, he still was not entitled to a salary commensurate with his level of education and that could not be justified by precedence. Yet the colonial government could not explain why Nyerere should not be the first person to receive this kind of salary and thereby set precedent that could be cited in the future to justify payment of salaries to other Tanganyikans with master's degrees at that degree level. It was obvious why they denied him what he was duly entitled to. The British governor, Sir Edward Twining, and other colonial authorities saw him as a troublemaker who had to be discouraged from pursuing his political goals. The party of the British settlers, the United Tanganyika Party (UTP) that was opposed to independence on the basis of majority rule, was seen as an antidote to Nyerere's crusade for independence. But it could not turn back the tide of history even with the support of the colonial government.

Nyerere's tenure at Pugu, and earlier at Tabora, as a teacher may not have prepared him for the rigors of political campaigning and politics in general. But it earned him the title Mwalimu, which means Teacher in Kiswahili; a titled he used and cherished for the rest of his life, explaining that he was a teacher by choice and a politician by accident. And as his first profession, teaching also continued to be an integral part of his political career as a national leader during which he was known for his extraordinary ability, humility and patience to explain things to diverse audiences with different levels of education and experience, sophistication and wisdom, in a language everybody including children could understand. I experienced this myself in the late 1950s when I was under 10 years old and listened to Nyerere address a mass rally in Tukuyu, my home. The rally was also attended by pupils from our primary school, Kyimbila, and others. But even with our immaturity, we had not difficulty understanding what he said, although he addressed a mostly mature audience as he campaigned for independence. He was the master teacher, *par excellence*, befitting his title Mwalimu.

The independence campaign he spearheaded took him to places beyond Tanganyika, including the United States. His airfare and other expenses were partly paid by Catholic priests - he was a Catholic himself - including William Collins, Al Nevins and John Considine from the money they raised in Tanganyika and from other sources. The three priests were among those who helped provide him with the money he needed for his journey to Europe and America to present his case for Tanganyika's independence before the United Nations for the second time in December 1956. He first appeared before the UN Trusteeship Council in March 1955. The Trusteeship Council was responsible for the administration of Tanganyika as a UN trusteeship territory under British tutelage, giving the British colonial authorities the mandate to "guide" the colony towards independence. The British claimed

Tanganyika would not be ready for independence until the seventies or eighties at the earliest; a view that contradicted the nationalist aspirations of the people of Tanganyika as articulated by Nyerere.

During his appearance before the United Nations in March 1955, the Trusteeship Council debated the third UN Visiting Missions Report on Tanganyika. Nyerere participated in the debate, presenting the case for Tanganyika's independence. It was during this debate that he won international recognition and esteem because of his brilliant performance. Although young, he was highly articulate and confident, and presented a strong case for Tanganyika's independence, winning support and sympathy from his audience and members of the gallery with his penetrating logic and strong presentation. He was uncompromising, yet argued his case without attacking the colonial authorities. As he calmly but forcefully stated: "The main object of my presence here is to prove the falsity of European press reports that the Tanganyikan population is opposed to the recommendations of the (UN) Visiting Mission."[5]

Nyerere spoke in his capacity as president of the Tanganyika African national Union (TANU) he and his colleagues formally launched the previous year on July 7, 1954, to campaign for independence. TANU grew out of the Tanganyika African Association (TAA), its predecessor, which was also led by Nyerere but with a limited agenda that did not include a demand for full independence as soon as possible.

When Nyerere returned to Tanganyika from New York after his impressive appearance at the United Nations, he had to make a choice that would have a significant impact on his personal and political life and on the future of Tanganyika; and, indeed, on the course of African history. The governor of Tanganyika, Sir Edward Twining, who was one of the last two governors (Sir Richard Turnbull was the last), forbade civil servants from being members of any political party or organization regardless of its agenda. But the law was actually intended to decapitate or neutralize the African nationalist movement led by Nyerere, leader of the largest political party in the country that quickly evolved into a national movement with mass appeal. Nyerere had to choose between politics and teaching. He refused to resign from TANU and gave up his teaching job at Pugu to devote himself to politics in order to wage a sustained campaign for Taganyika's independence.

It was a principled decision. And he knew his dilemma. He taught at a Catholic school. But because he was paid by the government, he was a civil servant by definition, hence a government employee, even though he taught at a mission school. And he was, of course, at the same time a member of a political party, TANU, and its leader. He was also fully aware that even if he had been allowed to continue teaching and being a member of TANU, he would not have been able to devote himself to his students as much as he should, and as much as he would have liked to, because of his commitment to the independence struggle. The campaign demanded full devotion as much as teaching did. He couldn't serve both. So, one had to go.

His decision to devote himself to the independence struggle caused financial hardship for his family. It meant loss of regular income from his teaching job. It also meant an uncertain future. But that is the kind of sacrifice he had to make to lead the independence campaign. And it is this kind of selfless devotion that came to define his political career. It became one of the most important qualities of his leadership, and won him profound admiration and intense loyalty from the people of Taganyika, later Tanzania, especially the masses who came to identify with him simply as "one of us." He was a revered statesman and world leader, yet a simple worker and peasant at heart.

After Nyerere resigned from his teaching job to devote himself to the independence struggle, he returned to his home village of Butiama in Musoma district in northern Tanganyika. After he returned home, he was asked to teach a Catholic priest Kizanaki, his native language. The priest was Arthur Wille, and the two remained close for the rest of Nyerere's life. In addition to teaching the priest Kizanaki - it was an intensive course, teaching him everyday for three months - and preparing for the independence struggle, Nyerere also used his literary skills during this time to compose English-Kizanaki grammar that came to be widely used by the foreign Catholic priests and other church members working in the area.

He also translated two catechisms into Kizanaki,

demonstrating a facility for languages that also served him well years later when he translated two works of Shakespeare into Kiswahili: *Julius Caesar* as *Juliasi Kaizari,* and *Merchant of Venice* as *Mabepari wa Venisi.* By translating these great works of literature, Nyerere demonstrated that Kiswahili was capable of serving as a vehicle for the articulation of ideas and concepts from other cultures that, regardless of their complexity, could be easily understood by Africans in their own native language. He also demonstrated the versatility of Kiswahili as an effective medium for the transmission of knowledge, including science and philosophy, from other civilizations; showing that it was truly an international - let alone a national - language in terms of its capacity to handle knowledge, ideas and concepts, from other cultures and civilizations. His translation of theological works from English, Latin, and even Greek, into Kizanaki demonstrated nothing less. It showed that African languages, dismissed as "primitive," were no less capable of handling abstract ideas and concepts and other intellectual tasks than European languages.

Nyerere also translated prayers and scripture readings for mass, an undertaking that enhanced his status as a Catholic but which could not be separated from his commitment as an African nationalist proud of his African heritage, of which Kizanaki, his native language, was an integral part. He also did other translations, this time into Kiswahili that he elevated to national status as a lingua franca for all Tanganyikans, later Tanzanians, when he became president a few years later:

> In 1955 there were no decent translations of either the Old Testament or the New Testament in Swahili. Julius started the translation of the Scriptures using the Douay Rheims Bible. The old English in this translation proved difficult. He then used the Latin Missal. One day he asked Fr. Wille if he had a Greek New Testament. He said, 'I find some of the passages in St. Paul difficult to understand.' When Fr. Wille asked him if he knew Greek, he answered 'Yes, I had a year of Greek in the university. I think I can handle it.'[6]

Such intellectual pursuits even in a theological context in response to demands from his faith only further confirmed his high stature as a scholar, without scholarly pretensions, besides being a politician committed to the liberation of his people from colonialism. A devout Catholic, he even wanted to be priest. But that was not his calling. It is interesting that another great African leader, Kwame Nkrumah, also wanted to be a Catholic priest. His first Christian name was Francis, given to him by a Catholic priest, but he later dropped it in preference of his African name Kwame from the Fanti ethnic group. Nkrumah himself was a Fanti. He even preached in black American churches when he was a student in the United States in the 1930s and 1940s, but abandoned his interest in trying to become a priest when he became involved in politics. Nyerere, on the other hand, remained a Catholic - while Nkrumah abandoned the faith - but also explained how he accidentally became one:

> He could laugh at how he became a Catholic as he said 'by chance.' When he went to begin primary school in Mwisenge at the suggestion of Chief Makongoro, he met there another boy who was also a Mzanaki. This boy, Oswald Marwa, was also the son of another Zanaki chief. Julius and Oswald immediately became friends. Since Oswald arrived at school ahead of him, he was able to show Julius around. When the bell for religion rang, Oswald told Julius 'It is time to study dini (meaning religion in Kiswahili). Let us go to the class with Padre'.... With Oswald's help Julius began to study the Catholic faith. Later he would tell Fr. Wille that when he went to Makerere University after his baptism, he would read a lot of Catholic philosophers and other authors in order to understand his faith better. At Makerere he became one of the leaders of Catholic students, organizing retreats and pilgrimages to the shrines of the Uganda martyrs. This interest in his faith would grow when he went to Edinburgh University.
>
> There, he corresponded with Fr. Walsh, his friend and sponsor, who had raised the money for his scholarship. In this correspondence, Nyerere wrote that he was considering becoming a priest. Fr. Walsh wrote back to him and told him that he did not think that he had a vocation to the priesthood. He knew of his keen interest in politics and advised him to continue on in this field.[7]

Nyerere had no doubt that the party he led, TANU, would one day win independence for Tanganyika. He also believed that the struggle against colonialism was supported by many members of the international community, especially in an age when colonialism had become anachronistic, and its demise a historical inevitability. But he was also concerned that the struggle for independence could lead to bloodshed, and wanted to avoid that as much as he could. He even told Arthur Wille, the Catholic priest, that he would gladly resign as leader of TANU and return to teaching and his life as a scholar if there was someone whom he believed could lead the party without causing bloodshed.

He was still living in his home district, Musoma, and making preparations for the independence campaign. It was also during this time that Oscar Kambona, the TANU secretary-general, wrote him a number of times asking him to return to Dar es Salaam and start to campaign for independence. As the party's secretary-general responsible for organization, Kambona was TANU's most prominent leader after Nyerere. He also became one of the country's most influential politicians until July 1967 when he left Tanzania and went into self-imposed exile in Britain.

Nyerere left Musoma and returned to Dar es Salaam and began to campaign for independence. Besides the overwhelming support he got from the people of Tanganyika as the campaign gained momentum, Nyerere also got a lot of help from other people in the initial phase of this crusade against colonial rule, as he did thoughout the independence struggle. Among them were members of the Maryknoll, a Catholic order, who had established themselves in Nyerere's home district of Musoma and in other parts of Tanganyika. They helped pay for his second visit to the United States where he appeared before the Fourth Committee of the United Nations on Decolonization on December 20, 1956, where he argued his case for Tanganyika's independence. The Maryknollers also arranged Nyerere's lecture tour of American colleges and universities, including Wellesley College in Massachusetts where he participated in a symposium and gave a lecture, entitled, "Africa's Place in the World."[8] He also appeared on American television with Eleanor Roosevelt on the Mike Wallace show; at this writing, in 2002, Mike Wallace, 83, was still a prominent television personality hosting "60 Minutes," a documentary program on CBS television.

After his appearance at the United Nations and lecture tour of the United States where he won great respect and admiration from his audiences for his masterly presentation and razor-sharp intellect, he returned to Tanganyika and continued to lead the independence struggle. Independence was five years away. And when the Union Jack was lowered at midnight on December 9, 1961, while the green, gold, and black national flag of the newly independent nation of Tanganyika went up, Nyerere became the youngest national leader in the world. He was 39. Tanganyika was also the first country in the region to win independence, and one of only two on the entire continent to win independence that year, and both from Britain. The other one was Sierra Leone on April 21, 1961.

Throughout the campaign for independence, Nyerere also worked diligently to prepare the people of Tanganyika to build a new nation free from tribalism and racism, and based on African values and culture that came to be collectively known as ujamaa, a Kiswahili word meaning familyhood; the bedrock principle of the extended family and communal living prevalent in African traditional societies he attempted to elevate and transform into a national virtue, but without much success. He did, however, succeed in building a nation where tribalism and racism were virtually banished from national life; an achievement unparalleled in the history of post-colonial Africa, as we will learn in the next chapter.

CHAPTER FOUR:

TANGANYIKA BEFORE THE UNION: CREATION OF A NON-RACIAL STATE

THE HISTORY of Tanzania is virtually indistinguishable from the political career of Julius Nyerere, the founding father of the nation, and one of the most influential leaders in the twentieth century. So is the history of Tanganyika since the fifties when the struggle for independence began as a coordinated campaign.

During the struggle for independence and in the following decades, Nyerere led a political party, which was more than just a political party but a national movement. It faced virtually no opposition across the country and was one of the most successful mass movements in colonial and post-colonial history, not only in Africa but in the entire Third World. The party was known as TANU, an acronym for Tanganyika Africa National union, founded by Nyerere and his colleagues on July 7, 1954. The day became a significant anniversary called Saba Saba - 7th day of the 7th month - celebrated every year throughout the country to commemorate the founding of the party, which led Tanganyika to independence.

Even after independence, TANU remained a liberation movement, as Tanganyika became one of the staunchest supporters of the independence struggle in the remaining African colonies and other countries under white minority rule on the continent. At the founding of the Organization of African Unity (OAU) in Addis Ababa, Ethiopia, in May 1963, Tanganyika was chosen as the headquarters of all the African liberation movements, based in the nation's capital, Dar es Salaam.

The struggle for the independence of Tanganyika itself was pursued mainly along constitutional lines, sparing the country the bloodshed that so much characterized the anti-colonial struggle led by Mau Mau in neighboring Kenya, another British colony like Tanganyika; in legalistic terms, Tanganyika was a UN Trusteeship Territory under British mandate, but a colony nonetheless.

The massive support for TANU in Tanganyika ensured victory at the polls. In the Legislative Council (LEGCO) elections of September 1958 and February 1959, candidates supported by TANU won overwhelmingly, paving the way for the establishment of a popularly elected government. The candidates included Tanganyikans of Asian (mostly Indian) and European origin. In December 1959, the United Kingdom, the colonial power, agreed to the formation of an internal self-government following general elections scheduled for August 1960. Nyerere became chief minister of the subsequent government. But the country was still under the British governor, since it was still a colony. Also because of that, Nyerere's government had no control over foreign policy - or the army - which remained under the jurisdiction of the Colonial Office in London overseeing all the colonies. The army then was known as the King's African Rifles (KAR), as were all the other armies in the rest of the British colonies across the continent.

In May 1961, Tanganyika became autonomous, and Nyerere became prime minister under a new constitution, which gave him more powers to his government. On December 9, 1961, Tanganyika became independent. It became a republic on December 9, 1962, and Nyerere became its first president. About one year and four months later, on April 26, 1964, Tanganyika united with Zanzibar to form one country. The new country was called the United Republic of Tanganyika and Zanzibar. It was renamed the United Republic of Tanzania on October 29 the same year.

The union helped protect and consolidate the freedom the people of Zanzibar won in the revolution, which ended Arab oppression in January 1964. With protection from Tanganyika, they no longer feared that their former oppressors would regain power on the islands and oppress them again.

But even in Tanganyika itself, there was deep concern by Nyerere and a number of his supporters that if left unchecked, racism would cause a lot of problems for the country. Racial animosity was not as intense as it was in Zanzibar. But it was serious enough to warrant immediate attention, and prompted Nyerere to take a very hard line against some members who wanted to institute a racial hierarchy in Tanganyika, in reverse, and even deny citizenship to non-blacks including those born in the country; a conception of nation reminiscent of Nazi Germany - and defined by German nationalist philosopher Johann Fichte as a manifestation of divine order - although not in all fundamental respects. Hitler's excesses in the African context, by analogy, were unparalleled until 1994 during the genocide in Rwanda in which about one million people, mostly Tutsi, were massacred by the Hutu at a rate five times faster than Hitler killed the Jews. It was the fastest massacre in modern history.

Conditions in Tanganyika in the early sixties soon after independence were not identical to Rwanda's but had the potential to degenerate into chaos, with possible "retaliatory" killings against Asians and other non-blacks, had Nyerere not actively intervened to halt this downward spiral. But the antagonism towards Asians and other non-blacks by black Tanganyikans was more economic than racial. The Asians were in a dominant economic position, controlling wholesale and retail trade and commerce, while Africans were predominantly poor peasants as they still are today. A significant number of them were also laborers in towns across the country. Some Tanzanians of Asian origin also acknowledge the economic dimension of the racial problem in the country to be the paramount factor. They include Professor Isa Shivji at the University of Dar es Salaam: "Issa Shivji (1976) acknowledges the importance of racial conflicts in Tanganyika but his structuralist analysis portrays Asian-African racial conflicts as reducible to antagonistic production relations determined by Asian dominance of the commercial sector."[1]

But such economic dominance assumed a racial dimension because wealth and social status associated with such wealth and other material possessions automatically coincided with racial identity; with Asians and other non-blacks on top, and blacks relegated to the bottom by poverty, and by a racially structured society conceived by the German and then the British colonial rulers. It could be a deadly combination, and Nyerere was fully aware of its combustible nature and all the incendiary elements.

Yet even some of the Tanganyikan leaders who capitalized on racial sentiments and put a premium on racial identity as a fundamental social category were not racist, *per se*, but simply nationalists who contended that race-neutral principles and policies would perpetuate the privileged position of Asians and other non-blacks to the detriment of the black majority who, throughout the colonial period, were on the periphery of the mainstream in spite of their numerical preponderance. The solution to this problem would have been affirmative action - not racism in reverse - for the disadvantaged majority, but still with an emphasis on individual not group rights, the latter being one of the main catalysts in ethnic and racial violence not only in Africa but in other parts of the world as well; including the unjust expulsion of Asians from Uganda - among them Uganda citizens of Asian origin - by Idi Amin in 1972, and the violence directed against Kenyans of Asian origin during the abortive coup attempt by some members of the Kenyan armed forces in 1982. Where a number of the early Tanganyikan leaders went wrong was in their advocacy of totally exclusionary policies, including outright denial of citizenship to non-blacks. They articulated this position before and after independence.

The 1958 racially-based elections highlighted the conflict between these two competing visions for Taganyika: racial and non-racial. TANU overwhelmingly won the elections, tipping scales in its favor so much needed in pursuit of its non-racial policies; race advocates, disenchanted with TANU's advocacy of race-neutrality, left the party and formed the opposition African Nation Congress (ANC) led by Zuberi Mtemvu, espousing an uncompromising racial doctrine; and Tanganyikans of Asian origin also won seats in the national legislature - called the Legislative Council (LEGCO) - since the elections were based on racial parity, to the detriment of the black African majority who were grossly underrepresented under this system. Each of the three racial categories - European, Asian, and African, in that descending order of social status - occupied a third of the seats in the legislature in which Europeans, constituting the smallest racial group, was over represented, followed by Asians. Given their numerical preponderance, Africans were not only grossly underrepresented but deliberately discriminated against, and ignored in decision making, because of this policy of "racial parity" which was, in fact, a policy of racial disparity.

The Asian Tanganyikans who won the election were also supported by TANU during the campaign, since they articulated the same position on race, advocating race neutrality in the new dispensation after independence which would replace the tripartite racial system instituted by the British colonial rulers, formalizing three racial categories: European, Asian (mostly Indian and Pakistani), and African, in that descending order of racial hierarchy.

I remember when I was growing up in Tanganyika, seeing signs saying "Europeans," "Asians," and "Africans," on toilets and other facilities. Arabs, and people of mixed racial backgrounds called half-castes in general in East Africa, did not fit in any of these fixed racial categories but could - and did - use toilets and other facilities designated "Asian"; while those assigned to Africans, which were also the worst, were beneath them. I was old enough to remember the signs well, but too young to understand their significance in a racial context reminiscent of apartheid South Africa. Independence ended this humiliation inflicted on us in our native land and the only place we knew as home. But, before the end of colonial rule, Nyerere and other leaders wanted to make sure that the roles were not reversed once Africans came to power. Everybody was to be treated equal.

During the struggle for independence, many Asians remained passive, apprehensive of the future once Africans assumed power. Conservative Asians were even to opposed the independence struggle, preferring the status quo, instead, which assured them a place next to the Europeans in the racial hierarchy instituted by the British. H.H. The Aga Khan, the spiritual leader of the Ismaili Asians who was also a close friend of the British governor of Tanganyika, Sir Edward Twining, reportedly gave money secretly to Asians opposed to independence. But nationalist-minded Asian Tanganyikans who led the Tanganyika Asian Association, as well as some of the members, actively supported Nyerere and even gave money to TANU to help fight for independence. So did their counterparts in Kenya who formed the Kenya Freedom Party, and those of the Uganda Action Group in Uganda. They also supported the independence movements in their respective countries.

But because of their proximity to Africans as a result of their daily contact in business transactions - most businesses in towns were owned by Asians but the largest number of their customers were Africans - as well as their privileged position in a racially stratified society, Asians became the primary target of hostility and impatient wrath by Africans who were dissatisfied with the slow pace of change in their social and economic status after independence. Nyerere and a number of his colleagues foresaw this danger long before independence, and moved swiftly in the early sixties to neutralize elements, which tried to capitalize on this discontent and fuel racial hostility towards Asians and other non-blacks, and even deny them citizenship rights. Compounding the problem was the fact that probably the majority of the Asian Tanganyikans, uncertain about their future under black majority rule after the British left, did not - if at all - actively support the struggle for independence. This left them open to the charge that they were not patriotic enough and could not be trusted to be loyal citizens of Tanganyika. It was a blanket charge, covering even those who supported TANU and the struggle for independence. Their citizenship was equally at stake. Race became a paramount factor.

The acrimonious debate over citizenship and the status of Asian Tanganyikans and other non-blacks reached a climax in the parliamentary debates in 1961. Nyerere and some of his colleagues wanted an inclusive citizenship law. Their opponents wanted citizenship exclusively based on race. No Asians, Arabs, Europeans or any other non-blacks would be granted citizenship. And those born in Tanganyika as citizens would have theirs revoked.

Yet, in spite of such hostility and heated rhetoric over race, Tanganyika adopted non-racial policies and was the only country in East Africa, which did not pass race-sensitive laws targeting Asians for exclusion from a number of areas, as Kenya and Uganda did. For instance, in Kenya soon after independence, the government excluded Asian Kenyans from high-level jobs in the civil service and other fields. Their citizenship as Kenyans became irrelevant to this gross violation of their fundamental rights. It gave them no protection under the law. The Kenyan parliament also passed laws denying Asian Kenyans opportunities in different sectors of the economy. The Trade Licensing Act was one of those highly restrictive and discriminatory laws directed against them. Uganda adopted similar measures under Dr. Milton Obote, with Idi Amin delivering the final blow when he expelled all Asians from

Uganda and seized their property without compensation.

Tanganyika was the only country in the region, which did not pursue policies of rapid Africanization, despite demands for such drastic measures by a number of African politicians who also did not want Asian Taganyikans to have citizenship and enjoy full citizenship rights. And the triumph of such moderation and color-blind policies was largely attributed to Nyerere. As he bluntly stated in the Tanganyika parliament in October 1961, about two months before independence:

> Because of the situation we have inherited in this country, where economic classes are also identical with race, we live on dynamite that might explode any day, unless we do something about it.[2]

And early in the struggle for independence, Nyerere explicitly stated that Tanganyika would be a non-racial society where people of all races would be entitled to citizenship and equal treatment under the law and as individuals. He also reassured Asians, Europeans, and Arabs as well as others that they were free to live in Tanganyika after independence, without any fear of being expelled from the country by the new government. And he emphasized: "What we want is a society where the individual matters, and not the colour of his skin or shape of his nose."[3] His reassurance was a welcome relief to Asians, especially, since they were the primary target of racial hostility. But Europeans and others who wanted to live in Tanganyika were equally relieved by Nyerere's magnanimous policies.

His racial tolerance was evident from the beginning when he founded TANU. The party did not allow Europeans and Asians to become members, thus employing a strictly racial criterion for membership, which was restricted to Africans. Nyerere and others were opposed to such racial exclusion but failed to make TANU membership open to all races. In 1956, TANU allowed people of mixed African and other racial ancestry - called half-castes - to become members, but still excluded Asians and Europeans because they did not have any African racial heritage. But Nyerere persisted in his quest for non-racial membership in TANU.

In October 1960, one Asian and one European became members of the TANU Executive Committee at Nyerere's insistence. And it should be remembered that some of the Asians who were denied TANU membership, purely on the basis of race, were not only Tanganyikans but actively involved in the independence struggle. They included Amir H. Jamal, who became one of the most prominent cabinet members for decades since independence, and one of Tanzania's most influential leaders nationally and internationally; M.N. Rattansey, and Sophia Mustapha. Rattansey, together with another Asian-Tanganyikan lawyer K.L. Jhaveri, also served as Nyerere's defence lawyers at his libel trial in July 1958. He won the case. As leader of TANU, he also threatened to expel from the party anyone who was engaged in racist practices, inciting animosities against Asians, Europeans and other non-blacks.

Leaders of the opposition party, the African National Congress (ANC), unequivocally stated that only Africans native to Tanganyika should be citizens, and the government should be composed of Africans only. But the party died a natural death in the early sixties after it was overwhelmed by TANU at the polls.

Although Tanganyika's attainment of independence was relatively peaceful, it was accompanied by an exodus of Europeans who were concerned about their safety in a country they no longer ruled. But there were many others who simply did not want to live under a predominantly black government, led by people who, not too long ago, were their subjects. And now that the Europeans were gone, it was the Asians who almost exclusively became the primary target of hostility by Africans because of their dominant economic position. The underlying theme of this hostility was that Africans were not yet free as long as they were economically dominated by Asians; and it resonated well among the masses and even in parliament where Nyerere and his colleagues faced stiff opposition to their non-racial policies from some members opposed to racial equality in a predominantly black nation. As Nyerere said in parliament:

> If we are going to base citizenship on colour, we will commit a crime. Discrimination against human beings because of their colour is exactly what we have been fighting against.[4]

There were other divisive elements in Tanganyika - tribal

loyalties, although not very pronounced; and religion, with even more potential for bloodshed, since Moslems felt they were being dominated by Christians in a country where each of the two groups constituted at least a third of the total population. But in spite of these factors and their potential for chaos and strife, the focus was on race as the most volatile and divisive element in Tanganyika, which was only a few weeks from independence. It was also a subject of intense debate in parliament in October 1961. The question was whether or not race should be the sole criterion for citizenship.

Even many members of TANU, not just those of the opposition African National Congress (ANC), argued in parliament that Asians and other non-Africans should not automatically become citizens like black Tanganyikans, simply because one was born in Tanganyika and had at least one parent also born in Tanganyika. Only African Tanganyikans should automatically qualify for citizenship under this liberal policy. One member of parliament, Mr. Mtaki, said in opposing the racially inclusive bill: "This is an African country and it has got to be ruled by looking to the interests of Africans."[5] He went on to say that non-Africans must first learn African customs and take an examination to qualify for citizenship, even if they were born in Tanganyika.

Christopher Kasanga Tumbo, the leader of the national labor movement and one of Tanganyika's most prominent members of parliament and a national leader who also within only a few years became one of Nyerere's fiercest critics, also demanded restrictive citizenship. There must be a distinction between Africans and non-Africans under the citizenship law. Non-African Tanganyikans should also be registered and naturalize themselves, even if they were born and brought up in Tanganyika. And the Council of Chiefs must approve or reject their applications for citizenship. As he emphatically stated: "One can be born here and yet he may not have the patriotism of this country. Therefore, if we judge citizens by birth I think we shall be selling our country."[6]

Another member of parliament, Michael Kamaliza who also became a cabinet member as minister of labor, expressed strong reservations about the Asians' loyalty to Tanganyika, and asked whether or not they would be willing to "shoot the Indians in

India for the sake of Tanganyikans." He also went on to say that "the common man" - euphemism for ordinary African, and nobody else - regarded Asians as having divided national loyalties, "with one leg in Tanganyika and one leg in Bombay."[7]

And another member, John Mwakangale, contended that after decades of exploitation by Europeans and Asians, "75 percent of [whom] still regard an African in Tanganyika as an inferior being," race-neutral laws guaranteeing equal rights for all would only perpetuate domination of Africans by Europeans and Asians and enable them to buy votes from blacks. He unequivocally stated that all European and Asian cabinet members should resign immediately. "We cannot be governed by foreigners!"[8] His definition of Tanganyikan Europeans and Asians captured the essence of the black nationalist sentiments articulated by many Africans across the country - not just those in parliament - who maintained that Tanganyika belonged to nobody else but them.

But several other members of parliament supported a racially inclusive law for citizenship. They argued that Asians and Europeans had also supported TANU in its campaign for independence, and dismissed fears of domination of the economy by non-Africans as no more than an admission of inferiority to non-blacks, as if this imbalance could not be redressed under race-neutral laws and a predominantly black government after independence. It also implied that Africans could not compete with members of other races on equal footing, thus justifying racial stereotypes about blacks as an inferior people. But such inferiority complex could not be used to deny equal rights to others. And one Asian member of parliament, Dr. Krishna, emphatically stated that he was a "loyal citizen of Tanganyika." He also went on to say that the non-racial citizenship bill presented by TANU and being debated in parliament was based on values of "the inherent dignity of man and the equal rights of development" enshrined in the United Nations Charter.[9]

Nyerere followed the debate closely, and gave a forceful response, clearly articulating his position diametrically opposed to that of the bill's opponents. "Julius Nyerere, typically quite calm, lost his temper during the course of the debate, accusing opponents of the bill of racism and talking rubbish and behaving like Nazis."[10] He made it clear that the issue at stake was a matter of principle, which cannot be compromised, and insisted that citizenship had to be based solely on loyalty to the country, not on race or any other criterion. He went on to say that those opposed to a racially inclusive law for citizenship, and to racial equality, were advocating policies, which were a threat to national unity:

> If we in Tanganyika are going to divorce citizenship from loyalty and marry it to colour, it won't stop there. We will go on breaking that principle...going downhill until you break up the country.... They are preaching discrimination as a religion to us. And they stand like Hitler and begin to glorify race. We glorify human beings, not colour.[11]

One member of parliament, Mr. Wambura, wanted the matter to be resolved in a referendum, but Nyerere rejected the proposal. The vast majority of the people across the country would probably have voted against the racially inclusive citizenship bill in favor of citizenship based on race, thus excluding Asians, Europeans and other non-blacks. Nyerere and his supporters eventually won, and the proposed legislation embracing non-blacks was passed by parliament. It was endorsed by an overwhelming vote. During the proceedings, Nyerere threatened that he and his government would resign immediately if the law was not passed; a threat that helped to get the bill accepted by his opponents in parliament. Yet his position on the matter did not reflect the sentiments of the average black Tanganyikan who was generally hostile towards Asians and other racial minorities.

But the sentiments of the average African, with his hostility towards Asians and other non-blacks, threatened to undermine national unity, and Nyerere had to take a principled - even if unpopular - stand not only to guarantee racial justice but also to save the country from civil strife. And expulsion of Asians - even racial attacks - instigated by unscrupulous politicians remained a distinct possibility in the absence of such strong leadership. Nyerere also took the same strong position on the highly controversial issue of Africanization. To many leaders and the majority of black Tanganyikans, Africanization meant racialization, giving jobs to blacks; transferring control of wholesale and retail businesses and everything else from Asians and others to blacks; and excluding Asians, Europeans and other non-blacks from the government and other areas of national life.

But to Nyerere, Africanization included Tanganyikans of all races who, as citizens of an African country, were also Africans by definition. It is a position he maintained throughout his tenure as president of Tanganyika and, later on, of Tanzania.

His vision of a non-racial state went beyond Tanganyika - and Tanzania - and was consistent with his opposition to all forms of discrimination anywhere in the world. In the African context, this vision was given full expression by his relentless support to the African liberation movements. And it had its most dramatic fulfillment when apartheid South Africa, the bastion of white rule on the continent, finally collapsed just five years before he died.

Yet it was East Africa itself, which became the arena for the fulfillment of some of Nyerere's earliest Pan-African ambitions, leading to the establishment of the union of Tanganyika and Zanzibar in 1964. It came only a few months after Kenya, Uganda and Tanganyika failed to form the East African Federation as the three East African leaders - Kenyatta, Obote, and Nyerere - promised they would before the end of 1963. It was one of Nyerere's biggest disappointments. But it also set the stage for one of his biggest achievements: the union of Tanganyika and Zanzibar.

CHAPTER FIVE:

UNION OF TANGANYIKA AND ZANZIBAR: NYERERE AS ARCHITECT OF FIRST AFRICAN UNION

THE UNION of Tanganyika and Zanzibar was the first merger of independent states on the entire continent and the only one that has ever been consummated. The Ghana-Guinea union formed on November 23, 1958, between the first black African country to win independence from Britain and the first to achieve it from France, and joined by Mali in 1961 to form the Ghana-Guinea-Mali union, was more symbolic than functional.[1] In the case of Tanzania, both Tanganyika and Zanzibar renounced their sovereignties and submerged their separate national identities in the new macronation. The establishment of Tanzania from this merger is also one of the most memorable achievements of the late President Julius Nyerere.

Tanganyika united with Zanzibar on April 26, 1964. For six months, the new country was simply known as the Union of Tanganyika and Zanzibar. It was also officially known by its much longer name as the United Republic of Tanganyika and Zanzibar, and was renamed the United Republic of Tanzania on October 29. Dar es Salaam, the capital of Tanganyika, which means Haven of Peace in Arabic and was founded by the Arab rulers, became the seat of the union government.

The union was preceded by the revolution in Zanzibar, which ended Arab hegemonic control of the islands that lasted for hundreds of years. The violent uprising was led by John Okello, a Ugandan who had settled in Zanzibar, and who saw himself as a messianic figure on a mission to free his people - blacks in Zanzibar - from Arab domination. And the role this self-styled field marshal played in the redemption of his race on the isles became a sub-text in the unfolding drama that eventually led to the consummation of the union. As Professor Haroub Othman, a Tanzanian of Zanzibari origin teaching at the University of Dar es

Salaam in Tanzania, explains:

> Nyerere states that he casually proposed the idea of Union to Karume when the latter visited him to discuss the fate of John Okello. According to Nyerere, Karume immediately agreed to the idea and suggested that Nyerere should be the president of such a union. In a New Year's message to the nation on 1 January 1965, Nyerere implied that even if the ASP (Afro-Sirazi Party led by Karume in Zanzibar) had come into power by constitutional means and not as a result of revolution, the Union would still have taken place.[2]

Even though a convergence of interests - Western (especially American and British) concern that Zanzibar was about to become "the Cuba of Africa," and Nyerere's Pan-African desire to unite with Zanzibar - may seem to have helped create a climate conducive to unification of the two independent African states; the union would probably still have been established on Nyerere's own initiative, even if there was no "communist" threat on the isles and independent Zanzibar - under black majority rule - was a capitalist haven, provided the leaders of Zanzibar also, like Nyerere, had the political will to do so. Nyerere had just failed, in 1963, to convince the leaders of Kenya and Uganda to unite with Tanganyika and form an East African federation. And now Zanaibar provided him with an opportunity to realize this Pan-African ambition, although on a smaller scale.

And American officials themselves who were in government service under President Lyndon B. Johnson during that time did not even claim credit for engineering the union. As Frank Carlucci, who was US consul in Zanzibar and later CIA director and American secretary of defense, stated in an interview in 1986:

> Nyerere had to do something about the Zanzibar problem. I don't know for a fact whether he came up with the idea himself, or whether we gave him the prescription. Whether our urging him to do something about Zanzibar had an effect on him.... I do know that the situation in Zanzibar was one of continuing deterioration. In the absence of action from Tanganyika, the place would have been completely controlled by the communists.[3]

The highly volatile situation in Zanzibar during that critical period provided momentum towards unification, but at a tempo influenced even if not dictated by Nyerere - the main architect of the union - and his colleagues in Tanganyika and Zanzibar, since it was they who stipulated the terms for unification. That the events in Zanzibar dictated the pace of this consensus building, between the leaders of the two countries, which led to the establishment of the union, is clearly demonstrated by the short time span in which the entire process was completed. The two countries united within three-and-a-half months: the proposal, negotiations, and consummation of the union, all took place within that short period. And some tough negotiations took place, since some Zanzibari leaders were opposed to the merger. As Professor Haroub Othman states:

> Discussions on the Union were conducted very secretively. From the archives, and the statements of those of those who were in the corridors of power at the time, it would appear that not many people in the Tanganyika Government, or the Zanzibar Revolutionary Council, knew what was happening. Apart from Nyerere and Karume, the only other people who might have been privy to these discussions were Rashidi Kawawa, Oscar Kambona, Abdallah Kassim Hanga and Salim Rashid. What is important is that the Articles of Union, signed by Karume and Nyerere on 22 April 1964, were subsequently ratified by both the Tanganyika National Assembly and the Zanzibar Revolutionary Council. Both Abdulrahman Babu and Khamis Abdallah-Ameir, the two former Umma Party leaders who were in the Revolutionary Council at the time, have confirmed that the matter was discussed in the Council and that, while there were reservations on the part of some members, these were overcome by Abdallah Kassim Hanga who made an emotional appeal in support of the Union.
>
> Presenting the proposal for a Union to the Tanganyika National Assembly on 25 April 1964, Nyerere based his argument on the proximity of the Islands to the Mainland, a common language, friendship between TANU and the ASP (Afro-Shirazi Party in Zanzibar), and common cultural traditions. But the ultimate ground for the Union was, he said, a commitment to the cause of African unity. Nyerere saw the Union with Zanzibar as a step towards federation in East Africa.[4]

With that step, Nyerere made a lasting contribution towards African unity and, after he died, left behind a very peaceful and stable nation; one of the very few on this turbulent continent. That Nyerere left behind such a cohesive entity he skillfully built - first as Tanganyika - and nurtured for more than 40 years, is probably is his most enduring legacy; yet the least appreciated among his most ardent critics who talk and write about his failed socialist policies more than anything else, while ignoring his achievements. But in spite of all this, his influence continued to grow, and he remained a towering figure on the national scene and in the international arena throughout his life.

Even after he voluntarily stepped down from the presidency in November 1985, he remained such a formidable figure on the national scene that, he not only provided guidance when needed but influenced the course of events in Tanzania until his death. His choice of his successors, Ali Hassan Mwinyi and Benjamin Mkapa, was easily approved by the ruling party, Chama Cha Mapinduzi (CCM), a Kiswahili name that literally means Party of the Revolution, or Revolutionary Party. His opposition to the establishment of a separate government for Tanganyika as demanded in the early 1990s by some members of parliament from mainland Tanzania, was equally supported by the ruling party - against prevailing sentiment within the party in favor of a separate government for Tanganyika - and probably saved the union which may not have survived with three governments: one for Zanzibar as has always been the case since the union formed; one for Tanganyika as proposed by some members of parliament in 1993 but rejected outright by Nyerere; and one union government for the whole country which has at the same time also served as the government of Tanzania mainland, hence Tanganyika, although the latter no longer exists as a political entity like Zanzibar still does. In fact, it is also politically unacceptable in a nationalist context for people on the mainland to call themselves Tanganyikans, unlike the people of Zanzibar who still call themselves Zanzibaris probably more than anything else when they affirm their identity, express their grievances against the union, and are nostalgic about the halcyon days when they were a separate independent nation.

That Nyerere was able to prevail in these and many other cases, was vindication of his status as the most powerful leader in Tanzania even after his retirement, and remained the final arbiter on the national scene until his death. And because of his formidable influence, there was some concern that the union of Tanganyika and Zanzibar would not survive without him. As President Benjamin Mkapa said when he announced the death of

Nyerere on national radio in Kiswahili:

> I know the death of the father of the nation will shock and dismay many. There are many who fear that national unity will disintegrate, the union will falter and our relations with our neighbours will deteriorate following the passing of Nyerere. But Nyerere has built a sustainable foundation for national unity, the union and relations with our neighbours.[5]

President Mkapa also issued a stern warning to those who may try to break up the union of Tanganyika and Zanzibar. He said they would be dealt with severely: "(Anyone) dreaming about breaking the unity of Tanzania, generating insecurity or stirring up tensions...will be dealt with ruthlessly and their activities curtailed."[6] Obviously, the warning was taken seriously, despite attempts by the Civic United Front (CUF) - the largest opposition party in Tanzania whose biggest support comes from Zanzibar, its stronghold - and by maverick politicians such as Christopher Mtikila, a Christian fundamentalist minister from the mainland and leader of a small opposition group, the Democratic Party, to destabilize and break up the union.

The union was consummated at the height of the Cold War, and there have been all sorts of speculations, allegations and innuendoes that the merger was externally engineered. The implication of these arguments is that Nyerere would not have formed the union had he not been prompted, prodded or manipulated by these external forces to do so. As Professor Ali Mazrui states in "Nyerere and I":

> Did Tanganyika unite with Zanzibar to form Tanzania under pressure from President Lyndon Johnson of the United States and Prime Minister Sir Alec Douglas Home of Britain who did not want Zanzibar to become another communist Cuba? Nyerere bristled when it was suggested that the union with Zanzibar was part of the Cold War and not a case of Pan-Africanism.[7]

The argument that Nyerere was coerced by the United States and Britain into uniting Tanganyika with Zanzibar to deprive communists of a base on the island nation is not validated by Nyerere's track record. And as we learned earlier, the American consul in Zanzibar during that time, Frank Carlucci, did not even claim that the United States - or any other Western power including Britain - engineered the union. Looking at Nyerere's record, we see that throughout his political career, he demonstrated a degree of independence in pursuit of his goals, which irritated and sometimes even infuriated both ideological camps, East and West, during the Cold War.

As far back as 1959, before he led Tanganyika to independence from Britain, he called for a boycott of apartheid South Africa because of her racist policies, at a time when both the United States and Britain and other Western powers were giving full and unconditional support to the apartheid regime which was oppressing black people and other non-whites. He was not intimidated by the West, and maintained his principled position on apartheid and other white minority regimes on the continent, as was clearly demonstrated when he invited the freedom fighters to establish their bases in Tanganyika soon after the country won independence from Britain on December 9, 1961. He did this contrary to Western wishes and interests, and in defiance of the West.

He also defied the West when he established strong ties with the People's Republic of China, the Soviet Union and other Eastern-bloc countries soon after independence. But he also annoyed communist nations when he continued to maintain equally strong ties with the West in pursuit of his policy of positive non-alignment. As he sharply responded to critics from the East and the West as far back as 1961: "We have no desire to have a friendly country choosing our enemies for us."[8]

Nyerere's commitment to African unity, like Nkrumah's, was well-known. And he lived up to that commitment; which had nothing to do with getting encouragement from the West to advance Pan-African goals. Those were the very same countries, which were intent on perpetuating their domination of Africa and were therefore opposed to any move, which would threaten or undermine their hegemonic control of the continent. A strong, united Africa would naturally not be in their best interest, since it would seek to end such domination. And Nyerere was one of the most implacable foes of imperial domination of Africa by both East and West. As he stated in August 1961, about four months before he led Tanganyika to independence:

I believe the danger to African unity is going to come from...external forces.... The rich countries of the world - both capitalist and socialist - are using their wealth to dominate the poor countries. And they are ready to weaken and divide the poor countries for that purpose of domination....

Whenever we try to talk in terms of larger units on the African continent, we are told that it can't be done; we are told that the units we would create would be 'artificial.' As if they could be any more artificial than the 'national' units on which we are now building!.... Many of them are deliberately emphasizing the difficulties on our continent for the express purpose of maintaining them and sabotaging any move to unite Africa.

The technique is very simple. One power bloc labels a move for unity a 'Communist plot' - not because it is Communist, but because they don't like it. Another power bloc labels another move for unity an 'imperialist plot' - not because it is so, but because they don't like it. What annoys me is not the use of these slogans by power-hungry nations, for this is something we do expect; but what does infuriate me is that they should expect us to allow ourselves to be treated as if we were a bunch of idiots![9]

In pursuit of his Pan-African goals, Nyerere had earlier, in 1960, offered to delay independence for Tanganyika due in 1961 so that the three East African countries of Kenya, Uganda, and Tanganyika would achieve independence on the same day and form a federation. Yet, no one would seriously suggest - if at all - that Nyerere offered to do so at the behest of the departing colonial masters in order to establish a federation. If the British wanted to form an East African federation - and undermine their interests in Africa by building a large, powerful macro-nation which would stand up to the West once free from colonial rule - they would have done so a long time ago. They had plenty of time, decades, to do that: at least since the end of World War I when Tanganyika, the last territory in the region to be colonized by Britain, came under the League of Nations mandate - and next designated as a UN Trusteeship Territory - ruled by the British after Germany lost the colony in the war. The British did, in fact, in the attempt in the 1930s to establish a giant federation stretching from East Africa all the way down to South Africa composed of all the British colonies in the region: Kenya, Uganda, Tanganyika, Zanzibar, Nyasaland (now Malawi), Northern Rhodesia (renamed Zambia), Southern Rhodesia (now Zimbabwe), Bechuanaland (today Botswana), Swaziland, Basutoland (renamed Lesotho), and South Africa. But they wanted to form such a federation for a different reason: to consolidate imperial domination. And the plan was strongly opposed and resisted by African nationalists.

But Nyerere's intention was not to perpetuate imperial domination of East Africa by the British when he strongly advocated formation of the East African federation and even offered to delay independence for Tanganyika if such a move could help achieve this goal. And the British as well as other Western powers definitely had more influence on Jomo Kenyatta than they did on Nyerere, if at all. Yet Kenyatta was the least enthusiastic of the three East African leaders about forming a federation - it was also reported in 1977 - 78 that he was on the CIA payroll, together with Mobutu Sese Seko and a number of other leaders. Nyerere was not one of them. Had Kenyatta and Dr. Milton Obote of Uganda been as enthusiastic as Nyerere was, the East African federation would have been formed before the end of 1963, as the three leaders promised in the declaration they signed in June in Nairobi, Kenya, the same year.

The failure of the three East African leaders to form a federation was one of Nyerere's biggest disappointments. But, undaunted in his quest for African unity, he went on to form the union of Tanganyika and Zanzibar the following year, and not because the Americans and the British asked him to do so. His track record in pursuit of African unity and independence, as we have just shown, contradicts this line of reasoning. And consummation of the union was one of his greatest achievements in the Pan-African context and in the area of foreign policy. It was also clear vindication of his non-aligned position in the bipolar world of the Cold War. The new nation of Tanzania went on to forge strong links with the Eastern bloc - the nemesis of the West, which supposedly inspired the union in its ideological war against the communist bloc - and continued to maintain equally strong ties with the West, contrary to the wishes of the Russians and the Chinese. In fact, Tanzania got more financial and technical assistance from the West than she did from the East, mainly because of historical ties.

It is also worth remembering that if Nyerere was subservient to - or took orders from - the West, as supposedly was the case when he formed the union of Tanganyika and Zanzibar, he would not have been able to expel American diplomats from Tanzania in 1964 when they tried to overthrow him; and they would not have tried to undermine his government, since he was their "ally." And he would not have broken ties with Britain in December 1965 over the Rhodesian crisis, the first African country to do so. Nor would he have curtailed ties with West Germany when the latter objected to diplomatic representation of East Germany in Tanzania; the West German ambassador was shown the door, and the Canadians came in to train Tanzania's fledgling air force after the Germans threatened to withdraw their aid to it. All these cases clearly show that Nyerere was an independent-minded leader who also demonstrated a degree of independence in his policy pursuits and initiatives rarely seen among Third World leaders.

Yet, in spite of all this evidence, the litany continues that the union of Tanganyika and Zanzibar was a product of Cold War intrigue, not of Nyerere's own initiative in pursuit of his Pan-African goals. If the communist threat prompted Nyerere to unite Tanganyika with Zanzibar, at the behest of Britain and the United States in order to stop communists from establishing a base in Zanzibar, why did he go on to establish strong ties with communist countries after the union was formed - instead of avoiding them? It seems he didn't pay very much attention to the British and the Americans who "told" him to form the union and avoid communists.

The union never served as a bulwark against communism - it did as a socialist state against capitalism - because it was never intended to be one. Nor did it serve as a launching pad for communist penetration of Africa from the east coast - it was never intended for that either. And communism never penetrated Tanzania in spite of the strong ties the country had with the Eastern bloc. It remained a non-aligned nation. Hence Nyerere's contention that we are not going to allow our friends to choose enemies for us. As he stated in a speech, "Policy on Foreign Affairs," October 16, 1967:

> We shall not allow any of our friendships to be exclusive; we shall not allow anyone to choose any of our friends or enemies for us. It should also be clear that we shall not allow anyone - whether they be from East or West, or from places not linked to those blocs - to try and use our friendship for their own purposes.[10]

Also, if Nyerere formed the union to neutralize communists in Zanzibar, and in Tanganyika itself, he not only would not have established strong ties with the People's Republic of China and other communist countries; he would also have tightened his grip on Zanzibar, the potential base for communists; and he would not have appointed to cabinet posts Zanzibaris who were known to have communist leanings. The president of Zanzibar who formed the union with Nyerere, Sheikh Abeid Karume, wanted a complete merger, hence a stronger union. But Nyerere refused to go that far. He preferred, instead, to have a weaker union in which Zanzibar would continue to have its own government and enjoy considerable autonomy, virtually as a sovereign entity in a number of areas except foreign affairs, defense, immigration, and others specifically placed under the jurisdiction of the union government. He was concerned that if a complete merger of the two countries and governments took place, the people of Zanzibar would feel that they had been swallowed up by Tanganyika, a much bigger country. It would not be a union of equals, since as a sovereign entity, Zanzibar was entering the union as an independent country, not as a junior partner. Another Zanzibari leader who was strongly in favor of a much stronger union was Kassim Hanga, who served as prime minister and vice president under President Karume, and was one of the leaders on the isles known for his communist sympathies.

Another leader from Zanzibar with known communist leanings was Abdulrahman Mohammed Babu, leader of the Umma (The People's) Party, who became minister of defense and external affairs under President Karume. Yet, in spite of his communist ties and ideological orientation, he was later appointed to cabinet posts in the union government by President Nyerere; and went on to become one of the most distinguished and influential leaders in Tanzania, whose influence as a scholar and Marxist theoretician extended beyond Tanzania. He held key ministerial posts, serving as minister of economic planning, and minister of commerce and industries between 1964 and 1972. He was also one of the strongest supporters of the union and African unity in general.

Nyerere's approach to unity between the two countries probably saved the union more than anything else. Had Zanzibar not been allowed to have its own government, and its own president who also served as the first vice president of the united republic - the second vice president automatically came from the mainland, according to the constitution - the union would probably have collapsed. Even soon after it was formed, there was strong opposition to the merger by some elements in Zanzibar who argued that their smaller country had been swallowed up by Tanganyika; in what amounted to annexation, as Professor Ali Mazrui has erroneously characterized the merger. Had Zanzibar indeed been swallowed up, without allowing it to have its own government, secessionist sentiments in the former island nation - which have existed since the union was formed - would have grown stronger and stronger, providing momentum to a separatist movement which could even have led to an insurgency on the islands, plunging the country into chaos.

But the secessionists were robbed much of this momentum by allowing Zanzibar to continue having its own government, under its own president, and enjoying extensive autonomy. Even such extensive devolution of power, if not properly managed, could have had unintended consequences by encouraging people opposed to the union to demand even more autonomy, progressively leading to a return to the status quo ante: restoration of Zanzibar's full sovereign status, hence dissolution of the union. Yet it was skillfully managed by Nyerere under what was essentially a unitary state which did not allow such extensive devolution of power to the regions on mainland Tanzania - except to the former island nation of Zanzibar.

Nyerere's consummation of the union was criticized even by some of his fellow socialists, although of the Marxist bent; Nyerere was not a Marxist. As Ann Talbot, a Trotskyite, stated in "Nyerere's Legacy of Poverty and Repression in Zanzibar":

The late President Julius Nyerere, the first president of independent Tanganyika,...formed a union with Zanzibar to create Tanzania in 1964.

Nyerere remains an icon of the Pan-Africanist movement and the limited welfare measures that he introduced in Tanzania are still held up by some as an example of the benefits of what was known as African socialism. To many he remains as saintly a figure as Nelson Mandela has become....

Nyerere formed the union with Zanzibar when a spontaneous popular uprising had just overthrown the government of large estate owners that Britain had given power to on independence. Neither of the two opposition parties, the

Afro-Shirazi Party (ASP), or the Umma Party, were in control of the uprising. Power fell into their hands because the movement lacked a program that represented the interests of the dispossessed estate workers or the workers on the docks....

Nyerere recognised that the uprising was a threat to his own position. In the weeks following it... encouraged by the events in Zanzibar, his army mutinied against its British officers.... The ease with which the mutiny had taken place revealed the weakness of his regime to popular opposition. Nyerere realised that if he could not control the political aspirations of the mass of his population, he would be of little use to Britain or any other imperialist power.... Nyerere had an object lesson close to hand in what happened to an African leader who could not control popular movements. Only four years before President (sic) Patrice Lumumba had been assassinated by Western agents because he could not maintain control of the volatile situation in the Congo.

Lumumba had appealed to the Soviet Union for military aid and in doing so had threatened to tip the balance of the Cold War in Africa. Now the new Zanzibar government had established relations with the Soviet bloc, allowed East Germany to open an embassy and accepting their help to train the army.

Nyerere was looking at Lumumba's fate when he initiated the union with Zanzibar. He knew that he would not survive if he allowed the movement in Zanzibar to continue and could not demonstrate his usefulness to imperialism by bringing Zanzibar into a union with Tanganyika.

For his part Zanzibar's President Abeid Karume, who led the Afro-Shirazi Party, saw the union with Tanganyika as a means of undermining his opponents in government. His particular target was Abdulrahman Mohammed Babu, leader of the Umma Party, who favoured close links with the Soviet bloc and Cuba. Babu, whose power base was on Pemba, as the CUF's (Tanzanian main opposition Civic United Front's) is today, was forced to take refuge on the mainland as Karume arrested or killed his opponents. In 1972 Karume was assassinated, probably at Babu's instigation.[11]

Factual errors aside - the army mutinies in all the three East African countries of Kenya, Uganda, and Tanganyika, took place in January 1964, therefore within days, not after weeks as Talbot says, following the Zanzibar revolution which took place on January 12; the first mutiny was in Tanganyika on January 20, and lasted for six days; and Patrice Lumumba was prime minister, not president, of Congo - there is a distinct ideological line, Trotskyite, Ann Talbot is pursuing in her deeply flawed analysis of Nyerere, instead of focusing on objective inquiry regardless of one's ideological preferences. It is these ideological blinders which have thrown her off track in what should be a scholarly pursuit involving dispassionate analysis. And Babu, of course, differs with

Talbot on the role of the Umma Party in the Zanzibar revolution. As he stated in "The 1964 Revolution: Lumpen or Vanguard?":

> Although the Umma Party did not fire the first shot of the uprising, it nevertheless rose to the occasion with revolutionary zeal and skill. It helped to transform a wholly lumpen - in many ways apolitical - uprising into a popular, anti-imperialist revolution, which, left to its own momentum, and without the external intervention that followed, would undoubtedly have opened up a new path - the road to socialism.[12]

The revolution itself was an indigenous expression of mass discontent, not a foreign-inspired uprising as some still maintain. And to contend, as Ann Talbot does, that Nyerere was an imperialist agent at the beck and call of the British and other imperialist powers - presumably the United States and other Western nations as well, since as a Trotsykite socialist, she would never conceive of a scenario in which she would see the Soviet Union, now dead, acting as an imperialist power - is, once again as I argued earlier, to deliberately ignore Nyerere's record of independent domestic and foreign policy initiatives which irritated and sometimes even infuriated both ideological camps at different times during his long political career; not only as a Tanzanian or African leader, but also as a Third World leader and one of the most influential world leaders in the twentieth century.

Yet, as a Trotskyite, Talbot is obsessed with "proving" in every conceivable way that Nyerere was "wrong" because he did not toe the Trotskyist party line (and I don't use the term Trotskyist in the disparaging sense in this context, as it is normally used) - he didn't the Maoist either. Trotskyites, like other Marxist-Leninists who include Maoists, see themselves as the standard-bearer of Marxism-Leninism, even though it is a discredited ideology as has been validated by experience and by the collapse of communist regimes around the world since the end of the Cold War. And any socialist - including Nyerere - who deviates from this or does not toe this party line, is considered to be an apostate or a traitor. Nyerere's independence from Marxism-Leninism - and unimpressed by Marxist-Leninist dogma - did not earn him endearment in the socialist camp anymore than it did in the West for his relentless criticism of Western imperialist policies towards Africa.

He demonstrated such independence even during the Congo crisis, as leader of Tanganyika before uniting with Zanzibar and after the two countries were united under his stewardship to form Tanzania, at a time when the East and the West were locked in the most bitter and intense rivalry on African soil right in the heart of the continent in the turbulent sixties. In spite of Tanzania's weakness, Nyerere openly supported the Congolese nationalist forces - followers of Lumumba - against the Western puppet regime in Leopoldville installed and supported by the CIA and other Western interests including French and British. He also allowed Cuban troops, led by Che Guevara, to use Tanzania as a conduit to enter the Congo, and even allowed them to have a rear base in western Tanzania to support the Congolese nationalists fighting the CIA-backed government in Congo.

Kigoma, a town on Lake Tanganyika, was used by Che Guevara as his rear base. Fidel Castro did not sneak Cuban troops and Che Guevara into Congo through Tanzania. He sent hundreds of Cuban troops, and Che Guevara, to Congo through Tanzania with the full knowledge and permission of President Nyerere and his government. And the CIA knew this. So did the British and other Western intelligence services, as did their governments, from Washington to London, Brussels and the rest. They also knew that Nyerere allowed the Russians and the Chinese to send weapons to the nationalist forces in the Congo through Tanzania. This doesn't seem to be the kind of leader who was a servant of Western imperialism as Ann Talbot contends, or as someone who took orders from the United States and Britain - the very powers he fought against - to form the union of Tanganyika and Zanzibar as others claim.

And it is worth remembering that even after the Congolese nationalist forces failed to dislodge the CIA-backed regime in Leopoldville, Nyerere never changed his position. He continued to oppose Western domination and exploitation of the Congo - and the rest of Africa - and supported the Congolese pro-Lumumbist nationalists and liberation movements in other parts of the continent. And when Che Guevara failed in his Congo mission, he retreated to Tanzania and stayed in Dar es Salaam, the nation's capital, for about five months, at least, during which he wrote the *Congo Diaries* before returning to Cuba. As Jorge Castaneda states in his book, *Companero: The Life and Death of Che Guevara:*

> His secretary during those crucial months in Tanzania... was... Colman Ferrer.... During the time he spent with Pablo Ribalta, the Cuban ambassador to Tanzania and his old comrade in arms, in the Tanzanian capital, Che made two crucial decisions: he would not return to Cuba, and his next destination was Buenos Aires....His wife arrived in Dar es Salaam. They were staying at the Embassy....
>
> Che spent his free time writing - his favorite activity, apart from combat and literature. Working from notes taken in the Congo, he began drafting...*Pasajes de la guerra revolucionaria (el Congo).* Colman Ferrer, a young secretary at the Cuban Embassy in Dar-es-Salaam, served as his assistant. Che dictated his text, Ferrer transcribed it, then Guevara revised and corrected the final manuscript. In the words of Ferrer, Che basically spent the days 'marking time, preparing the conditions for a change of scenery.' As Oscar Fernandez Mell recalls it, 'One of Che's great virtues was the way he enjoyed reading, though he also had more exacting tastes and ways of spending his time. He could read for hours; he had a good time even when he was alone.'
>
> He was extremely meticulous in his work. In Ferrer's words, 'he was careful in the things he was going to write, avoiding any mistakes. He took great care, he analyzed and reread the transcription repeatedly.' The book left little time for other activities. 'He wrote day and night. His only distraction was an occasional game of chess with me. One day when I was about to checkmate him, he looked at me as if he had not realized what was happening; it was obvious that he wasn't really in the game.'
>
> Finally, at the end of February or beginning or March 1966, Che agreed to leave.... 'Everybody returned to Cuba and he stayed on alone in Tanzania, and then I decided to get him out of Tanzania and take him to a safe place until he decided what he was going to do,' Ulises Estrada, (in) interview with the author (Castaneda), Havana, February 9, 1995.[13]

The CIA and other Western intelligence agencies knew Che Guevara was in Dar es Salaam, Tanzania, for months, after the failure of his Congo mission. He settled in Dar es Salaam in October 1965. And they knew when he left. Much as they hated him for spreading revolution to other parts of the Third World, they would have pressured Tanzania to expel him from the country if President Nyerere was their stooge, as Ann Talbot claims. And if they tried, then they failed to speed up his exit. Che Guevara left Tanzania when he was ready to do so. And he stayed in Tanzania for as long as he did because he was allowed to. Yet one can't think of him staying, even for one day, in a country whose leader was subservient to the West. He would have been expelled the same day, let alone allowed to have an operational base, as Che Guevara was, to support anti-Western nationalist insurgents in a neighboring country. That Nyerere allowed the Cubans to operate from Tanzania, and communist powers to funnel weapons through Tanzania to support nationalist forces in the Congo, demonstrated a degree of independence and his commitment to non-alignment one would hardly characterize - if at all - as a sign of weakness and subservience to the West.

And his opposition to American involvement in Vietnam during the Vietnam war, and to the invasion of Czechoslovakia in 1968 by the Warsaw Pact forces led by the Soviet Union, once again demonstrated his independence and commitment to positive neutralism without taking orders from either side of the Iron Curtain.

It is in this context that Nyerere's establishment of the union of Tanganyika and Zanzibar must be viewed, as a realization of his policy objectives, a triumph of Pan-Africanism, and a rejection of imperial domination by any of the world powers regardless of their ideologies. Yet, because of his modesty, even his adversaries underrated him. As Gamal Nkrumah, son of the late president of Ghana Dr. Kwame Nkrumah, stated in the obituary he wrote for Nyerere, "The Legacy of A Great African," in *Al-Ahram*:

Nyerere's presence at political rallies, remote poverty-stricken villages, academic conferences and international forums where he pleaded the case of the South always lit up the occasion. He had a way with the words.... He was the philosopher-king, intellectual, enlightened, the polar opposite of the despotic ruler so common in the Africa of his day. But he was also a man of the people....

Two years ago, at celebrations marking the 40th anniversary of Ghana's independence, I met and spoke to Nyerere for the last time. I would never have guessed that he was ill.... He was not only a man of integrity, but he also had the courage and modesty to admit to past mistakes. I have heard him speak in London, at the Commonwealth Institute, in several forums in the United States and at the United Nations, as well as in many an African setting. To me personally, Nyerere was always the attentive father figure, never missing an opportunity to remind me that my own father's vision for a united Africa was the only way forward.

With his wit, humour, sharp intellect and disarming sincerity, Nyerere was always a winning personality. But, to say that he was an uncontroversial character would be a grave mistake. From the beginning of his political career, Nyerere was widely seen as a moderate, and that at a time when more militant African leaders prevailed. As early as the late 1950s and early 1960s, official US documents, now declassified, interestingly reveal that America's Central Intelligence (CIA) regarded him as the only 'responsible' African leader. Nyerere himself was clever enough to realise that such a revelation was no compliment....

His greatest achievement is undoubtedly the successful unification of mainland Tanganyika with the Indian Ocean island of Zanzibar (and Pemba). The United Republic of Tanzania was born in 1964 out of that union with an overwhelmingly Muslim island-nation whose closest historical, economic and political ties were with Oman in particular and the Arab Gulf countries in general. Zanzibar was for two centuries the Omani official seat of government and the official residence of the Sultan. In contrast, Tanganyika...had a more mixed population, equally divided between Christians and Muslims. It was to Nyerere's credit that he managed to unite this most ethnically, linguistically and religiously diverse of nation-states and make it one of Africa's most politically stable countries.[14]

It is true that the United States denounced Zanzibar as "the Cuba of Africa,"[15] after the January 1964 revolution led by John Okello who toppled the Arab-dominated regime and transferred power to the predominantly black majority and their allies including a number of Arabs, Iranians (originally from Shiraz in Iran), and others. But it is also true that the people who led the revolution were not interested in substituting one master for another - capitalist or communist - and their uprising was not communist-inspired. It was an expression of indigenous aspirations triggered by the racial injustices the black majority suffered at the hands of the Arab-minority regime to whom the British transferred power at independence on December 10, 1963.

The communist threat in Zanzibar was overly exaggerated. Even the leaders who could have established communism on the isles dismissed this threat. They were explicit in their intentions, and would not have shied away from acknowledging that they were going to establish communism in Zanzibar - which would been an open secret, anyway, sooner rather than later. They included Abdulrahman Mohammed Babu, the most prominent leader with communist leanings on the islands and whom the CIA followed closely, as it did all the other leaders. According to one of the declassified documents in the US Archives written by the American ambassador to Nigeria, Averill Harriman, to President Lyndon B. Johnson and Secretary of State Dean Rusk on March 25, 1964:

In long talks with Prime Minister Abubakar (Tafawa Balewa) and Foreign Minister (Jaja) Wachuku,...both minimized concern I expressed for Communist takeover in Zanzibar, assured me that Karume was sensible and Babu was primarily African nationalist and would not permit Communist takeover. When I pressed Wachuku, he firmly insisted he could guarantee Babu whom he had personally known a long time.[16]

The preceding telegram was followed by other reports on the potential for communist penetration of Africa during the early years of independence in the sixties. Ambassador Harriman himself in another report to President Johnson on October 28, 1964, about nine months after the Zanzibar revolution and just one day before the Union of Tanganyika and Zanzibar was renamed Tanzania (on October 29, 1964), conceded: "Not a single new African nation has succumbed to Communist domination."[17] Officials in the Johnson Administration were convinced that communists had played an active role in the Zanzibar revolution on January 12, 1964, according to released documents contained in the 850-page volume of *Foreign Relations of the United States 1964 - 1968*. As one US State Department background paper, February 7, 1964, asserted: "There was obvious communist involvement in Zanzibar."[18] Yet, the same officials admitted that disturbances in other parts of East Africa - the army mutinies in Tanganyika, Kenya, and Uganda in January 1964 - around the same time did not appear to be communist-inspired. In fact, President Nyerere himself resolutely maintained that there was "no evidence whatsoever to suggest that the mutinies in Tanganyika were inspired by outside forces - either Communist or imperialist."[19]

But there was a common logic that linked the mutinies to the Zanzibar revolution. The revolution was an African uprising against Arab domination and had a distinct racial component (it was also a class conflict between dispossessed blacks and the merchants and landowners who were mostly Arab and Indian), as was clearly demonstrated during the revolution in which hundreds of Arabs and Indians, but mostly Arabs - probably no fewer than 2,000 - were massacred. Some estimates put the death toll at 13,000 and mostly come from supporters of the old Arab regime who are also opposed to the union of Tanganyika and Zanzibar.

The army mutinies in Tanganyika and in the other two East African countries (Kenya and Uganda), partly inspired by the uprising in Zanzibar, also had a racial dimension. In addition to demanding an increase in salary, the mutineers also demanded the replacement of British army officers with African ones to Africanize the armed forces in a true spirit of independence by eradicating the last vestiges of colonialism. But the mutiny in Tanganyika almost ended up as a military coup, according to the evidence gathered from an analysis of records and documents contained in the archives of the East Africana Collection at the University of Dar es Salaam, Tanzania:

(The) abortive military mutiny on January 20, 1964, (was) motivated by demands for higher pay and the replacement of British officers by Africans.

The six-day mutiny, which began at Colito Barracks (renamed Lugalo Barracks) in Dar es Salaam and spread to troops stationed at Tabora (and Nachingwea), appears to have been well planned. After arresting their British officers, soldiers built roadblocks at strategic points throughout the city, seized the State House (the president's official residence, although Nyerere did not live there but in a simple house on the outskirts of the city in Msasani, and used the State House, popularly known as Ikulu, only for official functions), police stations, airport, radio station, and railway station, and placed guards at critical postal, telegraph, and bank buildings. The Tanganyikan mutiny sparked similar uprisings in the Ugandan and Kenyan armies as well as the looting and pillaging of Asian shops in Dar es Salaam.

Hundreds of people were arrested during the looting in the commercial areas of the capital. Local forces of order were weakened by the government's earlier decision to send the Dar es Salaam Field Police (known by the acronym FFU - Field Force Units), a contingent of 300 men, to Zanzibar to help restore order on the troubled island. The fear that racial violence might escalate was linked to the revolution in Zanzibar, which took place in the preceding week and was accompanied by race riots, the murder of hundreds of Arab and Asian shopkeepers, and the mass exodus of Asians to the mainland. Field Marshal John Okello, who had seized power in Zanzibar, declared: 'We are friends of all Europeans and other foreigners. It is only the Ismailis and certain other Indian groups and people of Arab descent we do not like.' (*Tanganyika Standard*, January 17, 1964).

The racial antagonisms behind the army mutiny were evident in the behavior of the mutinous soldiers stationed in the town of Tabora, who beat up all Europeans and Asians who crossed their path. (Listowel, 1965: p. 433). During the looting of Asian shops in Dar es Salaam, 17 people were killed and 23 seriously injured. (*Tanganyika Standard,* January 22, 1964). Rumors spread throughout the capital that Nyerere had fled the country and a general strike was imminent. Nyerere, while still hiding, broadcast a radio message on the second day of the rebellion, to reassure the country that he was still in power.

Had they moved quickly, the mutineers could probably have seized control of the government, but the rebellious army units had no plans to launch a coup d'etat. Rebellious soldiers negotiated with Minister of Defense Oscar Kambona and agreed to release the 30 captured European (British) officers, who were quickly flown out of the country. Kambona had offered to replace all European officers with Africans and discuss wages, provided the troops release the officers and return to their barracks.

Nyerere's first public act, after he emerged from hiding on January 22, was to tour the city on foot, visiting the areas of looted Asian shops to express his condolences to Asian shopkeepers who had been targets of violence. (*Tanganyika Standard*, January 23, 1964).

Only after the mutineers began to negotiate with militant leaders of the trade union movement did the government reluctantly ask the British to intervene (the British were soon replaced by Nigerian troops at Nyerere's request at an urgent OAU summit he called in Addis Ababa, Ethiopia, to deal with the crisis). Trade union leaders hoped to take advantage of the situation and turn the mutiny into a coup d'etat. The two most prominent proponents of Africanization, trade union leaders Christopher (Kasanga) Tumbo, who had returned from Kenya, and Victor Mkello, met in Morogoro to plan a new government. (Listowel, 1965: pp. 437 - 38). On January 25, British troops quickly took control of the barracks and disarmed the rebels, killing five African soldiers in the confrontation.

The army mutiny proved to be a great embarrassment for the government, which was forced to call on troops of the former colonial power to restore public order. Yet the uprising also provided the occasion to move decisively against those who had continued to press for Africanization. After the abortive mutiny, the government arrested 50 policemen implicated in the uprising, reorganized the military (while Nigerian troops sent to Tanganyika by the Nigerian Federal Government provided defense for the country), and replaced British officers to defuse the issue of Africanization. It used Preventive Detention Law, rarely invoked since its passage in 1962, to order the arrest of more than 200 trade union leaders, many of whom were released after questioning. Fifteen soldiers were sentenced to prison for their role in the mutiny. The trade union movement was brought firmly under the control of the government by the dissolution of the Tanganyika Federation of Labour (TFL) and establishment in its place of the TANU-controlled National Union of Tanganyika Workers (NUTA). Several days after the suppression of the mutiny, on January 28, 1964, Nyerere announced the appointment of a presidential commission to pursue the plans that had been announced earlier to create a single-party state, subsequently instituted in the constitution of 1965.[20]

Therefore, from all available evidence, it is clear that communism - or any form of external involvement or manipulation - was not a factor in the army mutiny in Tanganyika or those in

Kenya and Uganda; three inter-related incidents in a chain reaction that almost plunged the three countries into chaos during those fateful days in January 1964. Probably more than anything else, even more than salary demands, the mutinies were inspired by black nationalism, and were a military expression of indigenous political aspirations. And so was the Zanzibar revolution, although it transcended race and included some Arabs and Persians in the vanguard in the quest for racial justice. But since the oppressive regime which was overthrown was Arab, oppressing and exploiting black people more than anybody else, the revolution assumed a racial dimension as an indigenous expression of the political and economic aspirations of the black majority - who did not need communism to wake them up to reality and show them that they were being oppressed and exploited by the Arabs because they were weak and black. Experience is the best teacher.

Although it is true that American policy towards Africa during the Johnson Administration (and preceding and future ones) was one of communist containment, there was little evidence to show that communism was gaining ground anywhere on the continent. Hence Ambassador Harriman's observation as early as 1964 that - "not a single new African nation has succumbed to Communist penetration"; and the conclusion, in the same year, by the US State Department that: "There is no hard evidence at this time that the trouble in East Africa (the army mutinies) was part of an inter-related communist plot to take over the area."[21]

A plausible explanation for American involvement in "facilitating" the establishment of the union of Tanganyika and Zanzibar may lie in the fact that the interests of the United States with regard to Zanzibar coincided with those of Julius Nyerere, who had always wanted all the countries in the region (including Zanzibar) to unite, and therefore the American government - at best - did not interfere and try to block the union from being formed; but not in the fact - the erroneous fact - that the union was conceived and engineered by the United States and Britain. Whereas the United States may have been concerned about the potential for the establishment of a communist regime in Zanzibar which could serve as a beachhead for communist incursions into the African continent and threaten her geopolitical and strategic interests on the continent and in the Indian Ocean as a world power

- since the island nation would be turned into a communist satellite dominated by the Soviet Union or the People's Republic of China; Nyerere, on the other hand, saw the establishment of the union as a step towards African unity and a realization of his Pan-African ambition to unite countries in the region; an ambition had had always cherished, long before the "communist-inspired" revolution in Zanzibar, and even long before Tanganyika and other countries in the region won independence.

But even if the Americans thought that by uniting Zanzibar with Tanganyika, communists would be deprived of a base in the island nation under a radical regime, they were not very comfortable with Nyerere himself, under whose leadership Zanzibar's radicalism was supposed to be contained or neutralized; thus raising questions why they would help such a leader unite his country with Zanzibar in the first place. Therefore, the legitimacy of the fundamental assumption - or argument - itself that Nyerere united Tanganyika with Zanzibar at the behest of the United States and Britain, and not on his own initiative, loses credibility. In fact, recently declassified documents show that President Lyndon Johnson and members of his administration, as well as many - if not most - members of the United States Congress, were not comfortable with Nyerere's socialist beliefs. According to a memo written by a National Security Council staff member, Ulric Haynes, on June 8, 1966: "Under the mercurial and fiery independent leadership of Nyerere, Tanzania is the bastion of radicalism in East Africa.... Soviet and Chicom influence is considerable, especially in Zanzibar."[22]

According to the documents released, the Central Intelligence Agency (CIA) was actively involved in covert operations in East Africa in the mid-sixties (and later, of course), although they don't specifically say what the activities were; and no one expects them to, given the clandestine nature of their operations. But such explicit admission by the CIA of its activities in East Africa only corroborated some of the accusations made against the United States in her attempts to sow dissension in the region. It also confirms the accusation by President Nyerere that the United States tried to undermine his government, leading to a deterioration of relations between the two countries, and prompting the expulsion of American diplomats from Tanzania. As Nyerere himself stated in 1966:

> We have twice quarreled with the US Government; once when we believed it to be involved in a plot against us, and again when two of its officials misbehaved and were asked to leave Tanzania.... The disagreements certainly induced an uncooperative coldness between us, thus suspending and then greatly slowing down further aid discussions. A comparison of American aid to Tanzania and other African countries supports the contention that at any rate our total policies (including support of the African liberation movements) have led to a lower level of assistance than might otherwise have been granted.[23]

Obviously because of his policies, the United States did not see Nyerere as an ally in the region, and therefore had no reason to help him establish and consolidate a union - of Tanganyika and Zanzibar - except in strategic "partnership" to thwart communist advances, of which there were actually none, and about which Nyerere was not worried as he clearly demonstrated when he forged strong ties with Communist China and, to a lesser degree, with the Soviet Union and her satellites. In many fundamental respects, his policies were the exact opposite of those of the United States. He was a socialist, opposed to capitalism. The United States was - and still is - capitalist, opposed to socialism. He was an implacable foe of apartheid South Africa and other white minority and colonial regimes on the continent - the Portuguese colonies of Angola, Mozambique, Guinea-Bissau and Cape Verde, and Principe and Sao Tome; Rhodesia (Zimbabwe); and South West Africa (Namibia) ruled by apartheid South Africa in defiance of United Nations resolutions which terminated its mandate to rule the former German colony. The United States, on the other hand, supported apartheid South Africa, Rhodesia, and Portugal as geopolitical and strategic allies in the Cold War and as a bulwark against communism in Africa - a red herring to perpetuate Western domination of Africa.

The United States also supported Portugal, a fellow NATO member, and refrained from criticizing her policies in her African colonies because the Americans were allowed to maintain a military base on the Portuguese-controlled Azores islands in the Atlantic Ocean northwest of Africa. The United States and other Western countries also supported apartheid South Africa, Rhodesia, and Portugal for racist reasons, taking sides with their kith-and-kin regardless of the immorality of such a stance. As Nyerere bluntly stated in his article, "Rhodesia in the Context of Southern Africa," published in *Foreign Affairs*:

> The deep and intense anger of Africa on the subject of Rhodesia is by now widely realized. It is not, however, so clearly understood. In consequence the mutual suspicion, which already exists between free African states and nations of the West, is in danger of getting very much worse....
>
> Successive Western governments have declared their hostility to apartheid, and their adherence to the principles of racial equality. They have frequently made verbal declarations of their sympathy with the forces in opposition to South African policies. But they have excused their failure to act in support of their words, on the grounds of South Africa's sovereignty. Africa has shown a great deal of skepticism about this argument, believing that it masked a reluctance to intervene on the side of justice when white privilege was involved. Now, in the case of Southern Rhodesia, legality is on the side of intervention. What is the West going to do? Will it justify or confound African suspicions?
>
> So far the West has demonstrated its intentions by the gradual increase of voluntary economic sanctions; there has been a refusal even to challenge South African and Portuguese support for Smith by making sanctions mandatory upon all members of the United Nations. And there have been repeated statements by the responsible authority that force will not be used except in case of a breakdown in law and order - which apparently does not cover the illegal seizure of power! What happens if the economic sanctions fail to bring down the Smith regime is left vague. The suggestion therefore remains that, despite legality, the domination of a white minority over blacks is acceptable to the West.... It is time...for Britain and the United States of America to make clear whether they really believe in the principles they claim to espouse, or whether their policies are governed by considerations of the privileges of their 'kith and kin.'[24]

Therefore, whatever help Nyerere got from the United States and Britain to form the union of Tanganyika and Zanzibar - and there is no tangible evidence of that - it did not have any moderating influence on his Pan-African militancy. And he continued to criticize the West, as he did the East, when he deemed it appropriate. And his criticism was not confined to their policies towards Africa. For example, when the Warsaw Pact forces led by the Soviet Union invaded Czechoslovakia in 1968, claiming they had been invited, Nyerere sharply responded: "Call an invasion, an invasion, not an invitation."[25]

On American involvement in Vietnam, he had this to say:

We are told that great principles are involved, and that the richest nation on earth is defending those principles against attack. What are these principles? There is the principle of self-determination for the people of Vietnam. For twenty years, with unparalleled courage and determination, the people of Vietnam have been fighting for a chance to implement this principle - first against the French, and now against the Americans....(And) if this is a civil war, what are outside nations doing in that conflict?

Again, we are told that democracy is being defended, and only last month (September 1967) there were some 'elections' in South Vietnam. But these elections only covered the 'pacified areas,' and no candidate could stand on a clear platform of opposition to the war! And in any case these were the first elections since 1956, when South Vietnam came into existence, and no one could possibly call the governments of Mr. Diem, or his military successors, democratic.

Or we are told that the outside power responded to a request for assistance from a legitimate government, which was threatened by aggression. One can only look at the figures of soldiers operating in South Vietnam and ask whose aggression?...

The USA must recover from the delirium of power, and return to the principles upon which her nation was founded. Those millions of Americans who are now opposing their government's policies in this matter, and calling for peace, are working for the honour of their country.[26]

On Britain:

We have quarrelled with the British Government on a number of issues, e.g. when we refused to associate ourselves with the Commonwealth communique on Rhodesia in June 1965; when we refused to support the proposed Commonwealth Peace Mission to Vietnam on the grounds that it was neither practical nor genuine; and when we received a Chinese offer to help with the building of the railway to Zambia while still discussing the possibility of British and American help on the same project.[27]

Tanzania was also the first African country to break diplomatic relations with Britain over Britain's unwillingness or refusal to take decisive action, including the use of military force, to end the rebellion by the white minority regime, which illegally declared independence in Rhodesia on November 11, 1965.

On relations with West Germany, Nyerere had the following to say:

East Germany wanted Tanzania to give diplomatic recognition to her, and West Germany wanted us to ignore the existence of the German Democratic

Republic and pretend there is no such administration over the Eastern part of Germany. In fact we refused recognition to the East German authorities but accepted an unofficial Consulate General from them - a formula which had been accepted in one other African country. As a result of our decision West Germany withdrew some types of aid - unilaterally breaking a five-year air training agreement - and announced that other aid was under threat if Tanzania did not change her policies. Tanzania refused to do this and told the West Germans to withdraw all their federal government aid.[28]

Nyerere continued to pursue an independent, non-aligned, foreign policy throughout his tenure as president Tanzania, just as he did when he was president of Tanganyika before the union with Zanzibar in April 1964. The union only widened the scope of his activities because of the merger itself as a subject of major interest in diplomatic circles and other international forums; also because it was the first union of independent states on the African continent, setting precedent; and because of the controversy over Zanzibar as a potential communist outpost, and the revolution itself as a phenomenal event in the history of African decolonization hailed across the continent for its Pan-African militancy.

And despite Nyerere's own commitment to African unity, which inspired him to unite Tanganyika with Zanzibar, the political dynamics in the island nation itself also played an important role in facilitating the establishment of this union. Therefore, even if Tanganyika did not have a leader of Nyerere's caliber and depth of Pan-African commitment, the unstable situation in Zanzibar only a few miles from the mainland - 25 miles or so - would perhaps have encouraged or compelled another leader to seek such a merger himself, even if it was just for the security of the mainland without any concern for African unity. And a communist threat would not be ignored anymore than would a threat from the West: penetration and domination of the island nation by the United States and other Western powers after the revolution to secure their geopolitical and strategic interests in the region and keep the Russians and the Chinese out. A threat to independence from the West is no more benign than a threat from the East; a "subtle" distinction that seems to have eluded many Westerners, including pundits, who think the West is a paragon of virtue. Otherwise African countries would have been happy to remain under Western domination as colonies, and would never have fought for independence.

There was also a racial element in the quest for unity. Black people in Zanzibar had been oppressed by Arabs for centuries. This oppression included outright enslavement. The January 1964 revolution won them freedom. But with freedom was the residual fear that their former masters could reclaim the islands one day and re-institute tyranny with the help of the Arab states, especially the Gulf States, Oman in particular where the majority of the Arabs in Zanzibar including the sultanate, came from. Their only hope for security was union with Tanganyika, a country much bigger and stronger than Zanzibar, and with more than 20 times the population, mostly black. This was undoubtedly a factor when the black leaders of Zanzibar promptly agreed to the merger, with Zanzibari President Abeid Karume calling for total unification; a formula rejected by Nyerere who felt that total renunciation of sovereignty by Zanzibar, without retaining extensive autonomy, would destabilize the union and even lead to its dissolution.

Therefore, the union was a product of a combination of factors, internal and external, but mostly internal. As Samir Amin said in the First Babu Memorial Lecture in honor of the late Abdulrahman Mohammed Babu (September 22, 1924 - August 5, 1996), one of the architects of the Zanzibar revolution and the union of Tanzania, in London on September 22, 1997:

> For me, speaking about Babu is speaking, not only of a comrade and an elder but of a personal friend whom I knew right from the post-war period - the whole of our generation in Africa. Babu was someone with whom I shared most political views for something like 40 years.... It was in London, in 1952, that we first met. Babu was then, like me, a young student, he was elder to me by a few years which at that point of time seemed a considerable difference - later of course the difference lost most of its meaning.
>
> We were both very active among African students in Britain and France trying to start a unified movement.... Babu was connected to the East African anti-colonialist committee....
>
> Babu did better than I (did in Egypt) because he was able... to participate in the creation of objective forces in his country - Zanzibar - which led to a revolution in January 1964, which potentially at least could go beyond nationalist populism.
>
> I knew of course what Babu thought of all this. We had been on the board of a magazine, *Revolution*, which was published in 62/63 i.e. just before the Zanzibar revolution.... We worked, both of us, with others on that magazine, to look at precisely this question. Is it possible and if so under what conditions

for nationalist populism to move to the left?... provided the popular classes organised independently go into conflict with the system and go ahead. Babu tried to do this in Zanzibar with some success.... (The) merger...(of) Zanzibar with Tanganyika to form Tanzania...was for reasons internal to Tanzania (Tanganyika) and Zanzibar.[29]

Even without external forces, internal factors alone - "reasons internal to Tanzania (Tanganyika) and Zanzibar," as Samir Amin put it, which also led to the merger of the two countries - constituted sufficient ground for the establishment of the union. But without the Zanzibar revolution - which was an expression of the collective sentiments of frustrated and downtrodden blacks, especially the young - the union of the two countries would probably not have taken place; at least not when it did, if at all. The revolution provided a powerful impetus to the merger of the two predominantly black nations, and the leader of the revolution, self-styled Field Marshal John Okello originally from Uganda, provided an equally powerful rallying point for the frustrated black masses groaning under Arab oppression.

The ouster of the oppressive Arab regime was carried out by only a few hundred men - figures range from 300 to 600, but it probably was 300 - led by John Okello. But after they seized the radio station and other vital installations including police stations where they seized more weapons, and Okello went on the air to announce the takeover, the majority of the African population welcomed the change and rallied behind the freedom fighters, giving overwhelming support to the revolution. Although the Afro-Shirazi Party (ASP) which represented African interests did not participate in the initial phase of the revolution, including its actual launching, it immediately gave full support to the uprising and acted as the official organ articulating the sentiments of the downtrodden black masses. It was joined by the Umma (People's) Party of Abdulrahman Mohammed Babu, with which it went on to form a coalition government.

Thousands of supporters of the revolution and the Afro-Shirazi Party (ASP) struck back at their former oppressors, attacking landowners and merchants - who were mostly Arab and Indian - and their property including private homes. And the killings spread further to include ordinary Arabs and Asians, by virtue of their position as members of the oppressive races. In addition to the hundreds killed, thousands fled the islands and sought refuge elsewhere in Arab countries, Europe, Asia, and even in Africa itself, especially North Africa; although many fled to Tanganyika as well, as they did to Kenya. In fact, the sultan of Zanzibar himself and his family and others fled to Dar es Salaam, Tanganyika, after they were denied entry into Kenya, at Mombasa, where they first sought refuge. Many other people also fled to the Comoro Islands.

Many of those targeted in the uprising were also originally from the Comoros, an island nation that has had historical ties with Zanzibar - and even with mainland Tanzania, formerly Tanganyika - for centuries. The Comorians are mostly of mixed Arab-Malay-African ancestry. And in the racially stratified society of Zanzibar, they were also above the Africans, together with the Arabs, and the Asians - mostly Indian. Also in addition to the historical ties between the Comoros and Zanzibar, there are also racial ties, especially Arab, and linguistic ties: the main languages spoken in the Comoros are Arabic and Kiswahili (which is itself heavily influenced by Arabic), just like in Zanzibar, although French is also spoken, since the islands were once a French colony.

But in spite of the fact that many Comorians have African ancestry, they did not - in general - sympathize with the plight of black people in Zanzibar, since they were members of a different "racial stock," or ethnic group, a confluence of three tributaries: Arab, Malay, and African. And because of their higher status in Zanzibar, as well as contempt for blacks they shared with Arabs and Indians, they were some of the primary targets during the revolution.

Estimates of the number killed vary. Some put it even as high as 20,000. But after some extrapolation, it was obviously in the hundreds, and may be no fewer than 2,000. It was virtually a one-sided conflict, with the Africans having the upper hand after Okello and his men seized weapons from the police barracks they had overtaken. Most of those killed were Arabs, Indians, Comorians and other minorities.

It was one of the bloodiest conflicts in the history of colonial Africa, and one of the most well known. But out of this bloodshed emerged a new nation, born out of a merger of two countries, Tanganyka and Zanzibar, a union that would probably not have been consummated had the revolution not taken place, prompting the Zanzibari Africans to seek immediate protection from Tanganyikans for their newly won freedom by uniting with them; lest their former oppressors launch a counter-attack some time in the future and re-impose tyranny on the islands.

Concern for security by blacks in Zanzibar; a deteriorating economic situation in the island nation; willingness - after some debate - of their leaders to unite with Tanganyika; the unstable political situation on the isles; Nyerere's desire to eliminate any threat to Tanganyika that may come from an unstable, economically non-viable and weak neighbor whose weakness would provide an opportunity for external forces to intervene and dominate the island nation - and that included possible intervention by the West, not just by the East; and his desire to unite all the countries in the region, probably more than anything else; all these factors combined to facilitate the unification of Tanganyika and Zanzibar on April 26, 1964, only three-and-half months after the revolution on January 12, leading to the establishment of the first union of independent states in Africa, a feat that has not been duplicated anywhere else on the continent.

After the union, Tanzania also became one of the most stable and peaceful countries in Africa under the leadership of Julius Nyerere. Before the union, he had also presided over the establishment and growth of Tanganyika, one of the most ethnically diverse countries on the continent, yet which became one of the most cohesive states in the history of post-colonial Africa. But in spite of all these achievements, most of Nyerere's critics give him little credit in this area, focusing, instead, on his failed economic policies he pursued along socialist lines.

There is no question that his socialist policies were a failure in most cases, good intentions notwithstanding; something even his admirers should admit, as many of them in Tanzania including this writer and others elsewhere indeed do. The evidence is overwhelming - it's all over Tanzania, as are many of his achievements. He did his best - which he himself once said would be a fitting epitaph for him after he died - and definitely meant well, as clearly demonstrated by his deep concern for the masses which even had a saintly dimension, in spite of all his flaws as a mere mortal, like the rest of us including hallowed saints themselves, and one of the most humble, unlike most. But his achievements must also be acknowledged and not overlooked or deliberately ignored because of his failed socialist policies. As Professor Ali Mazrui stated in his tribute to Nyerere at Cornell University in October 1999:

Julius Kambarage Nyerere's radical thought was multifaceted. He began as an anticolonial African nationalist on his return home, seeking the independence of Tanganyika....

Linked to Nyerere's nationalism from quite early was his Pan-Africanism, a commitment to the pursuit of African unity and the adoption of the principle of African solidarity whenever possible. Sometimes he put his Pan-Africanism ahead of his Tanganyika nationalism, as when in 1960 he offered to delay Tanganyika's independence if this would help achieve the creation of an East African federation of Tanganyika, Kenya and Uganda. In the end, there was not enough political will in the other two countries - Kenya and Uganda - to achieve such a union. African researchers need to investigate why it has been so difficult to achieve regional integration.

Nevertheless, Tanganyika played host to other major Pan-African activities. It became a frontline state for the liberation of southern Africa from Portuguese rule and from white minority governments. Politically the colony for a while hosted the Pan-African Freedom Movement for Eastern, Central and Southern Africa (PAFMESCA). Tanganyika subsequently established major training camps for southern African liberation fighters. Much later, Nyerere's Tanzania hosted the sixth Pan-African Congress (in 1974 at the University of Dar es Salaam, in Nkrumah Hall, named after another ardent Pan-Africanist leader), an attempt to re-establish the solidarity of Africa and its diaspora worldwide. This was the first of the Pan-African Congresses actually to be held in Africa. The fifth was in Manchester in 1945, with participants who included Kwame Nkrumah, Jomo Kenyatta, W.E.B. DuBois, and George Padmore. The Dar es Salaam Congress of 1974 was in a great Pan-African tradition....

Domestically in Tanzania he inaugurated three reforms - a political system based on the principle of the one-party state, an economic system based on an African approach to socialism - what he called ujamaa, or familyhood - and a cultural system based on the Sawhili language.

The cultural policy based on Kiswahili was the earliest and most durable. Tanganyika - and later Tanzania - became one of the few African countries to use an indigenous language in parliament and as the primary language of national business. Kiswahili was increasingly promoted in politics, administration, education, and the media. It became a major instrument of nation-building, and nation-building became the most lasting of Nyerere's legacies. Yet, Africana researchers have done little work on Nyerere's best contribution....

Why did ujamaa fail? Was it domestic factors? Was it external pressures? Was Nyerere building socialism without socialists? We need a postmortem on ujamaa....

(Also) Nyerere's Tanganyika did form a union with Zanzibar. This remains the only case in Africa of previously sovereign states uniting into a new country - and surviving as one entity more than three decades. What used to be sovereign Tanganyika and Zanzibar became the United Republic of Tanzania in 1964.

Nyerere strengthened the union when he united the ruling Afro-Shirazi Party of Zanzibar with the ruling party of Tanganyika (TANU - Tanganyika African National Union - in 1977) to form the new Chama Cha Mapinduzi, the Party of the Revolution. Will this union of Zanzibar and Tanganyika survive Nyerere's death? Once again have Africana scholars done enough to find out why Africans find it so hard to unite?

Has Nyerere's political behaviour sometimes reflected his upbringing as a Roman Catholic? One school of thought explains his recognition of the secessionist Biafra in 1969 as a form of solidarity with fellow Catholics against a Federal Nigeria, which would have been dominated by Muslims. This was in the middle of the Nigerian civil war. The Igbo of Biafra were overwhelmingly Roman Catholic. It seems much more likely that Nyerere recognized Biafra for humanitarian reasons.

What about the assertion that Nyerere's military intervention in Uganda in 1979 was motivated by a sectarian calculation to defend a mainly Christian Uganda from the Muslim dictator, Idi Amin? In reality, Nyerere might once again have been more motivated by a wider sense of humanitarianism and universal ethics. He was also defending Tanzania from Idi Amin's territorial appetites.

Most Western judges of Julius Nyerere have concentrated on his economic policies and their failures. Ujamaa and villagisation have been seen as forces of economic retardation that kept Tanzania backward for at least another decade.

Not enough commentators have paid attention to Nyerere's achievements in nation-building. He gave Tanzanians a sense of national consciousness and a spirit of national purpose. One of the poorest countries in the world found itself to be one of the major actors on the world scene.

Nyerere's policies of making Kiswahili the national language of Tanzania deepened this sense of Tanzania's national consciousness and cultural pride. Parliament in Dar es Salaam debated exclusively in Kiswahili. Government business was increasingly conducted in Kiswahili. The mass media turned away from English in favour of Kiswahili. Newspapers had not only letters to the editor but also poems to the editor in Kiswahili. And the educational system was experiencing the stresses and strains of the competing claims of English and Kiswahili. Nyerere's translation of two of Shakespeare's plays into Kiswahili was done not because he 'loved Shakespeare less, but because he loved Kiswahili more.' He translated Shakespeare into Kiswahili partly to demonstrate that the Swahili language was capable of carrying the complexities of a genius of another civilization.

Above all, Nyerere as president was a combination of deep intellect and high integrity...(and) was in a class by himself in the combination of ethical standards and intellectual power. In the combination of high thinking and high ethics, no other East African politician was in the same league.[30]

That is probably an understatement. Hardly any other politician on the entire continent was in the same league with Nyerere in terms of high ethical standards and intellectual prowess; a rare combination. And Nyerere's most enduring legacy is the nation he left behind as a united, stable entity; a phenomenon also rare on the continent. It all started with Tanganyika. He built Tanganyika into a cohesive state out of more than 126 different tribes and racial minority groups including Arabs, Asians, and Europeans. And he went on to create a larger nation, Tanzania, by uniting Tanganyika with Zanzibar during some of the most tempestuous times in Africa's post-colonial era. By the time he died, the union had survived 35 years. And it will always be remembered as one of his biggest achievements. Yet, as Nyerere himself conceded:

My greatest success is also my greatest disappointment. We have established a nation - Tanzania - that is some achievement. Stable, united, proud with immense clarity of what it wants to do, committed to the liberation of our continent. It has played an immense role - poor as it is - in the liberation of our continent and it will continue playing it. So that is what I think is our greatest achievement. But it is also our failure. I never wanted a Tanzania. I really do not believe that these African countries should establish different sovereignties. They are artificial creations, all of them.[31]

Africa is a natural entity. Achieving African unity is a goal to which he dedicated his life. As he said in Accra where he was invited by President Jerry Rawlings in 1997 to celebrate the 40th anniversary of Ghana's independence: "We are all Africans trying very hard to be Ghanaians and Tanzanians."[32]

He made that remark in a country whose founding father, Dr. Kwame Nkrumah, was one of the most uncompromising advocates of African unity and independence - twin Pan-African goals - and an ideological compatriot of Nyerere. As the first black African country to win independence since the partition of Africa at the Berlin Conference in 1885, Ghana set a precedent and became a source of inspiration to other African countries in their struggle to end colonial rule. Liberia was, of course, the first black African country to attain republican status, but in name only, and remained a virtual American colony throughout its history, as it still is even today: a client state, or America's "51st state" more or less like Puerto Rico.

While Nkrumah blazed the trail for the African independence movement by being the first leader of the first black African country to attain sovereign status, Nyerere also set a precedent by being the first leader on the continent to unite two independent countries to create one nation, Tanzania; and the first East African leader to lead his country to independence. And while Nkrumah preceded Nyerere in political activism and in the struggle for independence - born on September 22, 1909, and Nyerere on April 13, 1922, he was his senior by almost 13 years - the two became peers in the post-colonial era and two of the most influential African leaders in the twentieth century besides Nelson Mandela; with Nyerere also earning the title, "The Conscience of Africa." Yet, characteristic of his humility, he paid great tribute to Nkrumah when he visited Ghana after he stepped down as president of Tanzania. According to a Ugandan newspaper, *The Monitor*:

> Mwalimu Julius Nyerere paid a visit to Ghana shortly after his retirement in 1985 and reportedly berated the leadership of that country for the shabby way in which the republic's founder, Kwame Nkrumah, had been treated: 'This man is one of the greatest Africans that has ever lived. If you in Ghana don't respect him, the rest of us in Africa do. Independent Africa owes its liberty to this man. The least you can do is...give him a decent burial.'[33]

He also acknowledged the inspiration he drew from Nkrumah when he was still a student at Edinburgh University in Scotland earning his master's degree in economics and history, while Nkrumah was leading the independence struggle in Ghana. And in one of his last interviews in December 1998, about a year before he died, Nyerere remembered Nkrumah and talked about the relationship they had in the quest for African unity and independence. He also talked about his attempts to form the East African Federation with Mzee Jomo Kenyatta and Dr. Milton Obote. The interview was published in *The New Internationalist*:

It was events in Ghana in 1949 that fundamentally changed my attitude. When Kwame Nkrumah was released from prison, this produced a transformation. I was in Britain and, oh, you could see it in the Ghanaians! They became different human beings, different from all the rest of us! This thing of freedom began growing inside all of us. First India in 1947, then Ghana in 1949. Ghana became independent eight years later.

Under the influence of these events, while I was at university in Britain, I made up my mind to be a full-time political activist when I went back home. I intended to work for three years and then launch into politics. But it happened sooner than I planned....

For me liberation and unity were the most important things. I have always said that I was African first and socialist second. I would rather see a free and united Africa before a fragmented socialist Africa. I did not preach socialism. I made this distinction deliberately so as not to divide the country. The majority in the anti-colonial struggle were nationalist. There was a minority who argued that class was the central issue, that white workers were exploited as black workers by capitalism. They wanted to approach liberation in purely Marxist terms. However, in South Africa white workers oppressed black workers. It was more than class and I saw that....

Even now for me freedom and unity are paramount.... I respected Jomo (Kenyatta) immensely. It has probably never happened in history. Two heads of state, Milton Obote and I, went to Jomo and said to him: 'Let's unite our countries and you be our head of state.' He said no. I think he said no because it would have put him out of his element as a Kikuyu Elder....

It seems that independence of the former colonies has suited the interests if the industrial world for bigger profits at less cost. Independence made it cheaper for them to exploit us. We became neo-colonies. Some African leaders did not realize it. In fact many argued against Kwame (Nkrumah's) idea of neo-colonialism....

Let us create a new liberation movement to free us from immoral debt and neo-colonialism. This is one way forward. The other is through Pan-African unity....

Kwame Nkrumah and I were committed to the idea of unity. African leaders and heads of state did not take Kwame seriously. However, I did. I did not believe in these small little nations. Still today I do not believe in them. I tell our people to look at the European Union, at these people who ruled us who are now uniting.

Kwame and I met in 1963 and discussed African Unity. We differed on how to achieve a United States of Africa. But we both agreed on a United States of Africa as necessary. Kwame went to Lincoln University, a black college in the US. He perceived things from the perspective of US history, where 13 colonies that revolted against the British formed a union. That is what he thought the OAU (Organization of African Unity) should do.

I tried to get East Africa to unite before independence. When we failed in this way, I was wary about Kwame's continental approach. We corresponded profusely on this. Kwame said my idea of 'regionalization' was only balkanization on a larger scale. Later, African historians will have to study our correspondence on this issue of uniting Africa.

Africans who studied in the US like Nkrumah and Azikiwe were more aware of the Diaspora and the global African community than those of us who studied in Britain. They were therefore aware of a wider Pan-Africanism. Theirs was the aggressive Pan-Africanism of W.E.B. DuBois and Marcus Garvey. The colonialists were against this and frightened of it.

After independence, the wider African community became clear to me. I was concerned about education; the work of Booker T. Washington resonated with me. There were skills we needed and black people outside Africa had them. I gave our US Ambassador the specific job of recruiting skilled Africans from the US Diaspora. A few came, like you (the interviewer, Ikaweba Bunting, who had lived in Tanzania for 25 years when he interviewed Nyerere in his home village of Butiama where he returned in 1985 after stepping down from the presidency and buried in 1999). Some stayed; others left.

We should try to revive it (Pan-Africanism). We should look to our brothers and sisters in the West. We should build the broader Pan-Africanism. There is still the room - and the need.[34]

The Pan-Africanism Nyerere talked about embraced people of African descent in the diaspora, as did Nkrumah's. It also assumed another dimension when the Organization of African Unity (OAU) was replaced by the African Union (AU) in 2001, which was formally launched in 2002; the diaspora was represented in the OAU as it is in the AU. The transformation was intended to facilitate continental unification, and strengthen institutions of regional cooperation and Pan-African integration, leading to the establishment of a common market, a common currency, a continental parliament, a Pan-African court and an executive body as an enforcement mechanism responsible for implementing decisions binding on all countries across the continent.

And although the Ghana-Guinea and the Ghana-Guinea-Mali unions - formed by Kwame Nkrumah, Sekou Toure, and Modibo Keita - were more symbolic than functional, they served to inspire other Africans across the continent to pursue regional integration and keep the dream of African unity alive. The most successful of these efforts was, of course, the union of Tanganyika and Zanzibar formed by Julius Nyerere after he failed to convince the leaders of Kenya and Uganda - especially Kenya - to unite with Tanganyika and establish the East African Federation. And even if the union were to collapse, if secessionist elements (especially with ties to Oman and other Gulf States) in the former island nation of Zanzibar are not neutralized through extensive devolution of power and formation of coalition government or some other institutional arrangements but without unconditional accommodation for separatists, it will still be remembered as one of Nyerere's biggest achievements; and one of the most ambitious experiments in regional integration on the African continent and in post-colonial history anywhere in the world. As he said in an interview with the *Black World*, an African-American journal, in the early seventies when he was asked how he would like to be remembered after he died, he hoped that people would say: "He did his best."

CHAPTER SIX:

THE STRUGGLE FOR MOZAMBIQUE: THE FOUNDING OF FRELIMO IN TANZANIA

THE STRUGGLE for the liberation of Mozambique was led by FRELIMO, a Portuguese acronym for *Frente de Libertacao de Mocambique*, meaning Front for the Liberation of Mozambique.

It was founded in Dar es Salaam, the capital of Tanganyika, now Tanzania, in May 1962, just a few months after Tanganyika won independence from Britain on December 9, 1961. But it was not officially launched until June the same year, and in the same city, under the leadership of Dr. Eduardo Chivambo Mondlane.

President Julius Nyerere played a critical role in uniting the various Mozambican nationalist groups that led to the establishment of FRELIMO, one of the most successful liberation movements in colonial history. That was only about two years before he was to accomplish another memorable feat, uniting two independent countries, Tanganyika and Zanzibar, in April 1964 to form Tanzania; the first such union in Africa, and the only one that exists today. No other independent countries on the continent have united to form one country or even seriously attempted to do so.

And no other major liberation groups in any of the other white-ruled countries in southern Africa ever successfully united to form a single nationalist movement as the Mozambican nationalist organizations did in Tanzania under the aegis of Julius Nyerere. Instead, the trend was the opposite among a number of them. In South Africa, the Pan-Africanist Congress (PAC) was established under the leadership of Robert Mangaliso Sobukwe by members who left the African National Congress (ANC) in 1959. In Zimbabwe, the Zimbabwe African National Union (ZANU) was formed as a breakaway from the Zimbabwe African People's Union (ZAPU) in 1963, first under the leadership of Reverend Ndabaningi Sithole, and then Robert Mugabe. And in Angola the three main nationalist groups, the Popular Movement for the Liberation of Angola (MPLA) led by Dr. Agostinho Neto; the

Front for the National Liberation of Angola (FNLA) led by Dr. Holden Roberto; and the Union for the Total Independence of Angola (UNITA) led by Dr. Jonas Savimbi, went to war against each other. It was only in Mozambique that the various nationalist groups united to form a single nationalist movement, FRELIMO. Mozambique also had the distinction of being the first country in southern Africa - where liberation wars were fought - to win independence after waging an intense guerrilla campaign against the Portuguese colonial rulers for 10 years.

The groups which united to form FRELIMO in Tanzania in 1962 were an assorted lot, and themselves products of coalitions of even smaller groups, most of them without a clear ideological line. And not all of them were formed in Mozambique. But it was the conditions in Mozambique, of course, which were responsible for this political awakening among the Africans as a nationalist response to Portuguese oppression. For instance, in Cabo Delgado district in northern Mozambique among members of the Makonde tribe, a number of African leaders - especially from 1959 and early 1960 - tried to improve working conditions and wages of the laborers and extract concessions from the Portuguese authorities to make them more responsive to the needs of the African population. Instead, the authorities responded by arresting several of the activists after the local Portuguese administrator invited nearby villagers to air their grievances at a public meeting held at Mueda in the district. What happened at that meeting became one of the most important events in the history of Mozambique, and in the evolution of nationalist thinking among Africans, as recounted in Dr. Eduardo Mondlane's book, *The Struggle for Mozambique*:

> Certain leaders worked amongst us. Some of them were taken by the Portuguese - Tiago Muller, Faustino Vanomba, Kibiriti Diwane - in the massacre at Mueda on 16 June 1960. How did that happen? Well, some of these men had made contact with the authorities and asked for more liberty and more pay....
>
> After a while, when people were giving support to these leaders, the Portuguese sent police through the villages inviting people to a meeting at Mueda. Several thousand people came to hear what the Portuguese would say. As it turned out, the administrator had asked the governor of Delgado Province to come from Porto Amelia and to bring a company of troops. But these troops were hidden when they got to Mueda. We didn't see them at first.
>
> Then the governor invited our leaders into the administrator's office. I

was waiting outside. They were in there for four hours. When they came out on the verandah, the governor asked the crowd who wanted to speak. Many wanted to speak, and the governor told them all to stand on one side. Then without another word he ordered the police to bind the hands of those who had stood on one side, and the police began beating them. I was close by. I saw it all. When the people saw what was happening, they began to demonstrate against the Portuguese, and the Portuguese simply ordered the police trucks to come and collect these arrested persons. So there were demonstrations against this.

At that moment the troops were still hidden, and the people went up close to the police to stop the arrested persons from being taken away. So the governor called the troops, and when they appeared he told them to open fire. They killed about 600 people. Now the Portuguese say they have punished that governor, but of course they have only sent him somewhere else. I myself escaped because I was close to a graveyard where I could take cover, and then I ran away.[1]

The account of the massacre comes from Alburto-Joaquim Chipande who later became a prominent national leader in FRELIMO during the liberation struggle and after Mozambique won independence. Some questioned the accuracy and veracity of Chipande's account because of his involvement in the liberation struggle, especially as a member of FRELIMO, which did not exist at the time of the massacre. But other African sources corroborated his account that the massacre did indeed take place - there were just too many witnesses to dismiss it as a fabrication - and that it was large-scale; although these sources put the death toll between 400 and 500, contrasted with Chipande's figure of 600. Still, all the figures are within the same range.

The massacre at Mueda had a significant impact on African nationalist leaders and their supporters in Mozambique and helped galvanize them into action against the Portuguese colonial rulers. The brutality perpetrated by the colonial authorities against blacks clearly showed that the African majority had few options, if any, to ventilate their grievances let alone articulate nationalist aspirations in their quest for racial equality and full independence from Portugal. The leaders concluded that the only appropriate response to such oppression was armed struggle. Leading the struggle would be political parties they were going to form in neighboring countries.

The incident at Mueda may, indeed, have been a defining moment in the history of the anti-colonial struggle in Mozambique.

But it did not trigger an immediate armed response to Portuguese oppression. Instead, it helped create conditions for armed insurrection in the future; encouraged Africans to close ranks and mobilize forces in order to provide a united response to the colonial authorities; and heightened political consciousness among the masses, thereby solidifying the nationalist movement against increasing brutal oppression by the Portuguese colonial rulers. And as neighboring Tanganyika approached independence, the African population of Mozambique became increasingly restive, with political agitation becoming more widespread among the Makonde than any other ethnic group.

In 1961, leaders from the Makonde tribe in northern Mozambique, an ethnic group that straddles the Tanzanian-Mozambican border, formed the Mozambican African National Union (MANU) in Mombasa, Kenya, in preparation for an armed struggle against the Portuguese colonial rulers. Because of their proximity to Tanzania, which served as a rear base, the Makonde regions in northern Mozambique - with an excellent terrain for insurgency operations - proved to be critical to the liberation struggle after guerrilla warfare started.

Besides the acronym itself, MANU resembled TANU (Tanganyika African National Union) in Tanzania, and KANU (Kenya African National Union) in Kenya in political organization. And it became one of the most important groups in the coalition that led to the establishment of FRELIMO in Tanzania the following year. MANU itself was a product of a coalition of several smaller groups already in existence, including the Mozambique Makonde Union, and led by Mozambicans who fled to what then was Tanganyika, and to Kenya, where they sought and were granted asylum away from the Portuguese colonial authorities who were on their trail. Many of its leaders had also been actively involved in the independence movements of Tanganyika and Kenya. They included MANU's president, Matthew Mmole, and its secretary-general, Lawrence Malinga Milinga.

MANU's leaders also established strong ties with the leaders of Tanganyika and Kenya and gained a lot of experience - in political campaigning and mass mobilization - when they participated in their independence struggle, especially in neighboring Tanganyika. This knowledge and experience, and especially the close links they forged with the leaders of Tanganyika, proved to be an indispensable asset not only in the liberation of Mozambique but, by multiplier effect, in the liberation of neighboring Zimbabwe (then Rhodesia) and South Africa as well, after Mozambique became independent and served as an operational base for freedom fighters from these two countries.

Three organizations merged to form FRELIMO. Besides MANU, the other two were the National Democratic Union of Mozambique, known by its Portuguese acronym as *Uniad Democratica Nacional de Mocambique* (UDENAMO), and the National African Union of Independent Mozambique - *Union Nacional Africans de Mocambique Independente* (UNAMI). The people who formed UDENAMO and constituted the bulk of its membership were mostly migrant workers and disgruntled students living in Southern Rhodesia, what is Zimbabwe today. They came from central and southern Mozambique and fled their homeland because of Portuguese oppression. UNAMI was the smallest of the three. It was formed by Mozambicans who had fled to Malawi, which was then known as Nyasaland until July 1964 when the country won independence from Britain and changed its name. They came from Tete Province which borders Malawi.

The year 1961 became a turning point and an important milestone in the history of Mozambique. African nationalists in Angola, another Portuguese colony, had just launched an armed struggle against their colonial masters that year, prompting the authorities in Mozambique to intensify their campaign of terror and intimidation against black dissidents and agitators. But the crackdown had unintended consequences. It intensified nationalist feelings among the Africans, instead of neutralizing them, and triggered an outflow of even more refugees into neighboring countries; especially Tanganyika whose 500-mile border with Mozambique made it very easy for them to cross and seek asylum in this country. The long border also proved to be critical to the liberation of Mozambique when the guerrilla campaign started, enabling the freedom fighters to move and back forth at will and maintain secure supply lines for weapons and other material from their bases in what became Tanzania. Without such access, provision of weapons and other items to the guerrilla fighters would have been a logistical nightmare.

The new refugees, most of whom fled to Tanzania and did not belong to any of the three organizations - UDENAMO, MANU, and UNAMI - strongly urged the formation of a single nationalist organization transcending ethnoregional loyalties and other differences in order to fight for independence. Solidarity with other colonized Africans, especially in the other Portuguese colonies on the continent, helped facilitate the creation of a united front against the colonial regime in Mozambique. In 1961, the Conference of the Nationalist Organizations of the Portuguese Territories (CONCP) was held in Casablanca, Morocco. It was attended by representatives of UDENAMO, as well as delegates from the other Portuguese colonies besides Mozambique, and made a strong appeal for unity and concerted action by the nationalist organizations in their campaign against Portuguese colonialism. Marcelino dos Santos, a nationalist intellectual from Mozambique, was the secretary-general of CONCP and soon became a prominent leader of FRELIMO, and eventually Mozambique's vice president when the country won independence 14 years later. He attended the conference as a member of UDENAMO which he joined in April 1961.

The independence of Tanganyika in December 1961 had a profound impact on the nationalist leaders of Mozambique. All three organizations - MANU, UDENAMO, and UNAMI - moved their headquarters to Dar es Salaam, Tanganyika, and eventually merged to form a single nationalist movement, FELIMO, by the end of June 1962. The former leaders of MANU, UDENAMO, and UNAMI occupied key positions in FRELIMO which came to be recognized by the Organization of African Unity (OAU) as the sole legitimate representative of the Mozambican people, and the only recipient of aid from the OAU and African governments to the nationalist forces in Mozambique. Dr. Eduardo Mondlane was chosen to lead FRELIMO and became its first president. He was the ideal choice, and comments have been made that he was "hand-picked" by Julius Nyerere "for the tightrope walking job as head of a faction-formed movement."[2]

As a highly respected host, there is no question that Nyerere exercised considerable influence on the Mozambican nationalist leaders, as he did on all the other freedom fighters and their organizations based in Tanganyika, later Tanzania. And his preference as to who should be the leader of FRELIMO probably played a major role in choosing Dr. Mondlane as president of the nationalist organization. Dr. Mondlane also had one great advantage over his rivals for the top position in FRELIMO. He was not affiliated with any of the three Mozambican nationalist organizations and was therefore not seen as a partisan candidate for the job. FRELIMO was also in a unique position among the nationalist organizations in the Portuguese African colonies and other white-ruled territories in the continent. Not only did it get the best qualified leader but also had another major asset. The organization did not suffer a major rift or an open split, as had been the case in Angola, especially with the MPLA, although it was composed of members divided by many ideological differences. But they were all united by a common desire to fight a common enemy and achieve a common goal: independence for Mozambique after almost 500 years of Portuguese colonial rule.

It is interesting that although FRELIMO was formed in Dar es Salaam, Tanganyika, its formation was announced for the first time in Accra, Ghana, on May 29, 1962, by UDENAMO and MANU leaders. The two organizations had been negotiating for months in Dar es Salaam in order to reach a compromise and form a single nationalist movement. The negotiations had been strongly encouraged by the government of Tanganyika led by Julius Nyerere. The third organization, UNAMI, joined the negotiations before FRELIMO was formed, and formally launched in Dar es Salaam in June 1962. Although the three organizations were united by a common desire to end colonial rule, the compromise they reached to establish FRELIMO was essentially a marriage of convenience, clearly demonstrated by the continuing ideological differences within the nationalist movement, and struggle for power, all of which contributed to the assassination of Dr. Eduardo Mondlane in February 1969; schisms that were exploited by the Portuguese secret police who delivered the final blow by way of a mailed package bomb sent to Mondlane and which ended his life. Among the prime suspects in Mondlane's assassination was Reverend Uria Simango, FRELIMO's vice president. He was later arrested and imprisoned by FRELIMO and reportedly executed in

1983 together with others. Like any other nationalist movement, FRELIMO had traitors. Besides Uria Simango, there was the highly notorious Makonde leader Lazaro Kavandame who collaborated with the Portuguese, and who went on to wage war against the FRELIMO government, but whose insurgency in northern Mozambique was suppressed by the Mozambican army with the help of Tanzania's national army, the Tanzania People's Defence Forces (TPDF), and the Cubans.

Compounding the problem for the Mozambican nationalists was interference by a number of African governments, each with its own agenda on how to address continental issues including liberation of colonies. Such interference played a critical role in the consummation of this marriage between UDENAMO, MANU, and UNAMI.

The first organization to advocate armed struggle as the only viable means to end Portuguese colonial rule was UDENAMO, formed in Southern Rhodesia in November 1960. The nationalist struggle by Africans in Southern Rhodesia had a major impact on UDENAMO whose members had a working relationship with the National Democratic Party (NDP) led by Joshua Nkomo, father of African nationalism and of the independence movement in that British colony. UDENAMO was led by Adelino Gwambe, a 20-year-old from Inhambane, Mozambique. But he and his colleagues knew that they could not effectively, if at all, wage an armed struggle against Portuguese colonial rule in Mozambique from another white-ruled territory, Southern Rhodesia. They therefore decided to move to Tanganyika where they felt that they would be welcomed and allowed to establish bases once the country became independent in only a few months.

After it established itself in Dar es Salaam, UDENAMO continued to attract more members and supporters, many of whom were already living in Tanganyika, while others were new arrivals from Mozambique fleeing Portuguese oppression. In April 1961, UDENAMO's vice president, Fanuel Mahluza, wrote Dr. Eduardo Mondlane in New York where he worked for the UN Trusteeship Council and invited him to join the organization. But Dr. Mondlane did not join the group. He refused to join UDENAMO or any other nationalist organization because he had his own plans for Mozambique and saw the separate groups as divisive. He had recently visited Mozambique on behalf of the United Nations and saw that nationalist feelings were widespread, but preferred a non-violent approach towards independence, as opposed to armed struggle advocated by UDENAMO.

Mondlane was concerned over the possibility of a war being waged from Tanganyika because, as he put it in a report on his tour of Mozambique given to United States Undersecretary of State Chester Bowles: "One shudders at the consequences of such an eventuality, judging by Portugal's reaction to a similar situation in Angola."[3] The Portuguese colonial authorities responded with unconstrained fury to the nationalist uprising in Angola in 1961, and Mondlane did not want this to happen to the people within Mozambique, and to Tanganyika in retaliation for providing sanctuary to the Mozambican freedom fighters. Mondlane went on to say in his report:

> United States should be in a position to encourage Portugal to accept the principle of self-determination for the African peoples under her control; set target dates and take steps towards self-government and independence by 1965; and help formulate and finance policies of economic, educational, and political development for the people of Portuguese Africa and to prepare them for an independence with responsibility.[4]

Dr. Mondlane was already the most visible and articulate spokesman of the Mozambican nationalist movement, even at a time when the nationalist groups in the Portuguese colony had not formed a united front against their colonial rulers. He also saw himself as a leader of his country's independence struggle and a unifying figure needed to bring all the nationalist organizations together and form a single nationalist movement.

Another prominent Mozambican nationalist during the early sixties before FRELIMO was formed in 1962 was Marcelino dos Santos, a Marxist theoretician, unlike Eduardo Mondlane who was not a Marxist or attracted to communism. Ideologically, Mondlane was closer to the West than he was to the East but was fiercely independent in his quest for Mozambican independence. When the Conference of Nationalist Organizations of the Portuguese Territories - *Confereancia das Organizaceaoes Nacionalistas das Coloanias Portuguesas* (CONCP) - was held in

Casablanca in April 1961, Marcelino dos Santos was already living there and became involved in organizing the conference. It was in that capacity the he invited UDENAMO's president, Adelino Gwambe, to attend the conference and represent the organization. The Casablanca conference also led to the establishment of CONCP as an enduring umbrella organization charged with the responsibility of coordinating the liberation struggle in the Portuguese colonies against imperial rule.

Gwambe made a momentous decision and appointed Marcelino dos Santos as UDENAMO's secretary-general, when dos Santos invited him to attend the Casablanca conference, providing the organization with its most capable and articulate intellectual and organizer. The appointment of Marcelino dos Santos - who was then 32 - was to have profound influence on UDENAMO's destiny because of the central role this nationalist intellectual and theoretician played in the organization, giving it a higher profile it otherwise would not have attained without him. It was Marcelino dos Santos who drafted UDENAMO's constitution based on democratic centralism. And it was he who swayed the organization and convinced its other leaders to enter unity talks with MANU. His emergence on the Mozambican political scene also became highly significant because of the prominent role he played in the independence struggle as FRELIMO's chief spokesman in the international arena and its leading ideologue.

As UDENAMO continued to grow and establish international ties with an increasing number of groups and individuals, including some governments, strains began to show in its relationship with Tanganyikan leaders, its hosts, because of the direction in which its leaders were taking the organization. Tanganyikan officials were concerned over UDENAMO's ties to Ghana, established through the Ghanaian Bureau of African Affairs when UDENAMO was based in Southern Rhodesia. Ghana, the first black African country to win independence in 1957, was also the first country to provide the organization with financial assistance and invited UDENAMO's main leaders to visit Accra, Ghana's capital, on regular basis. The Ghanaian government also paid for Adelino Gwambe's visits to Conakry, Guinea, and to Helsinki, Finland, and provided an office for UDENAMO representatives in Accra.

Tanzania was ideologically aligned with Ghana, and the two countries agreed on most fundamental issues, including armed struggle for the liberation of white-ruled countries in southern Africa and of Portuguese Guinea (Guinea-Bissau) in West Africa. But the idea that Ghanaian President Kwame Nkrumah was trying to set the agenda for Mozambique and dominate - not just help - the nationalist organizations fighting for independence in that colony was unsettling to government officials in what was then Tanganyika. "Fearing that he could in fact pose a threat to Nyerere's desire to become the champion of southern Africa's nationalist cause, the Tanzanians took action."[5]

Tanganyika threw its weight behind MANU as a counter-weight to Ghana's support of UDENAMO. But it must also in fairness be stated that Tanganyika already had strong ties to MANU. Many of MANU's leaders had participated in the campaign for the independence of Tanganyika, long before Mozambican nationalist groups - MANU, UDENAMO, and UNAMI - were offered sanctuary in Dar es Salaam when the country became independent on December 9, 1961. It must also be emphasized that UDENAMO was still allowed by the government of Tanganyika to continue to operate and have an office in Dar es Salaam, despite its strong ties to Ghana and Nkrumah's undue influence on an organization that was in Nyerere's "backyard." Had it been a case of purely personal rivalry between Nyerere and Nkrumah, Tanganyika would have closed down UDENAMO's office and expelled its members. Instead, it went on to encourage the three Mozambican organizations - UDENAMO, MANU, and UNAMI - to submerge their differences for the sake of national unity and form a single nationalist organization to fight for independence.

But it is true that, of all the three organizations, MANU had the strongest ties to Tanganyika for geographical, historical and political reasons. Geographically, MANU was a northern organization, drawing its largest membership from the Makonde tribe found in both Tanganyika and Mozambique. And many of its members, including some of its leaders, were born and brought up in Tanganyika. In fact, in the early sixties, about 250,000 Mozambicans, mainly Makonde, were living in Tanganyika, which united with Zanzibar in 1964 to form Tanzania. And many of them were involved in trade union and political activities. The Makonde of Mozambican origin living in Tanganyika, Zanzibar, and Kenya were also affiliated with the Makonde African Association (MAA) with ties to Mozambique. Historically and politically, Tanzania and Mozambique have also been equally linked by the Makonde and other ethnic groups such as the Yao, the Makua, the Nyasa and the Ngoni which also - like the Makonde - straddle the Tanzanian-Mozambican border forming insoluble bonds between the two countries. But probably most significant of all this was the involvement of the Mozambican Makonde in the struggle for Tanganyika's independence. And their political activism became critical to the rise of Mozambican nationalism across the country as a whole, not just in Cabo Delgado Province, their traditional home and stronghold in northern Mozambique.

In January 1961, the Makonde African Association (MAA) branches in Dar es Salaam (Tanganyika), Mombasa (Kenya), and Zanzibar, merged to form MANU. The Tangayikan branch was led by Matthew Mmole; the Kenyan and Zanzibari branches, by Samuli Diankali and Ali Madebe, respectively. Matthew Mmole became MANU's president, and Lawrence Malinga Milinga, its vice president. Both were born in Tanganyika. Many MANU members, if not the majority, also wanted to unite Cabo Delgado Province with Tanganyika in order to establish a greater Makonde homeland.

UDENAMO, one of the other two Mozambican nationalist organizations, was still committed to armed struggle to free Mozambique but felt that prospects for such a campaign were not good. The government of Tanganyika cut off all assistance to UDENAMO and declared Adelino Gwambe, UDENAMO's president, *persona non grata* for announcing at a news conference just before Tanganyika won independence that arrangements had already been made for UDENAMO to launch a guerrilla campaign in Mozambique. Because of his status as an undesirable alien in Tanganyika, he had to leave for Accra, Ghana, but was allowed to return to Tanganyika soon. But when Ghana invited UDENAMO to attend the African Freedom Fighters Conference in Accra in May-June 1962, the government of Tanganyika refused to issue travel documents to UDENAMO delegates for them to go to Ghana. Instead, the Ghanaian High Commission (Embassy) in Dar es Salaam had to make the necessary provisions to enable its delegates to travel to Ghana and attend the conference.

Tanganyikan leaders were not the only ones who were suspicious of Nkrumah's intentions in supporting UDENAMO and for trying to actively intervene in Mozambique and southern Africa in general. Marcelino dos Santos, who had by then become a prominent Mozambican nationalist leader within a relatively short period of time since he joined UDENAMO in April 1961 during the Casablanca conference, was deeply offended by Nkrumah who did not see him as truly representative of the black people of Mozambique because he was a mulatto. Yet, he continued to play a major role and used his diplomatic skills - for which came to be widely acclaimed in the international arena - to prevent relations between Tanganyika and UDENAMO from deteriorating any further because of Nkrumah's undue influence in the organization. And being fully aware of Tanganyika's strategic position as a rear base critical to the liberation of Mozambique, he advised his colleagues in UDENAMO to unite with MANU and form a single nationalist organization. UDENAMO's president, Adelino Gwambe, dismissed the idea and refused to compromise. Marcelino dos Santos responded by threatening to leave UDENAMO and join MANU.

Other UDENAMO leaders, besides Marcelino dos Santos, were also fully aware of Tanganyika's strategic significance to the liberation of their country, and Tanganyika's support of their nationalist cause. If they had to wage a successful guerrilla war against the Portuguese colonial forces in Mozambique, they had to rely on bases and supply routes in Tanganyika. So, throughout October 1961, UDENAMO's Executive Committee held several meetings to evaluate the entire situation and agreed to unite with MANU. But they also used money to achieve this goal. In order to get MANU's support for the merger, UDENAMO leaders used their financial resources to virtually bribe members of the Makonde organization to join them and form one nationalist organization embracing all Mozambicans. To entice them even more, UDENAMO also included MANU leaders in its delegation to the African Freedom Fighters Conference in Accra. It was a brazen attempt to achieve solidarity, but it impressed MANU leaders and their supporters.

On May 24, 1962, at a ceremony held in Dar es Salaam under the auspices of the Tanganyikan government, UDENAMO and MANU announced that they had "decided to bring unity of all the patriotic forces of Mozambique by means of forming a common front," pending the return of the respective leaders from Accra. The merger was forged in Tanganyika with the active support of the Tanganyikan government, which had always enocuraged such unification. But because he was on Nkrumah's payroll, UDENAMO's president, Adelino Gwambe - in a move that amounted to a slap in the face of the Tanganyikan leaders - announced at a news conference in Accra five days after the merger that the decision to unite the two organizations was in response to Nkrumah's call for closing ranks for the liberation of Africa; while, actually, the driving force behind the merger was none other than Julius Nyerere.

It was Nyerere who invited Mozambican and other African nationalist groups to establish bases in Tanganyika soon after the country won independence from Britain in December 1961, and before the Organization of African Unity (OAU) was founded in May 1963 to support such groups among other goals. It was he who urged the Mozambican liberation groups to form a united front. And it was he who asked Dr. Eduardo Mondlane - back in the late 1950s when the two met at the United Nations in New York - to return to Africa and unite the Mozambican nationalist groups. He also asked him to establish a base in Dar es Salaam for Mozambique's liberation movement and promised him full support to liberate Mozambique from Portuguese colonial rule. After UDENAMO and MANU agreed to unite, it was the Tanganyikan government under Nyerere - not Nkrumah's in Ghana - which facilitated and skillfully guided the merger; a fact that has been acknowledged by Mozambican leaders through the years. As proposed by Fahnuel Mahluza, the new organization came to be known as *Frente de Libertacao de Mocambique* (FRELIMO). But both Adelino Gwambe and Fahnuel Mahluza left FRELIMO within a few months of its formation, driven by their personal ambitions transcending national interest.

While negotiations were going on between UDENAMO and MANU to unite the two organizations, the leader of UNAMI, Josea Baltazar Chagonga, arrived in Dar es Salaam where the talks were being held. In 1959, Chagonga formed the *Associaceao Nacional Africana de Moatize* (ANAM), ostensibly a cultural association of Moatize coal mine workers and Mozambican migrants in Northern Rhodesia (now Zambia), Nyasaland (Malawi today), and Southern Rhodesia (renamed Zimbabwe). But the organization was really nothing but an incubator of nationalism and propagated nationalist ideals among its members who now had a medium through which to articulate their nationalist aspirations. Chagonga advocated peaceful change and tried to ask the Portuguese colonial authorities in Mozambique to improve working conditions, which were becoming increasingly intolerable to African miners, laborers and other workers. He was detained for that and, after he was released, fled to Nyasaland where in May 1960 he renamed his organization UNAMI, one of the three Mozambican nationalist groups demanding independence, and which also united to form FRELIMO.

But while Mozambican nationalists to the Accra conference in Ghana were celebrating the merger of UDENAMO and MANU to form FRELIMO, they had no idea of what awaited them in Dar es Salaam once they returned days before the official launching of the umbrella organization, which took place on June 25, 1962. Dr. Eduardo Mondlane, who had resigned from his UN post to become a professor at Syracuse University in New York starting in September the same year, arrived in Dar es Salaam in the first half of June; encouraged by Nyerere to lead the Mozambican independence struggle.

Before he went to Taganyika in June 1962, Mondlane met with American State Department officials in Washington on February 8 the same year, and reiterated his intention to lead the struggle for Mozambique's independence. He also emphasized that he would be willing to negotiate with Portugal, but could only accept "the negotiations of equals." Mondlane was confident that he would be able to lead the independence movement and did not see UDENAMO and MANU as a serious threat to his plans. He dismissed UDENAMO's president, Adelino Gwambe, as a lightweight, and MANU as a group manipulated by Tanganyikans without solid nationalist credentials within Mozambique. He also concluded that should MANU lead any successful insurgency within Mozambique, the operation would be an "outside job," and could even lead to the secession of Cabo Delgado and Niassa Provinces by the Makonde who wanted to unite with their brethren in Tanganyika and establish a greater Makonde homeland.

But when Mondlane went to Tanganyika in the first half of June 1962, he encountered stiff opposition to his quest for leadership of the Mozambican nationalist movement. The opposition came from UDENAMO and MANU leaders. Adelino Gwambe wanted to lead FRELIMO and launch guerrilla warfare, supported by Ghana where some of his people had reportedly received military training. The challenge to Mondlane's leadership came from the very same people he had underestimated and who had been dismissed by many, including Mondlane himself, as lightweights.

On June 18, 1962, Dr. Mondlane had a meeting with Thomas Byrne, the acting American charge d'affaires in Dar es Salaam and told him that Adelino Gwambe was totally committed to Nkrumah and to communist countries; a commitment and ideological tilt he did not approve of as a Mozambican nationalist. Mondlane also said that the UDENAMO leader was not only commited to Nkrumah and to communist nations but also received on regular basis large amounts of money from Ghana and the Soviet Union, and had recently received $14,000 from the Ghanaian government. Mondlane also learned that MANU's president Matthew Mmole and his colleagues had virtually been bought by Adelino Gwambe and were being paid by him. But he also found out that a significant number of UDENAMO members were disgruntled because of Gwambe's tight control of the group's financial assets, virtualy turning them into his personal account.

Dr. Mondlane told Thomas Byrne that he had brought the matter to the attention of Oscar Kambona, then Tanganyika's minister of home affairs - later defence and foreign minister and the second most influential politician after Nyerere - and explained that if Adelino Gwambe continued to have a lot money, while the other two nationalist groups (UDENAMO and MANU) had almost nothing, this would mean that he was in full control of the Mozambican nationalist movement on behalf of the Ghanaians and the Russians who were paying him. Mondlane appealed to Kambona to do something about the situation. He also told him that if UDENAMO and MANU could get funds from the West,

Gwambe would no longer be able to dominate the two organizations with his Ghanaian and Soviet masters who were providing him with ample financial resources to control the two groups, hence the Mozambican nationalist movement, on their behalf.

Tanganyikan officials were glad to hear this. They were uncomfortable to have an organization based in their country, and in their capital on top of that, which was controlled by the Ghanaians. They also knew that of all the Mozambicans who had come to Dar es Salaam to carry on their nationalist activities or make plans to do so, only Mondlane seemed to be best qualified to lead the Mozambican independence struggle under a united front. He was mature, highly educated and articulate, with political and diplomatic skills; and in favor of a non-violent approach towards independence which was preferred by Tanganyika during that time because the country was not yet strong enough, as it became later on, to defend itself against military incursions and retaliation from Mozambique by the Portuguese.

In an attempt to neutralize Gwambe's financial control over UDENAMO and MANU members, Dr. Mondlane on his way back to Syracuse University from Dar es Salaam planned to visit Cairo, Tunis, Geneva, and London to get financial support through fund raising. The senior American diplomat in Tanganyika during that time, Thomas Byrne, stated: "As soon as he reaches the United States, Mr. Mondlane plans to get in touch with Deputy Assistant Secretary [State for African Affairs] Wayne Fredericks."[6] Dr. Mondlane planned to return to Dar es Salaam in September the same year (1962) and make his last attempt to be the leader of FRELIMO. But he did not have to wait that long to get his position.

A chain of events enabled Dr. Mondlane to secure the presidency of FRELIMO on June 25, 1962. When UDENAMO's president Adelino Gwambe was in India between the 17th and 25th of June, Mondlane took advantage of Gwambe's absence from Tanganyika to mobilize substantial support among Mozambicans in Dar es Salaam without encountering any serious opposition. He had earlier refused to join any of the three Mozambican nationalist organizations, contending that they were divisive and counterproductive, and would serve their people better by forming a united front against their colonial oppressors. And he continued to maintain this position. But as a matter of expediency in his quest for the presidency of FRELIMO, he decided to meet his fellow Mozambicans in Dar es Salaam as a member of UDENAMO, an organization headed by his arch rival, Adelino Gwambe, though an intellectual and political featherweight who was no more than a Soviet and Nkrumah's pawn in the Mozambican nationalist movement.

Mondlane had always shown great concern for the educational advancement of his people and, as a professor at a leading American university, served as an excellent role model. Because of his high status as a scholar, and his extensive ties to the United States including the United Nations, he was able to get the support of UDENAMO and MANU members in his bid for the leadership of FRELIMO by promising them scholarships to study in America. Adelino Gwambe had, up to that time, scared Mozambican refugees in Tanganyika away from applying for scholarships at the American embassy in Dar es Salaam, telling them that if they accepted these scholarships they would be kidnapped by Portuguese agents while on their way to the United States.

In spite of Gwambe's financial clout he used to buy and influence UDENAMO and MANU members, and his strong ties to Ghanaian officials, Dr. Mondlane told the American top diplomat in Tanganyika, Thomas Byrne - and this came from Byrne - that he had already convinced the Ghanaians through the Ghanaian High Commissioner (Ambassador) in Dar es Salaam that Gwambe was not the right person to lead FRELIMO. Mondlane also stated that Gwambe's subordinates and MANU leaders - all of whom were on Gwambe's, hence Nkrumah's and the Russians' payroll - had promised to oppose Gwambe's bid for FRELIMO's leadership provided Mondlane was able to find other sources of income for them to live on and carry on their activities. Their loyalty to Gwambe was predicated on monetary gain, and whatever other benefits could be derived from their relationship with him, not on genuine commitment to him as a credible and capable leader of the Mozambican nationalist movement. In the latter case, Dr. Mondlane had far more potential and without credible challenge to him within the movement.

On June 28, 1962, Mondlane again met the American charge d'affaires Thomas Byrne and asked him to inform United States Deputy Assistant Secretary of State for African Affairs, Wayne Fredericks, that he desperately needed some money to make sure that FRELIMO was no longer dependent on Ghana and beholden to Nkrumah who wanted to dominate - not just help - the liberation movement. To Mondlane and to the Americans, such domination by Ghana also meant a potentially dangerous situation of ideological control of FRELIMO by the Soviets, Nkrumah's allies and benefactors, and their nemesis who not only funded Nkrumah but supported other African governments. Mondlane went on to say that he had spent $1,000 of his own money to help FRELIMO become financially independent and no longer accept funds from Ghana and Soviet-bloc countries.

Mondlane's efforts to secure FRELIMO's leadership were successful. His name was on the list of candidates competing for the presidency of FRELIMO's Supreme Council whose members were to be elected on June 25, 1962. After UDENAMO's president Adelino Gwambe and MANU's president Matthew Mmole had signed an agreement which explicitly stated that they would transfer all assets owned and controlled by their organizations to FRELIMO's Supreme Council immediately after the council members were elected, a 20-man ad hoc committee composed of an equal number of UDENAMO and MANU members nominated Dr. Eduardo Mondlane, Reverend Uria Simango, and Josea Baltzar Chagonga, for the presidency of FRELIMO. Adelino Gwambe, UDENAMO's president, refused to enter the contest as long as Dr. Mondlane was still a member of UDENAMO.

The election was a big victory for Mondlane. Out of 135 ballots cast, Mondlane received 116 votes. Ethnic loyalties played a key role in Mondlane's election, more than his educational qualifications, his job as a professor, and his status as a former top international civil servant employed by the United Nations. Like Gwambe, Mondlane came from southern Mozambique. He was born in Gaza district in 1920. And with Gwambe out of the race for the presidency, UDENAMO members from southern Mozambique preferred to have him, a fellow southerner, as head of FRELIMO rather than Uria Simango, a member of the Ndau ethnic group from central Mozambique, in spite of the fact that Simango was a long-time member of UDENAMO; unlike Mondlane who joined the organization just a few days before the election in a strategic move to win FRELIMO's top position. Simango was elected vice president of FRELIMO, and other UDENAMO members secured key positions in the organization. David Mabunda became secretary-general, and Paul Gumane, deputy secretary-general. Dr. Mabunda ended up in Grand Rapids, Michigan, where he taught at Grand Rapids Junior College, and later at Muskegon Community College in Muskegon about 30 miles from Grand Rapids. I was living in Grand Rapids myself and talked to him in 1977. When I told him I was a Tanzanian, he said he had close ties to Tanzania and that his wife was from Moshi. He was one of the early luminaries in the Mozambican liberation movement, FRELIMO. He left Muskegon College in 1994 and moved to South Africa where be became director of Kruger National Parks.

Marcelino dos Santos was put in charge of the foreign affairs department of FRELIMO. Joao Munguambe was given defence and security, with Filipe Magaia serving as his deputy.
And MANU's president Matthew Mmole was elected treasurer, while MANU's secretary-general, Lawrence Milinga, became FRELIMO's executive secretary of the Scholarship Committee. The election of Mmole as treasurer reflected regional balance in an organization that was intended to be national in character, despite its southern tilt. But with the important post of treasury going to a northerner, a Makonde, the vice presidency to Simango from the central region, and the presidency to Mondlane, a southerner, there was at least a semblance of regional balance and ethnic diversity in the allocation of power in the hierarchy of FRELIMO.

After Mondlane secured the presidency of FRELIMO, he formulated a strategy to have Adelino Gwambe removed from the scene with the help of the government of Tanganyika, his host. He told Oscar Kambona that he and his wife, Janet, were being watched by armed men who supported Gwambe, and that Gwambe had told the Portuguese about Mondlane's travelling plans so that he could be kidnapped while in transit in Rome. The government of Tanganyika arrested Gwambe on June 27, 1962, but did not declare him *persona non grata*, as it did before, after it released him. Kambona assured Mondlane that Gwambe would not be allowed to re-enter Tanganyika after he left for Moscow on July 3 to attend a World Peace Council meeting.

On his relations with Ghana, Mondlane believed that they would improve since he had now been elected president of FRELIMO. He told Tomas Byrne, the American senior diplomat in Dar es Salaam, that the Ghanaian High Commission in Tanganyika had even invited him to visit Accra and given him plane tickets. As Byrne commented in a cable to the US State Department in Washington, D.C.:

> Dr. Mondlane's position as leader of the Mozambique Liberation Front appears at the moment to be strong. His future prospects will depend to a great extent upon how successful he is in obtaining money to carry on the party's activities here (in Tanganyika). Another as yet unclear factor is the sincerity of Kambona's assurance of support. If Ghana is now shifting its support from Gwambe to Mondlane, the latter's position should be secure.[7]

Mondlane's rise to the top as head of FRELIMO was facilitated by the fact that he was highly regarded by African leaders outside Mozambique and respected by the leaders of MANU, UDENAMO and UNAMI as a unifying force and capable leader. And he had a history of political activism and sympathy for nationalist causes even in his student days in South Africa, Portugal, and the United States, although he was not a radical. For instance, he was expelled from Witwatersrand University in Johannesburg, South Africa's most prestigious institution of higher learning, for being a "foreign native," and returned to Mozambique where he founded a student nationalist organization which was quickly and effectively contained by the Portuguese colonial rulers, as were the other student organizations advocating fundamental change in the status quo.[8]

Although he was exposed to communism in Lisbon, Portugal, when he was a student there in the late 1940s, and came to know fellow African students who were affiliated with the radical left and later became national leaders - Dr. Agostinho Neto of Angola, Amilcar Cabral of Guinea-Bissau, and others - he was never attracted to the communist ideology. And even his ties to the United States where he also attended school, worked, and met his wife in the fifties, did not sway him to embrace the West as a paragon of virtue. He was, instead, an independent-minded nationalist who wanted to see his country free from Portuguese colonialism and remain independent of both ideological camps, East and West, a quality he shared with Julius Nyerere. Dr. Mondlane also, like Nyerere, became convinced that the only way Mozambique would be able to win independence was by armed struggle.

Tanzania played a critical role in the liberation of Mozambique. Without Tanzania operating as a rear base for the freedom fighters, Mozambique would not have won independence as soon as it did, although it took more than 10 years of guerrilla warfare to liberate the country. But it would have taken much longer if Tanzania was also still a colony, therefore equally hostile to the freedom fighters; was led by someone like Mobutu Sese Seko or Kamuzu Banda who did not want to support freedom fighters anywhere in Africa; or did not commit as much resources and provide logistical support to the guerrilla fighters as it did under the leadership of Julius Nyerere. And if Kenya - another East African country like Tanzania and Mozambique - under the leadership of Jomo Kenyatta bordered Mozambique, or if Kenyatta was president of Tanzania, FRELIMO freedom fighters would not have been able to get as much support, if any, as they did from Tanzania under Nyerere. Kenyatta did nothing to support the African liberation movements, despite his image - highly inflated - as the embodiment of Mau Mau; the true leader of Mau Mau was Dedan Kimathi, not Jomo Kenyatta. He did not even talk about them, except in a perfunctory manner, and only on very few occasions.

Nyerere was exactly the opposite, and helped change the course of African history, especially in southern Africa because of his uncompromising support for the liberation movements. But probably nowhere else did he have such a direct impact as he did on Mozambique, because of the common border between Tanzania and Mozambique, providing direct, unimpeded access to the battlefield for the freedom fighters from their bases in Tanzania.

Tanzanian support of the liberation struggle in Mozambique and other countries in southern Africa involved commitment of troops to the battlefield. By the time Mozambique won independence from Portugal on June 25, 1975 on the 13th anniversary of the official launching of FRELIMO in Dar es Salaam on June 25, 1962 - it was "granted" a provisional government on September 20, 1974 - after waging guerrilla war since 1964 in which about 70,000 Portuguese troops fought against the freedom fighters, a significant number of Tanzanian soldiers had fought and died in Mozambique, together with FRELIMO guerrillas, fighting to end the oldest and last colonial empire in Africa: Portuguese. Thousands of people died in this conflict, mostly in Mozambique itself.

In addition to Tanzanian soldiers who died together with FRELIMO guerrilla fighters in the war against Portuguese colonial forces, Tanzanian civilians and Mozambican refugees living in southern Tanzania also died in the attacks, including aerial bombings, by the Portuguese backed by their Western allies including the United States and apartheid South Africa. A NATO member, Portugal was free to use weapons obtained from the United States and other Western powers in her wars against the freedom fighters and civilians in her African colonies and neighboring countries supporting the liberation movements. Tanzanian soldiers also fought and died in other liberation wars in southern Africa, including Zimbabwe and Angola; also an entire battalion of Nigerian soldiers fought in Angola in the seventies on the side of the MPLA against South African troops who invaded the country and attempted to capture the capital Luanda and install a puppet regime in place of the staunchly anti-colonial MPLA government. At least 5,000 Nigerian soldiers went into combat against the South African invaders. And as Tanzanian Minister of Defence and National Service, Professor Philemon Sarungi, stated in parliament on July 11, 2002, the bodies of Tanzanian soldiers who died in other African countries during the liberation struggle would be returned home for burial. According to Tanzania's *Daily News*:

> The government plans to return home remains of bodies of those who fought, died and were buried outside the country during the liberation wars of southern Africa and accord them a heroes' funeral in a heroes' square.... The Minister for Defence and National Service, Professor Philemon Sarungi,... told the National Assembly that Tanzanian soldiers were buried in countries including Mozambique and Zimbabwe where they fought in the liberation wars for these countries.
>
> Professor Sarungi also told the House that his ministry was planning to erect a monument where Tanzanian soldiers died in the Kagera War (in Kagera

Region in northwestern Tanzania) against Uganda's dictator Idi Amin. 'Those who have died in other places during wars will have their names listed on the monument in order to keep the records for future reference of the country's history in the liberation of the continent,' he said.... Sarungi said July 25 every year has been earmarked as the day for remembrance of national heroes at Mnazi Mmoja in Dar es Salaam.[9]

Without Julius Nyerere, or another leader of his caliber and depth of commitment, it is highly unlikely that Tanzania would have played such a critical role in the liberation of Africa. And without good leadership, even a country with enormous wealth and potential amounts to nothing, as has been tragically demonstrated in the case of the Congo, the bleeding heart of Africa, since independence in 1960. No one knows what Lumumba would have done had he lived and continued to lead the Congo for a number of years. But he showed a lot of promise and left his people with a sense of national identity and pride that is still sustained by his memory. Even a traitor like Mobutu invoked Lumumba's name to burnish his image. Everybody knows what Mobutu and his Western backers and masters did to the Congo and to Africa as a whole. And the world knows what Nyerere did for Africa. As the Zambian ambassador to the United Nations, Professor Mwelwa C. Musambachime, stated:

To Zambians, Mwalimu Nyerere holds an exalted place in the history of our country. He had a direct and personal contribution to our political independence and economic development. The Tanzania-Zambia Railway (TAZARA) and the Tanzania-Zambia Pipeline (TAZAMA) linking Ndola with Dar es Salaam, are some of the features that are closely linked to Mwalimu. Above all, every Zambian knows how close he was to our first President, Dr. Kenneth Kaunda. They were like twin brothers. To show the depth of their friendship, President Kaunda gave Mwalimu's middle name Kambarage to one of his sons....

Rarely is a person given the praises and high marks that Mwalimu received from people from all walks of life when still alive. In life, he was lionized by the people of Africa. He was given high accolade and status as one of the giants of a generation of leaders that has disappeared. That generation, sacrificed itself to the cause of the liberation of the African continent....

Mwalimu was not only a believer in Pan-Africanism; he was an actor who took very difficult steps to fulfill his total commitment to the liberation of Africa from colonialism and apartheid. Even though Tanganyika was not rich, Mwalimu readily shared the little that country had with the liberation struggle. All political parties in Central and Southern Africa received direct monetary and material support from Nyerere and the Tanganyika African National Union (TANU). This included vehicles, office equipment, housing, food, clothes, training and diplomatic passports and air tickets.

Soon after independence, Mwalimu opened up his country to the freedom fighters, a move that brought an end to racism and colonialism in South Africa, in Zimbabwe, Mozambique and Angola. For Nyerere, the move marked the beginning of an effective commitment to African liberation movements; later, he played host to the African National Congress (ANC) and the Pan-Africanist Congress (PAC) of South Africa, to Samora Machel's FRELIMO - battling against the Portuguese in Mozambique, Joshua Nkomo's ZIPRA (Zimbabwe People's Revolutionary Army) and later Robert Mugabe's ZANLA (Zimbabwe African National Liberation Army) forces, which opposed colonial rule in the then Southern Rhodesia. He did this fully knowing the risks involved. He was resolute and undeterred. He was, as Smith described him later, the initial 'evil genius' behind the liberation struggle and the guerrilla wars, which followed. The freedom fighters were trained not only in the military sphere. Many pursued academic studies that took them to various parts of the world to attain professional qualifications. Today many of these are holding very senior positions in government.

Thousands of political exiles swarmed the country.... There was always trouble in their ranks. Add to this, the dangers and actual infiltration by agents of hostile countries into their ranks, management problems, frustrations, challenges to the party leaderships, enemy attacks, and also the resentment that some Tanzanians began to cultivate for the exiles. Mwalimu and his countrymen overcame these problems and moved on.

Practically for its entire life, the Liberation Committee, an organ of the Organization of African Unity (OAU), charged with the responsibility of co-coordinating the liberation struggle, was based in Dar es Salaam, under a Tanzanian military officer, Colonel (later Major-General) Hashim Mbita. Tanzania's ability to continue to host it year after year was a great credit to the inspiration provided by Mwalimu. With his guidance, the Committee was able to register success after success as the countries of Southern Africa were liberated one after another.

Through his l Type your question here and then click Search eadership style, dress, speeches and writings as well as personal discussion, Mwalimu was able to exert a lot of influence on many African leaders in Southern Africa. These included Kaunda and Chiluba of Zambia, Marcel and Chissano of Mozambique, Robert Mugabe of Zimbabwe, Sam Nujoma of Namibia, Thabo Mbeki of South Africa and Uganda's Yoweri Museveni as well as the new breed of African leaders. He played an 'enormous' role in the fight for independence and the liberation of Southern African countries.

As a Pan-Africanist, he could not be faulted for putting his country in the forefront of the frontline states against white minority rule in Africa. He took a principled stand at a great loss to his country. Credit should be given to the people of Tanzania, for in spite of the problems this sacrifice brought, they never really complained. Tanzania became a home for exiled freedom fighters who are now the leaders and civil servants in a number of Southern African states. A few of them have become international civil servants in many multilateral organizations.

Mwalimu was an African leader who outgrew his country and his continent. He was an influential figure on the international scene and one of Africa's most respected elder statesmen.... Mwalimu was also a strong believer in African Unity. He was one of the founders of the Organization of African Unity (OAU) in 1963 and was one of the 32 signatories to the Charter of the Organization of African Unity. Later he served as chairman of the Organization of African Unity in 1984/85 and piloted the discussions on the independence of Namibia and the end to apartheid in South Africa. He left an indelible mark on the social and political history of the continent. He was an architect of the East African Community (EAC) and the Southern African Coordination Council now the Southern African Development Community (SADC).... He was also involved in seeking solutions to the many conflicts that raged in Africa. In 1995, the OAU asked him to devote his efforts to bringing peace in the troubled country of Burundi. Sadly, he was taken away without concluding his mission.

Aside from politics, Nyerere was a scholar with a formidable intellect of the highest repute. He contributed immensely to the area of education reforms and coined the term 'education for self-reliance' which found wide acceptance and currency all over the world. He was a poet of modest pretensions. His translation of Shakespeare's *Julius Caesar* (and *Merchant of Venice*) into Kiswahili, a regional lingua franca, was brilliant. He has left us with brilliant essays on political theory and political thought that have a great impact and influence on us....

Mwalimu was not only a Zanaki from Butiama, Musoma, a Tanzanian and an African, he was an internationalist.... We thank Mwalimu for teaching us the true meaning of being the servant of the people.[10]

The liberation of Mozambique, masterminded from Tanzania's capital Dar es Salaam where FRELIMO was founded in 1962, was but one example of the historic role Tanzania under the leadership of Julius Nyerere played in the liberation of Africa, and in the global context in general, especially with regard to North-South relations, protecting and promoting the interests of the Third World. One of the poorest countries in the world, the poorest of the poor, became one of the world's most significant players in international affairs. It was one of the world's 25 poorest, yet in political terms was described as one of the top 25. An economic featherweight, it became a political heavyweight in the international arena dominated by the big powers. As *The Washington Post* put it, Tanzania punched far above its weight.

And it did so, with a megaton punch, because of Julius Nyerere.

CHAPTER SEVEN:

THE RHODESIAN CRISIS: TANZANIA'S ROLE

TANZANIA was the first African country to break off diplomatic relations with Britain because of the refusal of the British government to intervene in Rhodesia to end the illegal seizure of power by the white minority regime, which unilaterally declared independence in that British colony.

The unilateral declaration of independence (UDI) by whites on November 11, 1965, under the leadership of Prime Minister Ian Smith, was a flagrant violation of the rights of the black majority who were denied racial equality and excluded from the government of their country. And it was strongly condemned by African countries, which demanded immediate action by Britain to end the rebellion in her colony. When Britain failed to do so by December 15, 1965, most African countries severed diplomatic ties with her in protest, and in fulfillment of a resolution adopted by the Organization of African Unity (OAU) requiring all African countries to take such action.

President Julius Nyerere set the tone for Africa's collective response to the crisis by being the most relentless and outspoken champion of black majority rule in Rhodesia among the leaders of the frontline states, which included Tanzania, Zambia, Botswana, Mozambique, and Angola. He was also chairman of the leaders of the frontline states, and Tanzania the headquarters of all the African liberation movements. Tanzania was also the first country in the region to win independence, as Tanganyika, in 1961, and immediately offered sanctuary to the freedom fighters and refugees from countries still under white minority rule. A large number of the freedom fighters and refugees who sought asylum in Tanzania came from Rhodesia.

Rhodesia's road to independence was filled with minefields, in the literal sense as well, and presented Britain with one of her most vexing problems mainly because of the pressure exerted on her by African countries - most of them independent by then - to end the rebellion by the white minority regime. But Britain was unwilling to take action due to a number of factors: economic interests, East-West ideological rivalry, security of the West, and racial considerations; with the vast majority of the whites in Rhodesia being British themselves.

In fact, South Africa was Britain's third largest export market and the recipient of one third of British overseas investment in the 1960s. And the vast majority of whites in South Africa, including the apartheid regime itself, were overwhelmingly in favor of UDI. The opposition leader in the South African parliament, Sir de Villiers Graaff, went so far as to say the government of Prime Minister Hendrik Verwoerd was not giving enough help to Rhodesia; Verwoerd himself being a fierce proponent of white supremacy. And because of her vested interests in South Africa, Britain was reluctant to support full mandatory sanctions - endorsed by the United Nations - against Rhodesia because she feared that this would generate momentum for a comprehensive embargo against South Africa as well. As Professor Richard Coggins of Oxford University states:

> Southern Rhodesia's Unilateral Declaration of Independence in November 1965 created arguably the most intractable problem in British foreign and colonial policy in the post-war period. For 15 years successive UK governments sought to end the rebellion by the white settler regime entrenched in Salisbury. Economic sanctions and political initiatives failed to convince the regime of Ian Smith to agree to concede power to the black majority in the country now known as Zimbabwe....
>
> Rhodesian independence raised several conflicting problems for Harold Wilson's Labour government.... Beset by ongoing economic crisis, the government had to reconcile backbench opinion, skeptical - if not hostile - criticism from the African Commonwealth, and pressure at the United Nations, with the need to dispose of the problem in a practicable way, taking into account essential economic interests in South Africa and Zambia. The principal dilemma for British policy makers was a classic one: balancing considerations of Realpolitik against fundamental principles of democracy for the black majority in Rhodesia.[1]

Besides South Africa, Britain also had significant economic interests in Zambia on whose copper supplies - at least 40 percent - British manufacturers and other businesses were heavily dependent. Therefore, ignoring Zambian demands over Rhodesia, and her security concerns, would jeopardize the relationship between the two countries and may even lead to curtailment of copper supplies to Britain.

And one of the considerations of Realpolitik which clashed with the fundamental principles of democracy for the black majority in Rhodesia was Britain's desire to neutralize Soviet and Chinese influence in Africa which was gaining ground because of Russian and Chinese support for the liberation movements across the continent, especially in southern Africa. Yet, Britain's unwillingness to end the Smith rebellion, by force if necessary as circumstances seemed to dictate, could not be reconciled with her desire to contain or neutralize Eastern-bloc influence in Africa, or with the universal assumption that race-neutral democratic principles were the accepted norm in international relations; at least in theory even if not in practice in all cases, and as an ideal to be attained. Britain's failure to aggressively advance the cause of freedom for the black majority in Rhodesia not only undermined British interests in independent Africa but enhanced the image of the Russians and the Chinese as well as their communist allies - the Cubans, the East Germans and others - as "true friends" of the Africans in the liberation struggle against white minority rule. It also provided the communists with ample ammunition to attack and portray Britain and other Western countries as racist (the same way the Soviet Union did to the United States when black Americans in the southern states were being attacked during the civil rights movement in the fifties and sixties) because of their friendly policies towards white minority regimes in Africa - including apartheid South Africa, the bastion of white supremacy - and their refusal even to help bring about fundamental change in white-dominated countries on the continent.

Therefore, the issue of racial equality in Rhodesia was not of paramount importance to British and her Western allies; nor was it to the Russians and the Chinese, although they used it effectively as a propaganda weapon against the West in their ideological rivalry at the height of the Cold War. But it was of utmost importance to Africa. And Smith's unilateral declaration of independence was an act of ultimate defiance of fundamental human rights, and of the wishes of the African majority, that could not go unchallenged by the independent African states. It was in this context that President Nyerere articulated his position on the Rhodesian crisis, one of the most urgent problems ever confronted by independent Africa.

And the refusal by Britain to use military force to end the rebellion was hypocritical. Britain herself used military force to expand and maintain her colonial empire. And that included Rhodesia itself in the 1890s, besides Ghana against the Ashanti, the Mau Mau in Kenya in the 1950s, and even the military campaigns against Germany in Africa and Asia in World I and World II. Yet, the British government refused to use force to end the Smith rebellion, even though that would have been the only and most effective way to do so, as clearly demonstrated 15 years later when a sustained military campaign by the freedom fighters compelled Smith to capitulate and relinquish power to the black majority.

Even in the 1960s, when the white minority regime illegally seized power in Rhodesia, Britain did not refrain from using military force in other parts of the Commonwealth to protect and promote her interests. She did so in Malaysia, Aden, South Arabia, and even in Tanganyika in January 1964 when President Nyerere requested British assistance to suppress the army mutiny as we learned earlier. So why not in Rhodesia? The argument that Britain did not militarily intervene in Rhodesia because dislodging Smith from power and ending his rebellion would have required a large military operation and troop commitment, is not supported by facts. Britain used massive military force in previous wars - in World War II and even in the Boer War in South Africa - yet refused to do so against Rhodesia.

It seemed obvious that Britain did not want to intervene militarily because the intervention would have been directed against fellow whites and would have ended white privilege enjoyed at the expense of blacks; an interpretation given validity by Britain's strong denunciations of President Robert Mugabe in the nineties and beyond against his seizure of white-owned land to correct historical injustices perpetrated against the African majority during British colonial rule, while maintaining virtual silence on despotic rule and other injustices committed by black leaders against blacks elsewhere on the continent if Britain's concern in the case of Zimbabwe was, indeed, simply a matter of justice and not racially motivated. Even the intelligence services of Britain, Rhodesia, and apartheid South Africa - the British M16, the Rhodesian Central Intelligence Organization (CIO), and the South African Bureau of State Security (BOSS) - worked together very closely; a concession also made by the head of the Rhodesian Central Intelligence Organization (CIO), Ken Flower, in his book, *Serving Secretly: Rhodesia's CIO Chief on Record.*[2] It was a tripartite alliance which amounted to a security pact of kinsmen to protect white interests in Africa.

There was no other explanation - besides race, why Britain did not intervene militarily in Rhodesia - that would convince Africans otherwise, including those in other countries across the continent. And that was the only plausible and credible explanation. Britain was stronger than Rhodesia. Therefore ending the rebellion by military force was a practical proposition. But Britain chose not to do so, thus incurring the wrath of African countries.

Dr. Kwame Nkrumah was one of the strongest proponents of military intervention in Rhodesia and strongly urged Britain to exercise this option. He even proposed mobilizing a Pan-African force to intervene in Rhodesia and oust Smith, thus paving the way to black majority rule, but was overthrown in February 1966 in a coup engineered and masterminded by the CIA, three months after Rhodesia illegally declared independence. In fact, Akwasi A. Afrifa, who led the coup, stated in his book, *The Ghana Coup,*[3] that one of the reasons why he and his fellow soldiers overthrew Nkrumah was that he was getting ready to send them to fight a war they had nothing to do with, and in a faraway country they knew nothing about; an inexplicable statement coming from an African.

Yet, the collective sentiment articulated across the continent was exactly the opposite of how Afrifa and his treasonous coterie felt. Military force was the only viable option in the Rhodesian context. Smith could not be ousted any other way, as African countries clearly showed when they gave full support to the freedom fighters, training and arming them. In the Commonwealth, the strongest exponents of military intervention to end the rebellion in Rhodesia were presidents Nkrumah, Nyerere, Obote, and Kaunda.

These leaders also knew that race was a factor in Britain's refusal or unwillingness to use military force in Rhodesia. In fact, it was highly unlikely that British soldiers would obey orders to go and fight their "kith and kin." And there was a strong possibility that South Africa would intervene on Rhodesia's side for the same reason, racial solidarity, a point underscored by Colin Legum in "Witness Seminar on Rhodesian UDI":

> The heated early arguments over whether Britain should have intervened militarily to stifle UDI at the beginning ignored two political factors as well as assumptions about the willingness of the army to obey an order to go to Rhodesia, and possible South African reactions.... Another political factor was that a military decision would not only have divided parliament between Labour and Conservatives but would also have polarised the British electorate over 'kith and kin' sentiments. (And) the anti-military interventionist made an issue about the possibility that South Africa would intervene militarily, directly or indirectly.
>
> Much was made of the assumption that the army would refuse to fight against 'kith and kin.' At the time I was engaged in lecturing at the four UK regional commands. At the Southern Command, the commanding officer at a mess lunch said emphatically that most of his senior officers would resign rather than accept an order to go to Rhodesia. On the other hand, the commanding officer at Scottish command was equally emphatic that it was unthinkable that the British Army would refuse a legal command. General Henry Alexander, who had experience in Ghana, Nigeria and the Congo, told me that he was prepared personally to take a brigade to Salisbury to take over and establish control over the international airport that would give the British Government a bargaining position to discuss terms with Smith.
>
> Contrary to official denials that a contingency plan for military intervention was ever prepared, I met an army team in Southern Command who had worked on a contingency plan, the outline of which was given to me.[4]

The fact that the British military, on orders from the government, worked on a contingency plan for military intervention in Rhodesia is indisputable evidence showing that the British government and armed forces believed that a military operation was a feasible undertaking; thus invalidating the argument that Britain did not intervene because the mission would have failed. It also lends credibility to the contention that the main reason why the British government refused to use military force against the white minority regime in Rhodesia was race.

Preparation for the contingency plan also showed that logistical problems were not an insurmountable obstacle to military intervention, had Britain decided to launch an operation. British officers who went to Zambia to asses the country's defence needs, because of the potential threat from neighboring Rhodesia, conceded that a large military intervention, including large-scale bombing to destroy the Rhodesian Royal Air Force (RRAF), would be necessary; so would a deployment of considerable military force of divisional strength. Zambian airfields would have to be used to launch an operation of such magnitude against Rhodesia, but the airfields' capacity was limited; and military helicopters taking off from an aircraft carrier in the Madagascar Strait would have had enough fuel to fly British soldiers to Rhodesia, but not to get them out if things went wrong - did anyone ever ask Tanzania, which is not very far from Rhodesia, if the helicopters en route to Rhodesia from the Madagascar Strait in the Indian Ocean could use her facilities to re-fuel to make sure they had enough fuel to fly back? But in spite of all those obstacles mentioned here, British military planners concluded that they would be able to launch a successful military operation against Rhodesia. That is why they drew up a contingency plan for military intervention, thus vindicating the position taken by African countries that the white minority regime in Salisbury could indeed be removed by force.

Even South African intervention on Rhodesia's side, however massive, could not have prevented the British military from carrying out a successful military operation against the Smith regime. Advanced as South Africa is, by African and Third World standards, her armed forces would still have been no match for British military might, had the British government been fully committed to its mission of ousting Smith by force. But it never embarked on this mission, triggering a sharp response from African countries and intensifying pressure on Britain to end the rebellion by any means possible. The military option remained one such possibility and the most effective one, if economic sanctions failed as they were bound to, because of sanctions-busting by a number of countries including South Africa, France, the United States (buying chrome and engaging in other anti-embargo activities), Portugal, Spain, Japan, Taiwan, Israel and others.

In the Commonwealth, the number of countries which took the most uncompromising stand on the Rhodesian crisis dropped to three after Ghana left the ranks following the ouster of Dr.

Nkrumah. They were Tanzania, Zambia, and Uganda. But they were soon joined by Nigeria when a military regime came to power and took a more militant stand on Rhodesia, including a threat to nationalize a major British oil company if Britain kept on dragging her feet over the Rhodesian crisis. The threat caused great concern in Britain. And pressure intensified on the British government to resolve the crisis:

> After 1970, Commonwealth summit conferences began to focus increasingly on the Rhodesian issue. Criticism, led by Tanzania's President Julius Nyerere, Sierra Leone President Albert Margai, and Uganda's President Milton Obote, condemned (British Prime Minister Harold) Wilson's negotiations with Smith on board Tiger and Fearless, fearing a sell-out. They invented the slogan NIBMAR - No Independence Before Majority Rule.
>
> The Commonwealth factor became increasingly important to the point where, under a Nigerian threat, Wilson's Foreign Secretary, James Callaghan, flew to Nigeria for a meeting, the result of which was Wilson's astonishing statement that sanctions would succeed in a 'matter of weeks.' At the time I was in close touch with W.A.W. Clarke, the official in the Commonwealth Office responsible for monitoring the progress of the sanctions programme; he told me that Wilson's statement disregarded all reports submitted to him and was devoid of reality.[5]

It was clear to African leaders that British Prime Minister Harold Wilson was not serious about ending the rebellion in Rhodesia, leaving them with only one option: supporting guerrilla warfare against the minority regime. President Nyerere was the most outspoken supporter of the freedom fighters and established military training camps for them in Tanzania, prompting rebel Prime Minister Ian Smith to describe him "the evil genius on the Rhodesian scene" and behind all the liberation movements in Africa. He equally incurred the wrath of apartheid South Africa, first by threatening in August 1961 that Tanganyika would not join the Commonwealth - after attaining sovereign status on December 9, 1961 - if South Africa remained a member. The threat was taken seriously by Britain and other countries and forced the apartheid regime to withdraw. Nigeria also played a major role in forcing South Africa out of the Commonwealth.

Nyerere also launched a sustained campaign to stop Britain from arming South Africa; opened up military training camps in Tanzania for freedom fighters from the land of apartheid and other countries under white minority rule; and provided the freedom fighters with an external service at Radio Tanzania, Dar es salaam (RTD), which became very effective in mobilizing forces and support against the white racist regimes on the continent. According to *Africa Contemporary Record*:

> The Rhodesian rebel Minister of Law and Order, Mr. Lardner Burke, extending the state of emergency at the beginning of 1968, said that the number of 'terrorists' waiting in Zambia and Tanzania to cross the Rhodesian border continued to mount. The South African Deputy-Minister of Police, Mr. S.L. Muller, said Tanzania posed 'the greatest potential threat to the Republic.' He claimed there were '40 camps in Tanzania for the training of terrorists and all the offices of subversive organisations.' In Zambia, he said, there were '19 training and transit camps.'
>
> An external service of Radio Tanzania was inaugurated in 1968 to assist in 'propagating the ideological principles of the liberation movements in Tanzania.'[6]

Tanzania's and Zambia's uncompromising stand and strong support for the freedom fighters triggered a sharp response from South Africa. On April 24, 1968, the former head of the South African Defence Force, Commandant-General S.A. Melville, threatened the two countries, contending that South Africa already had sufficient justification and provocation for retaliation against countries which "harboured" and encouraged "terrorists" to penetrate South Africa and South West Africa.[7] South West Africa, now Namibia, was a German colony the Germans lost in World War I. It was taken over by South Africa - under the League of Nations mandate - which continued to rule the former German colony in defiance of the United Nations which terminated its mandate in 1966.

The threat by Commandant-General S.A. Melville included South West Africa because it was a virtual colony, or province, of apartheid South Africa. The Minister of Defence P.W. Botha, who later on became president, used even more blunt language to threaten Tanzania and Zambia, saying countries which harbor and train "terrorists" should receive a "sudden hard knock."[8] Rhodesia itself, although weaker, was equally committed to the same policy of hot pursuit of the "terrorists" all the way back to the countries where they were based and trained.

South Africa and Rhodesia invoked sovereign rights to

justify their position and even their diabolical policies. It is true
that South Africa, even under apartheid, was a legal sovereign
entity and recognized as one by the international community. But
Rhodesia was not, and only claimed to be a legally constituted
state; its "legitimacy" derived from usurpation of power under the
Crown, which was tantamount to treason since it was legally still a
British colony. Yet, for all practical purposes, it functioned as an
independent state in spite of its dubious credentials; a matter that
was also addressed by the Rhodesian High Court but to the
satisfaction of no one in the African nationalist movement.
According to *Africa Research Bulletin*:

> The five judges of the Appellate Division of the Rhodesian High Court,
> hearing the constitution test case appeal, ruled on January 29th, 1968, by a
> majority of 3 to 2 that the Rhodesian Government was not yet a *de jure*
> government. But four of the judges agreed that it was in effective control of the
> country and therefore the *de facto* government. A minority of two of the judges
> found that the Government had acquired *de jure* status and one judge considered
> that Rhodesia was already a *de facto* republic.[9]

Although the Rhodesian High Court conferred legitimacy
on the Smith regime despite its treasonous acts, the fundamental
problem that there shall be no independence before majority rule -
a position maintained by African nationalists and other Africans
across the continent - was not even addressed by the court.
Therefore, what came to be known as the NIBMAR principle - No
Independence Before Majority Rule - articulated by President
Julius Nyerere and others - was collectively invoked by African
countries under the auspices of the Organization of African Unity
(OAU) as the rationale for armed struggle. And it became the
cornerstone of all the negotiations conducted through the years to
resolve the Rhodesian crisis, while the liberation war was being
prosecuted at the same time and used as a bargaining tool to extract
meaningful concessions from the white minority regime in
Salisbury.

The Rhodesian crisis became a test case for independent
Africa, and was the most urgent issue confronting the continent
since the chaos in the Congo. But the Rhodesian impasse was also
a test case for Britain to live up to her commitments. As Nyerere
stated on December 14, 1965 - before severing diplomatic ties with

Britain the next day over the Rhodesian crisis - in his speech to the Tanzania National Assembly, aptly entitled, "The Honour of Africa":

The policies of Tanzania, and of Africa, in relation to Southern Rhodesia, have always had one object, and one object only. That was, and is, to secure a rapid transition to independence on the basis of majority rule....

Africa maintains that Southern Rhodesia is at present a colony of the United Kingdom, and that ultimate responsibility for events there resides, in consequence, with the Government of the united Kingdom in London....(But) Britain has not shown serious determination either to get rid of those in Southern Rhodesia who have usurped British power, or to replace them with representatives of the people. For it is not the independence of Rhodesia that Africa is complaining about; it is independence under a racialist minority government....

Southern Rhodesia is a British colony; its constitution is subject to the will of the British Parliament. As an international entity Southern Rhodesia does not exist. Internationally, by both law and custom, there exists only Britain and its colony.

The colony of Southern Rhodesia has been self-governing since 1923; for 43 years increasing *de facto* power has been exerted by a government based in Salisbury. But the constitution under which that government operated reserved certain powers to the British Government and Parliament in London. The fact that successive British Governments did not use their powers to prevent acts which were contrary to the interests of the African people does not alter the existence of these 'Reserved Powers'; nor the ultimate responsibility of the British Government for the actions of the Southern Rhodesian government.

In saying this there is no need to argue abstract cases of law. Britain herself accepts responsibility for Southern Rhodesia. More, she claims that responsibility. Britain claims that she, and she alone, can decide what is to be done about Southern Rhodesia. The only time she has ever used her veto in the United Nations was when Ghana proposed a resolution which would have blocked the transfer to the Southern Rhodesian government of the Air Force which had been built up by the defunct Federation of Rhodesia and Nyasaland. In the Commonwealth Conferences of 1964 and 1965, the Government of Britain maintained this stand, and it was conceded by the rest of the Commonwealth - including the African members. And just over a week ago - on 6 December 1965 - Mr. Wilson, the Prime Minister of Britain, is reported to have said once again, 'Rhodesia is Britain's responsibility.'

There is thus no dispute between Britain and Africa about the British responsibility. What then of the manner in which that responsibility has been, and is being, exercised?

I do not propose to go back further than October 1964 in an examination of the British record. The record before that date is a shameful one; time after time the interests of the African majority were subjected to the selfish power hunger of the settler minority. Even after 1947, when other colonies in Africa began to feel some hope of ultimate freedom, the settlers of Southern Rhodesia were able to extend their sway. In return for some concessions on the periphery of power, some verbal acceptance of the theory of 'partnership,' they were able to secure dominance in a federation of Rhodesia with the countries, which are now Zambia and Malawi. In 1961, with the tide running hard against them, and when they were concerned to try and save their federation, they still managed to secure a constitution for Southern Rhodesia, which entrenched minority power while only appearing to make some concessions to the African population. And in 1963, at the break-up of the federation (which was established in 1953), they secured into their own hands the real instruments of power - the aeroplanes, the equipment, and the administration of the Army and the Air Force.

For the settler government of Southern Rhodesia even this was not enough. In 1963, and even more in 1964, they began to demand independence for themselves.

That was the position in October 1964....

On 27 October 1964, the Prime Minister of Britain said openly to Mr. Smith, the Prime Minister in the British colony, that a unilateral 'declaration of independence would be an open act of defiance and rebellion, and it would be treasonable to take steps to give effect to it.' These strong words meant that Africa was heartened despite the fact that the statement went on to speak only of economic consequences of such a declaration.

In November, however, the Smith government called for a referendum in support of independence for Southern Rhodesia under the 1961 constitution. He received 58,000 votes in support. I ask that this House should take particular note of that number; it is less than the total registered voters in the Dar es Salaam South constituency of Tanzania. And even that vote was only obtained after Mr. Smith had said that he was not asking for a vote in support of an illegal declaration of independence!

Threats of illegal action nonetheless continued to come from Salisbury, and apart from warnings about what would happen if they were carried out, nothing was done to those who made the threats.

Indeed, by the end of the year there were indications from London that independence might be granted without majority rule. Mr. Bottomley, the British Commonwealth Secretary, was reported as saying , 'We must be satisfied that the basis on which independence is to be granted is acceptebale to the people as a whole.' This ambiguous statement was clearly deliberate, and it succeeded in one of its designs. Africa thought that this was merely a tactical move, an endeavour to avoid provoking Smith before Britain was ready to deal with him....

Although UDI was declared to be an act of rebellion there was a studious avoidance by British Ministers of the statement that the rebellion would be brought down by all necessary means, including the use of force. The Smith group were never faced with that prospect. On several occasions British Ministers said, 'We shall not use force to impose a constitutional solution' to the Rhodesian situation. They never went further. Africa worried, and waited.

Even more serious for Africa was the deliberate vagueness about the ultimate objective of the negotiations (between Smith and the British government) and the opposition to UDI....

Britain's 'five principles' which had to be met before independence would be granted by the British Government did not specify the existence of majority rule. On the contrary, they clearly showed that if certain 'safeguards' were enshrined in a document, then majority rule would not be insisted upon. There was only one ambiguous statement in principle five, which many genuine people - including African leaders - believed provided a safeguard. Principle five stated that 'any basis proposed for independence must be acceptable to the people of Rhodesia as a whole.' Many of our friends said that the people of that colony could not possibly agree on an independence without majority rule, and that therefore, so long as this principle was maintained, Rhodesia would not become completely a second South Africa without hope of peaceful progress.

Tanzania was less sanguine; in the Commonwealth Conference I therefore demanded that the words *'independence on the basis of majority rule'* be included in the final communique. They were not included; and in consequence Tanzania disassociated itself from the Southern Rhodesia section of the communique. Our friends thought us needlessly suspicious. But it was quite clear to us that the British Government was willing to grant independence on the basis of minority rule.

Now it is one month after thet minority government of Rhodesia has seized power.... Have we yet had the assurance (of independence on the basis of majority rule), which Tanzania sought in June? The answer is no. The 1961 constitution remains in being, with some few powers having been resumed by the Government in London. This resumption having been forced upon Britain by Smith! Let me quote Mr. Wilson, the Prime Minister of the United Kingdom, speaking in the House of Commons, London, on 23 November 1965 - 12 days after the rebellion. He said - as reported in the *Times*:

'While we have power to revoke or amend sections of the 1961 constitution we have said we have no present intention of revoking it as a whole, and I cannot at this stage foresee circumstances in which we would do so.'

Mr. Wilson went on to deal with the role of this constitution in what he calls 'the resettlement period.' He said:

'When the Governor is able to report that the people of Rhodesia are willing and able to work on constitutional paths, we are prepared to work together with their leaders to make a new start. For this purpose the 1961 constitution remains in being, though the House will realize the need for those amendments which are required to prevent its perversion and misuse such as we have seen in the last fortnight, and those amendments, too, which are needed to give effect to the five principles to which all parties in this House have subscribed'....

Later in the same speech Mr. Wilson said:

'All along we have made it plain - we did all throughout the negotiations - that while guaranteed and unimpeded progress to majority rule is the policy of all of us, we dot believe it can be immediate.... But all of us are committed to an early attempt by the Rhodesian people to pronounce on their own future. That was the reason for the suggested referendum and for the Royal Commission.'

The thing, which I notice in the last statement, Mr. Speaker, is that this was not an assurance about majority rule; it was an assurance against majority rule.

At the end of last week the British Broadcasting Corporation (BBC) news service reported that Mr. Wilson had suggested that after all, when British authority was re-established in Southern Rhodesia, there might be a period of direct rule by the Governor with advisers from all races. As this would mean the end of the 1961 constitution I had a moment of hope; we would begin over again. But the report went on to say that Mr. Wilson stressed that majority rule could not come for a very long time - and still there was no suggestion that independence would be held up until this majority rule had finally been attained....

It is not the timing, which is causing Africa to become so angry; we could argue about time. Our anger and suspicion arise from the fact that Britain is not even now - 14 December 1965 - committed to the principle of 'independence only on the basis of majority rule.'

I must, however, now move to the question of whether Britain has shown serious determination to get rid of those in Southern Rhodesia who have usurped her power. Africa maintains that she has not....

What has Britain done since 11 November?

On that date Mr. Wilson used some strong words: he said, 'It is an illegal act, ineffective in law; an act of rebellion against the Crown and against the constitution as by law established.' But he then went on to instruct the civil servants of Southern Rhodesia to 'stay at their posts but not assist in any illegal acts.' He was unable to explain how they could do that when they were serving an illegal government.

As regards the use of force Mr. Wilson repeated his stock phrase despite the changed circumstances. Britain would not use force to impose a constitutional settlement he said, but he went on to say that the British Government 'would give full consideration to any appeal from the Governor for help to restore law and order.' Mr. Wilson refrained from explaining how the law could be more broken than it had been by the usurpation of power, that is to say, by treason. He refrained later from explaining how the Governor was to transmit his appeal once the telephone had been taken from him as well as all the furniture of his office, his staff and his transport.

Instead, Mr. Wilson obtained the approval of the British Parliament for economic action against the regime. Capital exports to southern Rhodesia were stopped; exchange restrictions were imposed; Commonwealth preference was suspended, and a ban was imposed on the British import of Rhodesian tobacco and sugar. The British Foreign Secretary was sent to the United Nations to secure international support for these actions.

The United Nations was highly critical: it demanded further action. Finally, on 20 November Britain accepted a Security Council resolution which included this phrase: 'Calls upon all states...to do their utmost in order to break all economic relations with Southern Rhodesia, including an embargo on oil and petroleum products'....

On 23 November Mr. Wilson spoke to the House of Commons, saying, 'We are going to study all aspects of trade and oil.... We are not going in for a trade embargo or oil embargo alone.' And in explanation of this, he said that there are many difficulties and 'there is the position of Zambia to be considered'! That Zambia had supported the resolution appeared irrelevant to the British Prime Minister, who clearly thought he knew the business of that independent African state better than President Kaunda. On 1 December Mr. Wilson again said, 'We are not contemplating an embargo immediately.'

What is Africa expected to think of this mockery of a UN resolution which was already - at Britain's insistence - less than a firm, binding declaration of determination to defeat Smith?

On 1 December, however, Mr. Wilson announced new and much sterner economic measures against Rhodesia. Ninety-five per cent of Rhodesia's exports to Britain were then blocked, and financial measures taken which could have had a fairly quick and fairly severe effect on the economy of that colony. But Mr. Smith of Rhodesia was yesterday reported to have said that these have come too late to affect Rhodesia's economy. I do not believe that he is bluffing. He has had weeks in which to prepare for these measures. But the timing is not my only criticism. I have argued that economic sanctions against Rhodesia will not work as long as South Africa is allowed to trade freely with the rebel colony. And it is Britain, which has blocked obligatory sanctions under Chapter 7 of the UN Charter....

The British Government has not shown serious determination either to get rid of those in Southern Rhodesia who have usurped British power, or to replace them with representatives of the people.... Britain... has failed to live up to the responsibilities she has claimed, and she has failed to protect...an independent state (Zambia) which is threatened because of her failure to immediately overthrow the rebel regime.[10]

On the next day, December 15, Tanzania broke off diplomatic relations with Britain because of Britain's unwillingness to end the rebellion in Rhodesia. The British government did not even ask for a multilateral force under UN auspices to intervene, if she did not want to do so alone and commit only British troops to combat. Nyerere became the first African leader to sever diplomatic ties with Britain in compliance with the OAU resolution adopted on December 2, 1965, in Addis Ababa, Ethiopia, by all independent African countries except two, including Malawi under Dr. Hastings Kamuzu Banda, a perennial opponent of OAU policies towards white minority regimes on the continent.

Tanzania was followed by Ghana under Dr. Nkrumah, and Egypt under Gamal Abdel Nasser, some of the strongest supporters of the African nationalist groups in Rhodesia and other white-ruled countries in Africa. They were also some of Lumumba's uncompromising supporters during the Congo crisis and sent troops to the Congo under UN command to help save his government. Nkrumah was also the first African leader to propose sending a Pan-African force to Rhodesia and offered Ghanaian troops for combat in the rebel colony to oust Smith from power.

Even before illegally declaring independence, Smith was confident of success. His confidence could largely be attributed to the fact that he did not believe Britain would send troops to Rhodesia to kill their "kith and kin"; also to the fact that not all countries around the world would abandon Rhodesia or enforce economic sanctions against his regime, even if they publicly condemned the unilateral declaration of independence (UDI). He calculated well, and was right on both counts. And after winning what came to be known as the "Constitution Test Case" before the Appellate Division of the Rhodesian High Court which conferred legitimacy on Rhodesia as an independent state, Smith felt vindicated in his claim that he had the electoral mandate to declare Rhodesia a sovereign entity; although only 58,000 voters, all white - out of a population of about 250,000 whites and more than 4 million Africans - endorsed his move, and only when he told them that it would not be illegal, although he knew full well that it was; since Rhodesia was legally still a British colony - therefore could not legally become independent without the approval of the British parliament. He totally ignored the wishes of the vast majority, the 4 million Africans who constituted more than 95 percent of the total population.

Zambian Minister of Foreign Affairs Reuben Kamanga expressed his government's "utter disgust" with the way the British government had handled the situation in Rhodesia "by resorting to ineffective means instead of bringing down the rebellion by force."[11] But demands in the UN Security Council by African countries that Britain should use force against the white minority regime in Rhodesia were rejected by British Prime Minister Harold Wilson on March 14, 1966. Lack of such action or any other effective measures to end the rebellion emboldened Rhodesian Prime Minister Ian Smith to say in a broadcast on March 24, 1966, that any personal doubts he had about Rhodesia becoming a republic had been "wiped out completely by the antics of Harold Wilson and his socialist Government." He went on to say that recent attempts by the British to interfere with the maintenance of law and order in Rhodesia, openly or by hiding behind the skirts of their Queen, were "one of the most despicable acts ever committed by a Government in Britain"; and defiantly added that things "are going well in Rhodesia and according to plan."[12]

But the "Constitution Test Case" won in Rhodesia had a different outcome in Britain where in July 1966 the Privy Council ruled that the emergency regulations passed by the Rhodesian government - and used to detain people - had no legal validity; and that the "usurping Government now in control (in Rhodesia) could not be regarded as the lawful Government."[13] However, the Rhodesian authorities dismissed the ruling as irrelevant, since their own high court had already ruled that Rhodesia was a legal sovereign entity, and therefore no longer subject to British law. Yet, despite its status as a pariah in the international arena where, at least officially, no country recognized this British colony as an independent nation, it continued to function as a *de facto* independent state and got a lot of support from apartheid South Africa which refused to enforce economic sanctions imposed by the United Nations on the white minority regime in Salisbury. South Africa also sent police and military reinforcements to Rhodesia to help the regime fight African nationalists and flatly refused to withdraw them when Britain asked the apartheid government to do so. Containing or neutralizing the nationalist insurgency in Rhodesia, with the help of South African forces, was also considered by the South African government to be in the best security interests of the apartheid state.

Emboldened by this crucial assistance from South Africa, Rhodesian Prime Minister Ian Smith became even more defiant in his public pronouncements, virtually daring African countries to go after him, as he continued to emphasize that there shall be no black majority rule in Rhodesia. Because of this unholy alliance between the two white-dominated countries - together with the Portuguese in their colonies of Angola, Mozambique and Portuguese Guinea (Guinea-Bissau) - African countries were confronted with what was essentially the same problem, only in different territories. Therefore, although the Rhodesian crisis was serious enough by itself, it could not be separated from the other crises in the region. And the destiny of all the countries in southern Africa became inextricably linked with that of the rest of the continent; as had indeed always been the case, only in a more pronounced way this time, with independent Africa being in a state of war with the white minority regimes.

The defiance of the Smith regime was also a negation of the principles of justice and equality independent Africa invoked to justify her existence. African countries constituted an indivisible whole. The dignity and freedom they were entitled to, was equally indivisible. And an insult to one was an insult to all. As President Nyerere stated in April 1966 - a few months after Rhodesia declared independence in November 1965 - in his article, "Rhodesia in the Context of Southern Africa," in *Foreign Affairs*:

The deep and intense anger of Africa on the subject of Rhodesia is by now widely realized. it is not, however, so clearly understood. In consequence the mutual suspicion, which already exists between free African states and nations of the West, is in danger of getting very much worse.

Before November 11th, 1965, African states, individually and collectively, had frequently expressed their great concern about the position in Southern Rhodesia. But it was with the unilateral declaration of independence by the Smith regime that this concern was transformed into impatient wrath. The catalyst of this changed attitude was the rebellion against British sovereignty. This was not because Africa wished Southern Rhodesia to remain a colony; Africa's earlier demands had been for action to end colonialism. Nor was it evidence of a deep-rooted objection to illegality in the anti-colonial struggle. It is a fact that Africa prefers to use constitutional, legal and peaceful methods in the campaigns for national freedom; but if these fail then other methods are accepted. Thus, for example, an Algerian Government-in-Exile was recognized by many African states long before France conceded independence to that North African state. And at the present time a Government-in-Exile, headed by Holden Roberto, is recognized by the Organization of African Unity as the rightful authority in Angola despite the fact that legally Portugal continues to dominate the area. Africa's objection is to this particular assumption of authority in Southern Rhodesia, not to illegality in general. It would be hypocrisy to pretend otherwise.

The hostility aroused by the Smith declaration of independence is based on a rational interpretation of its purpose and its effects in relation to the total and legitimate goals of Africa. For this rebellion is not an uprising of the people; it represents an attempt to expand the area, and strengthen the hold in Africa, of doctrines, which are inimical to the whole future of freedom in this continent. It represents an advance by the forces of racialism, fascism, and indeed, colonialism, in Southern Africa.

To the independent states of Africa this is not a development, which can be viewed with Olympian detachment. We are on the frontiers of the conflict with these forces, and our future demands their defeat. Gradually and somewhat painfully, colonialism and racialism have been pushed out of Northern and Central Africa. But while they remain in this continent none of us can really be free to live in peace and dignity, or be able to concentrate on the economic development, which was a large part of the purpose of our political revolution. The Smith declaration of independence represents a counter-attack by these forces, and it is in that context that Africa has reacted, and demands its defeat.

This should not be difficult to comprehend. It may have been possible for the Allied Powers to make peace with Hitler after France, Belgium, and Holland were liberated. They were not prepared to try. Still less were the Jews outside Germany willing to support any compromise which would have left their compatriots under the control of a Nazi regime - even had the ultimate horror of racial extermination been excluded. Both the states concerned, and the peoples who were being treated as racially inferior, realized that the war had to continue until Nazism was politically ended in Europe.

The parallels are almost exact. The separate freedom movements in Africa were but different arms of one liberation process. When Dr. Nkrumah said in 1957 that the independence of Ghana was incomplete until the whole of Africa was free, he spoke a truth, which is still valid for all of us. The struggle has to continue until final victory; colonialism must be wiped out in Africa before any post-colonial independent state can feel secure. And no citizen of Africa - white or black - can live in the comfort of his own self-respect while other African citizens are suffering discrimination and humiliation for being born what they are.

Yet at the present time the Portuguese colonies of Angola and Mozambique, together with South Africa, South West Africa, and Rhodesia, constitute almost one seventh of the landmass of Africa. About 12 per cent of Africa's population lives in these areas. And each of these territories in their different way are governed on the principles of racial inequality and minority domination.

Portugal pretends that her colonies are really part of Europe, and that she abjures racial discrimination. She claims instead to be in the process of making European Gentlemen out of the African inhabitants of those areas, and talks proudly of the policy of equality for the 'assimilado.' But Africans are not European, could not become

European, and do not want to become European. They demand instead the right to be Africans in Africa, and to determine their own cultural, economic, and political future. This right is what Portugal denies. The inhabitants of her colonies can certainly be 'African'; but if they are, then they are subjected to special laws, and special taxation and labour levies; their participation in the functions of their own government is ruled out.

In South Africa there is no longer even the pretence that citizens of different races are equal before the law, or in social and economic rights and duties. The 'separate but equal' concept, which was defeated in the United States in 1964, had been defeated in South Africa too; but there, inside Africa, it is the equality aspect, which has been abandoned. In providing separate facilities for people of different races, the judges have ruled that the separate schools, housing, waiting rooms and so on, do not have to be of equal standard; it is enough that they are separate. Africans can be - and are - treated as a sub-species of mankind. No legal or political restraint now prevents the white minority government in the Union of South Africa from imposing its harsh, discriminatory will upon the African majority. To be an African is to beg for a permit to live in your own country - or to leave it; it is to need permission to work in a particular place or in a particular job; it is to carry a pass at all times - day and night - and be subjected at any moment to arbitrary arrest. And it is to have no legal means whatsoever to participate in the determination of your own wages and conditions of employment, your own place, or conditions, of living - much less to participate in the governing of your country. To be an African in South Africa is to have permission - unlimited permission - to say 'Yes, Baas' - preferably even then in Afrikaans. It is to have permission to be humiliated by any man, woman, or child, who has a white skin just for the reason that they have a white skin.

It is conditions and attitudes of this kind, which free Africa is determined to fight. And there can be no questioning of the fact that (regardless of some reasonable criticisms of particular independent African states), the elimination of colonialism and racial domination in these countries to the South is justified by all the basic principles of mankind. Every principle of national and individual freedom, every principle of human equality, of justice, and of humanity, make it imperative that the rule of the minorities shall be ended. For they are judge, jury, prosecuting counsel, and lawmaker in their own dispute. And the question at issue now is whether Rhodesia shall for the foreseeable future be a state governed on that same basis of human inequality, or whether the existing, at present very slightly modified, version of racial discrimination, shall be replaced by progress towards human justice and equality.

THE POLITICAL SITUATION IN SOUTHERN AFRICA

While Africa is determined that the whole of Southern Africa shall be freed before the struggle ceases, it recognizes that the strategy and tactics of the fight will vary according to the particular circumstances of the three different areas (there are four if South West Africa in counted separately). The monster of 'unfreedom' in Southern Africa has three heads, and although they each draw strength and sustenance from the existence of the others, it remains true that each has its own separate vulnerability to determined assault by the world forces of freedom.

The best armoured, and in many ways the most tragic of the three heads in Southern Africa is the Union of South Africa itself. There, the racialism itself has become a self-justifying religion of survival, which demands ever-increasing ruthlessness to protect its adherents against the hatred it has induced. Its doctrines of superiority are inculcated into the white community from the moment of their birth; its teaching of inferiority dominates the lives of the non-whites from a similar moment. And it is in grave danger - if it has not already done so - of convincing all South Africans that there are not human beings in the world, but whites and non-whites. If it succeeds in this, there will also one day be learned the dreadful lesson that the whites constitute less than one fifth of the South African population, and that numbers provide strength. Yet because this religion of racialism has already been responsible for so much human humiliation and suffering, only a miracle could provide any real hope of its peaceful reversal and the growth of practical brotherhood. For it has already promoted hatred, and justified fear. It now appears inevitable that sooner or later an overwhelming internal explosion will occur in South Africa and bring the whole present edifice of apartheid to an end; we can only pray that it is not followed by a mere reversal of the racial discrimination, for that would be the logic of the doctrines which are now being propagated by the South African Government.

But if there is no hope of peaceful change from inside, it remains true that the Union of South Africa is an industrial state, inextricably involved in international commerce. It is also true that the South African Government's policies suffer the expressed disapproval of every major power political organization in the world. This disapproval, however, remains a verbal one; no action is taken to activate it. This is largely because of the international economic links of the capitalist world (and thus international business involvement in apartheid). This economic reluctance to take action is backed up by the fact that South Africa is a legally constituted, internationally recognized, sovereign nation. Fears of the implications of intervention from outside - through the United Nations or by any other means - have thus caused the democratic, and even the anti-colonial, nations of the West, to eschew, on grounds of legality, any deliberate activity designed to reverse the apartheid policies of South Africa. It is claimed that however reprehensible these may be, there must be no outside intervention in the internal affairs of a sovereign state. Legality is given paramountcy over morality. In consequence, the only prospect for the Union of South Africa is long-drawn-out suffering, violence and bitterness. For the struggle will go on until the cause of freedom ultimately triumphs.

The position in relation to Angola, Mozambique, and Portuguese Guinea, is different. This is, or should be, a classic colonial situation. The problem is that Portugal refuses to live in the twentieth century; she persists in believing that colonialism can be maintained, even by the poorest and most backward of the states of Europe. The problem in this case is, therefore, how to wake up Portugal to the facts of politics in the modern day.

Portugal's European and American allies could, of course, have great influence upon her - particularly if they were prepared to deny her the right to use their military strength in her defence while she uses her own (and their ammunition) in suppressing incipient revolt in her colonies. They could even help her to make the transition to the twentieth century by reviving her internal economy! But if the free countries of the West fail to try, or if they fail to succeed, then Africa will have to pursue this battle on her own, or with what allies she can find. Our own weakness means that we shall have only one way of doing that; by supporting guerrilla warfare until, after suffering and destruction, Portugal wakes up to her own realities.

Until November 11th, 1965, there was a hope that Southern Rhodesia would be able to avoid this dreadful path to freedom. Certainly the *de facto* government was a racialistic, racially constituted, minority government. Certainly apartheid under other names restricted the Africans' freedom to choose their place of living and working, and certainly separate educational, health and other public services, ensured that the Africans maintained their existing lowly position. But the vital difference was that Southern Rhodesia was legally a British colony; British surrender of power to the settler minority had been tragically real, but it stopped short of legal transfer. This meant that although she was faced with difficulties of implementation, Britain was the power responsible for the future in Southern Rhodesia. And Africa took comfort from the fact that Britain's declared policy, in relation to all her colonies, has been to bring them to democratic independence under conditions which safeguard the people from oppression from any quarter.

The legal power and responsibility of Britain therefore meant that Africa expected gradual constitutional advance towards democracy or majority rule. What appeared to be required was to make Britain realize the seriousness of a situation where Southern Rhodesia existed as an outpost of South Africa, but where she operated under the name and responsibility of the British crown. Once this was realized Africa expected that Britain would at last take steps to deal with the white settlers who were misappropriating power.

AFRICA'S DEMANDS FOR SOUTHERN RHODESIA

In other words, what Africa has been demanding from Britain in relation to Southern Rhodesia is a transition from the white minority domination in government to majority rule and, only after that, independence for the colony. This has been the position of the nationalist forces in the colony; it has been the position of all African leaders. The argument has not been about the timing of this transition - how long it would take, or how many steps are involved - but about the principle of it.

It is in that context that Africa looks at the unilateral declaration of independence by the white minority government in Rhodesia; it is because of these reasonable and justified expectations that the Smith move is of such importance. The settler regime has said, in effect, that the very existence of legal restraints upon the minority is unbearable. And as Britain refused to give them independence without asking for some assurances about the future development to majority rule, so they took the independence. And in so doing their leader had the temerity to paraphrase the greatest freedom document of all time - the American Declaration of Independence!

Mr. Ian Smith justified his seizure of power, and his quotations, by claiming that his move was 'anti-colonial,' and that his government is the defender of civilized standards - not racialistic at all. He has argued that because countries to the North with a black majority government were granted independence it is unreasonable that southern Rhodesia should remain a colony after 43 years of 'governing ourselves responsibly.'

The facts do not support Mr. Smith. The facts show that

Southern Rhodesia has been governed responsibly only as far as the white community is concerned, and that every aspect of that society is based on racial distinctions to the detriment of the African community. The facts prove, once again, that any elected government is responsive to the electorate, and only to the desires of the electorate; even if its Ministers wish to consider the interests of non-voters they are virtually powerless to do anything really effective.

Writing in *Punch* recently Mr. Smith said, 'Our Parliament is open to all races, our Civil Service offers senior posts on parity terms for all races, our University opens its doors to all races, and our voters' rolls are open to all races. Merit is, and must be, the only criterion....'

The fact of the matter is that of the 65 seats in Parliament, 50 are elected by the 'A' roll, and 15 by the 'B' Roll. To get on to the 'A' Roll it is necessary to have an income of 792 pounds per annum, or an income of 330 pounds per annum plus four years' secondary school education (or certain other intermediate combinations). To get on to the 'B' Roll the figures are lower; an income of 264 pounds per annum, or a combination of being 30 years of age with an income of 132 pounds per annum plus primary education. The registered voters in consequence showed that of the 94,080 people on the 'A' Roll, 89,278 were whites; Africans predominated in the 'B' roll with more than 10,000 voters as against 1,000 non-Africans on this Roll, but these actual figures are not very revealing as the nationalist organizations called for a boycott of the elections. The comparative population figures show that there are in Southern Rhodesia almost four million Africans, and less than 250,000 people of European descent.

The government of Southern Rhodesia is thus firmly in the hands of the white voters; and is likely to remain so. The 'B' Roll seats are not even sufficient to veto changes in the constitution. Neither are there in fact any Africans in senior positions in the Civil Service; and if there were, the existing legislation would force them to live in the designated 'African Areas' of the towns regardless of their income. And behind all this smokescreen of 'responsibility' and 'merit' is complete segregation, and absolute inequality, in the availability of education.

Schooling for non-African children is compulsory between the ages of 7 and 15 years; and in 1963 there were 19,898 European children in secondary schools out of the 53,000 total European school enrolment. Only 7,045 African pupils were attending secondary schools during that year, and only 81 of these were in Form VI where entrance to the university can be attempted. It is hard to argue that these differences of secondary school attendance are due to differences in innate ability when something like ten times more finance is allocated for each European pupil than each African pupil. The truth is that educational opportunities just do not exist for the African community in the way they do for whites. There are places in the sixth year class for only 50 per cent of the African children who attend school for the first five years; out of those who do pass that hurdle, only 25 per cent will find a place in a secondary school three years later.

It is not my purpose to deny that there are difficulties in providing the educational expansion, which is required in Africa now; Tanzania's problems are too real for that. But when this racial distinction is made in educational opportunities, it is rank dishonesty to talk of equality opportunity in other fields, which depend on an educational or income qualification. Neither is it realistic to expect the voters (i.e. the people in the upper income brackets, who have reserved educational opportunities for their own children) to break down the racial distinctions, which maintain their current privileged position.

Recent history in Southern Rhodesia supports this lack of expectation. Since 1957 there has been a steady electoral move towards political parties and groups, which have been most fierce in their declared intention to resist racial integration. The Rhodesian Front, which is the party of the present Smith regime, was elected when it opposed the United Federal Party proposal to amend the Land Apportionment Act (this, among other things, reserves 37 per cent of the land area of the country for European ownership). In its manifesto the Rhodesian Front also declared that it would bring about 'premature African dominance,' and the manifesto recognized the right of government to 'provide separate amenities for various (racial) groups.'

In fact, since the election successive Rhodesian Front governments have concentrated on political questions, and particularly on the question of independence. In the process they have gained, and used, all the powers of a police state. All African nationalist parties have been banned, and their leaders imprisoned or detained; meetings have been prohibited, demonstrations broken up by police violence. And since independence press censorship has been imposed on all media of public communication, and the harshest penalties imposed for any refusal to bow down to the behests of this minority and illegal administration. The regime has, in fact, moved consistently along the path it laid down for itself; the path which leads directly and in a short time to the imposition in Southern Rhodesia of an unabashed apartheid policy as it is operated in South Africa.

Many of these developments, and certainly the groundwork for them, had taken place before UDI. Independence merely represented a logical further stage; it had to come - legally or otherwise - or there had to be a reversal of direction. What independence under the present minority regime means, therefore, is that the Rubicon has been crossed. If this independence is sustained the hope of a peaceful (even if gradual) development to majority has been obliterated. The only hope now remaining is for the rebellion to be defeated by the legal power and a new start made on the road to peaceful progress.

THE INTERNATIONAL IMPLICATIONS OF UDI

The importance of this cannot be overestimated. A successful declaration of independence by the minority government of Southern Rhodesia represents an expansion of racialism and fascism in Africa, and a step backward in the drive for African freedom. It is as though one of the southern states in the United States of America now, in the year 1966, succeeded in enlarging and strengthening the segregation and discrimination within its area of jurisdiction. The reaction of the federal authorities, and of the civil rights organizations, can be easily imagined. They would know that their future was at stake, and that the battle was joined as surely as it was at Fort Sumter in 1861. So it is in Africa.

But the parallel does not stop there. Just as would be the case in America, so in Africa success by the Southern Rhodesian minorities would strengthen the forces of reaction in other parts of the continent. South Africa and Portugal must want the Smith rebellion to succeed. Their interest is one of ideological sympathy; but it is also of geography. The map of Africa shows their reasons for wanting white domination to be safely entrenched in Southern Rhodesia - just as it indicates the special interest of countries like Zambia and Bechuanaland that it shall not succeed.

Yet although South Africa and Portugal want white domination to be firmly established in Southern Rhodesia, the illegality of the present situation is an embarrassment to them. They cannot afford to intervene actively on the side of Rhodesia unless and until they are certain that the rebellion will succeed. For in supporting the illegal regime they are staking their own future on its success.

South Africa's strongest defence against international criticism of her policies is the legality of her government, the recognized sovereignty of her state, and the doctrine that the internal affairs of any nation are outside the competence of the United Nations or any other international official body. If she openly supports a rebellion against legal authority in another state, then it is infinitely more difficult for her to resist international intervention in her own affairs. Consequently, we have the position where the Verwoerd government claims to stand neutral in the conflict between the sovereign authority (Britain) and the *de facto* authority (the Smith regime) in Southern Rhodesia.

This official neutrality is at the moment possible because the economic sanctions are voluntary acts of each separate nation state. By refusing to participate in these sanctions South Africa is thus breaking no international commitment and infringing neither domestic nor international law. This situation would be changed if the United Nations adopted Chapter 7 of the Charter (even article 41 alone), which makes sanctions mandatory on all members. South Africa would then either have to co-operate, or she would draw upon herself the international action she is concerned to avoid. That is to say, she would either have to close her own trade with Southern Rhodesia and be prepared to answer questions about the ultimate destination of goods she is importing, or she would be liable to be included in the area covered by sanctions.

The implications of the present position are well understood by the present South African Government. They account for its failure to give the 'independent' Smith regime all the support it hoped for. Yet it is clear that white public opinion inside South Africa is willing to do at least some of the things the government fears to do - and that the government will not interfere. The 'Oil for Rhodesia' campaign depends for its success on publicity and is thus known outside Southern Africa. There is little doubt, however, that through private business deals with South African firms and citizens, the cutting edge of international sanctions against Southern Rhodesia is being - and will be - blunted. By these means South Africa is able, without risking her own position, to assist the white regime in Southern Rhodesia to survive.

Portugal, too, is hamstrung by the illegality of the present Southern Rhodesian position. She, too, is relying upon legalistic niceties to prevent Western pressure building up against her occupation of Mozambique, Angola and Portuguese Guinea. She can therefore hardly afford to defend and assist a rebellion in the territory of a major European ally. Yet again, it is (to say the least) highly probable that she is giving under-cover assistance to Rhodesia. As Sir Edgar Whitehead, a past Prime Minister of Southern Rhodesia, said in the *Spectator* of January 28th, 'Mozambique could not survive of an African nationalist government took over in Rhodesia, and would be utterly ruined if the Rhodesian economy collapsed.' Sir Edgar went on to refer to the oil refinery at Lorenzo Marques, and the assistance, which it can give quietly to the Smith regime despite the absence of crude oil for the Umtali refinery. Once again, this position exists because there is no international 'illegality' in trading with Southern Rhodesia. The situation would be changed if Chapter 7 of the United Nations Charter were adopted. For in that case Portugal (even more than South Africa) would be forced by her own needs to cease giving active support to the Smith regime.

South Africa and Portugal are thus unable to give open support to Smith because they depend upon claims of legality to defend their own positions. There is thus a weakness in the racialist Southern African front, which could be exploited by the forces of justice. And it is, in fact, this same question of legality which makes it imperative for Britain and the West generally to use this weakness and to defeat Smith and white domination in Southern Rhodesia.

Successive Western governments have declared their hostility to apartheid, and their adherence to the principles of racial equality. They have frequently made verbal declarations of their sympathy with the forces in opposition to South African policies. But they have excused their failure to act in support of their words, on the grounds of South Africa's sovereignty. Africa has shown a great deal of skepticism about this argument, believing that it masked a reluctance to intervene on the side of justice when white privilege was involved. Now, in the case of Southern Rhodesia, legality is on the side of intervention. What is the West going to do? Will it justify or confound African suspicions?

So far the West has demonstrated its intentions by the gradual increase of voluntary economic sanctions; there has been a refusal even to challenge South African and Portuguese support for Smith by making sanctions mandatory upon all members of the United Nations. And there have been repeated statements by the responsible authority that force will not be used except in case of a breakdown in law and order - which apparently does not cover the illegal seizure of power! What happens if the economic sanctions fail to bring down the Smith regime is left vague. The suggestion therefore remains that, despite legality, and despite the protestations of belief in human equality, the domination of a white minority over blacks is acceptable to the West.

WHAT DOES AFRICA REQUIRE IN SOUTHERN RHODESIA?

This suspicion about the sincerity of the West can only be eliminated by the defeat of the Smith regime, and a new start being made on the path to majority rule before independence. It would not be enough for Smith to resign and a different 'more liberal,' white dominated, independent government to be legally established. If Britain and her allies, with the support of Africa, defeat of Smith, then the minimum requirement must be the re-establishment of effective British authority, and an interim government, which is charged with the task of leading the colony to majority rule. This will inevitably require the presence of British civil servants and British troops - or, better still, United Nations administrators and forces. Experience in South Africa, and in Southern Rhodesia itself, makes it absurd for anyone to expect Africa to trust Rhodesian whites (even under nominal British sovereignty) with the task of effecting the transition to majority rule.

It is important, too, that there should be a public declaration about the intentions in Southern Rhodesia. It must be made clear that there will be a rapid move (even if in stages) to majority rule, with safeguards for human rights, and after that - but only after that - independence for the colony. This public declaration is essential. Its absence has already caused major diplomatic difficulties between Britain and Africa, because it leaves open the possibility of a simple return to the pre-UDI status quo in Rhodesia.

It is true that such a declaration would be opposed by South Africa and Portugal, and that the Rhodesian whites would be bitterly hostile. But this is what the present crisis is all about; is Southern Rhodesia to become a nation of equal citizens or is it to become an outpost of white racialism? The fears of Southern Rhodesia's minorities have been dealt with by the many assurances given by Britain about the transitional period after the rebellion comes to an end. It is now time to consider the fears of the African majority, both inside the country and elsewhere in the continent. It is time, in other words, for Britain and the United States of America to make clear whether they really believe in the principles they claim to espouse, or whether their policies are governed by considerations of the privileges of their 'kith and kin.'

By its unilateral declaration of independence, Southern Rhodesia has come out openly in support of racialism in Africa. The rest of Africa cannot, for the sake of its own future, acquiesce in this. But circumstances have meant that Southern Rhodesia's action is also a challenge to Britain and to the West generally. Their future relations with Africa and Africa's future attitude to them, depend upon this challenge being answered effectively. At present the world is willing to support them in meeting this challenge; for once no complications of the 'Cold War' or the 'International Communist Menace' enter into the problem. But if the West fails to bring down Smith, or having defeated him, fails to establish conditions, which will lead to majority rule before independence, then Africa will have to take up the challenge. In that case there will be no question of a transition to majority rule. And Africa's economic and military weakness means that she would have to find allies. It is worth considering whether, if that happens, it will then still be true to say that the Cold War does not enter into the situation, and that the 'Communist Bogey' is a nonsensical red herring.

It is vital that Africa's legitimate concern in this matter should be recognized. For each sovereign African nation has had to overcome the power of racialism in order to become independent. It is, to us, the ultimate horror. We can never surrender to it, or allow it to continue unchallenged on the African continent. Our own future is too much involved.

But the United States, Britain, and all other countries of the world are also involved in the issue of racialism. Smith has thrown a challenge at the world, and particularly at the Western powers. He has thrown it on behalf of the whole of Southern Africa. Free Africa is now waiting, with some impatience, to see whether the West really intends to stand on the side of human equality and human freedom.[14]

Smith's intransigence left no room for negotiations and served as a catalyst in the liberation struggle, igniting guerrilla warfare. Although the white minority regime continued to get steadfast support from South Africa, its survival also depended on other countries, including most Western nations - among them, Britain and the United States - which deliberately ignored the economic embargo imposed on Rhodesia by the United Nations. They continued to trade with Rhodesia, and even more so with apartheid South Africa where they had substantial investments. But guerrilla war began to have a significant impact on Rhodesia as time went on.

The war was mostly fought by the Zimbabwe African National Union - ZANLA (Zimbabwe African National Union Liberation Army) - guerrillas who first penetrated Rhodesia in 1966 and intensified their insurgency in 1972, launching attacks from Mozambique where they worked together with FRELIMO forces. FRELIMO was waging its own war against the Portuguese colonial rulers, but the campaign was an integral part of a wider struggle to free all the countries in southern Africa still under white minority rule.

Comprehensive economic sanctions, made mandatory by the United Nations in 1968, did not have the desired impact but continued to be advocated by a number of countries - including almost all African countries, even though quite a few of them such as Malawi, Ivory Coast, Congo-Kinshasa (renamed Zaire in 1971), Liberia and others continued to trade and maintain other ties with

South Africa, Rhodesia's strongest supporter on the continent; by trading with the apartheid regime, they therefore also indirectly traded - and sometimes directly - with and helped sustain the white minority regime in Rhodesia. On March 2, 1970, Rhodesia became a republic, but no other country, besides itself, accorded it official recognition. After Robert Mugabe was released from Gwelo prison in 1974 where he spent more than 10 years for his political activities fighting against racial injustice, he assumed the leadership of ZANU, replacing Reverend Ndabaningi Sithole, and intensified the armed struggle from bases in Mozambique.

The war had an impact on the white minority regime in Rhodesia whose South African and American allies urged rebel Prime Minister Smith to seek a negotiated a settlement to the conflict. After a meeting with American Secretary of State Henry Kissinger in Pretoria, South Africa, in September 1976, Smith announced that he had agreed to majority rule, and that it would be achieved within two years. It was a shocking revelation to his white supporters in Rhodesia and elsewhere; and a major concession by a leader who had only in March the same year vowed that there shall be no black majority rule in Rhodesia, not even "in a thousand years."

Following Smith's announcement, arrangements were made for Rhodesia's main African leaders to attend a conference in Geneva, Switzerland, on the future of their country. The conference was attended by Robert Mugabe, leader of ZANU; Joshua Nkomo of ZAPU; Ndabaningi Sithole, also of ZANU, but separate from the more militant breakaway ZANU led by Mugabe which advocated intensified guerrilla warfare; and Bishop Abel Muzorewa, leader of the African National Congress (ANC). Each led his own delegation to the conference. But after some negotiations, ZANU and ZAPU agreed to form an alliance, called the Patriotic Front, in order to present a united front against Smith at the talks in Geneva and afterwards on the battlefield if the conference failed to resolve the Rhodesian crisis.

After many weeks, the delegates failed to agree on the schedule for independence on the basis of majority rule. Muzorewa and Sithole ended their exile and returned to Salisbury - obviously to pursue their own secret deals with Smith - while the more militant leaders, Mugabe and Nkomo, continued to live in exile in neighboring countries: Nkomo in Zambia, and Mugabe in Mozambique and Tanzania.

Another attempt was made by Britain and the United States to resolve the Rhodesian crisis, and in mid-1977, British Foreign Secretary David Owen and the American ambassador to the United Nations, Andrew Young, presented the new proposals to Smith. The proposals were supposed to be a dynamic compromise intended to end the impasse and satisfy both sides. They called for a six-month interim period in which a British-appointed commissioner would assume full control of Rhodesia; a new national army would be created out of an integrated pool of the Rhodesian forces and guerrilla armies; all whites' property rights would be guaranteed; and whites would virtually be given veto power under a power-sharing compromise which would guarantee them a disproportionate influence over any decision by the coalition government, far in excess of their numbers in the total population. Thus, national policy would be formulated on the basis of bi-racial consensus, and not on majority basis.

It was an unacceptable formula to the African nationalists, and the war continued, as did white emigration and deterioration of the economy because of the conflict. In December 1977, Smith decided to reach an "internal settlement" to stop the downward spiral which threatened to spin out of control. He started to negotiate with Muzorewa, Sithole, and Chief Jeremiah Chirau of the Zimbabwe United People's Organization (ZUPO), a group formed by government-appointed chiefs to preserve their interests and maintain the status quo. On March 3, 1978, they signed an agreement that outlined a new constitution and created a transitional government to rule until December 31 when Rhodesia would become "independent" on the basis of a compromise formula "embracing" Africans.

The African leaders - Muzorewa, Sithole, and Chirau - who signed the agreement constituted a trio, whose most influential member was Muzorewa of the United African National Council (UANC), in pursuit of their own version of majority rule, with the black majority assuming "power" on December 31, 1978. And the signatories, including Smith, constituted the Executive Council with rotating chairmanship. But Smith retained the title of prime minister. The head of the UANC, Bishop Abel Muzorewa, joined

Smith's government, and blacks were named to each cabinet ministry, serving as co-ministers with the whites already holding these posts. Zimbabwe's nationalist leaders and African countries immediately denounced the compromise as a sell-out.

And it was from the beginning. The transitional government, headed by Smith, was to write a new constitution, which had to be approved by white voters. The Rhodesian Front, Smith's party representing white interests, had veto power in the coalition government. The three African leaders who signed the agreement - Muzorewa, Sithole, and Chirau - agreed that whites would be automatically guaranteed 28 out of 100 seats in parliament under the new constitution, totally out of proportion with their numbers in the total population: 250,000 whites versus 6.5 million Africans by then; veto power exercised by members of the Rhodesian Front in the government, over any legislation, would last for at least 10 years; all white property and pension rights would be protected, regardless of how the property was acquired, and however inequitable the allocation of pension rights - Africans had virtually none; whites would continue to control the civil service, the police, the judiciary, and the armed forces; and Smith would remain prime minister during the transitional period.

The new transitional government offered amnesty to the Patriotic Front (PF) guerrillas of Mugabe and Nkomo, but was rejected, and the war intensified. There was also schism within the coalition government, and among its few - very few - African supporters outside the government. Muzorewa and Sithole blamed Smith and other Rhodesian Front members in the government for vetoing any proposal to improve the living conditions of Africans. Faced with the prospect of increasing guerrilla warfare, continued sanctions and the collapse of the internal settlement he reached with Muzorewa, Sithole, and Chrau; Smith made an ingenious attempt in August 1978 to split the Patriotic Front and invited Nkomo to join the transitional government.

Nkomo met Smith on August 14, 1978, in Lusaka, Zambia, encouraged by President Kaunda, and by Nigerian, British and American officials to do so. The leaders of Tanzania, Mozambique, Angola and Botswana - the other frontline states together with Zambia - were not informed of the meeting. Nor was

Mugabe, Nkomo's partner in the Patriotic Front. Mugabe, who was then in Nigeria, flew to Zambia the following week. He was accompanied by Nigeria's Foreign Minister Joseph Garba (he died in 2002) who told him on the way that a meeting between Smith and Nkomo had taken place in Lusaka, and another one was going on in the same city. Feeling betrayed, Mugabe was angry and refused to negotiate with Smith secretly. The secret talks had also been held without the knowledge or approval of the Rhodesian Front members - Smith's colleagues - in the transitional government.

Just a few days before the secret meeting was revealed to the public, a civilian plane of Air Rhodesia was shot down. ZAPU guerrillas claimed responsibility. At least 48 people were killed, inflaming passions among whites, and dashing any hope that the secret talks held in Lusaka between Smith and Nkomo may bear fruit. In response to this, Smith launched sustained large-scale incursions into Mozambique and Zambia to destroy guerrilla bases and refugee camps, killing many innocent civilians as well.

The attacks on guerrilla bases and refugee camps only fueled the conflict as Rhodesia approached "independence" scheduled for December 31, 1978. And the transitional government was compelled to postpone elections until the third week of April because of intensified guerrilla activities, yet with no sign of de-escalation in the coming months. Also, all the three African members of the Executive Council who had signed the agreement with Smith to form a transitional government - Muzorewa, Sithole, and Chirau - were rapidly losing whatever support they had among their people because of their inability to help improve the condition of the masses. And in reality, the token leadership of the three African leaders in a government dominated by whites could not claim legitimacy without electoral mandate.

In late January 1978, the new constitution written by the white-dominated parliament and government was submitted for approval in a referendum in which only white registered voters - 90,000 in total - participated. The constitution also had another concession for whites. The country after "independence" would be renamed Zimbabwe-Rhodesia, instead of just Zimbabwe as previously agreed upon, at the insistence of the three African leaders who had now lost another battle to Smith who insisted on using the double name. About 70 percent of the white voters participated in the referendum on the new constitution, which received 85 percent approval. Africans - 6.5 million of them - had absolutely no say in approving the constitution, in spite of the fact that they constituted the vast majority of the total population. The referendum was held on January 30, as Rhodesia continued to be hit by guerrilla attacks, and the economy continued to deteriorate.

The elections for the new parliament in 1978 lasted for four days, from April 17 - 21, and were won by Bishop Abel Muzorewa's UANC, amidst tight security provided by 100,000 men under arms, mobilized by the government as a safeguard against possible disruptions by guerrilla fighters. The biggest loser was Ndabaningi Sithole, the most well known African leader living in the country at that time. He expected to win the elections and, only a few days before they were conducted, hailed them as "a great democratic experiment." But after he lost, he denounced them as "one big cheat." And the British All-Party Parliamentary Committee on Human Rights issued a searing verdict on the elections. In its report, the group said the elections were "a gigantic confidence trick," marred by intimidation and death threats against anyone who urged people not to vote. The elections were not democratic as the government claimed, and on April 29, the UN Security Council condemned them as illegal. It also called for continued sanctions but France, Britain and the United States abstained from the vote. Yet, four days later, the American permanent representative to the United Nations, Andrew Young, denounced the elections and said they were "rigged."

On May 29, 1979, Bishop Abel Muzorewa became the country's first black prime minister, and he tried to get the sanctions lifted and his country recognized as a legal sovereign entity, since he claimed to have the electoral mandate to rule, given to him by the majority of the African voters. About 1.7 million Africans voted for the first time, giving 51 parliamentary seats to Muzorewa's UANC. But Muzorewa did not have any credentials as a freedom fighter or true African nationalist, and was considered to be an accommodationist at best, compromising on the principles of genuine racial equality and helping whites retain their privileged status. The guerrilla fighters and other Africans, inside and outside Rhodesia, considered him to be a traitor. And the war continued with the full support of African countries including Tanzania, the headquarters of the OAU Liberation Committee and all the liberation movements.

In early May, not long after the election, Mugabe and Nkomo held a three-day meeting in Addis Ababa, Ethiopia, and agreed to establish a joint military command for their guerrilla armies under the umbrella of the Patriotic Front. But they also rejected a proposal by some of the frontline states that they form a provisional government, which would be recognized by them and other African countries, as well as by others around the world. The two leaders refused to form such a government, not because they were opposed to the idea as a matter of principle, but because they and their organizations - ZANU and ZAPU - were not prepared to form a genuine coalition transcending personality and ideological differences.

The Zimbabwe crisis was not yet resolved and, in August 1979, the Commonwealth conference held in Lusaka, Zambia, attempted to help all the parties involved reach a final settlement. Nyerere, Kaunda, and British Prime Minister Margaret Thatcher had intense discussions in Lusaka and reached a consensus on holding another meeting in London in May the same year, attended by all the parties to the conflict. The compromise agreement reached by the three leaders was endorsed and signed by all 39 members of the Commonwealth.

The talks did not begin until September 10, 1979, under the chairmanship of British Foreign Minister Lord Carrington at Lancaster House in London. They were attended by Ian Smith, Abel Muzorewa, Robert Mugabe, Joshua Nkomo, Ndabaningi Sithole and other Zimbabwean leaders. After three-and-a-half months of tough negotiations, the leaders reached a compromise and signed the Lancaster House Agreement on December 17, 1979. It was agreed that independence would be achieved in stages. On December 21, Muzorewa and the guerrilla leaders signed a peace agreement, and a cease-fire went into effect on December 28.

In addition to the cease-fire, the implementation phase of the Lancaster House Agreement included free elections, formation of an African-majority government, and attainment of full sovereign status. In elections held from February 27 - 29, 1980, about 94 percent of Zimbabwe's black electorate of 2.9 million people voted. The results were announced on March 4, and the ZANU-Patriotic of Robert Mugabe won control of parliament with 57 of the 80 seats reserved for blacks. Mugabe's victory surprised many observers, but was well-deserved, since it was his ZANU guerrilla fighters who did most of the fighting - as the MPLA did in Angola - and therefore played the most critical role in compelling Smith to make meaningful concessions at Lancaster House.

Mugabe won 63 percent of the vote, about the same as Nelson Mandela did in South Africa's first multiracial democratic elections in April 1994 when he won 62 percent of the vote. Joshua Nkomo's ZAPU-PF won 24 percent of the vote, and 20 seats, mostly in his home region of Matebeleland in southwestern Zimbabwe, just as Mugabe did in his ethnic stronghold of Mashonaland which is also the largest with about 80 percent of the country's population. Bishop Abel Muzorewa captured 3 seats, and none of the smaller African parties won any.

On April 18, 1980, Zimbabwe became independent and Robert Mugabe its first truly elected leader, with the title prime minister, and held that title until December 31, 1987, when he became president. After the country won independence, Mugabe formed a coalition government which included his main rival, Joshua Nkomo, whose party ZANU-PF was predominantly Ndebele, the country's second largest ethnic group constituting about 20 percent of the total population; Mugabe's ZANU-PF was equally dominated by members of his tribe, the Shona. Nkomo became minister for home affairs in the coalition government, but security forces were kept under Mugabe's - and ZANU-PF's - control. And two other ZAPU men were also included in the government, assigned minor ministerial posts. Whites were also represented in the cabinet: David Smith was appointed minister of commerce and industry, and Dennis Norman, minister of agriculture.

Mugabe's coalition government was just one aspect of his commitment to reconciliation in order to achieve and maintain national unity across racial and ethnic lines. He left the economic structures intact, instead of restructuring them to conform to his socialist vision. He left whites in management positions, and many of them decided to stay. One of his biggest problems was the resettlement of about one million refugees who had fled to neighboring countries during the liberation war, and the reintegration of the guerrilla fighters into the mainstream of society but who remained in their camps until the economy could absorb them. Many people expected an exodus of whites after blacks took control of the country, but the emigration rate was far lower than had been predicted. Those who left, mainly because they just did not want to live under a black government settled in apartheid South Africa more than anywhere else.

But despite President Mugabe's continued assurances of protection, promising whites that he would not seek retribution for the racial injustices perpetrated against blacks during white rule, many of them continued to leave in large numbers. At independence, Zimbabwe had about 250,000 whites, mostly British. Between 1980 and 1984 alone, more than 100,000 emigrated, mostly to predominantly white countries: Britain, Australia, New Zealand, the United States, Canada, continental Europe, as well as neighboring South Africa where the apartheid regime was still in power and assured the new arrivals of protection, guaranteeing them a privileged position over blacks and other non-whites.

By early 2002, the white population of Zimbabwe had dropped to 60,000, with further emigration prompted by the seizure of white-owned farms by Mugabe's government in his campaign to redistribute land to landless blacks in a country he had ruled for 22 years. In March 2002, he won another six-year term in a controversial election some observers considered to be seriously flawed. In the same month, Zimbabwe was suspended from the Commonwealth for one year, although Britain and other countries did not demand the same action when the government of President Frederick Chiluba of Zambia, Zimbabwe's neighbor, rigged the election in December 2001 in favor of its candidate Levi Mwanawasa who succeeded Chiluba in spite of the fact that he won a mere 29 percent of the vote; or when other Commonwealth members had perpetrated the same injustice through the years; leading to the inevitable conclusion that the only reason why Britain and other European countries and even the United States were so determined to punish Mugabe for disregarding the rule of law - rigging elections and unleashing violences against white farmers and their black workers, and against government opponents although the opposition also used violence, sometimes in retaliation or preemptively - was because of the large number of whites in Zimbabwe whose farms were being seized by the government for redistribution to landless blacks.

And it is a plausible argument. But it should not in any way be misconstrued as an endorsement of violence perpetrated by the government of President Robert Mugabe and his supporters against his opponents in the Movement for Democratic Change (MDC) led by Morgan Tsivangirai, and other government critics, while condemning the opposition for using the same tactics. Both should be equally condemned when they deserve condemnation. But it is also true that the same kind of conduct has been deliberately overlooked by Britain in other African countries and elsewhere who are also members of the Commonwealth, as much as it has been by other European countries. Military rule, rigged elections, systematic violence and other abuses of power by governments in Nigeria, Sierra Leone, Ghana, Malawi, Kenya - including ethnic cleansing instigated by President Daniel Arap Moi's government - through the years, did not lead to the suspension of any of these countries from the Commonwealth. And none of these countries, except Kenya, has a significant white population; a factor that should not be overlooked in Zimbabwe's suspension from the Comonwealth.

It is also not insignificant that among all these countries - and they are only a few examples - it is Kenya, a country with a large number of whites probably no fewer than 40,000 and mostly British, which was threatened the most with severe economic sanctions through the years, especially in the 1990s, because of corruption, economic mismanagement, and suffocation of dissent. Yet Nigeria, for example, was no better off than Kenya in all those areas, but has never had a large number of whites like Kenya. And she has plenty of oil, of course. Both factors have helped insulate her from severe condemnation by Britain, let alone expulsion from the Commonwealth; attempts to expel her during Sani Abacha's brutal dictatorship in the 1990s failed largely because of British intervention on Nigeria's behalf, thanks to oil. Other predominantly white nations, including the United States, have also soft-pedaled on Nigeria, while coming down hard on Zimbabwe.

Therefore, race is a prime factor in the equation. In fact, the countries which called for sanctions against Zimbabwe - including Britain, Australia, the United States, Germany, and France, among others - are the very same ones which opposed sanctions against apartheid South Africa. And one can't help but wonder whether they would have been just as vocal, if at all, in their condemnation had the people whose land was being taken away by Mugabe's government were black. Would they really have been just as concerned, anymore than they were about the plight of black victims groaning under brutal dictatorship, dying from persecution and in civil wars, and suffering from other scourges, in a number of African countries? As John Kamau, a Kenyan editor, stated in his article, "Anti-Mugabe Sanctions Hypocritical," in the *Daily Nation*:

Somebody should find a better reason for isolating Mugabe. Nobody should tell us it has anything to do with democracy. For if it had anything to do with good governance, virtually all countries in this part of Africa would be under European Union (EU) sanctions. And so the question remains: Why Zimbabwe, and not Uganda or Zambia, which also have a mockery of democratic regimes. Why not Kenya?

Most of us are wondering why the EU is shedding tears on the future of Zimbabwe. The recent elections (in January 2002) in Zambia were a total sham. Uganda's election last year was anything but democratic. We don't need a political scientist to tell us what constitutes free and fair elections and none of these states can masquerade to be democracies. And that is the reason we have to be blunt. The Zimbabwe row with Western states is about land ownership by whites and the methods Dr. Mugabe's government is using to address this land inequity.

To be frank, nobody in the West has ever cared how Africans vote or who leads what country as long as Western interests are not in jeopardy. Haven't we had Idi Amin Dada, Jean-Bedel Bokassa, Marcius Nguema, Mobutu Sese Seko, Kamuzu Banda, Laurent Kabila and Siad Barre? An elementary student of history would tell you that these coconut heads were maintained by Western support.

This, however, is not to condone the kind of thuggery that ZANU-PF youths initiate in Harare in the name of protecting the government. Yet, again, Zimbabwe is not the only government, which unleashes such thugs. Just here in Nairobi, we have had the Youth for

Kanu '92, Operation Moi Wins, Jeshi la Mzee (Kiswahili meaning the Old Man's Army or Militia), and so on, and none of the European Union (EU) members even dreamt of imposing sanctions on the Kanu Government.

The so-called 'smart' sanctions (against Mugabe and his colleagues) are an indicator of how the West reacts when its interests are threatened and it exposes its double standards.

Fancy this: When our own Attorney-General threatened to bring a new media Bill that would have gagged the Press in this country, these paragons of Press freedom did not speak out as they did when Dr. Mugabe tried to do the same. Journalists in this region have been jailed, beaten, harassed and even denied access to information. But the regimes that sustain this machinery go scot-free with no threat of sanctions.

If we are to believe that the sanctions were initiated out of a desire to force a free and fair election, then there must be uniformity all over.

Zimbabwe's land inequity is real and not part of Mugabe's fertile imagination. Zimbabwe has a population of about 12 million people. Of these, 98 per cent are black while 0.8 are white. The rest are Asian Indians and people of mixed races. When you look at the land distribution pattern, you find around one million black families occupy 16.3 million hectares. Compare that with 4,000 white commercial farmers who occupy 11.2 million hectares!

That means that 70 per cent of the population farm the poorest of the soil and nobody wants Dr. Mugabe's government to speak on the issue. No country, however democratic, would allow 50 per cent of its land to be occupied by a minority group that is less than one per cent of the population. The principles of natural justice demand that such inequity be addressed as fast as possible.

We all have to understand that the current crisis has its roots in Britain's racist colonial policies, and the fact that after Zimbabwe got its new constitution, it was left with colonial laws to work with. By throwing their support to white farmers, the Western nations have shown their tail!

The EU had better look again at the terms of the Lancaster House Conference on Zimbabwe. White farmers were given up to 1990 to develop their land or hand it over to the government. All those farmers who owned land that abutted communal lands were asked to dispose of it. It was written very clearly that after 1990, the Zimbabwe Government had a right to nationalise all lands that had not been disposed of or developed. Any time President Mugabe raised the issue of land and quoted that document, the white farmers cried sabotage. Mugabe led his troops and fought Ian Smith to get back this land. Should he go to the grave without fulfilling that ambition?

According to the Western media, sanctions were imposed on Zimbabwe because Mugabe is 'clinging to power.' Now, which president in Africa is not 'clinging to power'?

The monopolisation of Zimbabwe's best land question must be addressed. And the Movement for Democratic Change leader, Morgan Tsavingirai, the man the Western media says poses the greatest danger to Mugabe's presidency (which I doubt), must come out with a clear land policy. Land, he will quickly learn, is central to African politics and any politician who masquerades otherwise and dangles IMF statistics on inflation to the electorate without promising land would lose hands down. Which is why Tsavingirai could not even win a parliamentary seat!

This brings me back to the sanctions. We have to acknowledge that Zimbabwe has little capital to buy the land and there were cumbersome legal procedures required by Britain during the independence negotiations. With the sanctions in place, Mugabe will have free rein and will conclude the resettlement in his own way, which will be bad for the country's economy. The interests of white farmers cannot be allowed to overshadow the legitimate cry of the impoverished and landless majority in post-colonial Zimbabwe. No economy is worth talking about if it is built on grave injustice.[15]

John Kamau's sentiment was echoed in other African quarters, including neighboring Tanzania. What infuriated many Africans across the continent and elsewhere, prompting them to rally behind President Mugabe, was that his critics in the West and other parts of the world, but especially in the West, ignored the suffering of the Africans in Zimbabwe since the advent of colonial rule and the legacy of inequality they inherited and which continues to exist in the post-colonial era. They demonized Mugabe, gave the whites under siege ample coverage, focusing on their suffering, while paying little attention to the racial injustices perpetrated by whites against the African majority. As Reginald Mhango, a prominent Tanzanian journalist and managing editor of the *Guardian,* stated in March 2002 in an editorial, "Mugabe: Teaching White Rhodesians A Final Lesson or Two":

Robert Gabriel Mugabe, the man who in 1980, cut short white supremacist Ian Smith's 1,000 years prediction before blacks could rule themselves in Zimbabwe, the man who did what the British Government could not do; who restored the authority of the Queen of England over Rhodesia, who rid Africa of one of a scandal when a tiny settler white minority unilaterally declared independence is now high on the cross, condemned for trying to right a wrong his ancestors paid with blood.

In reality and cruel irony, some of the...opposition leaders are very young men and women, whom 78-year-old Mzee Mugabe lost his prime years in prison and the bush to liberate.... The opposition has never mentioned, raised or discussed the record of barbarism that characterised successive white regimes....

Smith with his customary arrogance declared to the world that 'never in a thousand years' would Africans rule in Rhodesia.... That was when the Nyereres and the Kaundas vowed to fight and fight they did. Like Smith in Salisbury, Nyerere and Kaunda took the liberation of Zimbabwe as a crusade. Smith saw this and made no secret of his hatred of particularly Mwalimu Nyerere, whom he labeled the communist devil. That People's China, a close ally of Tanzania was arming and training Mugabe's Zanu-PF fighters was not lost on Smith. He hated both with equal intensity....

In parliament, to which he was a member, Smith did little to hide his contempt for Mugabe and Nyerere. Mugabe too, saw his party's victory (just before independence in April 1980) as a sweet revenge on Smith and his fellow Rhodesians, as he still refers them today, 22 years after Uhuru....

Smith...openly vowed that the day Mugabe the communist was bundled out of power would be his best lived. This is the scenario Mugabe sees as happening in Zimbabwe now. He does not believe that Smith and his fellow Rhodesians are not trying to make good their vow to live for the day when his so-called communist party and government are ousted from power. Smith's own speeches in London last year and even in Zimbabwe to that effect have not helped matters.

President Mugabe himself has been quoted as saying that he will only resign from the presidency after he has taught some Rhodesians a lesson or two.[16]

His determination to win the presidential election in March 2002 showed that he still was not done teaching them a lesson. He felt that he needed years to do so, although with tragic consequences for the country - starvation, death, economic destruction - because of the way he implemented the land reform program, good intentions notwithstanding. There was need for land redistribution, but not the way it was done. It should have been done in an orderly way without violence, farm "invasions," and without disrupting the economy.

The people Mugabe tried to help are the very same ones who suffered the most. They were the most vulnerable. And many of them starved, while others - including farm workers - were attacked by his supporters. Yet, he remained an icon of African liberation across the continent. Even many of his critics still admired him because of what he did to liberate Zimbabwe and the role he played in helping liberate the rest of southern Africa, including South Africa itself, the citadel of white supremacy on the continent. But to many suffering Zimbabweans, he became a villain because of the devastation wrought as a result of his fast-track land reform program which disrupted the economy and spawned violence across the country, forcing many people to flee their homes and seek refuge in South Africa and elsewhere, only to be turned back in large number by their powerful southern neighbor, where there were also strong anti-foreign sentiments especially against fellow Africans from other parts of the continent who were accused of taking jobs away from black South Africans.

And in spite of the strong opposition he faced, Mugabe claimed victory in the presidential election he saw as a struggle between the forces of change, of which he was the embodiment, and those determined to perpetuate racial inequalities at the expense of the African majority for whom he fought so hard to liberate. He also reminded friends and foes alike that he went to prison for that. He also went to war, and won.

Much as many people condemned Mugabe, hardly any cared to construct a proportional perspective on the land crisis in Zimbabwe and on the nature of the opposition. Such bias and deliberate distortion of truth did little to facilitate a settlement of the crisis but, instead, only helped fuel the conflict. The balance sheet was clear. The government did unleash violence against its opponents and even against innocent civilians, including women and children. Mugabe's supporters must admit that. But violence also came from the other side. Mugabe's opponents must admit that. The opposition members were not innocent bystanders as they portrayed themselves to be, when they paraded themselves before the international media most of whose reporters focused on the plight of white farmers and Mugabe's opponents more than anything else.

Mugabe's opponents, even if on a smaller scale than what the government did, also used violence as a political weapon, and not always in self-defence as some of them claimed. They launched pre-emptive strikes. They blamed the government for all the violence across the country to make it look bad before the whole world in order to isolate it and bring it down. And they initiated violence in many cases themselves, yet denied their involvement as the culprits in these brutal attacks as if they were mere victims or some kind of saints singing hymns of martyrdom while they were being forcibly marched to their graves by Mugabe's storm troopers; all this in spite of Morgan Tsvangirai's own proclamation to the world before television cameras - broadcast by the BBC and other media - that "We are going to take violence to their doorsteps."

Also, a disproportionately large number of the people who bankrolled the opposition Movement for Democratic Change (MDC), led by Morgan Tsvangirai, were hardcore racists who couldn't have cared less if Africans were denied democratic rights, lived in anarchy, or even if the entire black population of Zimbabwe starved to death. These were the very same people who helped perpetuate white minority rule and were some of the staunchest supporters of the previous regime headed by Ian Smith. Many of them were also members of the notorious Rhodesian security forces who were responsible for brutal attacks, torture, and indiscriminate killings of countless innocent civilians in African villages during the halcyon days of white minority rule they now remembered with nostalgia, some of them even with tears in their eyes. The contrast is obvious. To Africans, those were *not* the good old days. As Malcolm X used to say, "A white man's heaven is a black man's hell."

And in spite of all the achievements under Robert Mugabe, few people cared to talk about that and give credit where credit is due. Instead, Mugabe's critics were busy compiling a catalogue of his evil deeds - many of them a litany of lies - as if he had done nothing good for the people in more than 20 years he had been in power. Yet here was a leader who did more for his people than all the previous colonial governments had since the conquest of Zimbabwe by white settlers - led by Cecil Rhodes and his fellow imperialists of the British South African Company he headed - from South Africa and Britain more than 100 years ago in the 1890s. They did nothing for blacks, except steal their land, rape, kill and exploit them.

Nothing is going to be solved unless the entire matter is put in its proper historical perspective. Many may say, all that is history. It is true, it is history. But the past is also the present. There is no present without the past. It is also a warning to others. The writing is on the wall. Next will be South Africa, and even Namibia, but especially South Africa where millions of whites enjoy a privileged life style at the expense of blacks, and occupy most of the fertile land at the expense of blacks even after the end of apartheid. If whites in neighboring South Africa can't see this, then they will have a rude awakening. As one prominent black South African leader ominously warned in 2001, what is going to happen in South Africa is going to make Zimbabwe's conflict look like a picnic. History is *not* being re-written. Only historical injustices are being corrected. Therefore the past is part of the solution. As George Shire, a Zimbabwe liberation war veteran and an academic working for the Zimbabwe Open University, stated in his article, "The Struggle for Our Land: Britain is Interfering in Zimbabwe in Support of Corporate Power and A Wealthy White Minority," in *The Guardian*:

The crisis currently gripping Zimbabwe has its roots in Britain's racist colonial policies, the refusal of a previous Labour government to act against the dictatorship of the white minority and the failure of Britain to stick to its promises after my people finally won independence 20 years ago. But instead of acknowledging their own responsibilities and helping overcome the legacy of the past, the British government and media - and their friends in the white Commonwealth - are fostering a flagrantly partisan mythology about the conflict in the country, while intervening in support of a privileged white minority and international commercial interests.

Take the continued white monopolisation of Zimbabwe's best land, which is at the heart of the upheavals and is routinely presented in Britain as a spurious pretext to keep a despot in power. In reality, the unequal distribution of land in Zimbabwe was one of the major factors that inspired the rural-based liberation war against white rule and has been a source of continual popular agitation ever since, as the Government struggled to find a consensual way to transfer land. My grandfather, Mhepo Mavakire, used to farm on land, which is now owned by a commercial farmer. It was forcibly taken from the family after the Second World War and handed to a white man. Many of my relatives died during the Zimbabwean liberation war, trying to reclaim this land. I joined ZANU-PF, which played the central role in the war, in the late 60s and there was never any doubt in my mind that it was both a duty and an honour to fight for that land.

Land reform is now a socio-economic and political imperative in Zimbabwe. The land distribution program of President Mugabe's ZANU-PF Government is aimed at redressing gross inequalities to meet the needs of the landless, the smallholders who want to venture into small-scale commercial farming and indigenous citizens who have the resources to go into large-scale commercial agriculture. These are modest but worthwhile objectives.

The Western-backed Movement for Democratic Change opposition, by contrast, is very reluctant to be drawn on how it would resolve the land question. Although middle England continues to be fed the tale that nothing was done about land until MDC began to challenge ZANU-PF's power base, the truth is that the white-dominated Commercial Farmers Union (CFU) has fought the Government's strategy for land distribution at every stage since the 80s. The CFU and members of the defunct Rhodesia Front, strongly represented in the MDC, could not care less who governs Zimbabwe as long as they keep the land and continue to live in the style to which they have become accustomed. The lack of money for land acquisition, cumbersome legal procedures required by Britain in the independence negotiations and the withdrawal of international donors in recent years - as well as the explosive political restiveness and farm occupations - have all combined to force the Zimbabwean Government to speed up resettlement.

But of course a process of land acquisition and resettlement of indigenous landless people cuts across the networks that link the farmers, the producers of agricultural inputs, the banks and insurance houses, all dominated by the white minority. And this network also spreads into the international capital arena. Many Zimbabweans believe that the interests of this white network have been allowed to overshadow the morally legitimate cry of the impoverished and landless majority in post-colonial Zimbabwe.

While I unreservedly condemn all form of political violence and criminality that have come to dominate the contemporary political culture of Zimbabwe, violence is, in fact, being perpetrated by people with links to both sides of the political divide.

In the last couple of weeks alone (January 2002), three people have been killed by MDC supporters, who also went on a rampage in Harare, petrol-bombing shops belonging to ZANU-PF supporters. Senior MDC figures have been implicated in the murder of a ZANU-PF official, Gibson Masarira, who was hacked to death in front of his family. And in Kwekwe, suspected MDC supporters burnt three ZANU-PF officials' houses. None of these events has been reported in the British media. Such MDC violence echoes the activities of the Rhodesian police and notorious Selous Scouts in the late 70s - which is perhaps hardly surprising since several are now leading lights in the MDC.

It was the Selous Scouts who killed refugees, men, women and children at Nyadzonia, Chimoio, Tembue, Mkushi, Luangwa, and Solwezi, where they still lie buried in mass graves. David Coltart, an MDC MP for Bulawayo South, was a prominent member of the Rhodesian police and he and his bodyguard Simon Spooner - recently charged with the murder of Cain Nkala, leader of the war veterans in Matebeleland - were attached to the Selous Scouts. The deputy national security adviser for the MDC, who rose to the rank of sergeant in the Rhodesian police, was likewise a handler of Selous Scouts operatives while based in Bulawayo. Mike Orret, another MDC MP, was also a senior police officer.

You would never know from the way Zimbabwean politics is usually reported in Britain that ZANU-PF supports a broadly social democratic program, focused on the empowerment of the landless and poor, and is opposed by supporters of neo-liberal economic policies. Among ZANU-PF's often overlooked achievements is a massive expansion in education in the past 20 years - from one university to 14, and from a handful of secondary schools to hundreds of six-form colleges. Sadly, the enormous progress that had been made in public health has been reversed by the HIV/Aids pandemic, which is reducing life expectancy. Nevertheless, the Zimbabwean Government has constructed 456 health centers, 612 rural hospitals and 25 district hospitals, as well as providing one provincial hospital in each of the country's eight provinces. Eighty-five percent of Zimbabwe's population is now within eight kilometers of a health facility. The 25 percent coverage of immunisation at independence has now been boosted to 92 percent, while antenatal coverage has risen from 20 percent at independence to the present 89 percent.

The MDC has no corresponding program for mass public health or education, or rural electrification, or the economic empowerment of indigenous people. The MDC has remained silent when asked about what it will do with the more than 130,000 families who have been allocated land through the fast-track process if it wins the presidency. Incidentally, beneficiaries of this process include known members of MDC, not just 'friends and cronies' of president Robert Mugabe.

Contrary to the received wisdom in Britain, the best chance of completing the unfinished business of land reform, and for improvements in public services, housing, education, clean water, support for people living with illness and dying of Aids, lies with a President Mugabe victory in the presidential elections. The past few days of vigorous cross-party debate about the freedom of the press in Zimbabwe's parliament have shown what a vibrant democracy the country in fact has, with ZANU-PF reflecting a broad range of political allegiances. The longer-term challenge ZANU-PF faces is to rethink itself, in the new conditions its victory might help to bring about.[17]

Although some observers and countries said the March 2002 presidential election in Zimbabwe was deeply flawed, African countries including the Organization of African Unity (OAU) observer mission on the scene led by former Tanzanian ambassador Gertrude Mongella concluded that the election was free and fair, and Mugabe was the legitimate winner of the most bitterly contested election in Zimbabwe's history since independence. Mugabe also rose to power after one of the bloodiest conflicts in colonial history. The guerrilla war lasted for about 15 years from 1965 - 1979 (started by ZAPU in 1965, and by ZANU in 1966), and claimed tens of thousands of lives, mostly black - including soldiers from the Tanzania People's Defence Forces (TPDF), Tanzania's national army, who joined the freedom fighters on the battlefield, as they did in Mozambique and Angola - before the white minority regime capitulated to African might and made concessions at the Lancaster House conference which eventually led to independence on the basis of majority rule under the leadership of Robert Mugabe.

Tanzanian troops also intervened in the Seychelles in 1977 in support of revolutionary forces against an inept regime; and in 1982 saved the national government of that island nation from being overthrown by mercenaries from apartheid South Africa who, with the help of the South African security forces, captured Victoria airport in the nation's capital and largest town, Victoria. President Nyerere also sent Tanzanian soldiers to the Comoros to reinstate an elected president who had been overthrown in a military coup. Therefore Tanzania's military involvement in the liberation struggle in Zimbabwe and elsewhere in southern Africa and other parts of the continent - including the ouster of Idi Amin by Nyerere, freeing the people of Uganda from tyranny, while other African leaders looked the other way or quietly applauded the burly Ugandan dictator; Tanzanian military officers training Congo's national army under Presidents Laurent and Joseph Kabila; and, at his insistence, the imposition of economic sanctions on Burundi in the 1990s by East and Central African countries to compel the Tutsi-dominated regime to share power with the Hutu majority on meaningful basis - was in keeping with Nyerere's Pan-African commitment he had consistently maintained throughout his tenure as president of Tanzania and as one Africa's most influential statesmen who came to be known as "The Conscience of Africa"; a point also underscored by President Robert Mugabe when he paid glowing tribute to Nyerere at his funeral for the indispensable role Tanzania played in the liberation of Zimbabwe and the rest of southern Africa. He described Nyerere as "the revolutionary, the visionary, the principled, indomitable and unyielding supporter of the struggle for our own and the region's independence."

Mugabe also took stewardship of one of the most developed and richest countries on the continent. As President Julius Nyerere told him: "You have inherited one of the jewels of Africa. Kept it that way."

CHAPTER EIGHT:

TANZANIA RECOGNIZES BIAFRA

HE WAS a staunch supporter of African unity, and lived up to his commitment to this Pan-African ideal. He was the first East African leader to call for federation and even offered to delay independence for Tanganyika in order for the three East African countries of Kenya, Uganda, and Tanganyika to attain sovereign status on the same day and form an East African federation. He also engineered the first union of two independent states, Tanganyika and Zanzibar - and the only one on the entire continent - which led to the creation of Tanzania, one of the most stable and peaceful countries in Africa. Yet, under his leadership, Tanzania also was the first African country to recognize the secessionist region of Eastern Nigeria as the independent Republic of Biafra, a move his critics denounced as anti-Pan-African by one of the strongest advocates of African unity. Only three other African countries recognized Biafra. They were Ivory Coast, Zambia, and Gabon. And one non-African country, France, did so.

Yet, Nyerere's decision to recognize Biafra, which he himself admitted had been made with great reluctance, was based on moral grounds. The people of Eastern Nigeria, especially the Igbos, no longer felt secure within the Nigerian federation after tens of thousands of them had been massacred by their fellow countrymen, especially in Northern Nigeria, while the authorities did nothing to stop the pogroms. Therefore to protect themselves, they decided to withdraw from the federation and establish their own independent state.

Unity is based on the willingness of the people to be part of the union, and on the willingness of the government to be fair to all its citizens. A government which refuses to protect some of its citizens cannot claim to be fair and has abdicated its responsibility. Therefore the people who have been rejected have the right to choose the type of government they want to live under, and in their own independent state where they can be guaranteed protection and feel secure. That was the case for Biafra.

Critics of Biafra's secession tried to draw parallels between Biafra and Katanga. But there were fundamental differences between the two. The secession of Eastern Nigeria was in response to the pogroms in Northern Nigeria and other parts of the federation, but mostly in the north, which claimed and estimated 30,000 - 50,000 lives in about three months in 1966. It was not foreign-inspired to break up Nigeria. By contrast, Katanga's secession was engineered by Western powers to secure their political and financial interests by detaching the mineral-rich province from the rest of the Congo, which they feared could be ruled by a staunchly pro-African nationalist government that would threaten their interests. Moise Tshombe, the Katangese leader and Western puppet, was a traitor. Colonel Chukwuemeka Odumegwu Ojukwu, the Biafran leader, was an African patriot trying to save his people from oppression and possible extermination by other Nigerians who hated the Igbos, reminiscent of the plight of the Jews under Hitler in Nazi Germany. As one of the two most educated ethnic groups in Nigeria and one of the most business-oriented, together with the Yoruba in Western Region, they were being punished for being successful. Even a number of Nigerian leaders made that clear. As one representative in the regional legislature of Northern Nigeria, Mallam Muhammadu Mustapha Maude Gyari, emphatically stated in the February-March 1964 session:

> On the allocation of plots to the Ibos, or the allocation of stalls, I would like to advise the Minister that these people know how to make money and we do not know the way and manner of getting about this business.... We do not want Ibos to be allocated plots, I do not want them to be given plots.[1]

He was roundly applauded by other representatives in the Northern Regional Assembly, including the Northern Premier himself, Sir Ahmadu Bello, the Sardauna of Sokoto, who was also the most powerful man in the Nigerian federation. The federal government was controlled by northerners who dominated the federal legislature where the Northern People's Congress (NPC) had the majority of the seats. Half of them were occupied by northerners. The party was dominated by Ahmadu Bello who also controlled Federal Prime Minister Alhaj Sir Abubakar Tafawa Balewa, a fellow northerner and leader of the Northern People's Congress (NPC) in the Nigerian federal parliament.

And it is important to remember that the anti-Igbo sentiments in the Northern Regional Assembly in February-March 1964 were expressed almost two years before the Igbo-led military coup of January 15, 1966, which triggered the massacre of tens of thousands of Igbos and other Easterners in Northern Nigeria in the following months. The anti-Igbo venom spewed in the Northern Legislative Assembly had also been preceded by the massacre of hundreds of Igbos in Jos in 1945 and in Kano in 1953. Therefore, there was a history of anti-Igbo hysteria in Northern Nigeria, and even in other parts of the country, long before the 1966 military coup; a history which puts in proper perspective the secession of the Eastern Region as an inevitable response to the cumulative impact of Igbophobia on the people of Eastern Nigeria that had infected large segments of the federation. It is also in this context that Tanzania's recognition of Biafra should be looked at, in order to understand why the government of Tanzania reached this momentous decision. As President Julius Nyerere stated in recognizing Biafra:

The Declaration of Independence by Biafra on the 30th May, 1967 came after two military coups d'etat - January and July 1966 - and two pogroms against the Ibo people. These pogroms, which also took place in 1966, resulted in the death of about 30,000 men, women, and children, and made two million people flee from their homes in other parts of Nigeria to their tribal homeland in Eastern Nigeria. These events have been interspersed and followed by official discussions about a new constitution for Nigeria, and also by continued personal attacks on individual Ibos who have remained outside the Eastern Region.

The basic case for Biafra's secession from the Nigerian Federation is that people from the Eastern Region can no longer feel safe in other parts of the Federation. They are not accepted as citizens of Nigeria by other citizens of Nigeria. Not only is it impossible for Ibos and people of related tribes to live in assurance of personal safety if they work outside Biafra; it would also be impossible for any representative of these people to move freely and without fear in any other part of the Federation of Nigeria.

These fears are genuine and deep-seated; nor can anyone say

they are groundless. The rights and wrongs of the original coup d'etat, the rights and wrongs of the attitudes taken by different groups in the politics of pre- and post-coup Nigeria, are all irrelevant to the fear which the Ibo people feel.

And the people of Eastern Nigeria can point to too many bereaved homes, too many maimed people, for anyone to deny the reasonable grounds for their fears. It is these fears, which are the root cause both for the secession, and for the fanaticism with which the people of Eastern Nigeria have defended the country they declared to be independent. Fears such as now exist among the Ibo people, do not disappear because someone says they are unjustified, or says that the rest of Nigeria does not want to exterminate Ibos. Such words have even less effect when the speakers have made no attempt to bring the perpetrators of crimes to justice, and when troops under the control of the Federal Nigerian authorities continue to ill-treat, or allow others to ill-treat, any Ibo who comes within their power. The only way to remove the Easterners' fear is for the Nigerian authorities to accept its existence, to acknowledge the reason fir it, and then talk on terms of equality with those involved about the way forward.

When people have reason to be afraid you cannot reassure them through the barrel of a gun; your only hope is to talk as one man to another, or as one group to another. It is no use the Federal authorities demanding that the persecuted should come as a supplicant for mercy, by first renouncing their secession from the political unit. For the secession was declared because the Ibo people felt it to be there only defence against extermination. In their minds, therefore, a demand that they should renounce secession before talks begin is equivalent to a demand that they should announce their willingness to be exterminated. If they are wrong in this belief, they have to be convinced. And they can only be convinced by talks leading to new institutional arrangements, which take account of their fears.

The people of Biafra have announced their willingness to talk to the Nigerian authorities without any conditions. They cannot renounce their secession before talks, but they do not demand that Nigerians should recognize it; they ask for talks without conditions. But the Federal authorities have refused to talk except on the basis of Biafran surrender. And as the Biafrans believe they will be massacred if they surrender, the Federal authorities are really refusing to talk at all. For human beings do not voluntarily walk towards what they believe to be certain death. The Federal Government argues that in demanding the renunciation of secession before talks, and indeed in its entire 'police action,' it is defending the territorial integrity of Nigeria. On this ground it argues also that it has the right to demand support from all other governments, and especially other African governments. For every state, and every state authority, has a duty to defend the sovereignty and integrity of its nation; this is a central part of the function of a national government.

Africa accepts the validity of this point, for African states have more reason than most to fear the effects of disintegration. It is on these grounds that Africa has watched the massacre of tens of thousands of people, has watched millions being made into refugees, watched the employment of mercenaries by both sides in the current civil war, and has accepted repeated rebuffs of its offers to help by mediation or conciliation.

But for how long should this continue? Africa fought for freedom on the grounds of individual liberty and equality, and on the grounds that every people must have the right to determine for themselves the conditions under which they would be governed. We accepted the boundaries we inherited from colonialism, and within them we each worked out for ourselves the constitutional and other arrangements, which we felt to be appropriate to the most essential function of a state - that is the safeguarding of life and liberty for its inhabitants.

When the Federation of Nigeria became independent in 1960, the same policy was adopted by all its peoples. They accepted the Federal structure which had been established under the colonial system, and declared their intention to work together. Indeed, the Southern States of the Federation - which include Biafra - delayed their own demands for independence until the North was ready to join them. At the insistence of the North also, the original suggestion of the National Council of Nigeria and the Cameroons (NCNC) that Nigeria should be broken up into many small states with a strong center, was abandoned. The South accepted a structure, which virtually allowed the more populous North to dominate the rest.

But the constitution of the Federation of Nigeria was broken in January, 1966, by the first military coup. All hope of its resuscitation was removed by the second coup, and even more by the pogroms of September and October, 1966. These events altered the whole basis of the society; after them it was impossible for political and economic relations between the different parts of the old Federation to be restored. That meant that Nigerian unity could only be salvaged from the wreck of inter-tribal violence and fear by a constitution drawn up in the light of what happened, and which was generally acceptable to all the major elements of the society under the new circumstances. A completely new start had to be made, for the basis of the state had been dissolved in the complete breakdown of law and order, and the inter-tribal violence, which existed.

The necessity for a new start by agreement was accepted by a conference of military leaders from all parts of the Federation, in Aburi, Ghana, in January 1967. There is a certain difference of opinion about some of the things, which were agreed upon at the conference. But there is no dispute about the fact that everyone joined in a declaration renouncing the use of force as a means of settling the crisis in Nigeria. Nor does anyone dispute that it was agreed that a new constitution was to be worked out by agreement, and that in the meantime there would be a repeal of all military decrees issued since January 1966, which reduced the power of the Regions. There was also agreement about rehabilitation payments for those who had been forced to flee from their homes, and about members of the armed forces being stationed in their home Regions.

The Aburi Conference could have provided the new start, which was necessary if the unity of Nigeria was to be maintained. But before the end of the same month, Gowon was restating his commitment to the creation of new states, and his determination to oppose any form of confederation. And on the last day of January, the Federal military authorities were already giving administrative reasons for the delay in the implementation of the Agreements reached at Aburi. It was in the middle of March before a constitutional decree was issued which was supposed to regularize the position in accordance with the decisions taken there. But unfortunately this Decree also included a new clause - which had not been agreed upon - and which gave the Federal authorities reserved powers over the Regions, and thus completely nullified the whole operation. Nor had any payment been made by the Federal Government to back up the monetary commitment for rehabilitation, which it had accepted in the Ghana meeting.

In short, the necessity for an arrangement, which would take account of the fears created during 1966 was accepted at Aburi, and renounced thereafter by the Federal authorities. Yet they now claim to be defending the integrity of the country in which they failed to guarantee the most elementary safety of the twelve million people of Eastern Nigeria. These people had been massacred in other parts of Nigeria without the Federal authorities apparently having neither the will nor the power to protect them. When they retreated to their homeland they were expected to accept the domination of the same people who instigated, or allowed, their persecution in the country which they are being told is theirs - i.e., Nigeria.

Surely, when a whole people is rejected by the majority of the state in which they live, they must have the right to live under a different kind of arrangement which does secure their existence. States are made to serve people; governments are established to protect the citizens of a state against external enemies and internal wrongdoers.

It is on those grounds that people surrender their right and power of self-defence to the government of the state in which they live. But when the machinery of the state, and the powers of the government, are turned against a whole group of society on grounds of racial, tribal, or religious prejudice, then the victims have the right to take back the powers they have surrendered, and defend themselves.

For while people have a duty to defend the integrity of their state, and even to die in its defence, this duty stems from the fact that it is theirs, and that it is important to their well-being and to the future of their children. When the state ceases to stand for honour, the protection, and the well-being of all its citizens, then it is no longer the instrument of those it has rejected. In such a case the people have the right to create another instrument for their protection - in other words, to create another state. This right cannot be abrogated by constitutions, or by outsiders. The basis of statehood, and of unity can only be general acceptance by the participants. When more than twelve million people have become convinced that they are rejected, and that there is no longer any basis for unity between them and other groups of people, then that unity has ceased to exist. You cannot kill thousands of people, and keep on killing more, in the name of unity. There is no unity between the dead and those who killed them; and there is no unity in slavery or domination.

Africa needs unity. We need unity over the whole continent, and in the meantime we need unity within the existing states of Africa. It is a tragedy when we experience a setback to our goal of unity. But the basis of our need for unity, and the reason for our desire for it, is the greater well-being, and the greater security, of the people of Africa. Unity by conquest is impossible. It is not practicable; and even if military might could force the acceptance of a particular authority, the purpose of unity would have been destroyed. For the purpose of unity, its justification is the service of all the people who are united together. The general consent of all the people involved is the only basis on which unity in Africa can be maintained or extended.

The fact that the Federation of Nigeria was created in 1960 with the consent of all the people does not alter that fact. That Federation, and the basis of consent, has since been destroyed.

Nor is this the first time the world has seen a reduction in political unity. We have seen the creation of the Mali Federation, the creation of a union between Egypt and Syria, and the establishment of the Federation of Rhodesia and Nyasaland. And we have also seen the dissolution of all these attempts at unity, and the consequent recognition of the separate nations, which were once involved. The world has also seen the creation of India and Pakistan out of what was once the Indian Empire. We have all recognized both of these nation states and done our best to help them deal with the millions of people made homeless by the conflict and division. None of these things mean that we like these examples of greater disunity. They mean that we recognize that in all these cases the people are unwilling to remain in one political unit.

Tanzania recognizes Senegal, Mali, Egypt, Syria, Malawi, Zambia, Pakistan and India. What right have we to refuse, in the name of unity, to recognize Biafra? For years the people of that state struggled to maintain unity with the other people in the Federation of Nigeria; even after the pogroms of 1966 they tried to work out a new form of unity which would guarantee their safety; they have demonstrated by ten months of bitter fighting that they have decided upon a new political organization and are willing to defend it.

The world has taken it upon itself to utter many ill-informed criticisms of the Jews of Europe for going to their deaths without any concerted struggle. But out of sympathy for the suffering of these people, and in recognition of the world's failure to take action at the appropriate time, the United Nations established the state of Israel in a territory, which belonged to the Arabs for thousands of years. It was felt that only by the establishment of a Jewish homeland, and a Jewish national state, could Jews be expected to live in the world under conditions of human equality.

Tanzania has recognized the state of Israel and will continue to do so because of its belief that every people must have some place in the world where they are not liable to be rejected by their fellow citizens. But the Biafrans have now suffered the same kind of rejection within their state that the Jews of Germany experienced. Fortunately, they already had a homeland. They have retreated to it for their own protection, and for the same reason - after all other efforts had failed - they have declared it to be an independent state.

In the light of these circumstances, Tanzania feels obliged to recognize the setback to African unity, which has occurred. We therefore recognize the state of Biafra as an independent sovereign entity, and as a member of the community of nations. Only by this act of recognition can we remain true to our conviction that the purpose of society, and of all political organization, is the service of man.[2]

The preceding statement by President Julius Nyerere was

issued by the government of Tanzania on April 13, 1968, the day
Tanzania recognized Biafra. It was also published in the ruling-
party's (TANU's) daily newspaper, *The Nationalist*, whose editor
during that time was Benjamin Mkapa who later on became
president of Tanzania from 1995 - 2005, and the country's third
head of state since independence in 1961. The statement was also
published in another daily newspaper, the privately-owned
Standard, whose editorial staff I joined in June 1969 when I was a
19-year-old high school student in Form V (standard 13, what
Americans would call grade 13). They were also the country's two
major newspapers and some of the largest and most influential in
East Africa.

President Nyerere also explained Tanzania's position on
Biafra in another statement, which was substantively the same as
the preceding one, but with other nuances to his central argument.
The statement was published in a British newspaper, in a country
that was the biggest arms supplier to the Nigerian federal military
government during its war against Biafra, and which played a
critical role in sustaining the conflict and wreaking havoc across
the secessionist region, as much as Soviet-supplied MIGs flown by
Egyptian pilots did. As Nyerere stated in "Why We Recognised
Biafra," in *The Observer*, London, April 28, 1968:

Leaders of Tanzania have probably talked more about the need
for African unity than those of any other country. Giving formal
recognition to even greater disunity in Africa was therefore a very
difficult decision to make. Our reluctance to do so was compounded by
our understanding of the problems of unity - of which we have some
experience - and of the problems of Nigeria. For we have had very good
relations with the Federation of Nigeria, even to the extent that when we
needed help from Africa we asked it of the Federation.

But unity can only be based on the general consent of the people
involved. The people must feel that this state, or this nation, is theirs; and
they must be willing to have their quarrels in that context. Once a large
number of the people of any such political unit stop believing that the
state is theirs, and that the government is their instrument, then the unit is
no longer viable. It will not receive the loyalty of its citizens.

For the citizen's duty to serve, and if necessary to die for, his
country stems from the fact that it is his and that its government is the
instrument of himself and his fellow citizens. The duty stems, in other

words, from the common denominator of accepted statehood, and from the state government's responsibility to protect all the citizens and serve them all. For states, and governments, exist for men and for the service of man. They exist for the citizens' protection, their welfare, and the future well-being of their children. There is no other justification for states and governments except man.

In Nigeria this consciousness of a common citizenship was destroyed by the events of 1966, and in particular by the pogroms in which 30,000 Eastern Nigerians were murdered, many more injured, and about two million forced to flee from the North of their country. It is these pogroms, and the apparent inability or unwillingness of the authorities to protect the victims, which underlies the Easterners' conviction that they have been rejected by other Nigerians and abandoned by the Federal Government.

Whether the Easterners are correct in their belief that they have been rejected is a matter for argument. But they do have this belief. And if they are wrong, they have to be convinced that they are wrong. They will not convinced by being shot. Nor will their acceptance as part of the Federation be demonstrated by the use of Federal power to bomb schools and hospitals in the areas to which people have fled from persecution.

In Britain, in 1950, the Stone of Scone was stolen from Westminster Abbey by Scottish Nationalists while I was still a student at Edinburgh. That act did not represent a wish by the majority of the Scottish people to govern themselves. But if, for some peculiar reason, that vast majority of the Scottish people decided that Scotland should secede from the United Kingdom, would the Government in London order the bombing of Edinburgh, and in pursuing the Scots into the Highlands, kill the civilians they overtook? Certainly the Union Government would not do this; it would argue with the Scots, and try to reach some compromise.

As President of Tanzania it is my duty to safeguard the integrity of the United Republic. But if the mass of the people of Zanzibar should, without external manipulation, and for some reason of their own, decide that the Union was prejudicial to their existence, I could not advocate bombing them into submission. To do so would not be to defend the Union. The Union would have ceased to exist when the consent of its constituent members was withdrawn. I would certainly be one of those working hard to prevent secession, or to reduce its disintegrating effects. But I could not support a war on the people whom I have sworn to serve - especially not if the secession is preceded by a rejection of Zanzibarins by Tanganyikans.

Similarly, if we had succeeded in the 1963 attempt to form an

East African Federation, or if we should do so in the future, Tanzania would be overjoyed. But if at some time thereafter the vast majority of the people of any one of the countries should decide - and persist in a decision - to withdraw from the Federation, the other two countries could not wage war against the people who wished to secede. Such a decision would mark a failure by the Federation. That would be tragic; but it would not justify mass killings.

The Biafrans now feel that they cannot live under conditions of personal security in the present Nigerian Federation. As they were unable to achieve an agreement on a new form of association, they have therefore claimed the right to govern themselves. The Biafrans are not claiming the right to govern anyone else. They have not said that they must govern the Federation as the only way of protecting themselves. They have simply withdrawn their consent to the system under which they used to be governed.

Biafra is not now operating under the control of a democratic government, any more than Nigeria is. But the mass support for the establishment and defence of Biafra is obvious. This is not a case of a few leaders declaring secession for their own private glory. Indeed, by the Aburi Agreement the leaders of Biafra showed a greater reluctance to give up hope of some form of unity with Nigeria than the masses possessed. But the agreement was not implemented.

Tanzania would still like to see some form of co-operation or unity between all the peoples of Nigeria and Biafra. But whether this happens, to what extent, and in what fields, can only be decided by agreement among all the peoples involved. It is not for Tanzania to say.

We in this country believe that unity is vital for the future of Africa. But it must be a unity which serves the people, and which is freely determined upon by the people.

For 10 months we have accepted the Federal Government's legal right to our support in a 'police action to defend the integrity of the State.' On that basis we have watched a civil war result in the death of about 100,000 people, and the employment of mercenaries by both sides. We have watched the Federal Government reject the advice of Africa to talk instead of demanding surrender before talks could begin. Everything combined gradually to force us to the conclusion that Nigerian unity did not exist.

Tanzania deeply regrets that the will for unity in Nigeria has been destroyed over the past two years. But we are convinced that Nigerian unity cannot be maintained by force any more than unity in East Africa could be created by one state conquering another.

It seemed to us that by refusing to recognise the existence of

Biafra we were tacitly supporting a war against the people of Eastern Nigeria - and a war conducted in the name of unity. We could not continue doing this any longer.[3]

Although the Igbos made the most determined attempt to secede from Nigeria, they were not the first of Nigeria's main ethnic groups to demand secession. They were, in fact, the last. The first people who wanted to pull out of the federation were Northern Nigerians, for no apparent reason, other than the fact that their region was more backward in terms of education and economic development than the other two regions - East and West in the south - and therefore could not compete with the rest of the country for jobs and other opportunities on the basis of merit. As far back as 1950, Northerners argued that amalgamation of the North and the South was a "a big mistake," and that the country should return to the boundaries established in 1914 when the two parts were virtually different colonies in terms of administration. Each had its own, separate, colonial administration. And throughout the 1950s, they continued to make secessionist demands, now and then, and seriously threatened to withdraw from the federation unless independence was granted on their terms and the federal government was dominated by them. Southerners conceded, in order to save the federation from falling apart. Even as late as the sixties, a few years after independence, Northerners wanted to secede and, in fact, almost did, during the second military coup of July 1966 executed by Northern military officers who, with the full backing of Northern politicians and other leaders, almost dissolved the Nigerian federation and declared independence for the North.

Besides Northern Nigeria dominated by the Hausa-Fulani, the predominantly Yoruba region of Western Nigeria also threatened to secede in the 1950s. In August 1953 at the constitutional talks held in London on the future of Nigeria - to whom should power be transferred at independence - attended by Nigerian leaders from all three regions, the leader of Western Nigeria, Chief Obafemi Awolowo, threatened to pull his region out of the federation if Lagos, located in the West, was not incorporated into the Western Region. Lagos, the federal capital of Nigeria until the 1980s, had been designated as federal territory by the colonial authorities since its founding, and was therefore not under the jurisdiction of the Western Region. And when British Colonial Secretary Oliver Lyttelton ruled that Lagos would remain federal territory, Awolowo stormed out of the conference in London, threatening secession of the Western Region from the rest of Nigeria. Had the British not been in control of Nigeria, the Western Region would probably have seceded from the federation.

Even as late as the 1990s, threats of secession came from all parts of Nigeria and continued through the years, although in varying degrees and in muted form in some cases, as different ethnic groups complained of marginalization by other groups in the giant federation. The Igbos, who never regained their former position when they were reintegrated into the Nigerian society after the end of the civil war (1967 - 1970), talked of another Biafra or an alternative arrangement - including confederation - which would give them complete control over their destiny and equal access to power and the nation's resources within the federation to end their marginalization. And other Nigerians, especially the Hausa-Fulani, were determined to keep the Igbos on the periphery after Biafra lost the war; a policy of marginalization and containment of the Igbos which continued through the years even after the 1990s. As George Ayittey states in his book *Africa in Chaos*:

> In Nigeria, this insidious tribalism has retrogressively evolved into what Nigerian columnist Igonikon Jack called a 'full-blown tribal-apartheid,' in which people of a particular tribal, regional, or religious origin enjoy more privileges than their fellow indigenous compatriots, the Christian Ibos of the Southeast. The Ibos, who lost the Biafran War, are the most disadvantaged and discriminated against. The Northerners, who are of the Hausa-Fulani ethnic group and predominantly Muslim, have ruled Nigeria for 31 out of 35 years of independence (won in October 1960) and the military, has also been dominated by the Northerners for 25 years.
>
> Nigerian journalist, Pini Jason, concurred: 'Since the North controlled political power, it also controlled, decided and manipulated the allocation of posts, resources and values. And with this power it kept the competition for the crumbs alive in the South and the cleavages and political disunity very wide. The fact that the North, like the Tutsis of Burundi (and of Rwanda since 1994), controls the military and uses its military might to monopolize political power, and is not willing to part with the privileges power has brought the North over the years, makes many Nigerians fear a possible blood-bath *a la* Burundi.'[4]

Northern political control of the Nigerian federation theoretically ended in May 1999 when former military ruler Olusegun Obasanjo, a Yoruba from the southwest, became Nigeria's democratically elected president after 16 years of military dictatorship by Northern soldiers. The last civilian government - also headed by a Northerner, President Shehu Shagari, a Fulani - was overthrown in December 1983, by a fellow Northerner, General Mohammed Buhari. But even Obasanjo's election did not end the Northerners' hegemonic control of the federation. His candidacy was backed and bankrolled by powerful Northern generals and politicians, including former military dictator Ibrahim Babangida - one of the richest men in the world, reportedly worth more than $30 billion siphoned off from petrodollars - who felt that, as a fellow soldier and former military ruler himself (he was Nigeria's head of state from 1975 - 1979), he would be sympathetic to them and protect their interests. And they were not disappointed.

But the transfer of political power to the south also had other consequences. Although northerners remained influential and the dominant force in the federation headed by a southerner - the vice president was a northerner, as was the defence minister and other key cabinet members and other high-ranking officials - the mere fact that the presidency had been handed over to the south rankled many Northern Nigerians, including former military rulers. They were determined to undermine the new dispensation and found a ready weapon in religion.

Northern Nigeria is overwhelmingly Muslim, and the south predominantly Christian and animist. But Nigeria is a secular state. Yet, northerners invoked religious rights guaranteed by the federal constitution to introduce Islamic law, known as *sharia*, in all the predominantly Muslim states, a move that virtually amounted to the establishment of theocratic regimes in a secular nation. And the defiance by northerners, clearly demonstrated by their refusal to abandon *sharia*, posed a serious challenge to the federal government. It was unquestionably a deliberate attempt by northerners to undermine federal law in the northern states, and a repudiation of federal authority tantamount to secession, even if in a limited way.

If the introduction of Islamic law in the northern states was of paramount concern to northerners, and religion the only reason why they introduced *sharia*, why didn't they do so when northern military officers and civilian rulers such as President Shehu Shagari were in control of the federal government? They didn't convert to Islam just recently, after Obasanjo, a Christian and a southerner, became president. It was only after a southerner, and a Christian on top of that, became president in 1999 that an Islamic revival swept the north, threatening all institutions of federal and secular authority in the region. All this, together with the marginalization of many ethnic groups in the federation, led many people to question whether Nigeria would really be able to survive as a nation, prompting some to ask: Should Nigeria break up?

The threat to Nigerian existence came from other groups as well, besides the three major ones - the Igbos whose independent Republic of Biafra lasted for about three years; the Yorubas who felt marginalized even under the democratic presidency of a fellow Yoruba, Olusegun Obasanjo, many of them believed was controlled by northern generals and political heavyweights; and the Hausa-Fulani and other northern Muslims who resorted to religion, employing Islamic law as a guerrilla tactic to undermine federal authority in their states and force southern Christians to leave Northern Nigeria and return to the south; a religious and ethnic conflict which cost thousands of lives between 1999 and 2002 in the northern states, especially Kano and Kaduna.

The Ogonis and other groups in the oil-producing states of the Niger Delta were, and continue to be, some of the most exploited and marginalized groups in Nigeria. In spite of the vast amount of oil pumped right from under their feet, earning Nigeria billions of dollars every year, they are among the poorest people in the world. They get nothing, or only a trickle, from the federal government and the oil companies. But such neglect also has had dire consequences. Groups of Ogoni and Ijaw youths among others have resorted to sabotage through the years, targeting pipelines and other oil installations, and kidnapping oil company employees, to dramatize their plight and extract concessions from the federal government and oil companies.

The militants have not only demanded money for development and provision of basis services, but also for cleaning up pollution. The environmental devastation wrought by the oil companies with the blessing of the federal government has taken a heavy toll on the people of the oil-producing states in terms of lost lives, disease, polluted water and fish supplies as well as vegetation. The neglect has been going on for decades since oil was found in the Niger Delta in the 1950s, and has prompted some members of these minority groups to demand secession. And their minority status in a federation dominated by the three main groups - the Hausa-Fulani, the Yoruba and the Igbo - only compounds the problem.

One of the Niger Delta residents who eloquently expressed their plight was Ken Saro-Wiwa, an Ogoni writer and activist of international stature, who was hanged in November 1985 by the putative military dictator Sani Abacha because of his relentless campaign against the depredations suffered by the people of the oil-producing states at the hands of the oil companies and the federal government; their plight compounded by their minority status. As he stated in one of his last statements, in an interview with a Nigerian newspaper, the Lagos-based *Guardian*: "My only regret is that I was born a minority in Nigeria."[5]

The idea of establishing independent ethno-states is probably very appealing to oppressed ethnic groups, but terrifying to African countries almost all of which are multiethnic societies. It may even be argued that they are multi-national states, if ethnic groups are considered to be nations, or micro-nations. Yet, in spite of this complex configuration of African nations or ethno-polities - characterized by ethnic diversity - built into their very architecture of national identity, the continent has not experienced major secessionist movements in the last 40 years or so since independence, except Katanga and Biafra. That is because, despite the tenuous bonds of national unity among the different tribes and racial groups in a given country, there is still some acceptance of the idea of a common national identity among the majority of the people, largely forged by a common history of colonial experience; the coercive power of the state to maintain national unity and territorial integrity at all costs; the capacity of the one-party system - the most dominant political institution across the continent for decades during the post-colonial era - to embrace all ethnic groups by eschewing divisive politics typical of multiparty democracy in the African context; and by the cultivation of a personality cult -

Nkrumah, Sekou Toure, Kenyatta, Mobutu, Banda - or the existence of a popular charismatic leader, such as Nyerere, who serves as a rallying point for the masses and the entire nation to forge a common identity and achieve national unity.

That is why even in the Democratic Republic of Congo, a country which has virtually ceased to exist and function as a state and as a nation, the people across this vast expanse of territory still identify themselves as Congolese - thanks to the enduring legacy of Patrice Lumumba, and a common history of suffering probably more than anything else, infused with a dose of Pan-African solidarity. And there has been no major secessionist threat since the sixties when Katanga, and then South Kasai Province led by Albert Kalonji, declared independence. Even the different rebel groups which in the late 1990s and beyond virtually carved up the Congo into fiefdoms dominated by warlords, plundering the nation's resources, did not say they wanted to break up the country into independent states; although their control of at least the entire eastern half of Congo by the late nineties and during the following years amounted to *de facto* partition, hence secession - in the practical, even if not in the legal, sense - from the central government in Kinshasa.

And tragically, Congo is only one example of the collapse of institutional authority and erosion of political legitimacy across the continent. What is needed in Africa, where - because of bad leadership - failed states are the norm rather than the exception, is an alternative configuration that will facilitate the establishment of institutional authority in many areas where the state is unable to function, or where it has abdicated its responsibility. In many parts of the continent, people rely on foreign-funded non-governmental organizations (NGOs) and civic institutions to provide them with goods and services, which they can't get on their own - more than they do on the government. But one thing they have not been able to provide is security. And it is this lack of security, especially for entire groups some of which have been targeted for ethnic cleansing, that can be a very powerful motivation for secession in a number of African countries.

The Igbos of Nigeria could have had all the goods and services they wanted and needed. But without security, all those would have meant absolutely nothing to them in terms of survival as a people. Theirs may have been a case of self-determination based on ethnicity, but precisely because they were targeted as Igbos, hence as an ethnic group. Yet, the independent Republic of Biafra they established also included other ethnic groups in the former Eastern Nigeria. The ethnicity of these other groups was also ground for secession from the Nigerian federation after they were also targeted for elimination in the pogroms directed against all Easterners by their fellow countrymen in Northern Nigeria. And in response to the charge by the federal government that the Igbos had forced minority groups to become part of Biafra, Biafran leader Odumegwu Ojukwu asked the federal authorities to conduct an internationally-supervised plebiscite if they sincerely believed that the minorities had been coerced into joining Biafra. But the Nigerian federal government refused to do so, thus losing its credibility.

But, besides its tragic aspect where ethnicity is seen as a liability and is used by some people to discriminate against some groups and even target them for extermination, ethnicity also has positive attributes which cannot be overlooked and must be acknowledged as an enduring feature of the African political landscape, and not the ugly phenomenon it is portrayed to be. As Professor Christopher Clepham states in his essay, "Rethinking the African State," in *Africa Security Review*:

> Ethnicity, quite regardless of arcane academic debates over its 'primordial' or 'constructed' character, has likewise developed into an enduring feature of African life, and provides a ready basis for the consolidation of political identities.... Critical to the relationship between ethnicity and statehood is not just the existence of an ethnic identity as such, but more importantly the substantive *content* of this identity in terms of shared attitudes toward issues of political authority and control that it embodies.... The decay of viable and effective states has created massive political violence.[6]

Although the Nigerian federal state was not weak when the Igbos were being massacred in Northern Nigeria and other parts of the country, it was an accomplice to their persecution because of its unwillingness to stop the massacres and provide security for the victims. It was this total disregard for their lives by federal and Northern Nigerian authorities, which forced them to withdraw from the federation. They felt that the only way they could be safe was by establishing their own independent state, in their home region, under their own government. And it is in this overall context that the secession of Eastern Nigeria must be looked at, in order to understand why Tanzania recognized Biafra, a decision President Nyerere admitted was a painful one to make, yet necessary if we were to remain true to our conviction that "there is no other justification for states and governments except man."

The secession of Biafra and subsequent civil war was a horrendous tragedy. But it also had an important lesson for Africa, especially for countries facing major secessionist threats; for example the Oromo Liberation Front in Ethiopia, which is fighting to establish its own independent state whose jurisdictional boundaries coincide with the ethnic identity of the people who want to secede. The Oromo, like other Ethiopians, live in a country which, at least in theory, has acknowledged the imperative need for ethnic confederalism as the basis for national unity.

Yet, true unity cannot be achieved by force, and Africa may have to concede the legitimacy of major secessionist movements as one of the ways to resolve conflicts on the continent and guarantee equality and justice for oppressed and neglected groups. Such a concession is a first step towards conflict resolution, which entails: conflict management, containment, reduction, and finally, resolution. One of the best ways to resolve conflict is to address the grievances of the people who want to secede, and therefore prevent secession.

Trying to force them to remain in a country from which they want to secede will only exacerbate and perpetuate conflict and lead to national instability. But secessionist movements can be robbed of momentum if the regions which want to secede, are granted extensive autonomy enabling them to rule themselves while remaining an integral part of the nation they want to break away from. Such extensive devolution of power can be achieved under federation or confederation far better than it can under a unitary state whose very nature is to centralize power, while assigning a peripheral role to its constituent units.

But the right to self-determination, hence secession, must also be enshrined in the constitution of every African country as a bargaining tool for oppressed groups to extract genuine concessions from the central government, short of secession.

Therefore the intent here is *not* to encourage secession, but to discourage secession in African countries. Paradoxically, the right to secede serves to neutralize the very tendency it seems to encourage. More often than not, people want to secede, not just because they want to separate; they want to secede because they are ignored, oppressed, exploited, and even rejected by their government and by their fellow countrymen. And usually, there is a long record of historical injustices, which serves as a catalyst for secessionist movements, fueled by contemporary oppression.

In Nigeria, had the grievances of the Igbos - who had also been the victims of earlier massacres in Jos in 1945 and in Kano in 1953 - been addressed during those critical months in 1966 when their people were being systematically slaughtered in Northern Nigeria, and even in many parts of Western Nigeria, it is highly probable that they would not have seceded; especially if the federal government had agreed to extensive devolution of power to the regions under genuine federalism or even confederalism, as it did in the Aburi Agreements. But those grievances were never addressed, forcing Easterners to secede. The Nigerian military head of state, General Yakubu Gowon, even reneged on his promise to implement the Aburi Agreements agreed upon by all the military governors, and Gowon himself, at a meeting in Aburi, Ghana, in January 1967, which could have prevented Biafra's secession and the subsequent civil war, had they been fulfilled. And the Biafran leader, Colonel Ojukwu, was explicit in his condemnation of Gowon for refusing to implement the Aburi Agreements, which granted more autonomy to the regions and rescinded any decrees which curtailed the power of regional governments and other institutions of authority to manage their own affairs. It was a betrayal of trust on the part of Gowon, and nothing was done through the years after the civil war to seriously address the grievances of the Igbos. As Ojukwu said in an interview with the BBC, 13 January 2000: Nothing had really changed since the war. The cause of the war was never addressed:

> None of the problems that led to the war have been solved yet. They are still there. We have a situation creeping towards the type of situation that saw the beginning of the war....
>
> At 33 I reacted as a brilliant 33-year-old. At 66 it is my hope that if I had to face this I should also confront it as a brilliant 66-year-old.

Responsibility for what went on - how can I feel responsible in a situation in which I put myself out and saved the people from genocide? No, I don't feel responsible at all. I did the best I could.[7]

He articulated a sentiment shared by many Igbos, and even by members of other groups who feel that they are marginalized in a federation still dominated by northerners. Ojukwu's candor on this incendiary subject on a number of occasions prompted a sharp response from President Obasanjo who accused the former Biafran leader of again fomenting trouble and threatening secession, and warned that secessionists would pay dearly as they did in the last war (July 1967 - January 1970). In fact, it was Obsanjo himself, then a senior army officer in the federal offensive against Biafra, who accepted the surrender of the Biafran forces after they capitulated to federal might on January 15, 1970. Although the Igbos suffered tremendously during the war, the majority of them continued to support Ojukwu because they believed that they had no other choice besides continued domination and oppression at the hands of the Hausa-Fulani, their nemesis, who were determined to control the federation perpetually. As Ojukwu stated in July 1999, almost 30 years after the war, in an interview with *USAfrica*:

It was a Hobson's choice for Igbos and other Biafrans. What else could we have done? Line up, bare our necks, shave it if possible, and say 'come on' to the Hausas, Kanuris, Tivs, Fulanis and other members of the Nigerian army and civilians who were killing our people of Eastern Nigeria, later Biafra? No!....We never declared war on anybody....It was simply a choice between Biafra and enslavement.[8]

Even today, hatred of the Igbos is an enduring obsession among a large number of them, and with it potential for ethnic cleansing, not only of the Igbos but other groups as well, in different parts of the giant federation.

The war itself remains a contentious issue in Nigeria and elsewhere, especially in other African countries where secession is a potential threat that could galvanize some groups to demand their own independent states, as happened in Casamance Province in Senegal, Cabinda in Angola, Caprivi Strip in Namibia, Anjouan and Moheli islands in the Comoros, Bioko island in Equatorial Guinea, and in Nigeria itself, especially in the Niger Delta, in

Yorubaland in the west as well as in the former short-lived independent Republic of Biafra in the east. Although Biafrans lost the war because they were outgunned, they are still fighting another war on a different front for inclusion in the Nigerian polity as equal members of society instead of being treated as traitors and outcasts because they fought for an independent homeland. They are also fighting against distortion of history about what really happened and what the war was all about. As Ojukwu said about the conflict and the distortion of historical facts about the war in an interview with Paul Odili of the *Vanguard*, Lagos, Nigeria, November 4, 2001, entitled "Ojukwu at 68 on State of the Nation: Why We Can't Have Peace Now":

> It is clear to me that many things are going on particularly in the recent interventions, by some of the ex-military officers, that Nigeria is not yet ready for the truth....They know that the distortions are deliberate....
>
> Let me ask you, who mounted the coup of 1966? Clearly, it was Ifeajuna, but for their own reasons, some northern officers are insisting that it was Chukwuma Nzeogwu; against all the facts. Let me ask you again, who was the rebel in the crisis that befell Nigeria in 1966? Everybody knows actually that the rebel was Gowon. But no, they prefer to say that it was Ojukwu. How could it be me? I was a loyalist serving the army in Kano.
>
> On the radio, I heard my name (that I had been) appointed governor of the East, by somebody who was legitimately appointed head of state. By the way, if Ironsi was not legitimately appointed head of state, then Gowon's appointment under Ironsi would have been illegal too. But I continued the task assigned to me legitimately. The fact that Gowon decided to assume the position of head of state was a major departure from both military discipline and accepted norm. Now, everybody knows that. Gowon knows that, Danjuma knows that, Obasanjo knows that. So, why keep pretending?
>
> I rejected the coup; that is an honourable act. And it is for that reason that I keep telling people that Gowon will go down in the *Guinness Book of Records* as the man who perhaps mounted the longest coup ever. In that actually, the war could be looked at as Gowon consolidating the coup, which he mishandled. Yoy see Gowon mounted a counter-coup...and never got complete control of Nigeria. He then proceeded to force the entirety of Nigeria to go under his command. I refused, and my refusal got to a point that he thought he should now fight me. And he never got control of Nigeria until he won that war. So it was a continuation of his coup actually.[9]

In the interview, Ojukwu was also asked: "When Gowon maintained his position, you initiated the MidWest invasion?" To which he responded:

Absolute lie. I was in Enugu and it is on record that Gowon ordered the troops into the East. They had a two-prong entry. One from Nsukka and one from Afikpo axis. The war had been (going) on for months, before I mounted an attempt at capturing Lagos or destablising Lagos through the Mid-West. How can that be that I took the initiative? I suppose your answer should be that I should stay in the East and do nothing. Again that is part of the lie. Everywhere you go, they say Ojukwu waged, mounted, declared war against Nigeria. But it is a lie. I had the opportunity of declaring war. I had the opportunities of doing so many things, check.... Gowon is a liar....

He had already prior to that (declaration of independence by Biafra) committed certain acts that were tantamount to acts of war. How do you stay in Nigeria, if you were under a total blockade? Tell me....

There is no way Nigeria can move forward in peace and harmony, without some restructuring. There is no way we can all feel part of Nigeria, if we do not go through a quasi re-negotiation of Nigeria, and our Nigerianness. In saying this, I want to make it clear, because I am the most misunderstood Nigerian. Nigeria itself, there is nothing wrong with it, nothing. It is our position in Nigeria that we do not like. There is nothing wrong with Nigeria; it is what we suffer in Nigeria that we can't accept. There is nothing wrong with Nigeria; there is nothing wrong with West Africa. What we continue to oppose is the oppression in Nigeria of Ndigbo, that's all. So, as far as I am concerned, a national conference is to make us feel better in Nigeria. Restructuring is to make Ndigbo feel part of Nigeria. That is how Ndigbo look at it....

I cannot help being sentimental about a Nigeria that has done me no good.[10]

That probably sums up the way many Igbos feel, although one cannot be sure exactly how many. But it is a collective sentiment shared by a significant number of Igbos, as demonstrated by their continued support of the ideals which inspired the emergence of Biafra on the international scene; they even had an office in Washington D.C. in the 1990s and beyond which some people - supporters and detractors - erroneously called "an embassy," as if Biafra were a legal sovereign entity recognized by the United States and other countries, a far cry from reality. However, this collective sentiment of Igbo nationhood, and marginalization in the Nigerian context, is a sentiment articulated by a man - Ojukwu - who is one of the most influential Igbo leaders in modern times and who continues to command allegiance among his people across the spectrum decades after the war when he emerged on the international scene as their savior, leading his troops against the federal army. It was David against Goliath. And besides the differences in the interpretation of what actually happened - Biafra's versus Nigeria's and vice versa - what Ojkwu said clearly shows that bitter memories of the war continue to poison relations between many Igbos and the rest of the Nigerians because of the injustices that were never corrected and which continue to be perpetrated against them as one of the most marginalized groups in the country; in spite of their high qualifications in many fields and their status as an integral part of the nation like the rest of their fellow countrymen.

Had the cause of the war been addressed, and had the grievances of the secessionists been redressed through the years since the end of the war, the Igbos would not be marginalized as they are today. And the Nigerian federation would be much stronger than it is now, and even more so if all the other groups shunted to the periphery of the mainstream were treated fairly. Interestingly enough, the situation is analogous to that of Tanzania, the first country to recognize Biafra, where secessionist sentiments in the former island nation of Zanzibar have grown stronger in recent years because of what many Zanzibaris consider to be their marginalized status in the union. Whether Zanzibar really plays a marginal role in the conduct of union affairs, as a junior and not as an equal partner as a former independent nation, is highly debatable. But many Zanzibaris, rightly or wrongly, believe this. And they have other complaints, chief among them - restoration of their sovereign status that ended when the union was consummated in April 1964. There is no question that if their grievances are not addressed, the union of Tanzania may face very serious problems in the coming years, even if it does not break up.

Should Zanzibar be allowed to secede? It depends on what the people want; a point also underscored by President Nyerere, the architect of the Tanganyika-Zanzibar union, when he explained why Tanzania recognized Biafra, as we learned earlier: "As President of Tanzania it is my duty to safeguard the integrity of the United Republic. But if the mass of the people of Zanzibar should, without external manipulation, and for some reason of their own, decide that the Union was prejudicial to their existence, I could not advocate bombing them into submission. To do so would not be to defend the Union. The Union would have ceased to exist when the consent of its constituent members was withdrawn."

If a referendum were held in the former island nation and the majority of the people in Zanzibar voted to dissolve ties with Tanganyika and return to the status quo ante, that would be the end not only of the union but of any hope of even forming a confederation under which members enjoy far greater autonomy than they do under federation. As a Tanzanian myself and strong believer in African unity, I don't want to see the union dissolved anymore than I would like to see any other African country break up. But there are cases when such dissolution of ties may be necessary. If people are abused, oppressed, and discriminated against by their fellow countrymen that's grounds for secession, unless the injustices are stopped. Otherwise there is no reason why they should not be allowed to secede, and if that is the only way they can live in peace and security in their own independent state. If you don't want them to secede, stop oppressing them and denying them equal rights. And if the right to self-determination has to be enshrined in the constitution of every African country as one of the best ways to guarantee equal treatment of oppressed groups, by threatening secession, so be it: "Treat us fairly. Or else, we are gone."

Therefore, in a paradoxical way, the right to secession may not only prevent secession. It can also help maintain and strengthen unity by using the threat of secession to demand and get justice and equal treatment from the government which has failed or refuses to protect oppressed groups who have also been rejected by their fellow citizens. And it will enable all citizens to hold their leaders accountable for their actions. Otherwise they will have nobody left to lead.

But unlike Biafra, the case of Zanzibar presents a unique problem for Tanzania because there are many people in the former island nation who want to maintain the union. The secessionists on the islands - of Pemba and Zanzibar, but especially Pemba - are not motivated by any genuine desire to correct whatever injustices may exist, but to restore historical ties with the Gulf States, especially Oman, reminiscent of the era when the islands were an integral part of the Arab world and Zanzibar the seat of the sultan of Oman. Islamic fundamentalists want to turn Zanzibar into a theocratic state and use it as an operational base from which they will be able - or try - to export their radical ideology to the mainland in a country which is constitutionally a secular state. And contrary to what the agitators say, the majority of Zanzibaris - most of whom are Muslim - are not Islamic fundamentalists and, therefore, do not support the agenda for a theocratic state based on a radical interpretation of the Koran.

Yet, secessionist sentiments may continue to grow on the isles if the islanders are not granted far greater autonomy than they now enjoy. Tanzania may have to learn a lesson from one of the neighboring countries, the island nation of the Comoros, which also has had historical ties with Zanzibar for a long time. In fact, many Zanzibaris are of Comorian origin, as are many Tanzanians on the mainland. And Kiswahili, Tanzania's national language, is also spoken in the Comoros where the overwhelming majority of the people are Muslim just like those in Zanzibar.

Two islands, Anjouan and Moheli, seceded from the Comoros in 1997. Federal troops failed to suppress the insurgency. The Comoros, a federation of three islands, was left with one island, Grande Comoro, which is also the largest and the seat of the federal capital. In 2001, the federal government and the secessionist islands agreed to hold a referendum on a new constitution which would give extensive autonomy to all the islands in the federation. An overwhelming majority of the people, at least 75 percent, approved the constitution, and the secessionists rejoined the union. Extensive devolution of power saved the federation, although in some cases, it can be recipe for disaster, fueling secessionist movements if not carefully managed within well-prescribed limits. But such extensive autonomy, short of sovereign status, may also dampen and neutralize secessionist sentiments and tendencies in Zanzibar and strengthen the union of Tanzania. It also could have saved Nigeria from exploding into civil war in the sixties, thus preventing the secession of Biafra and its aftermath including loss of at least one million lives, had the federal authorities implemented the Aburi Agreements to transform the highly centralized Nigerian federation into a confederation; a transformation that would have assured Igbos and other Easterners that they would be guaranteed security in their own autonomous region under their own jurisdiction, but without attaining full sovereign status.

It is a tragic irony that more than 40 years after

independence, African countries have not yet adequately addressed the question of ethnicity in a continent whose very traditional societies, the building blocks of African nations, are ethnic entities. Ethnic differences and loyalties are always and will always be exploited by unscrupulous politicians to promote their own partisan interests. Yet, ethnic groups have an enormous potential to serve as a solid foundation for stable nations, provided all the tribes and other groups in every African country, including racial minorities - Arab, Asian, European - in countries such as Kenya and Tanzania, are treated equal and have equal access to power and the nation's resources. It is denial of such equality, and exclusion of some groups from participation in the political and economic arena, that has served as a lightning rod in many conflicts ignited across the continent. As Dr. Sam Amoo, a Ghanaian scholar and United Nations specialist in conflict resolution, states in "The Challenges of Ethnicity and Conflict in Africa: The Need for a New Paradigm":

> Conflicts arise from dysfunctional governance or socio-political systems that deny or suppress the satisfaction of a group's ontological needs, such as the universal needs for identity, recognition, security, dignity and participation. This denial generates conflict, which can only be resolved through alterations in norms, structures, institutions and policies. The causes and remedies of conflicts in Africa therefore essentially relate to the socio-political structures of the particular state....
>
> Sources of conflicts in Africa are located in basic human needs for group - ethnic - identity, security, recognition, participation and autonomy, as well as in the circumstances, policies and institutions of political and economic systems that attempt to deny or suppress such basic needs.[11]

The significance of ethnicity in African life across the spectrum cannot be ignored or underestimated. Attempts to ignore it, or gloss over it, have only exacerbated conflicts where they already exist, and generated new ones where there weren't any. Like the English, the Scots, the Irish and the Welsh in the United Kingdom, African ethnic groups are not going to disappear, and would be a tragic loss if they did. That is because they are Africa itself. They constitute the African organic entity and the spirit that animates its very being. They are natural entities, not artificial constructs like the countries across the continent created by the colonialists.

The Kikuyu, the Luo, the Kamba and others existed before

Kenya was created; the Ewe and the Ashanti before the Gold Coast, now Ghana; the Igbo, the Yoruba, the Hausa, the Fulani, the Ijaw, the Tiv and the rest of the ethnic groups in Nigeria and other African countries - they all existed, at different levels of social and political organization, long before Europeans came and created the countries we have in Africa today. Europeans did not teach us our customs and traditions. Nor did they teach us our languages. Instead, they tried to destroy all that, one way or another, and exploited ethnic differences to consolidate their hegemonic control over Africa. The question is how all these groups can be harmonized as corporate entities, functioning smoothly as interlocking units that constitute an interdependent whole, without tearing African countries and the continent apart. And this requires a new - yet old, traditional - approach to nation-building and conflict resolution in Africa.

Therefore, there is a need for a paradigm shift in Africa; one that incorporates into its analytical framework the salience and primacy of ethnicity as an organizing concept, but one that does not nullify the legitimacy of the nation-state; one that also sees ethnicity as a basis for nation-building, and for power and resource allocation where it has generated and has the potential to generate conflict; and as a mechanism for conflict resolution through consensus building within a specific ethno-polity and across ethnic lines, with primary emphasis on the use of traditional institutions of authority as the key players in resolving conflicts. If Africa takes this approach, she may be on her way towards reducing and ending civil wars and other conflicts which have devastated the continent for years, as hundreds of millions of her people continue to suffer, and look helpless, in a world which couldn't care less if they vanished today from the face of the earth.

In the Nigerian civil war, the Igbos would have suffered even more casualties - far more than the 1 to 2 million who had already died, mostly from starvation - had they not capitulated to federal might after fighting a brutal war for almost three years to sustain their short-lived independent Republic of Biafra. It was an unnecessary war, which could have been avoided. But after it started and kept on going, recognition of Biafra by Tanzania became a moral imperative. And President Nyerere made that clear. Denying Biafra recognition would have been tantamount to sanctioning genocide against a people whose only crime was their desire, and right, to be safe and free in their own homeland.

CHAPTER NINE:

THE OUSTER OF IDI AMIN BY TANZANIA

THE RISE of Idi Amin to power in Uganda introduced a destabilizing factor on the East African political scene as never before. And his ouster by Tanzania eight years later also set a precedent as the first case of direct intervention by one African country in another in the post-colonial era; besides incursions by apartheid South Africa into neighboring countries which were supporting South African freedom fighters, and the apartheid regime's almost successful takeover of Angola in the seventies, until Fidel Castro sent Cuban troops to halt the advance. South African troops penetrated deep into Angola and were headed towards the capital, Luanda, before they were pushed back by the Cubans. Tanzania's intervention in Uganda was also the first time that an African country captured the capital, and overthrew the government, of another country on the continent.

Amin came to power in a military coup on January 25, 1971, which would probably not have been launched, let alone succeeded, without external help. In announcing his seizure of power in Radio Uganda, Amin made a short speech and tried to assure his fellow countrymen in the following terms:

> Fellow countrymen and well wishers of Uganda. I address you today at a very important hour in the history of our nation. A short while ago, men of the armed forces placed this country in my hands. I am not a politician, but a professional soldier. I am therefore a man of few words and I shall, as a result, be brief. Throughout my professional life, I have emphasized that the military must support a civilian government that has the support of the people, and I have not changed from that position.[1]

The contradiction is obvious. And the people who placed Uganda in Amin's hands, to paraphrase what he said, were not just the Ugandan soldiers but Israeli agents as well, with the support of the British government. The British supported the coup against President Milton Obote because of his uncompromising stand on apartheid South Africa and Rhodesia. His policies towards the apartheid regime in South Africa were diametrically opposed to those of Britain, which was friendly towards the racist government and did not want to impose severe economic sanctions on the white-dominated country because of her large investments there. African countries demanded such sanctions in order to force the apartheid regime to abandon its racist policies. In the case of Rhodesia, the British government was hostile towards President Obote because of his uncompromising stand on the white minority regime in Salisbury, demanding that Britain actively intervene in her colony with military force to end the rebellion by Prime Minister Ian Smith who had unilaterally declared independence, excluding the African majority from power.

Britain also supported the coup against Dr. Obote because he nationalized British companies in Uganda after he adopted socialist policies in pursuit of economic independence. And Western countries in general, including the United States, supported the coup against Obote as a containment strategy to neutralize "communist penetration" of East Africa through Tanzania which was friendly towards the People's Republic of China and other Eastern-bloc nations more than any other country in the region; a false accusation, since Tanzania was not communist or communist-oriented but fiercely independent, a stance that antagonized the West as much as Uganda's under Obote who was also a close friend of President Julius Nyerere of Tanzania. Obote's Pan-African militancy and socialist policies as well as his friendship with Eastern-bloc countries, like Nyerere's, were anathema to the West and could be neutralized only by ousting him from power.

It was a grand conspiracy, further confirmed when Western countries were the first to recognize Amin's regime, and before any African country did. Britain was the first Western country to do so; an implicit admission of her involvement in Obote's ouster, or, at the very least, of her strong desire to see him ousted. But Britain's complicity and involvement in the coup was obvious; a point underscored by Western analysts as well, including the *Executive Intelligence Review*:

> General Amin came to power in Uganda, in a military coup against

President Milton Obote. British sponsorship of the semi-illiterate Amin, son of a sorceress, was quickly evident; Britain was one of the first countries in the world to recognize the Amin government, long before any African country. And when relations with Britain had soured after Amin expelled the Asian business community from Uganda, British intelligence operative Robert Astles remained as Amin's mentor in Uganda until the very end. Amin's tyranny, lasting until 1979, trampled Uganda's political and economic institutions, leaving the country a wreckage from which it has never recovered.[2]

Israel's involvement in the Ugandan military coup was even more direct. The coup was masterminded by Israeli agents working in Kampala, Uganda. It could not have succeeded without them. As Dr. Milton Obote stated:

> It is doubtful that Amin, without the urging of the Israelis, would have staged a successful coup in 1971... Israel wanted a client regime in Uganda, which they could manipulate in order to prevent Sudan from sending troops to Egypt.... The coup succeeded beyond their wildest expectations.... The Israelis set up in Uganda a regime, which pivoted in every respect to Amin, who in turn was under the strictest control of the Israelis in Kampala.... The Israelis and Anya-Anya were hilarious; the regime was under their control.[3]

The Israelis wanted to prevent Sudan from sending troops to Egypt - a frontline state in the Arab League against Israel and the most powerful in the Arab world - by tying down her troops in a war against the rebels, known as Anya-Anya, fighting for self-determination in southern Sudan against the Arab-dominated government in Khartoum in northern Sudan. Israel's support of the black rebels was motivated by self-interest more than anything else including humanitarian concern. So was the coup against President Obote.

The ouster of Dr. Milton Obote had striking similarities to the coup against President Kwame Nkrumah of Ghana five years earlier on February 24, 1966. Both leaders were ardent Pan-Africanists and strong supporters of liberation movements in Africa. Both antagonized the West because of their Pan-African militancy and the socialist policies they pursued. And both were overthrown - with Western help including the CIA - when they were outside their countries: Nkrumah, while on his way on a peace mission to Hanoi at the invitation of Vietnamese President Ho Chin Mihn to help end the Vietnam war (and in pursuit of

Nkrumah's ambition to make Africa an important player on the global scene and in major international affairs); and Obote, when he was at the Commonwealth conference in Singapore where he had gone, at the urging of President Julius Nyerere, to make a strong case against Britain because of her insistence on selling arms to apartheid South Africa and her unwillingness to take stern measures against the apartheid regime and the white minority government in Rhodesia.

Obote did not want to go to Singapore because of the internal political situation in Uganda which he felt, and rightly so, that his enemies would try to exploit in his absence. And there has been some speculation that had he not left Uganda, as urged by Nyerere, he probably would not have been overthrown. Nyerere was undoubtedly outraged by the coup against Obote who was also his friend and ideological compatriot. But to say that he took military action against Idi Amin in order to reinstate Obote - hence make amends for his "mistakes" - because he had contributed to his downfall by urging him to go to Singapore to attend the commonwealth conference, is to distort history.

Idi Amin invaded Tanzania on October 30, 1978, and announced on November 1 that he had annexed 710 square miles of her territory in the northwest region of Kagera, triggering a counterattack by Tanzania, which eventually drove him out of Uganda. The atrocities perpetrated by Amin through the years in which hundreds of thousands of people were massacred were ignored by most African leaders and by the international community; a situation Nyerere found to be unacceptable, thus prompting him to intervene in Uganda to stop the atrocities by getting rid of Amin.

Therefore, even if President Obote had died in office and Amin or someone like him had usurped power and went on to perpetrate unspeakable horrors, as Amin did, Nyerere would still have intervened in Uganda out of humanitarian concern to stop the madness. He did not need Obote to be overthrown to do this. Obote could even have resigned, which is highly speculative, and Nyerere would still have intervened if Obote's successor - Amin or somebody else - went on to unleash terror on a scale Idi Amin did. It is in this largest context that Nyerere's outrage against the military coup by Amin should be viewed; a perspective that eludes a number of analysts or is deliberately distorted to conform to their interpretation of events at that critical juncture in Ugandan history. As Professor Ali Mazrui states in "Nyerere and I":

> In 1971, did Julius Nyerere convince Milton Obote to leave Uganda and go to Singapore to attend the Commonwealth conference of Heads of State and government? Milton Obote had hesitated about going to Singapore because of the uncertain situation in Uganda. Did Nyerere tilt the balance and convince Obote that he was needed in Singapore to fight Prime Minister Edward Heath's policy towards apartheid South Africa? Obote's decision to go to Singapore was disastrous for himself and for Uganda. In Obote's absence, Idi Amin staged a military coup and overthrew Obote. Eight years of tyranny and terror in Uganda had begun.
>
> I never succeeded in getting either Nyerere or Obote to confirm that it was Nyerere who convinced Obote to leave for Singapore. But we do know that Nyerere was so upset by the coup that he gave Obote unconditional and comfortable asylum in Tanzania. Nyerere also refused to talk to Amin even if the policy practically destroyed the East African Authority which was supposed to oversee the East African community. Was Nyerere feeling guilty for having made it easy for Amin to stage a coup by diverting Obote to Singapore?
>
> I shall always remember Nyerere's speech in Tanzania upon his return from Singapore. I was in Kampala listening to him on the radio. Nyerere turned a simple question in Kiswahili into a passionate denunciation of Idi Amin. Nyerere's repeated question was   'Serikali ni kitu gani?' ('What is government?').   This simple question of political science became a powerful speech to his own people and against the new 'pretenders' in Kampala.
>
> I visited Milton Obote at his home in Dar es Salaam during his first exile. Obote and I discussed Idi Amin much more often than we discussed Julius Nyerere....
>
> In 1979, Nyerere paid his debt to Milton Obote. His army marched all the way to Kampala and overthrew the regime of Idi Amin. My former Makerere boss, Prof Yusufu Lule, succeeded Idi Amin as President of Uganda. But Nyerere was so keen on seeing Obote back in power that Nyerere helped to oust Lule. Was Nyerere trying to negate the guilt of having encouraged Obote to go to Singapore for the Commonwealth conference way back in 1971? Was that why Nyerere was so keen to see Obote back in the presidential saddle of Uganda in the 1980s?
>
> Unfortunately, Obote's second administration was catastrophic for Uganda. He lost control of his own army, and thousands of people perished under tyranny and war. Was Julius Nyerere partly to blame?[4]

If Nyerere was partly to blame for Obote's ouster, then he was equally guilty of the atrocities perpetrated by Idi Amin, since he "helped" pave the way for Amin's rise to power by encouraging Obote to go to Singapore to attend the Commonwealth conference;

a far cry from reality, and a stretch of the imagination even Idi Amin - let alone his sponsors - would have found to be laughable. The Israelis and Western powers would still have tried and might even have succeeded, sooner or later, in overthrowing Obote with Amin's help even if he had not gone to Singapore, and even if Nyerere did not exist on the political scene to "influence" Obote one way or another. Whatever the case, the coup which catapulted Amin into power was one of the biggest tragedies in Africa's post-colonial history and one of the most tragic cases of foreign intrigue on African soil by outside powers. And an illiterate who never went beyond standard two - what Americans call second grade - took over the leadership of one of the most prosperous countries in Africa, and ruined it.

Yet, in spite of his wicked nature and bestial character, Amin was also capable of presenting himself in an amiable way as someone who could be trusted, although he could not hide his ignorance. As Henry Kyemba, who once served as Amin's private secretary and health minister before fleeing to Britain, said about him: "Amin never knew anything about how a government is run. He could not write and he had problems reading. So it was very hard to work with him."[5] Kyemba also described Idi Amin, whom some people called the Black Hitler, as one of the friendliest people he ever met, yet had the rage of a wounded buffalo. And his government and army were dominated by illiterates who were no better than he was. As another former Amin's cabinet member, Birgadier Moses Ali who later served as Third Deputy Prime Minister under President Yoweri Museveni, also bluntly stated: "Illiterates and sycophants were some of the people who spoilt Amin's government. They could not even read maps, they excelled in praising him, they were no better than Amin himself."[6]

Amin's willingness to be used by external powers to overthrow Dr.Obote - one of Africa's most prominent and influential leaders - was one of the most treasonous acts in the history of post-colonial Africa. As an expression of gratitude to those who had sponsored the coup, Amin took a strong pro-Western stance immediately after he seized power and declared that Israel and Britain were his close allies. The United States, like Britain, also supplied him with weapons. And the CIA as well as Britain's M16 intelligence service, together with Israel's intelligence agancy Mossad, trained Amin's security forces; including the dreaded and notoriously brutal Public Safety Unity and the State Research Bureau, euphemisms for secret police. They also provided them with weapons and other supplies. And Israeli troops also trained the Ugandan army and air force even when Obote was president, giving them a strategic advantage when they helped Amin execute a military coup a few years later. And Amin himself once received paratrooper training in Israel.

A former CIA official publicly confirmed in March 1978 that the coup against Obote was planned by the British MI6 and the Israeli Mossad intelligence services. And it had been confirmed earlier that a British agent operating under diplomatic cover at the British High Commission in Kampala, Uganda, planned the failed assassination attempt on President Obote on December 18, 1969.

Israel's role in the execution of the coup proved to be critical when, on the advice of an Israeli colonel in Israel's army and with the help of Israeli agents in Uganda, Amin was able to secure control and command of a mechanized battalion - of paratroopers, tanks, jeeps and armored vehicles - which was able to overwhelm the majority of the soldiers and officers in the Ugandan army still loyal to President Obote. Firepower compensated for numerical disadvantage to Amin's benefit. And the ease with which the coup was carried out also confirmed Obote's suspicion that the Israelis had played a direct and critical role in his ouster.

Obote may still or may not have been overthrown had he stayed in Uganda to mobilize support among his followers against any uprising. And although he knew that the security situation in Uganda was not very stable when he left for Singapore, he agreed with Nyerere that he would be needed at the Commonwealth conference to help present strong opposition to the sale of weapons to the apartheid regime of South Africa by Britain. The strongest opponents were Nyerere and Kaunda, and Obote provided much needed support to them at the conference where other African leaders were also opposed to the sale.

At a meeting in Singapore during the conference, Nyerere, Kaunda and Obote told British Prime Minister Edward Heath that their countries would withdraw from the Commonwealth if Britain proceeded with the sale of arms to the apartheid regime. In the ensuing debate, Heath is reported to have told the three leaders: "I wonder how many of you will be allowed to return to your own countries from this conference?"[7] It was an ominous warning, confirmed shortly thereafter, when Obote learned in Nairobi, Kenya, on his way back to Uganda from the conference that he had been overthrown. And it directly implicated Britain in the coup. Britain's involvement in the coup was further confirmed only a few days later when the British government became the first to recognize Amin's military regime exactly one week after he seized power.

The British also rejoiced at Obote's ouster and gave Amin extensive good coverage in the media, portraying him in a very positive way as Uganda's savior. According to *The Daily Express*: "Military men are trained to act. Not for them the posturing of the Obotes and Kaundas who prefer the glory of the international platform rather than the dull but necessary tasks of running a smooth administration."[8] And *The Daily Telegraph* bluntly stated: "Good luck to General Amin."[9] The thrill in government circles was equally evident, as reported by *The Times*: "The replacement of Dr. Obote by General Idi Amin was received with ill-concealed relief in Whitehall."[10] And Amin wasted no time in reciprocating these feelings.

He earned British confidence when he reversed Obote's policies in a number of areas. Unlike Obote, he supported the sale of weapons to apartheid South Africa by Britain. He also returned to private ownership British companies and other businesses nationalized by Obote. In return, Britain increased economic aid to Uganda, supplied weapons and provided further training to the Ugandan army. But the honeymoon was short-lived, and Britain as well as the United States and Israel soon learned that Amin was not the kind of leader they thought they could manipulate at will.

Amin had expansionist ambitions to conquer Tanzania and ostensibly gain access to the sea. He also toyed with the idea of annexing parts of western Kenya bordering Uganda, and even parts of Sudan, prompting Sudanese President Gaafar Nimeiri to remind Amin that he was Sudanese himself - Amin's small Kakwa tribe straddles the Ugandan-Sudanese-Congolese border, with part of Amin's lineage being on the Congo's and Sudanese side. He also threatened to destroy neighboring Rwanda. He antagonized almost all his neighbors, including Kenya whose western province, the burly dictator claimed, belonged to Uganda. But his immediate goal in this expansionist scheme was to conquer Tanzania, mainly because Nyerere had offered sanctuary to Amin's nemesis, Obote. And he became incensed when Britain refused to supply him with jet fighters and other sophisticated weapons to fulfill his mission.

Amin's desire to "flatten Tanzania," as he put it, became an obsession, which made him turn to Israel to seek weapons he needed to accomplish his mission. He asked for Phantom jets and other advanced weapons. But because these weapons were manufactured in the United States and sold to Israel with permission from the American government, the Israelis could not transfer or resell them to Uganda without Washington's approval. But Israel did not even go that far. The Israeli government refused to sell the weapons to Amin, saying that his request "went beyond the requirements of legitimate self-defence." The rejection of Amin's request was a prime factor in the expulsion of the Israelis from Uganda in April 1972, and in his unconditional support of the Palestinian cause and solidarity with Arab countries - and fellow Muslims - in their conflict with the Jewish state. And the failure to acquire the weapons he felt he needed, did not in any way discourage him from pursuing his expansionist ambitions to conquer Tanzania and secure a corridor to the sea.

Although he did not get the weapons he needed to inflict heavy damage on Tanzania, in his misguided belief that he would be able to conquer and occupy such a large country several times Uganda's size in terms of both area and population and which was believed to be militarily the strongest country in East Africa, Amin was provided with strategic advice and information in pursuit of this goal from an indispensable source. The advice came from a British major, working with the British intelligence service, who lived in the Tanzanian-Ugandan border on the Kagera River. He was in touch with Amin who frequently flew in a helicopter to the border for consultations with him on the planned invasion of Tanzania.

The British major had been an officer in the Seaforth Highlanders and a member of the International Commission of Observers sent to Nigeria during the 1967 - 70 civil war to investigate complaints by the Igbos and other Easterners in the secessionist territory of Biafra that they were victims of a systematic campaign of genocide by the federal military government. But he was expelled from the international observer mission because he compromised his neutral observer status when he offered his services to the Nigerian military regime as a mercenary in the war against Biafra. But at a hearing on his dismissal before the National Insurance Tribunal in England where he protested his expulsion from the observer mission, the major made a "startling" revelation that his real mission in Nigeria was to collect intelligence for the British government and provide strategic military advice to the Nigerian federal forces in their campaign against the Biafran secessionists and their supporters. The British government vehemently denied this, but the tribunal accepted his testimony and described him as a "frank and honest witness."[11]

He also proved to be an indispensable tool for Amin, as a spy, collecting vital intelligence for Amin's planned invasion of Tanzania. "The Major took Amin's invasion plan of Tanzania seriously, undertaking spying mission to Tanzania to reconnoiter the defences and terrain in secret. He supplied Amin with a strategic and logistical plan to the best of his abilities, and although lack of hardware was an obstacle, evidence that Amin never gave up the idea came in the fact that the invasion of Uganda by Tanzanian and exiled Ugandan anti-Amin forces in late 1978 which eventually brought his rule to an end on 10 April 1979, was immediately preceded by an abortive invasion of Tanzania by Amin's army."[12] Full-scale war between Tanzania and Uganda began after Idi Amin announced on November 1, 1978, that his troops had captured and annexed 710 square miles of Tanzanian territory in the northwestern part of the country, Kagera Region.

Amin would not have been able to invade Tanzania and cause a lot of destruction in Kagera Region had he not been kept in power, and armed, by outside powers. British and Israeli involvement has received more attention than America's But the United States' role in sustaining Amin's brutal regime cannot be underestimated. In July 1978, Jack Anderson, a hard-hitting American columnist, revealed in one of his columns that 10 of Amin's henchmen from the notorious Public Safety Unit were trained at the International Police Academy in Georgetown, a suburb of Washington, D.C. The academy was run by the CIA, one of the three foreign intelligence agencies - together with Britain's M16 and Isreal's Mossad - which helped sustain Amin in power, especially during the early years of his brutal eight-year reign. And as *The Economist* remarked, concerning the relationship between Britain and Amin's regime, "The last government to want to be rid of Amin is the British one."[13]

And following the invasion of Tanzania and annexation of part of her territory by Amin's forces, the Tanzanian government was probably the only one in the world, which was most interested in getting rid of Amin. Among the least interested were the Islamic states, including Libya and Saudi Arabia, which gave Amin substantial material and diplomatic support. For instance, even when Amin was launching raids across the border including aerial bombings through the years - as far back as 1972 when I was still a news reporter at the *Daily News*, Dar es Salaam, Tanzania - Arab governments in Africa did not use their considerable influence with the Ugandan dictator to moderate his behavior and dissuade him from pursuing his expansionist ambitions to conquer Tanzania. And when full-scale war began in November 1978, Saudi Arabia rebuffed Tanzania's request to stop supporting - let alone help oust - Amin. And Libya under Qaddafi sent troops - at least 2,500 - to Uganda to help Amin invade Tanzania; in addition to the military hardware, including Soviet-made combat aircraft, the Libyan Islamic regime had already sent to Uganda to be used in the invasion. A number of Palestinians and other Arabs from different Arab countries and elsewhere also supported Amin because of his shared hostility towards Israel.

Amin's expansionist ambitions were also fueled by his animosity towards Tanzania because of Nyerere's support of Dr. Milton Obote who lived in exile in Tanzania's capital Dar es Salaam after he was overthrown in January 1971. Obote, with the help of Tanzania, attempted to reclaim power in Uganda in the early seventies, but was not successful. His Ugandan supporters who also lived in Tanzania were not well prepared for the mission. The failure of these attempts emboldened Amin to pursue his wild ambition to conquer and occupy Tanzania, and even had him convinced that Tanzania had neither the will nor the capacity to fight back. It was a terrible mistake. As one of the senior officers in the Ugandan army, Colonel Bernard Rwehururu, who played a leading role in the war against Tanzania, stated in "Fighting for Amin":

In September 1972, as Ugandan authorities were putting final touches to the mass deportation of all British passport holders and Ugandans of Asian origin, the Kenyan Special Branch announced that it had received intelligence reports that Tanzanian troops and Ugandan guerrilla forces were planning an invasion of Uganda. Two days later, a combined force of guerrillas of Yoweri Museveni's Front for National Salvation (FRONASA) and the late Oyite Ojok's Kikosi Maalum fighters invaded Uganda.

Many of the officers had dismissed the Kenyan Special Branch reports with a contempt that they surely did not deserve. The attack therefore took many of them by surprise, contributing to the invaders' initial successes. A combined force of fierce fighters from both Simba Battalion Mbarara and Suicide Regiment Masaka was later assembled and placed under the command of Lieutenant Atanasius. They met the invaders at Kalisizo and routed them, forcing them to beat a hasty retreat back to Tanzania.

Amin ordered the air force to carry out reprisal air raids on Tanzanian towns. Bukoba and Mwanza were bombed ferociously, forcing Tanzania to reach a truce with Uganda. Hostilities ceased and the two countries agreed to pull back their troops from the border by at least 10 kilometers

Still, many us believed that it was only a matter of time before Amin ordered a full-scale invasion of Tanzania. This belief was lent credence by the fact that word from the Nubian, Kakwa and Lugbara officers who were close to him, was that he was becoming increasingly impatient with the numerous real and perceived subversive activities that were being traced back to Tanzania. The military planning unit and the army high command were ordered to work out multiple contingency plans of how best to attack and neutralise Tanzania. The plans were expeditiously drawn up and the best fighting units were put on red alert.

Early in 1973, several announcements were broadcast over Radio Uganda and the Uganda television service, alleging that a combined force of Tanzanian soldiers and Ugandan exiles estimated to be 10,000 in number had been assembled for an invasion of Uganda. Troops were deployed nearer the border and munitions transferred from Magamaga Ordinance Depot to Masaka, Mutukula and Mbarara in readiness, but the order to attack did not come...

In 1978... reports that an attack on Uganda was in the offing kept filtering into the headquarters of Masaka Mechanised Specialist

Reconnaissance Regiment, which was also known as Suicide Headquarters. The reports incensed the foreign legions, the Sudanese and the Congolese in the army high command. Led by Brigadier Malera, Taban Lupayi and Juma Butabika, they started calling for a pre-emptive attack on Tanzania. Then, in October 1978, Juma Butabika, with a handful of some of the Malire troops, left his unit and took command of the troops that had been permanently stationed at the border before advancing into Tanzania.

The attack took the few ill-equipped Tanzanian troops stationed at Mutukula and Minziro by surprise and they fled the area. Encouraged by the lack of resistance, Butabika who claimed to have been in Masaka by accident, rang Amin, claiming that Tanzanian troops had made an incursion into Uganda, prompting him to take command at the border guard in order to repulse the invaders. Amin fell for the lie, largely because it presented an opportunity for him to annex chunks of Tanzanian territory. He speedily sanctioned Butabika's southward march to Kyaka Bridge through Kasambya. Though the troops did not cross the Kyaka Bridge, they had effectively sealed off the entire Kagera salient and on November 1, Amin went on the air and announced that his government had annexed the Kagera salient.

Two days later, Butabika and his men, ignorant of military amphibious operations and the availability of emergency pontoon bridges, asked Amin to sanction air raids on the bridge. Approval was immediately given, but the inadequate firepower and poor marksmanship of our jet pilots meant that it was only after ballistics experts from Kilembe mines were ordered in that the bridge was finally blown up, sparking off wild celebrations. Gang rape, murder and the looting of all manner of goods and household property followed the celebrations....

A few weeks later, Amin ordered the immediate withdrawal of all Malire and Suicide regiment troops from the border area. As they returned to their respective units, he ordered the transfer of army recruits who had been undergoing training in Masaka to Mutukula. I had been hearing cases brought before the Economic Crimes Tribunal sitting in the Governor's Lodge in Jinja town, when one day, returning to the Crested Crane Hotel, I got a call from commanding officer Masaka, Lieutenant-Colonel Tom Asiki. Our dialogue was brisk. 'Rep to my loc imm,' he ordered, short for 'Report to my location immediately.' 'Wilco,' I replied.

The following day when I reported to Masaka, Asiki informed me that the tasks of guarding and patrolling the border as well as training the recruits who had been transferred to Mutukula had been placed on my shoulders and that I was to start at once. On arrival at Sanje near

Bigada parish, where I established my tactical headquarters, I found everything in a state of chaos. While a large number of recruits had been transferred there, no training had been going on. There was no established command structure and no way of differentiating between recruits and the soldiers who had already made their bones. To make matters worse, the men and officers mixed freely with the recruits. Luckily, I found that I had either trained many of the serving officers and men in Mbarara and Kabama or worked closely with them in diverse places. This simplified the task of regularising the administrative structure.

Barely a week after arriving in Bigada, intelligence reports indicating that Tanzania was building up positions started trickling in. We duly passed them on to our superiors in Masaka, but none of those reports was taken seriously. It was then that I realised that since the people on the ground were not taking the reports seriously, the Ugandan Prisons Services corporal cum tractor driver who had become the Chief of Staff would not react to those reports with the seriousness that they deserved.

A few days later, the Tanzanian troops acquired a BM Katyusha artillery piece, which later came to be known as Saba Saba in Uganda. The Tanzanians now began testing deep within their territory. Every night, the artillery fire drew closer to the border area. We intensified patrols on the border, dug more trenches and prepared for a fight.

On the other side of the border, having mastered their Katyusha, the Tanzanians lifted their range of fire. Rockets rained down on our defensive positions. A combination of good luck, poor artillery skills and being well dug saw us escape the initial wave without any casualties, but we knew that we wouldn't continue being so lucky. The shelling went on for weeks, seriously affecting the morale of my men. It was then that we requested air support against the mysterious Saba Saba artillery, the idea being to locate and destroy it. But the enemy had acquired SAM7s (surface-to-air missiles) that harassed and destroyed some of the MIG fighter jets dispatched for the operation. The mission aborted. We remained in our trenches, waiting for divine intervention.

By then we had lost touch with what was going on around us. We lost track of time and went about our duties mechanically. We ate food without paying any attention to what it was or what it tasted like.

About three weeks before the Tanzanians finally launched an infantry attack on Ugandan territory, we learnt by a stroke of luck the type of weapon they were using. One of the rockets aimed at Lukoma airstrip exploded only partially. We dispatched it to Army headquarters for identification, where a Soviet military advisor identified it as a BM

21 Katyusha multi-barrel. The Soviets offered to deliver superior artillery pieces, but Amin apparently viewed them with suspicion because of the ideological similarities between Nyerere's socialist government and that of the Soviet Union.

A few days later, Asiki sent me a message inviting me to attend a meeting in Republic House (in Kampala). During the meeting, attended by the Secretary of Defence, Major-general Emilio Mondo, Issac Malyamungu, Lieutenant-Colonel Godwin Sule, Gore and numerous others, I briefed the senior officers about the devastating impact that the Katyusha was having on troop morale. It was unanimously agreed to purchase powerful support weapons.... The Bank of Uganda was contacted and ordered to release the money in different European currencies. The cash was brought to Republic House. Uganda Airlines was ordered to reserve seats for an unspecified number of officers who were to immediately leave for Europe on the shopping trip, and our embassies abroad were cabled. Another group of officers was dispatched to Tripoli to collect a consignment of bombs promised earlier by the Libyan leader. One of our ambassadors also received two million US dollars to procure more hardware.

When I got back to my unit, news of what happened at Republic House boosted the morale of my soldiers. But as the weeks dragged on and the Tanzanians continued shelling our positions, the soldiers became impatient.... The enemy, having shelled Mutukula on a daily basis for more than two months, decided it was high time they crossed the border into Uganda.

The attack on Mutukula and Minzilo was a frontal one, coming east of Mutukula near where River Kagera joins Lake Victoria. On January 21, 1979, at 10 in the night, in heavy downpour, we started exchanging fire. It was difficult to distinguish the sound of small arms fire from that of a Katyusha. One could only distinguish lightning from the artillery fire - the lightning came zigzagging towards the ground, while the artillery fire moved through the sky in a huge arc.

As the fighting intensified, I thought it wise to get in touch with the Chief of Staff, but no one picked up the phone, even when I tried to get him at his residence... Towards morning, I rang Amin on 2241 Entebbe. I explained that the Tanzanian forces had at long last decided to move across the border into Uganda. Amin did not sound surprised. What seemed to shock him was that his Chef of Staff, who was meant to keep direct and open communication with the troops, could not be reached. He promised to get back to me.

In the early hours of the morning, as the Tanzanian troops approached the forward edge of the battle area, he rang back, and promised to order heavy air support and an immediate reinforcement of our position. The message lifted the spirits of the soldiers. By this time the invaders, most of them young boys... enlisted into the TPDF (Tanzania People's Defence Forces), had reached the forward edge of the battle area in the hope of capturing Mutukula Prison. Our troops were than ready to give them the bashing of their lives.

Armed with Yugoslav-made assault rifles which we fondly referred to as Yugos, our troops opened fire on the advancing enemy, mowing them down in their hundreds. But they came on in droves. Their bodies littered the Mutukula Prison grounds, but their commanders continued pouring more and more men into the attack. Though expensive in human lives, the gamble paid off. By the end of the first battle, which lasted more than six hours, they had overrun Mutukula.... Few of our artillery pieces had survived the long hours of fighting....

Many of us started praying that the Tanzanians would make a tactical withdrawal. An immediate enemy advance would mean both total defeat and another perilous drop in the morale of our fighters.... Many of the soldiers had come to the conclusion that their failure to defend Mutukula and the forced abandonment of Lukoma, Bigada, Kibale, Nazareth and Naluzale, was the fault of the army top brass....

At the barracks, I found that my family had already left and most of our fellow officers also evacuated their families. My wife had sought sanctuary in a small village located along the Masaka-Kalungu Road, where I found them at the home of a friend. By then, most of the Mbarara-Maska road had already been taken over by the enemy....

The enemy resumed shelling our positions and advancing towards Sanje, where we had left the First Infantry Regiment. In Kampala, despite the news that Mutukula had fallen and that the enemy was advancing deeper into our territory, members of the army high command, including my commanding officer, were busy celebrating the eighth anniversary of Amin's rule.[14]

They did not realize that they were also celebrating the last anniversary of Amin's blood-soaked reign of terror. Nor did Amin himself who had already declared himself life-president.

The ouster of Idi Amin became one of President Nyerere's main Pan-African objectives, to rid Africa of a brutal tyrant and an international buffoon who had become the laughing-stock of the world and an embarrassment for the entire continent, and who happened to be just across the border, thus making his presence even more intolerable for Tanzania. The decision to topple Amin was also one of Nyerere's most daring foreign policy initiatives and set a precedent that was followed by other African leaders years later. When the Tanzanian army finally ousted Amin and stayed in Uganda for six months to restore and maintain stability, Tanzania was strongly condemned by a number of African countries, mostly those with large Muslim populations, since Amin was a Muslim himself. Nyerere, one of the founders of the Organization of African Unity (OAU), was accused of violating one of the cardinal principles of the OAU: Non-interference in the internal affairs of another state. Yet, when Amin's forces made cross-border raids since the early seventies, violating Tanzania's territorial integrity, none of these countries condemned Idi Amin for that. And when some countries condemned him, condemnation of his aggression was not equally swift and was even muted in many cases. Since the countries, which criticized Tanzania for invading Uganda were mostly Muslim, including Arab ones, it seems obvious that religion was a factor in this condemnation. They were defending a fellow Muslim who had been ousted by a Christian president, although Tanzania itself has at least as many Muslims as Christians, and Nyerere's decision to get rid of Amin was definitely not based on religious considerations. His interest was, first and foremost, to defend the territorial integrity of Tanzania.

Tanzania's invasion of Uganda - which was more of a counter-thrust than an invasion and was totally justified to drive Amin's forces off Tanzania's territory - was also vehemently condemned by some African countries for another reason. It led to the overthrow of an African government by another African country, the first such case on the continent, and whose troops also stayed on as "an army of occupation" - not as a peacekeeping force, according to this rationale - for at least six months to help its "client regime" consolidate itself in power. Yet, in a reversal of fortunes, the ouster of Mobutu Sese Seko of Zaire almost exactly eighteen years later in May 1997 (Idi Amin was kicked out in April 1979) by the invading armies of a number of African countries - in which Tanzania also played a major role - was roundly applauded across the continent. The invasion followed a precedent set by Tanzania about two decades before - do what has to be done - and thus vindicated Nyerere's position, when he ordered the Tanzanian army to go into Uganda and get rid of Amin's regime, that principles of non-interference in the affairs of another state - whether those principles are OAU or UN principles or any other - should *not* take precedence over human lives and well-being. And Ugandans who lived under Amin during his reign of terror were grateful for that.

But even if Nyerere had not viewed Amin's brutalities and policies as well as stupidity in a Pan-African context as a shame on Africa, he had an immediate concern for his country's security. As long as Idi Amin remained in power, he would continue to be a threat to Tanzania, especially with the help he got from other countries to attack Tanzania; hence the need to get rid of him. And Tanzania was determined to do so. Annexation of her territory by Amin provided Tanzania with a justification to launch a counter-invasion and go to the source, all the way to Kampala, Uganda's capital, where all the trouble began at the instigation of Amin. As Nyerere said at a press conference in Tanzania's capital, Dar es Salaam, in November 1978 when the war broke out: "Tanzania has the reason, the capacity, and the determination" to fight and defeat Amin, and warned other countries to stay out of the conflict.[15] When Amin annexed the Kagera salient, Nyerere said such annexation amounted to a declaration of war on Tanzania.

Tanzania's security, and the honor of Africa - whose reputation had been badly tarnished because of the refusal or unwillingness of most African leaders to speak out against atrocities perpetrated in African countries, as in Uganda - were not the only reasons why Nyerere decided to oust Idi Amin from power. The suffering of the people themselves in Uganda under Amin's brutal regime, which included torture and murder of members of different tribes and the expulsion of people of Asian origin including those who were Ugandan citizens, also prompted President Nyerere to take action and get rid of Amin.

Therefore the ouster of Idi Amin was also a moral imperative as much as the struggle against apartheid in South Africa was. Nor was it motivated by religion - Nyerere as a Christian going against Amin, a Muslim, as some people have claimed - anymore than Nyerere's recognition of Biafra was. As Professor Ali Mazrui, a Muslim himself like Amin, states:

Has Nyerere's political behaviour sometimes reflected his upbringing as a Roman Catholic? There is a school of thought, which explains his recognition of the secessionist Biafra...as a form of solidarity with fellow Catholics against a Federal Nigeria, which was potentially dominated by Muslims. This was in the middle of the Nigerian civil war (Tanzania recognized Biafra on April 13, 1968, the first country to do so). The Igbo of Biafra were overwhelmingly Roman Catholic. Less convincing is the assertion that Nyerere's military intervention in Uganda in 1979 was motivated by a sectarian calculation to defend a mainly Christian Uganda (which is only 10 percent Muslim) from the Muslim dictator Idi Amin. In reality, Nyerere might have been motivated by a wider sense of humanitarianism and universal ethics. He was also defending Tanzania from Idi Amin's territorial appetites... (And) I personally did not share the suspicion that Nyerere recognized Biafra because the Igbo were fellow Roman Catholics claiming to be threatened by Muslim Northerners in Nigeria... It seems much more likely that Nyerere recognized Biafra for humanitarian reasons.[16]

It should also be remembered that although Nyerere was a Christian, he strongly supported the Palestinians - most of whom are Muslims - in their quest for justice and for a homeland in the Middle East, as much as he supported the existence of Israel as a homeland for Jews to live within secure borders and under their own government. Had he been biased as a Christian, he would not have supported the Arabs in their struggle against Israel but would have, instead, supported only Israel because of its biblical significance as the Holy Land for Christians. His support for both Israel's existence and the Palestinian cause was strictly based on principles of justice, which have universal validity. And as in the case of Biafra where about 100,000 Eastern Nigerians, mostly Igbos, had already died in the civil war at the hands of the federal military government by the time Tanzania recognized the secessionist region, Nyerere strongly felt that it was necessary to take a strong stand against the murderous regime of Idi Amin who was killing people in Uganda everyday; an average of 150 per day, killed by his henchmen. Failure to do so would have been tantamount to condoning the atrocities; just as failure or refusal to recognize Biafra would have been a virtual endorsement of the massacre of the Igbos and other Biafrans by the Nigerian federal military government - and in the name of unity, which did not even exist between the two sides.

Nyerere was also the only African leader who vehemently

condemned Idi Amin for his brutalities. He was also the only African leader who denounced Amin as a racist for expelling Asians from Uganda and seizing their property. Presidents Kenneth Kaunda of Zambia and Samora Machel of Mozambique also condemned Amin, but not as much as Nyerere did. Nyerere was also the only leader - not only in Africa but in the entire world - who took decisive action against Amin. He was also highly critical of fellow African leaders for their silence, and accused them of applying a double standard; reminding them that they were quick to condemn injustices committed by whites, but not when similar atrocities were being perpetrated by fellow black Africans. As he bluntly stated: "There is this tendency in Africa to think that it does not matter if an African kills other Africans. Had Amin been white, free Africa would have passed resolutions condemning him. Being black is becoming a certificate to kill fellow Africans."[17]

Most African leaders and other Africans were amused by Amin's antics and buffoonery - as much as non-Africans were, of course, who also saw Amin as a comedian - and took great delight in what he did because, being one of their own, they saw him as a fearless African twisting the white man's nose. The shoe was on the other foot, was the rationale, regardless of what it entailed in this context. Amin said things they wanted to say, but couldn't, the way he did, in a blunt and crude way. But they were able to do so, vicariously, through him. He became their mouthpiece. The imperial logic had been reversed, an the white man was no longer on top in Africa, best symbolized in a bizarre way - Idi Amin's style - when the Ugandan dictator ordered British diplomats to carry him on a forced march, barefoot, through the streets of Kampala in 1977. The story and picture of this circus made international headlines in major publications including *Time* and *Newsweek*, as many Africans applauded, although not all of us did. But a highly disproportionate number of them did, instead of being ashamed of a leader who continued to tarnish the image of our continent.

While all this buffoonery was going on, and his admirers applauded, Amin's henchmen - and on many occasions with the participation of Amin himself   - were killing about 150 - 200 people everyday, as African leaders remained silent or simply looked the other way. Even when Amin's atrocities made headlines, and irrefutable evidence showed what was going on, African leaders still refused to take measures against Amin and said nothing in condemnation. Instead, they applauded him privately, and continued to derive satisfaction from his antics and humiliation of Africa's former colonial masters and other whites as well as Asians - people of East Indian and Pakistani origin in East Africa - who were accused of exploiting Africans. He became the most "outspoken" African leader and one of the most brutal in the post-colonial era, also with expansionist ambitions, prompting Nyerere to take action and end such madness. He described Amin's reign of terror as an "eight-year regime of mass murder, cruel and ruthless torture, economic destruction, and deliberately imposed misery still leaves its shadow over the people of Uganda, years after he was overthrown."[18] He was a disaster of immense proportions.

From a regional perspective - to facilitate regional integration - we also see that there was another Pan-African dimension to Nyerere's campaign to oust Amin, besides his desire to restore Africa's credibility that had been severely eroded because of the refusal of most African leaders to stop atrocities on the continent - which prompted him in the late seventies to say the Organization of African Unity (OAU) was nothing but "a trade union of tyrants." Idi Amin was a major obstacle to East African cooperation - between Kenya, Uganda, and Tanzania - because of his erratic policies and irreconcilable differences with Nyerere. He could not work with Nyerere - nor could Nyerere work with him - as one of the three members of the East African Authority that oversaw the East African Community. The presidents of the three countries constituted the Authority. But because Nyerere and Amin could not work together, the East African Community could not function smoothly.

Also, there were fundamental policy differences between Kenya and Tanzania, capitalist versus socialist, which proved to be another major obstacle to East African cooperation and even prompted Tanzania to close the border with Kenya in 1977 in a dispute over Community assets and the shutting down of the East African Airways (EAA) that had been jointly owned by the three East African countries. When the East African Community collapsed in 1977, Kenya kept the bulk of the Community assets, including the East African Airways (EAA), which had its headquarters in Kenya's capital Nairobi, prompting Tanzania to retaliate by closing the border.

But Amin presented another serious problem to the Community because of the violence and instability in his country, making full cooperation among the three countries virtually impossible; in addition to the differences between him and Nyerere which precluded any possibility of cooperation between the two leaders. As Nyerere stated after Amin was thrown out of Uganda and forced into exile: "Tanzania now has greater opportunities to develop itself, and much less excuse than formerly for any failure to exploit to the full the possibilities of bilateral cooperation across the Ugandan-Tanzanian border."[19] Cooperation between the two countries was restored within a short time after Amin was overthrown by a combined invasion force of the Tanzania People's Defence Forces (TPDF) and Ugandan exiles, spearheaded by Tanzania.

During his eight-year reign of terror, drenched with blood, Amin killed between 300,00 and 500,000 people. Some estimates go as high as 800,000. The victims included some of his wives and very close relatives and friends, as well as hundreds of army officers in his own army. He trusted nobody. One of the few prisoners to come out alive from one of Amin's notorious torture chambers in a dungeon right in the capital Kampala, was James Kahigirizi, a civil servant. As he explained what amounted to hell on earth under Amin: "There were men taken out every night. Whenever a guard stood there at night, some of us covered our faces, thinking they were going to call you at that time to go back. Idi Amin was a devil."[20]

The State Research Bureau constituted the nerve center, and the heart, of Amin's terror state; its torture chamber in dungeons being notorious for countless deaths and some of the most extraordinarily cruel punishment ever inflicted on man. Among his biggest victims in his first year in office were soldiers from the Langi and Acholi tribes whom he suspected of being loyal to Obote. Obote was a Langi, and a fellow northerner like Amin who was a member of the small Kakwa tribe. Amin's feelings of insecurity were compounded by an inferiority complex attributed to his lack of education. He was very paranoid and ignorant. As Henry Kyemba - he once worked under Obote and was with him at the Commonwealth conference in Singapore and in Nairobi, Kenya, on their way back to Uganda when they heard that Amin had seized power - who served as Amin's principal private secretary and then as minister of health until he fell out with the dictator in May 1977, stated:

After the coup, it became more obvious that Amin was grossly inadequate for the high office of president. He was also illiterate, his English was poor, he read very badly and clearly had a hard time just signing prepared documents! As his first Principal Private Secretary, I never received a handwritten note from him! Amin had no idea of how governments were run. He had no experience of civil service procedures or of modern economies. in the early days, the very thought of speaking in public made him break out into a sweat!....

He refused to take the advice of his ministers and simply ignored the economic realities of life. Anyone not complying became a saboteur and enemy. Amin's reign of terror spread rapidly from the barracks to every facet of life in the entire country. (Hundreds of) thousands were murdered and a few managed to escape into exile including myself but the vast majority of Ugandans remained at the mercy abd whims of Amin's military machine. In my book, *The State of Blood*, which I dedicated to the memory of one hundred friends murdered by Amin, written in 1977while I was in exile in London, I listed some of those I knew were dead.

The list included among others my elder brother R.L. Kisajja, the late Honourable Shaban K. Nkutu, Chief Justice Benedicto Kiwanuka, Archbishop Janan Luwum, Frank Kalimuzo (Vice-Chancellor of Makerere University), late Honourable Basil Bataringaya, late Honourable John Kakonge, Professor Emiru, Henry Kagoda, Mrs. Dora Block and Bank of Uganda Governor Joseph Mubiru. Amin's reign of terror will continue to be a subject of debate for many years to come. How can one explain such man's inhumanity to man? Amin's friends and foes alike met the most grotesque deaths.... Chief Justice Benedicto Kiwanuka: I remember his case very well because he was grabbed at the High Court on the same day as my own brother was bundled away from his place of work at Nytil Jinja for a similar fate.... The Chief Justice...was seized in broadlight at the High Court....

Internationally, Uganda achieved a terrible image. The East African Community collapsed and the expulsion of the Asian community disrupted our commercial and industrial life....

In all this, there was clearly no alternative but to remove the dictatorship in its totality. Not merely Amin as a person. The occasion offered itself with Amin invading the Kagera triangle of Tanzania in 1978. What followed is a familiar history.[21]

The fall of Idi Amin on April 11, 1979, when Tanzanian soldiers and Ugandan exiles captured the capital Kampala marked the end of one of the most brutal regimes in modern history. It was also welcomed with jubilation in the capital and in other parts of Uganda as the news of Amin's downfall spread across the country. And it became a day of remembrance to honor those who died; and celebrate the end of a brutal tyrant whose murderous regime tarnished the image of a country Sir Winston Churchill called "the pearl of Africa."

And when Uganda celebrated the 23rd anniversary of Amin's downfall, the people of Uganda also paid tribute to the late President Julius Nyerere of Tanzania, not only for liberating them from Amin's tyranny, but also for his relentless effort to try to bring peace and stability to the entire Great Lakes region of East-Central Africa which had been plunged into chaos following decades of ethnic conflicts between the Hutu and the Tutsi in Rwanda and Burundi; conflicts which culminated in the Rwandan genocide in 1994, plunging the whole region into turmoil on an unprecedented scale. According to a Ugandan newspaper, *New Vision*: "Uganda will soon host 14 heads of state in...a regional symposium to remember former President Mwalimu Julius Kambarage Nyerere's peace efforts, mark 23 years after the fall of President Idi Amin and bolster the search for peace in the troubled Great Lakes Region."[22]

It is this bloodshed - especially in Burundi - that Nyerere worked tirelessly to bring to an end, and continued to do so until his last days; as much as he did years earlier when he was the only African leader who took decisive action against Amin's despotic regime and succeeded in ousting him from power, thus rescuing the people of Uganda - and Africa as a whole - from the tight grip of a blood-soaked tyrant, one of the worst in the twentieth century.

Amin was also the most flamboyant leader Africa has ever produced, and gave himself the title: "His Excellency President for Life Field Marshall Al Hadj Dr. Idi Amin Dada, VC (Victoria Cross), DSO (Distinguished Service Order), MC (Military Cross), Lord of All the Beasts of the Earth of and Fishes of the Sea, and Conquer of the British Empire (CBE)." He also called himself King Termite, King of Africa, and ruler of the universe.

As Nyerere bluntly put it: "He's an idiot."

CHAPTER TEN:

AMERICAN INVOLVEMENT IN ANGOLA AND SOUTHERN AFRICA: NYERERE'S RESPONSE

AMERICAN INVOLVEMENT in Southern Africa was dictated by economic interests more than anything else; rivalry with the Soviet Union and other communist-bloc countries; and strategic partnership with apartheid South Africa which was regarded as an integral part of the West and an embodiment and custodian of Western values and civilization in a non-Western region of the world. It was also influenced by racial considerations to protect the interests of the white minorities regardless of the racial injustices committed against the black majority and other non-whites.

This involvement assumed its most blatant form during the Angolan conflict in a proxy war with the Soviet Union in which American surrogates - apartheid South Africa and UNITA rebels - wreaked havoc across Angola in an attempt to oust the legitimate MPLA government from power; a government that had also been recognized by the organization of African Unity (OAU) and other countries besides those in the communist bloc. Although American intervention became a prime factor in determining the future of Angola especially during the war, we should not overlook the fact that the United States was not really new on the Angolan scene, although it made a dramatic "entry" during the seventies in terms of confrontation with the Soviet Union in this proxy war. American involvement in Angola goes way back to the sixties with regard to cultivating ties with potential future leaders of that country once it became independent; and long before then in terms of relations with Portugal as an ally and fellow member of NATO, while turning a blind eye to her brutal colonial policies in Angola and other Portuguese colonies in Africa.

American engagement in Angola on the nationalist side started when the United States established ties with Holden Roberto - of GRAE, later FNLA - in the sixties. The intention was not to support the liberation struggle. That's one thing the United States never did in Africa. Instead, it supported colonial and white minority regimes. But American officials felt that it was important to establish ties with potential future African leaders because Portugal would not be able to maintain colonial rule in Agola and elsewhere in Africa, including Mozambique whose nationalist leader, Dr. Eduardo Mondlane, had strong ties to the United States. Portugal's position was contrasted with that of the apartheid regime in South Africa which American leaders believed was firmly in control of its territory, although they were proven wrong only a few years later when the racist edifice gradually began to fall apart in the seventies after the Soweto uprising by black students in 1976. The CIA and American leaders felt that Holden Roberto was their man whom they could easily buy and manipulate, and went on to put him on the CIA payroll around 1961 or 1962.

Yet at the same time, they continued to support the colonial regime. In the following years, the United States provided weapons and ammunition, and counter-insurgency training, the Portuguese colonial rulers needed to contain and if possible neutralize the nationalist forces of the MPLA and the FNLA, which were fighting for independence. The devastation caused by American-supplied weapons used by the Portuguese against Africans including innocent civilians - women and children being among the victims - was extensive. As John Marcum, an American scholar who walked 800 miles through Angola and visited FNLA training camps in the early sixties, wrote:

> By January 1962 outside observers could watch Portuguese planes bomb and strafe African villages, visit the charred remains of towns like Mbanza M'Pangu and M'Pangala, and copy the data from 750-point napalm bomb casings from which the Portuguese had not removed the labels marked 'Property U.S. Air Force.'[1]

Super-power rivalry also became a prime factor because of American and Soviet involvement in Angola. But unlike the United States, the Soviet Union never supported Portugal in her war against the nationalist forces not only in Angola but in Mozambique and Portuguese Guinea (Guinea-Bissau) where Africans were also waging guerrilla warfare against the colonial armies. And this gave the Soviets credibility, which the Americans lacked, as friends of Africans helping them to become free. The Soviets had also supported Holden Roberto but left him because, among other reasons, he had helped Moise Tshombe - a pariah on the African continent - in the Congo, and also substantially curtailed his guerrilla campaign under pressure from the United States. He was already on the CIA payroll and from 1969 was getting a $10,000-per-year retainer from the agency. His brother-in-law, President Joseph Mobutu - later Mobutu Sese Seko - of Congo, was also on the CIA payroll.

In 1964, the Soviets embraced Dr. Agostinho Neto of the MPLA as a more credible nationalist. But they also supported him for another reason: ideological. Since his student days in the 1940s in Portugal, Neto had established ties with radical elements, many of them communists, and came to embrace Marxism, the state ideology of the Soviet Union which he felt would also be appropriate for Angola and help transform the country into a better society.

Then in 1966 another nationalist party, UNITA, emerged on the scene, led by Dr. Jonas Savimbi. It was supported by the People's Republic of China, and initially also got support from Tanzania and Zambia but abandoned it later on because of its ties to anti-colonial forces in the West and apartheid South Africa. At first, all three groups - FNLA, MPLA, UNITA - professed to be socialist. But only the MPLA was more committed to socialism than the other two. Yet, although it embraced Marxism, it was not really Marxist but nationalist more than anything else and ready to accept help from anywhere - including the West - to achieve its goals of liberation and economic development. In fact, in December 1962, Dr. Neto went to Washington to argue his case for Angola's independence before the American government and told American officials that it was wrong to call the MPLA communist.

American involvement in Angola dramatically increased in 1975 when the country was about to win independence. In January the same year, the CIA was authorized to give Holden Roberto and his group, the FNLA, $300,000. And shortly thereafter in March, FNLA forces attacked the MPLA headquarters in Luanda. A total of 51 unarmed, young MPLA recruits were gunned down, murdered in cold blood. The attack could not have taken place without the knowledge or approval of the United States, and it helped ignite a full-scale war in which UNITA, another American client, joined forces with the FNLA in an attempt to destroy the MPLA. Yet, it is a war in which the United States denied its involvement, let alone helping start it.

The $300,000 given to the FNLA in January 1975, and the attack by its forces that followed shortly thereafter in March to try to destroy the MPLA, played a critical role not only in starting the Angolan civil war but in plunging the country into chaos from which it has never recovered. And the United States - not Cuba or the Soviet Union - was directly responsible for this, despite repeated denials by American officials including Secretary of State Henry Kissinger. They lied. It was after this happened that the Soviet Union sent the first large shipment of arms to the MPLA in March. Even the investigating committee of the United States Congress conceded: "Later events have suggested that this infusion of US aid [$300,000], unprecedented and massive in the underdeveloped colony, may have panicked the Soviets into arming their MPLA clients."[2]

The Soviet Union was probably also influenced by China in its decision to send a large shipment of weapons to the MPLA. In September 1974, the Chinese sent a huge shipment of arms to the FNLA in Angola and more than 100 military advisers to neighboring Zaire - another American client - train FNLA soldiers only one month after the coup in Portugal which speeded up the desalinization process when the new military government of young leftist soldiers in Lisbon announced their intention to end colonial rule in Africa. The CIA escalated the conflict and further alarmed the Soviets when it sent its first major shipment of arms to the FNLA in July 1975; knowing full well that the Soviets would respond with their own shipment at least to match, if not exceed, the American infusion of military aid to Holden Roberto and his forces.

American involvement in the Angolan conflict had another dimension. Besides giving weapons to the FNLA and UNITA, the United States also trained the soldiers of the two groups, and American pilots and other personnel flew many times between Zaire and Angola on supply and reconnaissance missions. Kinshasa, the capital of Zaire, then had the largest CIA station and contingent in Africa. And their client, President Mobutu Sese Seko, did everything he could to impede the liberation of southern Africa and Angola at the behest of the United States and France and other Western powers. The CIA during that time also spent more than one million dollars to recruit and train mercenaries for its Angolan mission. Many of those mercenaries were Americans. Others were Portuguese, French, South African, and British including the notorious George Cullen who shot 14 of his fellow mercenaries dead because they had mistakenly attacked the wrong side; the MPLA, after consolidating its position as the government of Angola, executed him. Yet Henry Kissinger told the United States Senate that the CIA was not involved in mercenary activities in Angola, during the very same time when the agency was busy recruiting and training soldiers of fortune for the Angolan mission.

Besides the recruitment of mercenaries by the CIA, the agency also had more than 100 agents and military officers operating in Zaire, Angola, South Africa and Zambia, moving back and forth, directing military campaigns and other activities including a sustained disinformation campaign. It also recruited journalists working for major news organizations to help carry on the campaign through false reports - from the CIA - about Soviet military advisers in Angola; "atrocities" - including rape and murder - committed by Cuban soldiers against African civilians, and other lies. UNITA was one of the main sources of these reports generated by the CIA. But some major newspapers, such as *The New York Times*, *The Washington Post*, *The Guardian* (London), were on guard and pointed out that the only source of these reports was UNITA. The implication was obvious. The papers were careful not to give credibility to such reports, implying they were fabricated. But there were other journalists who did not do this. Instead, they tried to give credence to these false reports generated by the CIA in order to discredit the Soviets and the Cubans.

Yet, in spite of all this, the CIA clients - FNLA and UNITA - had little chance of defeating the MPLA, the most organized and best led of the three groups. It also controlled the capital Luanda and was recognized by the majority of the African countries, thus casting the United States in a very bad light across the continent, while the Soviets and the Cubans gained credibility as supporters of the legitimate government of Angola. Compounding the problem for the United States was the fact that apartheid South Africa supported the same groups - FNLA and UNITA - the Americans did. The MPLA definitely had the upper hand, but the United States still opposed a negotiated settlement of the Angolan conflict simply because the Soviet Union was on the winning side, not only of the MPLA but of the majority of the African governments who - through the Organization of African Unity (OAU) - had accorded it recognition as the government of a sovereign entity which was also a member of the OAU. And when the MPLA tried to establish relations with the United States, American officials said they would do so only if their country was allowed to replace the Soviet Union as the most influential power in Angola.

American involvement in Angola, and in southern Africa in general, assumed yet another dimension with the direct engagement of South African troops in the Angolan war with the encouragement of the United States; although the apartheid regime also had its own interests when it intervened in order to create a buffer zone between independent African countries supporting the freedom fighters and white-ruled South Africa by installing a puppet government in Angola to block guerrilla fighters from entering South West Africa (Namibia) and South Africa itself. The United States asked South Africa to actively intervene in Angola because it was American policy - implemented by the CIA and the National Security Agency (NSA) - since the sixties to cooperate with South Africa's intelligence service, hence the apartheid regime itself, in pursuit of Western interests in the region; including neutralizing Soviet presence and influence in Angola and elsewhere on the continent, but mainly in southern Africa which was the combat theater.

One of the main reasons why the United States wanted to actively collaborate with the apartheid regime in intelligence activities was the existence of the African National Congress (ANC) on the South African political scene as the dominant nationalist organization fighting to end apartheid, and whose most prominent leader was Nelson Mandela. Although banned, it wielded great influence not only within South Africa but in other African countries as well, and abroad, especially among anti-apartheid groups. It was also supported by the Soviet Union, thus making it a prime target for the CIA, which wanted to undermine it, and, if possible, destroy it. CIA involvement in South Africa reached a dramatic point in 1962 when Nelson Mandela, returning from Tanganyika where he met Julius Nyerere, was arrested by the South African police. The South African authorities were able to locate Mandela based on information about his movements and disguise, and his hideout, provided by CIA agent Donald Rickard. Mandela was eventually sentenced to life imprisonment and spent almost 28 years in confinement.[3]

During his visit to Tanganyika in 1962, the first to an independent African country to seek financial and military assistance - Tanganyika was also the first country in eastern and southern Africa to win independence - Mandela was somewhat disappointed when Nyerere told him that he and his organization, the African National Congress (ANC), should wait until Robert Mangaliso Sobukwe was out of prison before starting the armed struggle against the apartheid regime. Sobukwe, a professor at Witwatersrand University, South Africa's leading academic institution, was the leader of the Pan-Africanist Congress (PAC) formed in 1959 as a breakaway from the African National Congress (ANC). Although Mandela was discouraged by Nyerere's response to his request for military help, urging postponement so that the ANC and the PAC should wage a coordinated campaign once Sobukwe was freed, he was at the same time encouraged by the fact that Nyerere told him he would get in touch with Emperor Haile Selassie and ask him to help. So Mandela went to Ethiopia, traveling on documents issued by the government of Taganyika and authorized by Nyerere, where he got some military training. It was the same travel documents he used to go to other African countries and to Britain. As he states in his autobiography, *Long Walk to Freedom*, the government of Tanganyika assumed responsibility for his travel, giving him a document which said: "This is Nelson Mandela, a citizen of South Africa. He has permission to leave Tanganyika, and return here." And he did. But when he returned to South Africa, it was an entirely different story. Had it not been for the intelligence information provided by CIA agent Donald Rickard on Mandela's whereabouts and disguise, he probably would not have been found where he was hiding, and therefore would not have been arrested and sent to prison for almost three decades.

American involvement in southern Africa continued when the CIA set up a covert operation in 1975 to deliver weapons to South Africa for the South African armed forces. The weapons were also used in Angola by America's surrogate forces - FNLA and UNITA - against Soviet-Cuban-backed MPLA forces which were also supported by African countries such as Nigeria, Tanzania, Mozambique, and Congo-Brazzaville but opposed by Zaire under Mobutu, Tanzania's and Congo-Brazzaville's as well as Angola's neighbor and the most important American client state in the region and, indeed, on the entire continent. In a reciprocal arrangement with the United States, South Africa helped transport American weapons from Zaire to Angola for the FNLA and UNITA forces in acknowledgment for the military assistance the apartheid regime was getting from the American government. Yet American officials - Kissinger, CIA Director William Colby and others - continued to deny such involvement and even lied to the United States Congress about it.

Although the United States was deeply involved in Angola, it still was unable to turn the tide against the MPLA. By February 1976, with the crucial assistance of Cuban combat forces and Soviet military hardware, the MPLA had virtually defeated its rivals and was in full control of the capital Luanda. There has been much controversy over the sequence of events, which led to Cuban intervention, much of it generated by American denials and attempts to reverse the sequence and rewrite history. American and South African officials went in, they claim, in response to large-scale Cuban military intervention, instead of the reverse being the case; they went in surreptitiously at first. As Wayne Smith, director of the US State department's Office of Cuban Affairs from 1977 to 1979, wrote later: "In August and October [1975] South African troops invaded Angola with full U.S. knowledge. No Cuban troops were in Angola prior to this intervention."[4]

Even when UNITA leader Dr. Jonas Savimbi tried to reach an accommodation with the MPLA, mainly because he lost the war, the United States told him to keep on fighting simply because Angola had a government American leaders didn't like and which was getting help from their nemesis, the Soviet Union; in spite of the fact that they had a reliable client next door, Mobutu, and the largest CIA station on the entire continent based in Zaire's capital Kinshasa. Zaire also had its own reason why it was opposed to the MPLA government. Zairean leaders wanted a government they could manipulate or influence and prevent it from allowing Katanga rebels from using Angola as a sanctuary and springboard from which to launch attacks on Zaire. In fact, Katanga *gendarmes* fled to Angola and settled there after losing the war in the sixties. Determined to keep them out of Zaire, Mobutu sent his poorly trained, but American-equipped armed forces into combat to support the FNLA against the MPLA, although Holden Roberto, Mobutu's brother-in-law, and his army were an incompetent lot, and of little use to Zaire and to the United States except as a nuisance to the Soviets and the Cubans. As Professor Gerald Bender, a renowned American authority on Angola, said in his testimony before the United States Congress in 1978:

> Although the United States has supported the FNLA in Angola for 17 years, it is virtually impossible to find an American official, scholar or journalist, who is familiar with that party, who will testify positively about its organization or leadership. After a debate with a senior State Department official at the end of the Angolan civil war, I asked him why the United States ever bet on the FNLA. He replied, 'I'll be damned if I know; I have never seen a single report or memo which suggests that the FNLA has any organization, solid leaders, or an ideology which we would count on.' Even foreign leaders who have supported Holden Roberto, such as General Mobutu, agree with that assessment. When asked by a visiting U.S. Senator if he thought Roberto would make a good leader for Angola, Mobutu replied, 'Hell no!'[5]

The United States continued to justify its intervention in Angola and southern Africa by using convoluted logic, lying, and rarely telling the truth. Secretary of State Henry Kissinger testified before Congress that one of the main reasons for the American policy in Angola was to maintain stability in Zaire under Mobutu. Yet this was not a convincing explanation. It did not explain or justify large-scale American intervention in a third country, Angola. The United States could have directly poured massive aid into Zaire itself to strengthen Mobutu's regime. The stability and security of Zaire was, or could be maintained, within Zaire itself not in Angola. Kissinger's testimony before the US Congressional investigating committee could not be reconciled with what the United States was actually doing or how Mobutu felt after he discovered a plot to undermine his regime. In June 1975, a month before the United States sent a large amount of weapons to the FNLA, Mobutu accused the American government and the CIA of trying to overthrow and assassinate him and expelled the American ambassador. Yet this was the very same leader Kissinger claimed the United States was helping maintain stability in his country and sustain in power.

Even when the MPLA government provided security to American and other employees of Gulf Oil and its installations, the United States was still determined to undermine it and fuel the civil war, although Gulf Oil, an American corporation, accepted MPLA's security arrangements. Instead, the CIA and the US State Department exerted enormous pressure on Gulf Oil to stop royalty payments to the MPLA government for the oil it was pumping out of the Cabinda enclave. And contrary to what American officials said, Fidel Castro did not send Cuban troops to Angola at the behest of the Soviet Union but in pursuit of his own foreign policy objectives as a supporter of liberation movements, champion of the Third World, and as an internationalist. Hostility towards the MPLA, and refusal to accept it as the legitimate government of Angola, continued to be prominent features of American policy towards Angola even after the government had been internationally recognized by many countries as the true representative of the Angolan people, and exercising institutional authority over its territory, however tenuous in many areas because of the war. And the United States and her allies continued to work on plans to destabilize and overthrow the MPLA government. As William Blum states in his book, *Killing Hope: US Military and CIA Interventions Since World War II*:

In 1984 a confidential memorandum smuggled out of Zaire revealed that the United States and South Africa had met in November 1983 to discuss destabilization of the Angolan government. Plans were drawn up to supply more military aid to UNITA - the FNLA was now defunct - and discussions were held on ways to implement a wide range of tactics: unify the anti-government movements, stir up popular feeling against the government, sabotage factories and transport systems, seize strategic points, disrupt joint Anglo-Soviet projects, undermine relations between the (MPLA) government and the Soviet Union and Cuba, bring pressure to bear on Cuba to withdraw its troops, sow divisions in the ranks of the MPLA leadership, infiltrate agents into the Angolan army, and apply pressure to stem the flow of foreign investments into Angola.[6]

In pursuit of these objectives, the Reagan Administration announced in January 1987 that it was providing UNITA rebels with Stinger missiles and other anti-aircraft weapons. And, as far back as 1984, UNITA's official representative in Washington proudly stated that UNITA had "contacts with US officials at all levels on regular basis." And when UNITA lost the election to the MPLA in September 1992, the rebel group launched a full-scale war against the government with the help of South Africa and American "private" and "relief" organizations including conservative American leaders, despite the fact that the elections had been certified to be free and fair by the United Nations, the Organization of African Unity (OAU) and other international observers. As one senior US State Department official said in January 1993 a few months before the United States finally accorded the MPLA government full recognition in May the same year: "UNITA is exactly like the Khmer Rouge: elections and negotiations are just one more method of fighting a war; power is all."[7]

And the fact that the United States and South Africa intervened in Angola months before Castro sent troops in 1975, but lied about it claiming the Cubans went in first, raises serious questions about the credibility of American - and South African - officials throughout this engagement. It also raises serious questions about American claims that Washington was concerned about the well-being of Africans when it supported groups which were trying to destroy and replace an organization - the MPLA - which did most of the fighting during the liberation war against the Portuguese colonial forces and whose government was recognized by the majority of the African countries and the organization of African Unity (OAU). And the devastation wrought by America's surrogate forces - FNLA, UNITA, and apartheid South Africa - with American weapons, razing entire villages and killing countless innocent civilians, shows how much Washington really cared about Africans.

If the United States cared about the well-being of Africans, she would have supported them during the independence struggle and would have exerted a lot of pressure on Portugal, her NATO ally, to relinquish her colonies. Instead, she did exactly the opposite, yet expected to impress Africans not only in Angola but across the continent with its military intervention against the MPLA government. Worst of all is that the lies about American involvement in Angola were used by Kissinger and the United States government to justify American intervention which plunged the country and the entire southern Africa into civil war which lasted for almost 30 years, wreaking havoc and causing untold suffering on an unprecedented scale costing at least one million lives in Angola alone; with economic devastation amounting to hundreds of millions of dollars in a country which had the potential to become one of the richest not only in Africa but in the entire Third World. But for 30 years, all that potential went down the drain, thanks to the lies told by Dr. Henry Kissinger and other American officials to justify American intervention in an attempt to prevent the MPLA, a Soviet and Cuban ally, from assuming power.

Had the United States not intervened, the MPLA would have consolidated its position as the legitimate government of Angola from the time it routed its rivals - UNITA and the FNLA - back in 1976, and country would have embarked on the road towards stability and economic recovery and would probably have made significant progress during the next 30 years when it was, instead, mired in conflict. Yet American officials were so determined to prevent the MPLA from taking over Angola that they didn't care what they did to the country or what kind of lies they told; lies Kissinger continued to maintain through the years as if they were Gospel truth. He even told the same lies in the third volume of his memoirs, *Years of Renewal*,[8] published in 2002. As Professor Piero Gleijeses in the School of International Studies at Johns Hopkins University, who used the Freedom of Information Act to uncover documents about American covert operations in Angola and who was the first American scholar to have access to the archives in Havana, Cuba, on the Angolan conflict, states:

> When the United States decided to launch the covert intervention, in June and July (1975), not only were there no Cubans in Angola, but the US government and the CIA were not even thinking about any Cuban presence in Angola. If you look at the CIA reports, which were done at the time, the Cubans were totally out of the picture. (But in the reports presented to the US Senate in December 1975) what you find is really nothing less than the rewriting of

history.... Kissinger had the CIA rewrite its report to serve the political aim of the administration, and so the poor CIA ended up lying.[9]

Not only did Kissinger deny earlier American involvement in Angola; he also maintained then, and in his memoirs almost 30 years later, that the American government did not even know that South African troops invaded Angola posing as mercenaries in 1975. And although he claimed that the United States intervened in Angola (in July 1975) in response to a massive infusion of Cuban troops earlier, about 30,000 of them, declassified CIA papers for August-October 1975 say there were only a few Cubans in Angola during that time trying to pass themselves off as tourists. As Nathaniel Davis, Assistant Secretary of State for African Affairs under Kissinger but who resigned in July 1975 over American intervention in Angola, said: "Considering that things came to a head over covert action in the US government in mid-July, there is no reason to believe we were responding to Cuban involvement in Angola."[10]

A CIA-funded operation was launched from Zaire in July 1975 to support FNLA and Zairean forces in their invasion of Angola against the MPLA, during the same time when South African armed forces invaded the country in support of UNITA. They were not mercenaries, although the CIA leaked reports claiming that they were foreign mercenaries, probably funded by disgruntled elements in the former Portuguese colony. It was a well-coordinated attack masterminded by the CIA and the South African intelligence service. It was not until November 4, 1975, that Cuban President Fidel Castro decided to send troops to Angola - at the request of the MPLA in an urgent plea - in response to the South African invasion, which almost led to the capture of the capital Luanda, until the Cubans arrived in massive numbers and turned back the tide. The arrival of 30,000 Cuban troops tilted the civil war in favor of the MPLA, which was already in control of the capital. South African troops remained in Angola fighting the Cubans and the MPLA but were forced to withdraw in March 1976. They did not, however, stay out of Angola and continued to support UNITA rebels through the years, as much as the United States did, until the late 1980s.

Yet even such large-scale invasion of Angola by the South

African armed forces in July 1975 was not enough to make Kissinger tell the truth when he testified before Congress in 1976 on American covert operations in Angola. As Professor Gleijeses states: "The key element of the covert operation was cooperation with South Africa. Kissinger went to the extreme of saying he only learned a couple of weeks later that South Africa had invaded."[11]

Even the former CIA station chief in Angola from August to November 1975, Robert Hultslander, conceded later that American intervention was responsible for the chaos and destruction that ensued: "It was our policies which caused the destabilisation. Kissinger was determined to challenge the Soviet Union, although no vital US interests were at stake."[12] Hultslander also said US officers on the ground believed at the time that the MPLA was the "best qualified movement to govern Angola."[13] But Kissinger and others decided that it was not in the best interest of the United States for the MPLA to remain in power, despite its credentials as the legitimate government of Angola and the most competent group among the three contending factions (MPLA, FNLA, and UNITA). In fact, at a National Security Council meeting on June 27, 1975, Defence Secretary Dr. James Slazenger said the United States should "encourage the disintegration of Angola."[14] It was at that meeting that Kissinger indicated that the CIA had authorized provision of money and shipment of arms to American surrogate forces in Angola, months before the Cubans intervened in November the same year.

American intervention in Angola plunged the entire southern Africa into chaos from which it has not recovered after almost 30 years of war. The loss in human lives and destruction of property was enormous. All the countries in the region, including Tanzania, were affected one way or another. The flood of refugees alone fleeing into neighboring countries from the civil war in Angola became a major humanitarian crisis requiring massive international relief efforts - well into the late 1990s and beyond - unprecedented in the history of the region. Millions of Angolans became internally displaced, in addition to the one million who died, and untold numbers of others who sought refuge in Zambia, Zaire (renamed the Democratic Republic of Congo), Congo Republic (popularly known as Congo-Brazzaville), Namibia,

Botswana and other countries. America's determination to confront the Soviets wherever they were - except in their citadel, the Soviet Union itself and its satellites - turned Angola into a battleground it otherwise would not have been. As Julius Nyerere said on American television ABC program, "Issues and Answers," when he was asked in an interview in Dar es Salaam, Tanzania, in June 1976, why he thought the CIA was behind the fighting and chaos in Angola: "Who else is doing it? Who else could be doing it? Why do we keep hearing these whispers from Washington that let us create another Vietnam for Russia in Angola?...You are causing us trouble." Nyerere also articulated his position on American involvement in the region in his article, "America and Southern Africa," published in July 1977 in *Foreign Affairs*:

The dominant element in American foreign policy since 1946 has been opposition to communism and to the communist powers. As far as Africa was concerned, responsibility for pursuing these objectives was delegated to America's trusted allies - Britain, France, Belgium, and even Portugal - whose policies in the area were therefore broadly supported despite minor disagreements which arose as American business became interested in Africa's potential. Inevitably this placed America in opposition to an Africa, which was trying to win its independence from those same powers; but when political freedom could be achieved peacefully, America was able to appear to Africa like a bystander. It was therefore able to adjust its policies and accept the new status quo of African sovereign states without any difficulty. Notwithstanding these adjustments, however, America has continued to look at African affairs largely through anti-communist spectacles and to disregard Africa's different concerns and priorities.

And in southern Africa events did not force any readjustments of American policies during the 1960s; so none were made. Practical support for the status quo continued unabated until after the Portuguese Revolution in April 1974. Thus, despite America's verbal criticism of Portuguese colonialism, American arms and equipment were used by Portugal in its military operations in Angola, Guinea-Bissau and Mozambique. Despite the verbal opposition to apartheid, American trade and investment in South Africa were expanded, and America opposed any effective U.N. demonstration of hostility toward the apartheid state. The United States has also fought a hard, and largely successful, rearguard action against the demands for international intervention against South Africa's occupation of Namibia. And on Rhodesia,

America has trailed behind British policies, emasculated the sanctions policies it had endorsed at the United Nations, and criticized Africa for the vehemence of its opposition to the minority Smith regime.

This general approach to African questions, and particularly to southern Africa, culminated in the American government's support for the FNLA/UNITA forces in the dispute between the Angolan nationalist movements.

Throughout the anti-colonial war in Angola that is from 1960 to 1974 America had supported Portugal, not any of the nationalist forces. Supplies to the FNLA of money and other equipment while desalinization was taking place were thus a rather blatant attempt to place 'friends' in political power in the new state. Not surprisingly, it was the least effective of the contending nationalist groups, which was open to this kind of purchase; success therefore depended upon the quick collapse of the MPLA, under assault. But the MPLA did not collapse. Instead it asked for and received more arms from those who had been helping it for the ten years of its anticolonial war; to meet the simultaneous South African invasion of Angola, the MPLA also welcomed Cuban troops. And when the FNLA demanded more help than the American Administration alone could give it, the U.S. Congress - with the lessons of Vietnam still fresh in its mind - refused finance.

It is not cynicism, which attributes the beginnings of the 'Kissinger initiative' in April 1976 partly to this experience. Nations, like people, sometimes need to be shaken out of habitual modes of thought. Nor was the Angolan debacle the only factor leading toward a reassessment of traditional U.S. policies in southern Africa. Some Americans had for long been urging support for the anti-racialist and anticolonial struggle, and American blacks were beginning to take greater interest in these matters. Further, trade with independent Africa has been growing, and now includes oil from Nigeria. The possibility that this trade might be jeopardized by pro-South African actions is no longer of merely academic interest to the United States. And the guerrilla war in Rhodesia has been intensified since mid-1975, arousing fears of a repetition of the Angolan experience.

Africa welcomed the Lusaka statement by Dr. Kissinger that majority rule must precede independence in Rhodesia, and that America would give no material or diplomatic support to the Smith regime in its conflict with the African states or the African liberation movements. With some hesitation, Africa also cooperated with the Kissinger 'shuttle diplomacy' later in the year. For Africa hoped that, even at that late stage, the use of American power in support of majority rule could enable this to be attained in Rhodesia without further bloodshed.

The 'Kissinger initiative' did force Ian Smith to shift his ground, but it did not succeed in its declared objective. Neither did it remove Africa's uncertainty about the depth and geographical limitations of America's new commitment to change in southern Africa. For decades of history cannot be wiped out by one speech and a few months of highly individualistic one-man diplomacy. They cannot even be eradicated by the clear sincerity of a new President's commitment to supporting human rights, and the sympathetic understanding shown by the Ambassador he has appointed to the United Nations.

II

The United States of America is the most powerful nation on earth. Africa is weak, economically and militarily; its unity in action is still fragile. Africa does therefore naturally desire the friendship and cooperation of the United States; it does need trade, and economic assistance.

But overwhelming everything else in Africa is the sense of nationalism, and the determination of all African peoples that the whole continent shall be free and relieved from the humiliation of organized white racialism. Within Rhodesia, Namibia, and South Africa, and within the nations immediately bordering them, the commitment to the struggle against minority or colonial rule overrides all other matters.

This basic fact is important to America, as it is to the rest of the world. For power is not all-powerful. Nationalism cannot be overcome by it. Nationalist wars have no end except victory, however long that takes to achieve, whatever the cost and the inevitable setbacks. All that can be affected by the actions of its opponents is the character of the nationalist state and society after victory. The harder and longer the struggle for freedom, the more austere and radicalized the new state is likely to be. It may also be more intolerant. For wars are liable to destroy everything except hatred and mutual suspicion - which they nurture.

The United States, like other nations of the world, has a legitimate interest in the future as well as the present societies of southern Africa. It must be concerned about America's continued ability to buy the goods it needs, and its ability to sell sufficient goods to pay for its imports. America must be interested in whether or not these states will determine their own foreign policies according to their own interests after winning their freedom, or whether they will be dominated in these matters by states hostile to the United States. And America, like the rest of the world, will continue to have a legitimate interest in the status of human rights in southern Africa as well as elsewhere. None of these things will it be able to control in a state which is really independent - that is the meaning of independence. But one would expect that current American policies toward the nationalist struggles in southern Africa would be determined with these long-term interests in mind. And it does not seem to Africa that these factors have determined American policies in the past. At least they have not done so on any intelligent assessment of the paramountcy of nationalism in shaping the future.

III

One thing is quite certain. The status of human rights could not be worse in the independent states of southern Africa than it is now. The very idea of there being 'human rights' presupposes the basic acceptance of human equality. Yet colonialism is in principle a denial of equality. It means that the interests of the colonized are subordinate to the interests of the colonizers, or at the very least are interpreted and judged by the colonizers. Support for human rights therefore involves opposition to colonialism, regardless of how gentle, well intentioned, or selfless the colonial government may be. Greater urgency in ending this status is imparted to the situation when, as in Namibia and Rhodesia, colonialism has none of these virtues. Two hundred years after Americans fought their own kith and kin to end colonialism, it should not be necessary for Africa to try to convince America that Africans find colonialism intolerable.

Human rights are also inconsistent with the practice of racialism. They are denied by any law or practice, which distinguishes the rights and duties of men and women according to their racial origin. And in South Africa there is hardly a law, which does not make this distinction; the entire state machinery is directed at organizing and upholding the domination of one racial group over all others. This would be inconsistent with human rights if the majority racial group were using racial discrimination as a means of controlling a dissident minority. It is not made more consistent when 83 percent of the South African population is denied elementary political, economic, and social justice by legislation and economic power used by and in the interests of the whites.

Every aspect of the South African state organization is thus inconsistent with the American philosophy of human equality and freedom. But this is not simply an internal South African matter. Without the kind of practical support, which the South African government and society have been receiving - and are still receiving - from their relations with America and its allies, the present apartheid structure could not be sustained for very long. And therefore minority rule in Rhodesia and Namibia could not continue.

Thus, for example, South Africa has a continuing and large deficit in its foreign trade, which is financed by capital imports, both long and short term. American investment in South Africa has more than tripled since 1966 and now stands at more than $1,600 million. All these investors profit from apartheid and the discriminatory wage structure - and thus have an interest in sustaining it.

Further, until now America has continued to act in the United Nations and elsewhere as if South Africa were a bastion against Soviet infiltration into southern Africa, and against the spread of communism in Africa. This image is carefully fostered by the apartheid regime, which prides itself on its anti-communism, and had defined a communist as 'anyone who supports any of the aims of communism' - including the declared aim of human equality!

Yet by identifying itself in practice with the apartheid regime and its satellites, America is liable to bring about the very things it most fears - the growth of communist influence, the radicalization of the opposition to apartheid and colonialism, and the damage to its own economic interests. For opposition to the regimes in southern Africa is inevitable. Men will not indefinitely accept humiliation, exploitation, and tyranny. Sooner or later, by one means or another, the dominant minority will lose its ability to control the country and run the economy in its own interests. It is natural that Africa should seek American help in ending its humiliation. Americans should not find it natural when their country aids the oppressor instead of the oppressed.

The organizational and material weakness of the nationalist forces in southern Africa, which results from decades of ruthless oppression, does, however, have two consequences of international relevance. First, nationalists cannot be particular about the means through which they carry on the struggle; they have to take advantage of any opportunities, which they can find. Secondly, they have to accept help from wherever they can get it. The stronger apartheid and minority rule become, and the more supporters those forces enlist, the greater becomes the nationalists' need for outside help.

IV

When seeking external support for their struggles, it is natural that African nationalists should look first to the African countries, which have already secured their own freedom. And it is equally natural that free African states should give that support. No independent African state can rest secure while colonialism continues in Africa, for colonialism is a denial of its own right to exist. Further, the human dignity of all Africans is denied when Africans anywhere are humiliated because of their race. On the principle of giving assistance to the freedom movements in southern Africa, therefore, the whole of free Africa is united. But in comparison with South Africa, free Africa is weak. All African states are poor, some are almost overwhelmed by the task of trying to make independence economically meaningful and beneficial to their people. Further, no African state has an armaments industry of its own. The nationalist movements of southern Africa therefore need more help than Africa alone can give them.

Outside Africa, however, experience has shown that communist countries are almost the only ones, which are both able and willing to assist the nationalist movements of southern Africa. The major countries of the Western bloc urge patience and nonviolence as if these had not been tried for the past 30 years; simultaneously they continue to bolster South Africa's economic and military strength by trade, investment, and political cooperation. Some of the Nordic countries give humanitarian assistance to the freedom fighters. Only the communist countries are willing to make arms and other military help available when an armed struggle becomes the only way forward.

Why the communist states are willing to assist the freedom movements is for them to say. Africa knows why it needs that assistance, and what it will be used for if it can be obtained. Anything else is, at this stage, irrelevant to us. If the West decides to give us similar aid, I for one would not question its motives. Africa is concerned with existing oppression, not with hypothetical dangers in the future. Any new threats to freedom will be dealt with after it has been won - not before! In the war against Nazism the United States and the Soviet Union were allies.

But the peoples of southern Africa are not asking others to fight their liberation battles for them. They know that a people can only free themselves; they cannot import freedom. The peoples of these countries are asking only for appropriate support for the freedom struggle they are themselves conducting. Whether that support needs to be political, economic, or military - or all three - depends upon the type of struggle, which has to be waged before, victory is achieved. It is in this respect that the differences in the political and economic situations of Rhodesia, Namibia, and South Africa become relevant to current policies for other nations of the world.

Yet although the three countries do present different problems, and opportunities, it is pointless to try to treat each one in isolation. The objective is freedom for the whole of southern Africa. This means independence on the basis of majority rule in Rhodesia; independence on the basis of majority rule for Namibia as a single political unit; and an end to apartheid and minority rule in South Africa itself. So it is one struggle, with three geographical areas.

Therefore, South Africa cannot be regarded as an ally in the fight for majority rule in Rhodesia, any more than Rhodesia could be expected to support the anticolonial movement in Namibia. Rhodesia and South Africa are natural allies to each other. The most which could be achieved is for South Africa to recognize the differences between its own position and that of the Smith regime, and therefore to buy time for itself by refraining from direct assistance to minority rule in the British colony.

V

In Rhodesia, or Zimbabwe - to use its African name - we now have to face the fact that this is 1977, not 1965. A liberation war has started. Government 'reforms,' or reductions in the intensity of racial discrimination, which would have given hope of change fifteen or even ten years ago and thus prevented war, are now irrelevant. Options which existed at the time of Rhodesia's unilateral declaration of independence (UDI) no longer exist.

This should not be strange to Americans who know their own history. Very few inhabitants of the American colonies were calling for independence when the dispute with the British government arose in the 1760s. According to John Adams, one-third of the colonists remained opposed to the rebellion even during the War of Independence. Yet concessions made by the British government in 1770 were already too late to avert conflict. And once the war had begun it could have only one end. So it is in Rhodesia now. Ian Smith's unilateral 'package of reforms' announced in March of this year will not even buy him time.

The only question which remains open is whether independence on the basis of majority rule will be achieved by a fight to the finish, or whether that same end can be achieved by a minimum of bloodshed leading to negotiations.

Therefore negotiation cannot now be about the principle of majority rule before independence. Nor can it be about the establishment of an 'interim government' under white control. The nationalists are insisting that the 270,000 whites cannot be allowed to continue governing 5,800,000 Africans, whatever promises the former make about organizing an 'orderly transfer of power,' or anything else. For the argument now is about power, not about promises; the fighting, which has started, will not end until a transfer of power from the minority to the majority has actually taken place. A ceasefire without such a transfer of power was tried in December 1974; it led to a strengthening of the minority regime.

What was possible until the collapse of the Geneva Conference in December 1976 was a delay in independence. For in accordance with the British tradition of decolonization, the nationalists had separated independence from internal self-government under majority rule. The latter they were demanding immediately, with some minority representation in an interim nationalist government. But they had agreed on a delay of 12 months before independence, in the hope that effective British sovereignty during that period would allow members of the minority community either to adapt to majority rule, or leave the country. For in this connection it is relevant to remember that more than one-third of the 270,000 whites at present in Rhodesia have immigrated during the past 11 years - they can hardly be regarded as committed to the country.

These demands were rejected by Smith, as were the British government proposals. The British government then abandoned the Conference, showing that despite their legal responsibility for decolonization in Rhodesia, they regarded themselves merely as umpires between Smith and the nationalists, not as participants in a struggle against the Smith   regime.

That opportunity for a negotiated settlement has therefore been lost. The attempt of the new British Foreign Secretary to organize talks on another basis has thus to overcome still more suspicion. And even if agreement between the British and the nationalists is reached at new talks, the removal of Smith, and the dismantling of his power structure, still have to be achieved before any political agreement can be converted into the reality of majority rule.

The world in general, and Africa in particular, does, however, still have an interest in bringing the Rhodesian war to a rapid end. Ian Smith and his supporters have no such interest. On the contrary, their objective is the continuation of war until South Africa, and possibly even the United States, come to their support.

Ian Smith recognizes that, on a long-headed assessment of South Africa's own interest, Prime Minister Vorster does not want to get directly involved in the Rhodesian conflict. But in any guerrilla war, civilian casualties are likely to occur; they are already happening in Zimbabwe. If the dead women and children begin to include large numbers of whites, then Smith knows, because Vorster has admitted it, that the Pretoria government will come under pressure from its own electorate to increase South African material support for the Smith regime. And as the casualties begin to include South African citizens who live or visit Rhodesia, Smith believes that his armed forces will be strengthened by direct South African military intervention.

Direct South African military involvement would make a great change in the balance of forces in Rhodesia. It would not defeat nationalism. But it would increase the difficulties of the freedom fighters. The nationalists would therefore be forced to seek increased external help; and it is only communist states, which are likely to give whatever assistance is required. Even if an intelligent American government is then able to withstand the consequent pressure to intervene 'against communism' and to maintain its opposition to Smith, the conflict would have been internationalized. Smith desires this. Africa does not. Whether the internationalization of a limited war of independence is in America's interests is for America to judge.

But America is not a helpless bystander to events in Rhodesia. It is a powerful nation, and influences developments there. It can frustrate Smith's attempts to escalate the war, and can even help to get the war ended.

First, it has to make it quite clear that the United States will give no support of any kind to the minority regime of Rhodesia, at any time, and regardless of the progress or possible escalation of the war.

Second, as evidence of this determination, it has to follow up the rescission of the Byrd Amendment by active steps against all sanctions-breaking (whether by American firms or others), and by greater efforts to prevent the Rhodesian recruitment of American citizens into the regime's army.

And third, the United States has to put pressure on the South African government to desist from further help to the Smith regime. It is not realistic to expect Vorster to act against Rhodesian minority rule; but he can be prevented from propping it up - at least more than he is already doing. The United States has sufficient leverage to do this without treating South Africa as if it is an ally in the struggle for justice in southern Africa.

No one is suggesting that there are quick, or painless, solutions to the problems in Rhodesia. In the 11 years, which have passed since UDI, many opportunities have been lost, and new forces have arisen which now have to be taken into account. Thus, it is true that the Zimbabwe nationalists do not control all the forces, which will influence Rhodesian events in the near and far future. But no settlement of this problem can now be reached without their participation in drawing it up, and their active support in its implementation. In 1977 it is in that context, and only in that context, that America or Britain - or Tanzania - can work for an end to war in Rhodesia.

VI

Namibia is politically different from Rhodesia in two major respects. First, if Prime Minister Vorster really accepted the principle of majority rule outside South Africa, as he has sometimes claimed, it is within his power to introduce it in Namibia. And if he really wants Namibia 'off his back,' as he once asserted, he has the power to make the necessary arrangements. Namibia is not a 'client state' like Rhodesia; it is completely under the de facto control of the South African government and armed forces.

Secondly, Namibia is de jure a Trusteeship Territory. The United Nations has, by General Assembly and Security Council decision, withdrawn the authority of South Africa over Namibia. It has established the U.N. Council for Namibia, and appointed a full-time Commissioner, whose task is to arrange for an orderly transition to Namibian independence on the basis of political unity and majority rule and periodically to report progress to the United Nations. Also the General Assembly has recognized the South West African People's Organization (SWAPO) as the sole representative nationalist movement of Namibia.

Apart from these two respects, however, the situations in Rhodesia and Namibia are becoming increasingly similar. A united nationalist party now exists, and cannot be ignored. An armed struggle has started in Namibia, although it is not as yet very intense.

South Africa is still trying to evade the necessity of negotiating the form of Namibian independence with SWAPO under the auspices of the United Nations. In response to a threat of action by the United Nations if its resolutions were not observed, South Africa organized the 'Turnhalle Constitutional Conference' in 1975. Representation was by 'ethnic group' (i.e., South African-designated racial and tribal groups), and political parties were barred. The outcome of 'Turnhalle,' not surprisingly, is a set of proposals, which basically maintain the structure of 'tribal homelands' and 'White areas,' and would leave intact the existing racialist domination by the 99,000 whites among the 850,000 population. The South African government is proposing to present the result to the United Nations as an act of 'decolonization.'

Proposals such as these will not solve the problem in South West Africa. Nationalism in Namibia cannot be overcome by establishing another independent apartheid state. The choice for the world, and for South Africa, remains unaffected by such maneuvers. The choice is: either a transfer of de facto power by South Africa to the United Nations, which can then negotiate an independence constitution with SWAPO; or negotiations between South Africa and SWAPO under U.N. auspices; or an intensified war, with all the dangers to world peace which that will bring.

Once again, America cannot control these events. But it could use its considerable influence to avert the dangers of a serious war of liberation in Namibia. In order to do this, America would first have to accept that SWAPO is the only Namibian nationalist organization, and that no settlement is possible without its agreement. Then it would apply some pressure on South Africa to negotiate with SWAPO under U.N. auspices. Alternatively it would give active American support to the struggle at the United Nations for a South African withdrawal from Namibia, and the introduction of an effective transitional U.N. administration.

What America must not do, if it aims to prevent a major war in Namibia, is to give any encouragement to the 'Turnhalle' Conference, its participants, or South Africa's espousal of its proposals. For time is running out. If the Namibian war has to be intensified - as it will be if there is no progress - the time available for an orderly transition from minority to majority rule will again be exhausted before the work has begun.

VII

South Africa is an independent state. It is not a colony of anyone, and within the boundaries of the Republic there are no colonies to be granted independence. But its organized denial of human rights to all but 17 percent of its people, on the grounds of their race, make South Africa's 'internal affairs' a matter of world concern. For nations have learned, and mankind has learned, that the hope for world peace and justice precludes indifference in the face of organized racialism.

The official reply to all demands that the world should put South Africa into quarantine has been that apartheid is best countered by diplomatic and other contact with more open societies. Unfortunately, however, the South African whites are correct in saying that their society is unique. Nowhere else has the privileged life-style of the dominant minority ever rested so completely and exclusively on racial oppression. Other experiences of gradual desegregation, in the southern states of the United States or elsewhere, will therefore do no more to persuade the whites of South Africa to change their policies than has the polite criticism of Western statesmen since the last world war.

Policies are also based upon the argument that provided foreign investors pay a living wage to their employees; they will be increasing the pressures against apartheid because economic growth shows up the inefficiency of things like racial job reservation and migrant skilled labor. Quite apart from the fact that these are only a small aspect of apartheid, the evidence of the past 30 years - and longer - should by now have dispelled that illusion also. South Africa has been getting economically stronger and more developed at a rapid rate. Racial oppression has been increasing even faster. For the stronger the economy, the more can be spent upon suppressing the majority without any economic sacrifice being demanded of those who benefit by white supremacy. A strong South African economy strengthens the government, not the victims of its oppression.

The South African economy needs to be weakened, not strengthened, if apartheid is to be overthrown. South Africa therefore needs to be isolated economically, politically, and socially, by the rest of the world until there has been a change in political direction. The sooner that change begins, the less violence and chaos there is likely to be.

No one can doubt the desire of the people of South Africa to end apartheid. Organized opposition by the non-whites has been smashed, but the Soweto and Cape Town 'riots' are only the latest of a long series of spontaneous uprisings. And they will not be the last outburst of frustration. For despite everything which the South African state can and will do, instability is inherent in a situation where the majority of the people are excluded from the benefits of a society which depends upon their work. Change can be delayed by an intensification of oppression and human suffering. But apartheid is doomed. The only question is whether the society subsides into chaos, or whether there is an orderly but speedy movement toward justice.

At present there may still just be time for the Republic to avoid ultimate economic and social collapse if the whites can be woken up to their own danger. They would have to begin by setting free, and then entering into a dialogue with, the real leaders of the non-white peoples who are now being held in jails, detention centers, and Restriction - people like Nelson Mandela, Robert Sobukwe and their colleagues. For it is only such people who would have a chance of organizing and channeling the irresistible opposition of the black peoples to their present humiliation.

So far there has been no evidence that the South African white government intends to guide the country in this direction - on the contrary. The whites remain self-confident in their strength and their racial arrogance; and they do this partly because the world continues to talk with them and support them in action. They have not been shocked into a reassessment of their position. They have not yet realized their need to talk with non-white South Africans about their common future. Instead they are able to talk with the rest of the world, and solve their economic problems by new foreign investment, new trade, and new immigration.

VIII

Each nation has to decide for itself what will be in its own interests, and these will determine its policies. But no one is asking that America should fight for the freedom of southern Africa. Africa is simply asking that America should stop supporting racialism and unfreedom in that area.

For the penalty, as well as the opportunity, of America's great power relative to that of any other nation, is that every American action, or failure to act, has an effect upon the timing and the nature of developments outside its own borders. This is not to say that America can impose its will on an unwilling world; only that it cannot avoid involvement in events elsewhere. When Tanzania trades or fails to trade, or indicates support or opposition for another government, the world goes on unchanged and unruffled. When America does any of these things it is affecting what will happen elsewhere. One may like this or not; it remains a statement of fact.

Thus, America cannot prevent men from struggling against colonialism and racialism in southern Africa. But American actions will either ease the inevitable triumph of the freedom struggle, or strengthen the resistance to it and thus force the anticolonial and anti-racist movements into a hard, ruthless, and hostile mold. There is no way in which powerful America can avoid doing one or the other of these things, as long as it needs to have commercial and state relations with the rest of the world.

Africa is therefore asking that America should recognize the conflict in southern Africa as the nationalist struggle which it is, and that it should refuse to be taken in by the communist bogey paraded by the racialists. It is asking that America should refrain from profit making out of apartheid. South Africa needs the United States; but the United States does not need South Africa. Africa is asking that America should carry its declared support for human equality and dignity into policies which will weaken the forces of racialism and colonialism in southern Africa, so that the peoples of those areas can triumph more quickly and with less bloodshed.

With or without American support during the struggle, freedom in southern will not mean the birth of ideal democracies, where all citizens enjoy human rights, civil liberty, and a consumer society to boot. Popular governments in Rhodesia, Namibia, and later in South Africa, will face immense problems of poverty, disruption and unrealizable expectations. They will also inherit a legacy of mutual hostility and bitterness. The racial prejudice, which has been inculcated by years of deliberate indoctrination, and by bitter experience, will not disappear when majority rule begins.

But it is only after freedom has been won in the states of southern Africa that the positive struggle to build human equality and dignity can begin there. We in Africa hope that the new Administration of the United States will fulfill its early promise, and help the peoples of southern Africa to get to the position where they can make a beginning. At the very least, we hope that America will not continue to use its power and prestige to hinder the movement for freedom and humanity in the south of this continent.[15]

Nyerere's stand on southern Africa influenced the policies of the Organization of African Unity (OAU) more than that of any other African leader, especially in his capacity as chairman of the frontline states of Tanzania, Zambia, Botswana, Mozambique, and Angola in a concerted effort to end white minority rule on the continent. White rule finally ended with the collapse of the apartheid regime in 1994, five years before Nyerere died. Nyerere was also - although no longer president of Tanzania - one of the world leaders, including Fidel Castro whose intervention in Angola played a critical role in containing the apartheid regime, who attended the inauguration of Nelson Mandela as president of South Africa. The end of apartheid was a crowning achievement, culmination of an effort, in a struggle in which Dr. Julius Nyerere played a central role more than any other leader in independent Africa, and a tribute to a man who dedicated his life to the liberation of the continent during a political career that spanned almost half a century.

CHAPTER ELEVEN:

NYERERE AND NKRUMAH:
TOWARDS AFRICAN UNITY

THEY WERE some of the most influential African leaders in the twentieth century; probably the most influential. They also shared a vision of a united Africa under one continental government. But they differed on how to achieve this goal.

Kwame Nkrumah led the Gold Coast to become the first country in sub-Saharan Africa to win independence as Ghana on March 6, 1957. Four years and nine months later, Julius Nyerere led Tanganyika to become the first country in East Africa to win independence on December 9, 1961. Both countries won independence from Britain.

In May 1963, the Organization of African Unity (OAU) was founded in Addis Ababa, Ethiopia, by the African heads of state and government from 32 independent countries. The other 21, out of a total of 53 African countries, were still under colonial or white minority rule. The founding of the OAU was also marked by another event: publication of Kwame Nkrumah's book, *Africa Must Unite*.[1] The book was released around the same time African leaders met in Addis Ababa in May 1963. It was a timely release of a book that said Africa Must Unite at the very same time that African leaders met to form the Organization of African Unity. Nkrumah thought the book was appropriate for the occasion, to capitalize on the momentum provided by the founding of the OAU towards achieving continental unity under one government.

Most of his colleagues thought otherwise. They saw it as an attempt by Nkrumah to dominate Africa and realize his ambition to become the president of a United States of Africa. Earlier in 1960 during the Congo crisis, his proposal for an African high command to defend Africa with a continental army and liberate the remaining colonies and other countries still under white minority rule - South Africa, South West Africa, and Rhodesia - had been equally rejected by other African leaders, except a few, who believed that

Nkrumah would control and dominate the Pan-African force and use it to overthrow them. In many fundamental respects, he was ahead of his time and most of his colleagues, but was later vindicated by history when Africa remained weak and powerless as a divided continent composed of non-viable independent states because they did not heed his call to unite under one government as he urged them to, back in 1963. If he were alive today, in his 90s, he would probably be tempted to say, "I told you so!"

While Nkrumah advocated immediate continental unification, Nyerere sought a regional approach as the more realistic way to eventually achieve continental unity under one government, and became the strongest proponent of an East African federation as a step towards achieving this goal. Because of his opposition to this approach which he called "balkanization on a grand scale," and for other political reasons as Nyerere's rival whom he felt posed a challenge to his leadership of the continent and would make history - before he did - as the first African leader to unite independent countries even if on a regional scale, Nkrumah intervened in East Africa to thwart attempts by Nyerere to form an East African federation. As he stated in *Africa Must Unite*:

> The idea of regional federations in Africa is fraught with many dangers. There is the danger of the development of regional loyalties, fighting against each other. In effect, regional federations are a form of balkanization on a grand scale.[2]

Nyerere dismissed Nkrumah's opposition to regional federations as "attempts to rationalize absurdity." As he stated on the third anniversary of Tanganyika's independence on December 9, 1963 - the three East African countries of Kenya, Uganda, and Tanganyika had agreed to form a federation before the end of that year but failed to do so - reiterating his call for an East African federation as an imperative need and as a step towards African unity:

> We must reject some of the pretensions that have been made from outside East Africa. We have already heard the curious argument that the continued 'balkanisation' of East Africa will somehow help African unity.... These are attempts to rationalize absurdity.[3]

Nkrumah's opposition to the East African federation, and his interference in East Africa in an attempt to thwart any efforts towards consummation of such a union, tarnished more than enhanced his image as a Pan-Africanist in the eyes of many people, and was seen as an attempt on his part to further his own political ambitions. It also vindicated the position of many African leaders who felt that Nkrumah wanted to undermine their governments and replace them with those subservient to him, while professing African unity to hide his real intentions. As Basil Davidson says about Nkrumah's involvement in East Africa and his attempts to block formation of the East African federation, in his book, *Black Star: A View of the Life and Times of Kwame Nkrumah*:

> Some, like Julius Nyerere of Tanzania, chastised Nkrumah for his interference. East Africa, Nyerere believed, could best contribute to continental unity by moving first towards regional unity. Although knowing little about East Africa, Nkrumah not only disagreed but actively interfered to obstruct the East African federation proposed by Nyerere.... It was one of Nkrumah's worst mistakes.[4]

Although the three East African countries failed to form a federation in 1963, Nyerere never gave up and continued to advocate African unity at the regional level, as well as on a continental scale. He told Jomo Kenyatta, the least interested of the three East African leaders, that Tanzania would renounce her sovereignty right away if Kenya was ready to unite. And he reiterated that in different forums. As he stated on June 25, 1965, in an address to the International Press Club during his visit to London for the Commonwealth Conference: "We stand for unity in Africa. In particular we still urgently desire an East African Federation. If Mzee Kenyatta today says he is ready, then we will federate tomorrow."[5] And as Jaramogi Oginga Odinga, Kenya's vice president under Kenyatta but who resigned to form the opposition Kenya People's Union (KPU), states in his book *Not Yet Uhuru*:

> As late as 8 July 1965, Nyerere said that Tanzania was still ready for East African Federation no matter that outside influences had interfered in the hope of blocking its formation. He said 'If we listen to foreign influence we should be made to quarrel with Kenya and Uganda, but this we will not do.' He

had already told President Kenyatta that if his country was ready to unite, Tanzania was also ready.[6]

But, in spite of their differences on the East African federation and regional federations in general, Nyerere and Nkrumah continued to work closely because of their ideological affinity and the Pan-African vision they shared. They even corresponded on numerous occasions on a number of issues, including ways to achieve African unity, as Nyerere himself said in an interview with Ikaweba Bunting in 1999 not long before he died, published in the *New Internationalist*, and cited earlier in this book. They may have taken divergent paths - immediate continental unification for Nkrumah, and a gradualist approach for Nyerere - but were united in their passionate quest for one government for the whole continent. Nyerere was not, on principle, opposed to immediate continental unification as advocated by Nkrumah, but felt that Nkrumah underestimated the suspicion and animosity such an approach generated among other African leaders - most did not trust him - and would not get the necessary support needed to achieve a continental union immediately; a point he underscored during the 40th anniversary of Ghana's independence in March 1997 when he was invited to Accra by President Jerry Rawlings as one of the honored guests to participate in the celebrations on that momentous occasion, as we will learn later on. He also told his audience in Ghana that African leaders should have set up a special committee under the auspices of the Organization of Africa Unity (OAU) to work on ways to achieve continental unification in the same way the OAU Liberation Committee was created to coordinate the struggle for the liberation of the countries still under white minority rule on the continent. It was Nyerere who first proposed and introduced a resolution at the OAU summit in Cairo in July 1964 to retain the colonial boundaries inherited at independence. The resolution was adopted by his colleagues and became one of the bedrock principles of the OAU, also enshrined in the OAU Charter, maintaining territorial integrity of the new African nations and barring interference in the internal affairs of another state. Unfortunately, other African leaders saw this as a way of maintaining their separate sovereignties and consolidating their independence without pursuing continental unity, something Nyerere never intended. He remained firm in his commitment to continental unification, a Pan-African goal and ideal he shared with Nkrumah more than any other African leader, besides Obote, Sekou Toure, Modibo Keita, and Kenneth Kaunda. As he stated in 1999 in an interview with the *New Internationalist*:

> Kwame Nkrumah and I were committed to the idea of unity. African leaders did not take Kwame seriously. I did. I did not believe in these small little nations. Still today I do not believe in them. I tell our people to look at the European Union, at these people who ruled us who are now uniting.

> Kwame and I met in 1963 and discussed African Unity. We differed on how to achieve a United States of Africa. But we both agreed on a United States of Africa as necessary. Kwame went to Lincoln University, a black college in the US. He perceived things from the perspective of US history, where 13 colonies that revolted against the British formed a union. That is what he thought the OAU should do.

> I tried to get East Africa to unite before independence. When we failed in this, I was wary about Kwame's continental approach. We corresponded profusely on this. Kwame said my idea of 'regionalization' was only balkanization on a larger scale. Later, African historians will have to study our correspondence on this issue of uniting Africa.[7]

Nyerere and Nkrumah worked closely on other issues, especially the liberation of southern Africa. Together with Nasser, Ben Bella, Sekou Toure, and Modibo Keita, they even had their own group, known as the Group of Six, within the OAU and coordinated their efforts on a number of issues, such as the Congo crisis during which they were infuriated by Tshombe and his Western backers, and had little regard for other OAU members whom they felt were not doing enough to unite and liberate Africa. Kenya, for instance, did virtually nothing for the liberation struggle in southern Africa. And President Jomo Kenyatta even hardly spoke on the subject - let alone contribute material and financial support to the freedom fighters - in spite of his status as the Grand Old Man of the African independence movement who inspired, though he did not lead, Mau Mau in Kenya. He was just one of the leaders the Group of Six found to be useless in pursuit of Pan-African goals, especially the liberation of southern Africa and Congo from Western domination. As Ben Bella said about the Congo crisis, progressive forces had arrived too late in the Congo.[8]

He was equally blunt on the Group of Six in an interview in 1995 with Jorge Castaneda, who became Mexico's minister of foreign affairs in the late 1990s. As Castaneda states in his book *Companero: The Life and Death of Che Guevara:* "According to Ben Bella, these leaders had a group of their own within the OAU; they regularly consulted and conspired among themselves."[9]

Before he died in October 1999, Nyerere was one of only two surviving members of the Group of Six. The other one was Ben Bella who outlived Nyerere but lived in exile in Swtizerland. He was overthrown in June 1965 and was imprisoned for 15 years. But he did not continue to have much influence like Nyerere who remained a revered international statesman even after stepping down from the presidency in November 1985. The other members of the Group of Six who died before Nyerere were Nasser who died of a heart attack in Egypt in September 1970; Nkrumah, of cancer, at a hospital in Romania in April 1972; Modibo Keita in Mali in May 1977 under house arrest since he was overthrown in November 1968 - mass demonstrations at his funeral against the government of President Moussa Traore (military-turned-civilian head of state) who overthrew him led to the invocation of emergency powers by the despotic regime; and Sekou Toure during an emergency heart operation in the United States in March 1984. Nyerere remained on the scene as the most ardent supporter of African unity and the liberation movements on the continent.

And just as Nkrumah released his seminal work *Africa Must Unite* in 1963, Nyerere's article on the same subject was published about two months before Nkrumah's book was. The article was entitled, "A United States of Africa," and was published in *The Journal of Modern African Studies* in March 1963, about two months before the African heads of state and government met in Addis Ababa, Ethiopia, and formed the Organization of African Unity (OAU) towards the end of May. In that article, Nyerere advocated continental unification but, unlike Nkrumah, took a regional approach as the most practical way to achieve this goal.[10] The two leaders had a heated exchange on the subject the following year at the second summit of the OAU in Cairo in July 1964 - Malcolm X also addressed the conference and asked African leaders to raise the issue of racial discrimination and injustices in the United States at the UN - and Nyerere won majority support for his approach towards continental unification. As he put it: "When you set out to build a house, you don't begin by putting on the roof; first you start by laying the foundations."[11]

Nkrumah, on the other hand, contended that a regional approach towards continental unification would only benefit the enemies of Africa as they continued to exploit the weaknesses of a divided continent. It would also make it impossible for the whole continent to unite. And time was critical. Africa must unite *now*. The proposed East African federation would accomplish exactly the opposite. And he probably underestimated Nyerere and did not expect a sharp response from him and saw him as his junior, given the age difference between the two, 13 years apart; and because of his status as the trail-blazer of the African independence movement, having led Ghana to become the first black African country to win independence in 1957. And as Professor Ali Mazrui states:

> Nkrumah pointed out that his own country could not very easily join an East African federation. This proved how discriminatory and divisive the whole of Nyerere's strategy was for the African continent.
>
> Nyerere treated Nkrumah's counter-thesis with contempt. He asserted that to argue that Africa had better remain in small bits than form bigger entities was nothing but 'an attempt to rationalize absurdity.' He denounced Nkrumah's attempt to deflate the East African federation movement as petty mischief-making arising from Nkrumah's own sense of frustration in his own Pan-African ventures.
>
> Nyerere was indignant. He went public with his attack on Nkrumah. He referred to people who pretended that they were in favour of African continental union when all they cared about was to ensure that 'some stupid historian in the future' praised them for being in favour of the big continental ambition before anyone else was willing to undertake it.
>
> Nyerere added snide remarks about 'the Redeemer,' Nkrumah's self-embraced title of the Osagyefo.
>
> On balance, history has proved Nkrumah wrong on the question of Nyerere's commitment to liberation. Nyerere was second to none in that commitment.
>
> At that Cairo conference of 1964 Nkrumah had asked 'What could be the result of entrusting the training of Freedom Fighters against imperialism into the hands of an imperialist agent?' Nyerere had indeed answered 'the good Osagyefo' with sarcasm and counter-argument.[12]

Despite their shared Pan-African vision, and genuine Pan-African commitment, there was rivalry between the two leaders, fueled by their strong personalities and charisma as well as militancy. And their different approaches to African unity only intensified this rivalry, as did Nyerere's increasing prominence on the African political scene Nkrumah saw as his exclusive domain and himself as the brightest black star in the African firmament:

> In reality Nkrumah and Nyerere had already begun to be rivals as symbols of African radicalism before the coup, which overthrew Nkrumah. Nkrumah was beginning to be suspicious of Nyerere in this regard. The two most important issues over which Nyerere and Nkrumah before 1966 might have been regarded as rivals for continental pre-eminence were the issues of African liberation and African unity.... The Organization of African Unity, when it came into being in May 1963, designated Dar es Salaam as the headquarters of liberation movements. The choice was partly determined by the proximity of Dar es Salaam to southern Africa as the last bastion of colonialism and white minority rule. But the choice was also determined by the emergence of Nyerere as an important and innovative figure in African politics.
>
> Nkrumah's Ghana did make the bid to be the headquarters of liberation movements but Nkrumah lost the battle....
>
> The great voice of African self-reliance, and the most active African head of government in relation to liberation in Southern Africa from 1967 (after Nkrumah was overthrown in February 1966) until the 1980s was in fact Nyerere.... He became the toughest spokesman against the British on the Rhodesian question. His country played a crucial role at the OAU Ministerial meeting at which it was decided to issue that fatal ultimatum to Britain's Prime Minister, Harold Wilson - 'Break Ian Smith or Africa will break with you.'[13]

While Nyerere will always be remembered as the most relentless supporter of the liberation movements in Africa among all the heads of state on the continent after Nkrumah was overthrown; Nkrumah will, on his part, be always acknowledged not only as the leader who blazed the trail for the African independence movement when he led the Gold Coast (renamed Ghana) to become the first country in black Africa to win freedom; he will also be always remembered for his bold initiatives, including his call for immediate continental unification, a Pan-African quest given eloquent and forceful expression in his seminal work, *Africa Must Unite*. As he stated from exile in Conakry, Guinea, on April 22, 1970, almost exactly two years before he died in April 1972:

> The wave of military coups, and the stepping up of imperialist and neocolonialist aggression in Africa since 1963, when *Africa Must Unite* was first

published, have proved conclusively the urgent need for political unification. No single part of Africa can be safe, or free to develop fully and independently, while any part remains unliberated, or while Africa's vast economic resources continue to be exploited by imperialist and neo-colonialist interests.

Unless Africa is politically united under an all-African Union Government, there can be no solution to our political and economic problems. The thesis of Africa Must Unite remains unassailable.[14]

Nkrumah's thesis that Africa Must Unite indeed remains unassailable. But why has Africa failed to unite? Africa has failed to unite because of nationalism more than anything else. Countries on the continent jealously guard their independence and don't want to surrender their sovereign status to a higher authority for the sake of African unity. That Africa is still not united 40 years after the Organization of African Unity (OAU) was formed in 1963, also vindicates Nyerere's position that immediate continental unification was not a realistic goal - more than just a tough proposition - and would have been rejected by most African leaders, as it indeed was, back in 1963 and through the decades.

But it also vindicates Nkrumah's position that if African countries don't unite *now*, they probably never will, but will only drift farther and and farther apart. Ironically, Nyerere shared the same position, in terms of divided loyalties as each country consolidated its independence and separate identity the longer it took to unite, even regionally, thus making it virtually impossible for them to form such a union. That is one of the strongest arguments he made when he called for the establishment of the East African federation right away at independence or soon thereafter. But after the three countries - Kenya, Uganda, and Tanganyika - failed to unite, he no longer saw such an approach, immediate unification, as a practical proposition. The concrete blocks of nationalism built since independence had to be whittled away, and transcended, gradually in order to achieve continental unity. Otherwise Africa will never unite.

And it is an approach that has been accepted by most African leaders, thus vindicating Nyerere, and has been validated by experience even in contemporary times; as has been clearly demonstrated by the formation of such regional blocs as the Economic Community of West African States (ECOWAS); the Southern African Development Community (SADC); and the

Common Market for Eastern and Southern Africa (COMESA). It is our hope that these regional bodies will one day merge to form a continental union under one government as advocated by Nkrumah and Nyerere; two African titans who remain an embodiment of Pan-African ideals cherished by millions across our beleaguered continent whose only salvation lies in unity.

Although dismissed as a utopian ideal, Nkrumah's quest for immediate continental unification had emotional and rhetorical appeal on this divided continent, especially among the young. And his Pan-African militancy resonated well across the continent. It inspired many people, especially in the euphoric sixties soon after independence and during the liberation struggle in southern Africa, to pursue higher goals that transcended parochial nationalism to affirm what Nkrumah called the African personality in a world where Africans are not accorded due respect. Nelson Mandela is one of those who greatly admired Nkrumah, as he states in his autobiography, *Long Walk to Freedom*.[15] So did Robert Mugabe. And they still do, as do millions others across Africa and beyond. He remained a source of inspiration to them during their years in prison, as Nyerere was, and through the liberation struggle in southern Africa. In fact, Mugabe even went to live and taught in Ghana during Nkrumah's reign and got married to a Ghanaian who became Zimbabwe's First Lady when Mugabe became president.

Nyerere also saw Nkrumah as an embodiment of Pan-African ideals he shared with him and strongly condemned those who overthrew him in February 1966. Tanzania never recognized the government that replaced Nkrumah. And Nkrumah himself paid tribute to Nyerere for his support and for his bitter condemnation of the Ghana coup, as he states in the book he wrote in exile in Conakry, Guinea, after he was overthrown, and appropriately entitled, *Dark Days in Ghana*.[16]

And both went down in history probably as the most revered statesmen Africa has ever produced, together with Nelson Mandela who was also a close friend of Nyerere. Tragically, they died before their goal of African unity was realized.

The quest for African unity is going to be the biggest challenge Africa faces in the twentieth-first century. Without unity, all talk of an African renaissance is no more than empty rhetoric. African countries are too weak to be viable entities. They just don't make any sense. None.

CHAPTER TWELVE:

THE LAST OF THE INDEPENDENCE LEADERS: LIFE UNDER NYERERE FROM A PERSONAL PERSPECTIVE: END OF AN ERA

THE DEATH of Julius Nyerere in October 1999 marked the end of an era in more than one way.

He was one of the pioneers in the struggle to end colonial rule after the end of World War II. He was also one of the first African leaders who led their countries to independence in the late fifties and in the sixties. And he was one of the last surviving leaders who spearheaded the struggle for African independence; among them, Kwame Nkrumah, Jomo Kenyatta, Nnamdi Azikiwe, Sekou Toure, Modibo Keita, Patrice Lumumba and others. And he outlived most of them. The only surviving former African presidents who led their countries to independence in the sixties, and who outlived Nyerere, were Ahmed Ben Bella of Algeria, Dr. Kenneth Kaunda of Zambia, and Dr. Milton Obote of Uganda who were also his ideological compatriots like Dr. Nkrumah, Sekou Toure, Modibo Keita, and Lumumba.

It was the era of "Big Men," the founding fathers, and the life of Julius Nyerere as a political leader of international stature epitomized the best among them, despite a number of failures during their tenure. They will be remembered as the leaders who not only led their countries to independence but who also maintained national unity, especially in the early years after the end of colonial rule, laying the foundation for the nations we have across the continent today. They will also be remembered as the leaders who - besides Azikiwe and a few others - introduced the one-party system to fight tribalism and consolidate nationhood, and socialism to achieve economic development.

Nyerere will be remembered for both, probably more than any other African leader. His one-party state was probably the most successful in transcending tribalism and maintaining national unity. Tribalism never became a prominent feature of national life in Tanzania under Nyerere, unlike in other African countries wracked by war and other conflicts. And besides Nkrumah, he was also the most articulate exponent and theoretician of one-party rule. A firm believer in socialism until his last days, he was also one of the strongest proponents of socialist policies for decades. And he lived and dies as a socialist, probably more than any other African leader. Even after his socialist policies failed to fuel and sustain Tanzania's economic growth, he remained a firm believer in socialism, and responded to his critics in rhetorical terms: "They keep saying you've failed. But what is wrong with urging people to pull together? Did Christianity fail because the world isn't all Christian?"[1]

It is not the purpose of this chapter to examine the successes and failures of Nyerere's socialist policies but to look at how life was under Nyerere in one of the poorest and most ethnically diverse countries in Africa and, indeed, in the entire world. These are my reflections on Tanzania, the land of my birth (it was then called Tanganyika and still a British colony), and on the life and death of Julius Nyerere, a leader my fellow countrymen and I came to know through the years as a patron saint of the masses, and as one of the world's most influential leaders in the twentieth century.

His socialist policies were mostly a failure, but not his ideals of equality and social justice. My life in Tanzania, like that of millions of other Tanzanians, was shaped and guided by those ideals. It is these ideals which sustained Tanzania and earned it a reputation as one of the most stable and peaceful countries in Africa, and one of the most united; a rare feat on this turbulent continent. It was Nyerere's biggest achievement, as he himself said. And it was, even more so than the unification of Tanganyika and Zanzibar in 1964, although this also was a feat of singular significance on a divided continent.

Tanzania stands out as the only country in Africa formed as a union of two independent states. No other union has been consummated on the entire continent, setting Nyerere apart. It was he who engineered the union of Tanganyika and Zanzibar. And it was he who played the biggest role in maintaining stability of the union, and even in sustaining the union itself because of his sense of fairness and extraordinary ability in consensus building as a basis for national unity. Although the union was indeed a big achievement, there was no question that Nyerere had other goals in that area. His biggest failure, he said, was that he did not succeed in convincing his fellow leaders in neighboring countries to form an East African federation.

But in fairness, it must be stated that it was the other East African leaders who failed to live up to their Pan-African commitment to form the federation. Kenyatta and Obote agreed with Nyerere in June 1963 to form the East African Federation before the end of the year, but never did. The other two leaders were not as enthusiastic as Nyerere was. Kenyatta was the least enthusiastic. Obote was ideologically close to Nyerere and in his comitment to a political union of the three East African countries and, in fact, went with Nyerere to see Kenyatta and asked him if he was ready to unite. They also told him that he should be the president of the new macro-nation, once the three countries united. But Kenyatta refused, as Nyerere said in an interview with the *New Internationalist*[2] in December 1998 we cited earlier. So, Obote would probably have united Uganda with the other two countries. But internal opposition to his rule, especially from the Buganda kingdom, precluded any possibility of fulfilling his Pan-African commitment to form the East African Federation.

Although failure to form the East African Federation was one of Nyerere's biggest disappointments in the Pan-African sphere and in foreign policy, he also had one major achievement in these two areas as the most prominent and relentless supporter, among all African leaders, of the liberation movements in southern Africa. And he lived up to his commitment. Tanzania under his leadership became the headquarters of all the African liberation movements and provided material, diplomatic, and moral support to the freedom fighters through the years until the end of white minority rule. But without strong domestic support, Nyerere's efforts to help free southern Africa and pursuit of his foreign policy initiatives would not have been successful. It was Tanzania's stability and mass support for Nyerere as a national leader, which made the realization of these goals possible. And it is to this domestic arena that we now turn, in my reflections on Tanzania and on the life and death of Julius Nyerere.

My life as an African has a lot in common with the lives of

my fellow Africans across the continent. We all live in countries affected by one form of strife or another, differing only in degree. And we all, at least most of us, belong to one tribe or another. I am a Nyakyusa, one of the few tribes in Tanzania - including the Sukuma, the largest, with more than 7 million, the Nyamwezi, the Chaga, the Hehe, the Haya - with more than one million people in a country of 126 different tribes. Yet I am a Tanzanian first and foremost, transcending my tribal identity. Still, the tribe is an enduring entity and an integral part of Africa. You can't define Africa without it, or even begin to understand Africa without comprehending its nature and the central role in plays in life across the spectrum in most African countries.

Call it an ethnic group, a term sometimes more acceptable than tribe because of the latter's derogatory connotation, applicable mostly in the African context, while deemed inappropriate and irrelevant in Europe despite the existence of tribes there as well, but which Europeans and others prefer to call ethnic groups to set them apart from "primitive" Africa. Or call it a clan, like in Somalia. It is still a tribe in all its manifestations in terms of malignancy associated with tribalism. Therefore countries like Kenya and Nigeria, Rwanda and Burundi, which have had serious ethnic conflicts ignited and fueled by power struggle between different groups, are not unique in this continent of polyethnic societies. They all face basically the same problems, but differ in the way they tackle them, if at all. In many cases, they do nothing.

But there are a few, in fact very few, exceptions where tribalism has not been a major problem in Africa. Tanzania is one of them. Growing up in Tanganyika - later Tanzania - in the sixties was a unique experience in this part of Africa where many of our neighbors were going through turmoil, rocked by tribal conflicts and other forms of strife, during the very same time when we were enjoying relative peace and stability in my country.

The Hutu and the Tutsi in neighboring Rwanda and Burundi were at each other's throat, killing each other, a perennial problem in these two countries. The town of Kigoma, where I was born and which is on the shores of Lake Tanganyika, became a hub for refugee activities; and for decades the entire western region of Tanzania has been a sanctuary for refugees from Rwanda and Burundi as well as Congo. The former Belgian Congo, another neighbor, was also torn by civil war, ignited and fueled by ethno-regional rivalries, secession, and intervention by outside powers including the United States and other Western countries especially Belgium, France, and apartheid South Africa as well as Rhodesia both of which also belonged to the Western camp. The Soviet Union and the People's Republic of China also intervened in the Congo. All these highly combustible elements in one of Africa's biggest, potentially richest and most strategically located countries, which slid into anarchy soon after independence on June 30, 1960, would have been too much for any leader to handle without solid national support for a strong central government. The Congo had neither. The country was split along ethno-regional lines, making it impossible for any leader to mobilize national support for central authority. And the central government itself was weak, and national allegiance to it tenuous at best.

I remember listening to short-wave radio broadcasts from Congo's capital, Leopoldville (renamed Kinshasa by Mobutu in 1971), and from Elisabethville (now Lubumbashi), capital of the secessionist Katanga Province under Moise Tshombe which is about 300 miles west from my home province, Mbeya Region, on the Tanzania-Zambia-Malawi border in southwestern Tanzania. I was in Rungwe District then, in the Great Rift Valley, ringed by misty blue mountains in this region in the Southern Highlands of Tanzania. The broadcasts were in Kiswahili, the national language of Tanzania and one of the languages spoken in Congo, and the war in that country dominated the news in the sixties. The Simba rebellion (*simba* means lion in Kiswahili), the capture of Stanleyville (now Kisangani) by Belgian paratroops with American support; the "disappearance" and subsequent assassination of Lumumba; the Kwilu rebellion led by Lumumba's heir-apparent Pierre Mulele and his subsequent assassination by Mobutu's henchmen (he was reportedly chopped up and his body pieces fed to the crocodiles in the Congo River in October 1968); the battle for Katanga between Tshombe's army as well as mercenaries and the United Nations peacekeeping forces; these are some of the most memorable events I can easily recall even if I don't cherish the memory because of the devastation wrought in this bleeding heart of Africa.

Those were the turbulent sixties when the Congo was in the

news everyday. Besides the radio broadcasts coming directly from Leopoldville and Elisabethville everyday about the war, we also got ample news about the same events on our national radio, TBC (Tanganyika Broadcasting Corporation), Dar es Salaam, later renamed RTD (Radio Tanzania, Dar es Salaam). The conflict in the Congo was one of the dominant stories even in Tanganyika, almost everyday. But there were other crises in the region.

Uganda, another neighbor of Tanzania and Congo, also had to contend with separatist threats by the Buganda kingdom; although not as serious as those in the Congo but serious enough to prompt Prime Minister Milton Obote to use military force to contain the danger. In May 1966, he swiftly deposed the Kabaka Edward Frederick Mutesa (who was Uganda's president, but only as nominal head) and declared a state of emergency in the Buganda kingdom. And in June 1967, he abolished all four kingdoms and declared Uganda a republic. That was when he also became president. The other traditional centers of power in the kingdoms of Toro, Ankole, and Bunyoro, and in the princedom of Busoga, had their own well-established political institutions like the Buganda kingdom and were equally suspicious of the national government which wanted to centralize power under a unitary state; thus stripping traditional rulers of authority over their own people. But they did not pose as big a threat to national unity as King (Kabaka) Edward Mutesa did.

Another neighbor, Kenya, under the leadership of Mzee Jomo Kenyatta, had just emerged from Mau Mau, and the Kikuyu were consolidating their position as the dominant tribe across the spectrum at the expense of their rivals, the Luo, and other tribes; culminating in the assassination of 39-year-old Tom Mboya, a Luo and Kenyatta's heir-apparent, in July 1969. I remember the day he was assassinated in broad daylight in Kenya's capital, Nairobi. It was Saturday afternoon, and I was at work then, as a reporter at the *Standard*, Dar Es Salaam. The assassination is still vivid in my memory because of the magnitude of the tragedy itself. It was also one of the major assassinations in East Africa and, indeed, in the entire continent in the post-colonial era.

Tom Mboya's assassination threatened to plunge Kenya into chaos, a country already rife with ethnic tensions and rivalries. No one knew how members of his tribe, the Luo, and other

Kenyans opposed to Kenyatta's leadership and domination by the Kikuyu, would react. Nahashon Njenga Njoroge, a Kikuyu and the man arrested and accused of shooting Tom Mboya, said after he was captured: "Why don't you go after the big man?" The implication of who exactly "the big man" was, besides Kenyatta himself and other Kikuyu political heavyweights of national stature such Mbiyu Koinange who was also close to Kenyatta, added to the confusion as tempers flared especially among the Luo, Mboya's fellow tribesmen. Large-scale violence was a distinct possibility. Fortunately, nothing of the sort happened, much of this domestic tranquility attributed to Kenyatta's dominant personality as the revered father of the nation, and to his tight grip on the nation he ruled with an iron fist.

But from then on, a cloud hung over Kenya, and prospects for peaceful co-existence between the country's two main ethnic groups and their allies remained bleak. The problem was compounded by the mistreatment of Jaramogi Oginga Odinga, another prominent Luo politician of international stature, who resigned as Kenya's vice president under Kenyatta and in March 1966 formed the opposition party, the Kenya People's Union (KPU). But he was effectively neutralized as an opposition leader. His passport was withdrawn, preventing him from going to the United States in 1968 to deliver a lecture at Boston University, entitled, "Revolution As It Affects Newly Independent States." He was also denied permission to go to Tanzania where he had an ideological compatriot, President Julius Nyerere.

On October 27, 1969, Oginga Odinga was put under house arrest following an anti-government demonstration by KPU supporters and, three days later, the KPU was banned, leaving the Kenya African National Union (KANU) led by Kenyatta as the only legal party in the country. And on November 11, 1969, Kenyatta was re-elected to a second term. All this took place only about three months after Mboya was assassinated in July. Yet, Oginga Odinga was one of Kenya's most revered politicians. He was also one of the most prominent leaders of the independence movement, not only in Kenya but in Africa as a whole. And it was he who led KANU when Kenyatta was in prison. It was also Oginga Odinga who led the Kenyan delegation - which included Tom Mboya - to the constitutional talks in London on Kenya's transition from colonial rule to independence. Many Kenyans and others also remember him as the author of the best-selling book, *Not Yet Uhuru*,[3] meaning "Not Yet Independence" (*uhuru* means freedom or independence in Kiswahili), which he wrote after he resigned as Kenya's vice president. President Julius Nyerere wrote the introduction to the book, as he did years later to that of President Yoweri Museveni who said he considers himself to be a disciple of Nyerere. But although Odinga was silenced, he remained a highly respected leaders in Kenya. And he remains a revered figure in Kenyan politics even today on the same level with Kenyatta.

There were more crises in the region. In Zambia, formerly Northern Rhodesia before independence, just across the border from my home region in the Southern Highlands of Tanzania, violence also erupted on a significant scale. The country had just won independence from Britain on October 24, 1964, highly optimistic of the future under the leadership of Kenneth Kaunda, a former school teacher and an apostle of non-violence and author of a book, *Zambia Shall Be Free*.[4] Yet, just before and after independence, the country was rocked by violence instigated by members of an anarchist independent church movement known as the Lumpa Church led by a prophetess, Alice Lenshina, which claimed hundreds of lives and disrupted the lives of thousands of people. The church members refused to pay taxes and rejected secular authority. They clashed with the government and fortified their villages, and refused to surrender to security forces. And they invoked the Scriptures to justify their defiance and refusal to submit to temporal authority.

The Lumpa Church and its leader Alice Lenshina became "household" names. And clashes between government forces and the church members was one of the major stories in the early sixties in that part of Africa, with the short-wave radio as an indispensable medium. Zambia also had to contend with separatist threats in the western province, also known as Barotseland, which was and still is a powerful kingdom, and in the southern part of the country, which was also the opposition stronghold of Zambia's main opposition leader Harry Nkumbula of the African National Congress (ANC). Maluniko Mundia, leader of the United Party (UP), was another prominent opposition figure. He came from

Barotse Province - Barotseland - where he was allied with the powerful traditional rulers including the king of the Barotse people. His party was banned in 1968 because of its sectarian politics, threatening national unity.

And just 30 miles from my home in the misty blue mountains of Rungwe District in the Great Rift Valley, across the border in Malawi (known as Nyasaland until July 6, 1966, when it won independence from Britain and changed its name), Life-President Dr. Hastings Kamuzu Banda, had instituted a reign of terror, persecuting and killing his former compatriots, including leading cabinet members some of whom sought asylum in Tanzania. They included Yatuta Chisiza who was assassinated. Malawian officials claimed he was trying to enter the country from Tanzania in order to subvert the government with the help of the Tanzanian authorities. Another one was Malawi's Minister of Foreign Affairs Kanyama Chiume who also sought asylum in Tanzania. When I was a reporter at the *Daily News* in Dar es Salaam, Kanyama Chiume was at *The Nationalist*, a daily newspaper owned by the ruling party TANU (Tanganyika African National Union), where he worked as a features writer and editor, together with Ben Mkapa who was the managing editor before President Nyerere appointed him editor of the *Daily News*. Years later, Mkapa himself was elected president of Tanzania fro two five year-terms from 1995 to 2005.

Under Nyerere, Tanzania became a haven for asylum seekers and refugees from many African countries and others; and I attended Songea Secondary School in Ruvuma Region in the southern part of the country with some of the sons and relatives of these exiled cabinet members from Malawi, such as Henry Chipembere, who was minister of education under President Banda. Other students at the school included the nephews of former Tanzanian Minister of Foreign Affairs Oscar Kambona who came from that region and who himself went into exile in Britain in July 1967 where he continued to be a fierce critic of Nyerere until his death in 1998, following his return to Tanzania in 1992 to form an opposition party after the introduction of multiparty democracy in 1993. And at our newspaper, the *Daily News*, we also had reporters from other countries including South Africa, Rhodesia (renamed Zimbabwe at independence in April 1980),

Zambia, Kenya, Nigeria (from former Biafra), and Britain.

Dr. Banda also claimed substantial parts of Tanzania, including my home district - Rungwe - and the rest of Mbeya Region in southwestern Tanzania, as Malawian territory. He also claimed the entire Eastern Province of Zambia, provoking a curt response from Zambia's president, Dr. Kenneth Kaunda, who challenged Banda to "Go ahead and declare war on Zambia."[5]

And President Nyerere dismissed Banda's claim of large chunks of Tanzanian territory as "expansionist outbursts, which do not scare us, and do not deserve my reply." The outlandish claim also drew a sharp response from Nyerere who said Dr. Banda was "insane." But, he warned, "Dr. Banda must not be ignored; the powers behind him are not insane."[6]

So, that was the situation in these neighboring countries in the sixties when I was in my teens, and thereafter. The situation in Mozambique, another neighbor, was somewhat different but equally explosive. Mozambique was still a Portuguese colony, and, because Tanzania gave full support to the freedom fighters who used our country as an operational base and headquarters of their liberation movement FRELIMO (Portuguese acronym for Mozambique Liberation Front), the Portuguese attacked parts of southern Tanzania, especially Mtwara Region, as well as Ruvuma Region where I attended Songea Secondary School from 1965 to 1968. But the attacks only strengthened our resolve to support the freedom fighters; an unwavering commitment that continued until Mozambique finally won independence on June 25, 1975, after almost 500 years of Portuguese colonial rule.

One of the casualties of this liberation struggle was Dr. Eduardo Mondlane, founder and first president of FRELIMO, who was assassinated in Dar es Salaam in February 1969 when he opened a parcel, rigged with a bomb and mailed to him from Japan. The bomb, hidden in a book of Russian essays, was traced back to the Portuguese secret police in Lisbon. I was then a student at Tambaza High School (formerly H.H. The Aga Khan High School) in Dar es Salaam. I was in standard 13 (Form V) that year. Our high school system had two grades, standard 13 and standard 14 (Form V and Form VI), covering two years, what Americans would call grade 13 and grade 14, after completion of secondary school in standard 12. This is roughly equivalent to what

Americans call junior college, but with a concentration in three subjects, after which you went to university if you passed the dreaded final exams in standard 14. It was patterned after the British school system we inherited from our former colonial masters.

Many students, including myself, attended Mondlane's funeral at Kinondoni Cemetery within walking distance from our high school. President Nyerere was at the gravesite, together with Mondlane's widow Janet and their two little children, a boy and a girl. Leaders of all the African liberation movements based in Dar es Salaam and members of the diplomatic corps also attended the funeral, one of the saddest moments in our   history.

But the assassination of Dr. Mondlane did not in any way interfere with the liberation struggle. President Nyerere, who had asked Mondlane to come to Tanganyika and establish an operational base in our country for the liberation of Mozambique when the two met at the United Nations where Mondlane worked and when Nyerere argued our case for Tanganyika's independence, vowed to continue supporting the freedom fighters until Mozambique was finally free. Mondlane returned to Africa in 1962 and settled in Dar es Salaam, Tanganyika, where he went on to unite the various Mozambican nationalist groups to form FRELIMO, one of the most successful liberation movements in colonial history. Nyerere's invitation to the freedom fighters was typical of him. As he stated in his address to the Tanganyika Legislative Council (LEGCO) on October 22, 1959, even before our country became independent:

> We the people of Tanganyika, would like to light a candle and put it on top of Mount Kilimanjaro which would shine beyond our borders giving hope where there was despair, love where there was hate, and dignity where before there was only humiliation.[7]

And he went on to fulfill that pledge. Without Tanzania functioning as a rear base and as a conduit for material support to the freedom fighters, Mozambique would probably not have won independence when it did, and the liberation of other countries in southern Africa including the bastion of white rule on the continent, South Africa, would have been equally affected, only in varying degrees. In spite of her poverty as one of the poorest countries in the world, Tanzania still contributed a significant amount of resources to the liberation struggle far more than many other and richer African countries did. Many people used to say that Tazania contributed far more than its share; let other countries play their part. I also remember talking to a Malawian surgeon, Dr. Geoffrey Mwaungulu, in Detroit, Michigan, when I was a student there in the early seventies, who said "Tanzania is doing too much," overburdening herself, while many other African countries - including his, Malawi - are doing nothing or very little to support the liberation struggle in southern Africa and Portuguese Guinea (Guinea-Bissau) in West Africa. A graduate of Temple University in Philadelphia, Pennsylvania, he worked at Ford General Hospital in Detroit, and was one of a large number of African immigrants living in Detroit, including professors, lawyers, engineers and other professionals in the city and in other parts of the metropolitan area.

There were even some people in Tanzania who said President Nyerere was devoting himself too much to the liberation struggle and pursuits of other foreign policy goals while overlooking domestic problems. Yet there was no contradiction between the two. His commitment to the well-being of Tanzania was not in any way compromised by the active role he played in the international arena. And he could not have succeeded in the pursuit of his foreign policy objectives - including support of the liberation movements - without the unwavering support of the vast majority of Tanzanians. As David Martin, a renowned British journalist with *The Observer*, London, who was the deputy managing editor of the *Standard*, Tanzania, and the one who first hired me as a reporter in June1969 when I was still a high school student, stated in December 2001, two years after Nyerere died:

I arrived in the Tanzanian capital of Dar es Salaam as a journalist on 9 January 1964. Three days later there was a revolution in Zanzibar by the African majority against the Arab minority put in power by the retreating British colonialists just one month earlier. An African-driven union between Tanganyika and Zanzibar followed three months later and the country's name was changed to Tanzania. Despair, hate and humiliation had begun the painfully slow process of retreating.

Dar es Salaam in those days was the headquarters of the Organization of African Unity (OAU) Liberation Committee. Living in the city were the leaders of the liberation movements of southern Africa such as the ebullient Eduardo Mondlane from Mozambique, more taciturn poet, Dr. Agostinho Neto, and a host of others. Nyerere was their beacon of hope.

He was uninhibited by the paranoid attitudes that gripped the east and west at the height of the Cold War. And although he was not adverse to using westerners to achieve his vision, he sought for the continent to have African solutions created by African people. He did not tolerate fools and was a masterly media manager. He could go for months without seeing the press. But, whe he had something to say, as he did in 1976 during two visits by the US Secretary of State, Dr. Henry Kissinger, he astutely ensured that his version of events got across.

I remember one day sitting in his office questioning that a number of African countries had not paid their subscriptions to the OAU Liberation Committee Special Fund for the Liberation of Africa. He looked at me for some moments, thoughtfully chewing the inside corner of his mouth in his distinctive way. Then, his decision made, he passed across a file swearing me secrecy as to its contents. It contained the amount that Tanzanians, then according to the United Nations the poorest people on earth, would directly and indirectly contribute that year to the liberation movements. I was astounded; the amount ran into millions of US dollars.

It was the practice among national leaders in those days to say that their countries did not have guerrilla bases. Now we know that Tanzania had man such bases providing training for most of the southern African guerrillas, who were then called 'terrorists' and who today are members of governments throughout the region.... Tanzania was also directly attacked from Mozambique by the Portuguese. But, in turn, each of the white minorities in southern Africa fell to black majority political rule and Nyerere saw his vision for the continent finally realized on 27 April 1994 when apartheid formally ended in South Africa with the swearing in of a new black leadership.[8]

Mozambique was the first country in the region to win independence by armed struggle, six years after Dr. Mondlane was assassinated. His assassination in February 1969 was one of the two major political killings in the region that year, followed by the assassination of Tom Mboya only a few months later in July, about a month after I was first hired as a news reporter of the *Standard*, renamed *Daily News* in 1970. I started working full-time on the editorial staff in 1971 after completing high school and National Service.

As a reporter, I used to go to the headquarters of the Mozambique Liberation Front, FRELIMO, on Nkrumah Street in Dar es Salaam for the latest developments on the guerrilla war in Mozambique and to pick up press releases. The office of the African National Congress (ANC) of South Africa was also on the same street, on the opposite side, not far from FRELIMO's, just a few minutes' walk, probably not more than five minutes. The person I always spoke to when I went to FRELIMO's office was Joaquim Chissano who later became president of Mozambique after the tragic death of President Samora Machel in a plane crash in October 1986.

President Machel and his entourage were on their way back to Mozambique from Harare, Zimbabwe, when the plane crashed just inside the South African border not far from Maputo, the Mozambican capital. The South African government was immediately implicated in the crash, and subsequent investigations showed that the "accident" was an act of sabotage by the apartheid regime. The South African government was also behind the assassination of Swedish Prime Minister Olof Palme on February 28, 1986. Palme, who was shot by a gunman as he was walking home with his wife from a movie theater, was a strong supporter of the African liberation movements in southern Africa, as was his country, which -especially under his leadership - reportedly contributed more than $400 million to the liberations struggle in terms of financial and non-military support.

Chissano was in charge of the FRELIMO office in Dar es Salaam, and became Mozambique's minister of foreign affairs after his country won independence. He held the same ministerial post until he became president after Samora Machel was killed. Marcelino dos Santos who also used to live in Tanzania during the struggle for Mozambique's independence, remained vice president, under Chissano, as he was under Samora Machel. Our interaction with the FRELIMO office in Dar es Salaam as reporters was facilitated by Chissano because he also spoke English, besides Portuguese. He also learned and spoke Kiswahili, our national language. So, it was easy for us to communicate with him, as much as it was with most of the freedom fighters from other countries at their headquarters in Dar es Salaam who also spoke English, and some of them Kiswahili.

Dar es Salaam during those days was the center of seismic activity on the African political landscape and beyond. The list of the names of those who came to the city, who lived there, and those who just passed through during the liberation wars, is highly impressive to say the least. It was here, in Tanzania, where Nelson Mandela first came in 1962 to seek assistance for the liberation struggle in South Africa. And Nyerere was the first leader of independent Africa he met. Tanganyika was also the first country in the region to win independence, in 1961. Mandela also had his first taste of freedom after he arrived in Mbeya, a border town in southwestern Tanzania (then Tanganyika) and the capital of the Southern Highlands Province (later split into Mbeya and Iringa Regions) where, as he states in his autobiography *Long Walk to Freedom*, he was not - for the first time in his life - subjected to the indignities of color bar as he automatically would been in his native   land.[9]

Almost all the leaders in southern Africa who waged guerrilla warfare to free their countries from white minority rule, lived or worked in Tanzania at one time or another. Thabo Mbeki, who became vice president and then president of South Africa, first sought asylum in Tanganyika when he fled the land of apartheid in the early sixties. So did others, including many leaders in South Africa today besides Mbeki. They include the Speaker of the South African Parliament Dr. Frene Ginwala who once was editor of our newspaper, the *Daily News*, appointed by President Nyerere before Sammy Mdee replaced her. She lived in Tanzania for many years and is the person who received Mandela in Dar es Salaam when he first came to Tanganyika in 1962.

President Robert Mugabe also lived in Tanzania and Mozambique during Zimbabwe's liberation war. So did Dr. Agostinho Neto, the first president of Angola, and Sam Nujoma, president of Namibia, and many of their colleagues in government. I remember interviewing Sam Nujoma in 1972 at the office of his liberation movement, the South West African People's Organization (SWAPO), on Market Street in Dar es Salaam, only a few minutes' walk from our newspaper office on Azikiwe Street and from the offices of three other liberation movements: Zimbabwe African National Union (ZANU), Popular Movement for the Liberation of Angola (MPLA), and the Pan-Africanist Congress (PAC) of South Africa. I talked to Nujoma just before he left for New York to address the United Nations Decolonization Committee and speak in other forums in his quest for Namibian independence. Looking very serious, and highly articulate on the subject, he was very optimistic about the future. He was, of course, vindicated by history. But little did he or anybody else back then know that it would be almost 20 years before Namibia would be free.

Many other leaders found sanctuary in Tanzania. They include those from the Seychelles and the Comoros, two island nations on the Indian Ocean east and southeast of Tanzania, respectively; and President Yoweri Museveni of Uganda who attended the University of Dar es Salaam and lived in Tanzania for many years and who - after he became president - continued to express profound respect and admiration for Nyerere whom he acknowledged as his mentor.[7] Mwalimu Nyerere even wrote an introduction to one of Museveni's books, *What Is Africa's Problem?*[10]

The late President Laurent Kabila of the Democratic Republic of Congo also lived in Tanzania for more than 20 years since the sixties after the assassination of Patrice Lumumba, his hero, and even owned houses in Dar es Salaam where he was also known by different aliases including Mzee Mwale. His son Joseph Kabila who succeeded him as president was born and raised, and attended school in Dar es Salaam and in Mbeya, Tanzania. In fact, many Congolese refused to accept him as their leader when first became president because they saw him as a foreigner, a Tanzanian, who did not even speak Lingala or French, the main languages spoken in Congo, but instead spoke only English and Kiswahili, Tanzania's national language, although Kiswahili is also widely spoken in   Congo.

Even President Kenneth Kaunda of Zambia forged ties with Tanzania early in his life. He spent some time in Mbeya in the southwestern part of what was then Tanganyika, and with his friend Simon Kapwepwe who also spent some time in Mbeya and later became his vice president, used to dream of the day when

Northern Rhodesia (Zambia) would be free one day. The two were childhood friends in Chinsali, their hometown and district, in Northern Rhodesia, renamed Zambia.

The list of people who found asylum in Tanzania goes on and on. They include many who became leaders in Rwanda, Burundi, Ethiopia, Eritrea, Somalia, Sudan, Ghana, Nigeria, Guinea, Congo, Zambia, besides those in southern Africa - Mozambique, Zimbabwe, Angola, Namibia, South Africa - and other countries. Even Che Guevara spent months in Tanzania. He was in Dar es Salaam for about five months from October 1965 to February 1966, besides the time he spent in the western apart of the country during his Congo mission. And it was when he was in Dar es Salaam that he wrote his famous book, the *Congo Diaries*,[11] while staying at the Cuban embassy during those critical months. In fact, before he embarked on his Congo mission, it was Che Guevara himself who recommended Pablo Ribalta - his friend and compatriot since their guerrilla war days in the Sierra Maestra during the Cuban revolution - to be Cuba's ambassador to Tanzania because he felt that Ribalta's African ancestry would facilitate his mission to the Congo. And during his military engagement in the Congo, Che sometimes used Kigoma in western Tanzania as one of his sanctuaries. But he had a very low opinion of Laurent Kabila - whom he said had no leadership qualities and lacked charisma - and other Congolese nationalist leaders including Gaston-Emile Sumayili Soumialot. He accused them of abandoning their troops in eastern Congo preferring, instead, to live in comfort in Dar es Salaam.

But in spite of the fact that Tanzania was the headquarters of all the African liberation movements, and a place which attracted many liberals and leftists from many parts of the world including black militants from the United States such as the Black Panthers, and Malcolm X who also visited Tanzania and had a meeting with President Nyerere and attended the OAU conference of the African heads of state and government in Cairo, Egypt, in July 1964 (where he almost died when his food was poisoned, probably by CIA agents who followed him throughout his African trip); our country still enjoyed relative peace and stability, not only during the euphoric sixties soon after independence, but during the seventies as well, when the liberation wars were most intense in southern Africa, with Dar es Salaam, our capital, as the nerve center.

Therefore, besides the raids by the Portuguese from their colony of Mozambique on our country; a sustained destabilization campaign by the apartheid regime of South Africa whose Defence Minister P.W. Botha said in August 1968 that countries which harbor terrorists - freedom fighters in our lexicon - should receive "a sudden knock,"[12] a pointed reference to Tanzania and Zambia, and by the white minority government of Rhodesia (Prime Minister Ian Smith called Nyerere "the evil genius" behind the liberation wars), all of whom had singled out Tanzania as the primary target because of our support for the freedom fighters; the influx of refugees from Rwanda, Burundi, and Congo into our country; and Malawian President Banda's claims to our territory; in spite of all that, Tanzania was, relatively speaking, not only an island of peace and stability in the region but also an ideological center with considerable magnetic pull, drawing liberal and radical thinkers from around the world, especially to the University of Dar es Salaam which became one of the most prominent academic centers in the world with many internationally renowned   scholars who strongly admired Nyerere and his policies.

Among the scholars drawn to Tanzania was the late Dr. Walter Rodney from Guyana who first joined the academic staff at the University of Dar es Salaam in 1968 and, while teaching there, wrote a best-seller, *How Europe Underdeveloped Africa*;[13] the late distinguished Professor Claude Ake from Nigeria who died in a plane crash in his home country in 1996; Professor Okwudiba Nnoli, also from Nigeria (secessionist Biafra); Professor Mahmood Mamdani from Uganda and one of Africa's internationally renowned scholars; Nathan Shamuyarira who - while a lecturer at the University of Dar es Salaam - was also the leader of the Dar-es-Salaam-based Front for the Liberation of Zimbabwe (FROLIZI) headed by James Chikerema, a Zimbwean national leader. Shamuyarira went on to become Zimbabwe's minister of foreign affairs, among other ministerial posts. Many other prominent scholars from many countries around the world, and from all continents, were also attracted to the University of Dar es Salaam. C.L.R. James from Trinidad & Tobago, one of the founding fathers of the Pan-African movement who knew Kwame Nkrumah when

Nkrumah was still a student in the United States, and who introduced him to George Padmore when he went to Britain for further studies before returning to Ghana (then the Gold Coast) in 1947, was also attracted to Tanzania. So was Kenyan writer Ngugi wa Thiong'o, disenchanted with the Kenyan leadership, and Ghanaian writer Ayi Kwei Armah, an admirer of Nkrumah and Nyerere, who has also called for the adoption of Kiswahili as the continental language just as Wole Soyinka has.

Besides Malcolm X, other prominent black American leaders who came to Tanzania included Stokely Carmichael (originally from Trinidad) who as Kwame Ture lived in Guinea for 30 years until his death in November 1998; Angela Davis of the Black Panther Party and others in the civil rights movement including Andrew Young and Jesse Jackson. A number of revolutionary thinkers fro Latin America, Europe, and Asia were also drawn to Tanzania and lived in Dar es Salaam which was the center of ideological ferment and provided an environment condicive to cross-fertilization of ideas stimulated by Nyerere's policies and ideological leadership. And Tanzania's prominent role in the African liberation struggle and world affairs because of Nyerere's leadership put the country in a unique position on a continent where few governments looked beyond their borders, with most of them content to pursue goals in the narrow context of "national interest," which really meant securing and promoting the interests of the leaders themselves.

Tanzania was therefore an anomaly in that sense, on the continent, as a haven and an incubator for activists and revolutionaries from around the world. And it remained that way as a magnet throughout Nyerere's tenure. It was also his leadership more than anything else, which played a critical role in forging and shaping the identity of our nation and in enabling Tanzania to play an important part on the global scene, far beyond its wealth and size, especially in promoting the interests of Africa and the Third World in general. The fact that Nyerere himself was chosen as chairman of the South Commission, a forum for action and dialogue between the poor and the rich countries on how to address problems of economic inequalities in a global context, is strong testimony to that. And it was in this crucible of identity, a country that would not be what it is today had it not been for Nyerere that my own personality was shaped.

In some fundamental respects, it is an identity and an ethos like no other on the continent: an indigenous national language, Kiswahili, transcending tribalism and not claimed by any particular ethnic group as its own - all the tribes and racial minorities contributed to its creation and growth, a unique phenomenon; social equality as an egalitarian ideal implemented by Nyerere through the decades; national unity - and stability - that has virtually eliminated tribalism and racism as major problems in national life, and in a country where speaking tribal languages in front of other people who don't understand those languages is frowned upon. Kiswahili helped Tanzania's 126 different tribes and racial minorities - Arab, Asian, mostly of Indian and Pakistani origin, and European - to develop a sense of national unity and identity which has remained solid through the years regardless of what the country has undergone since independence in 1961. And the egalitarian policies of President Nyerere reduced social inequalities across the nation and guaranteed equal access to health, education, and other services on a scale probably unequalled anywhere else on the continent.

But probably more than any other asset, it was Nyerere's leadership which proved to be most useful at a time when we needed it most to forge a true sense of national identity, maintain national stability, and consolidate our independence; as much as Mandela's magnanimity and wisdom proved to be an indispensable asset in South Africa's transition from apartheid to democracy at a time when the country could have exploded, engulfing it in a racial conflagration. The pundits and laymen alike who predicted this were proved wrong largely because of Mandela's astute leadership, like Nyerere's. Therefore it's not surprising that they are the only two African leaders who are favorably compared to each other with equal international and moral stature - hence Nyerere's honorific title, "The Conscience of Africa." There is nobody else in their league.

I remember Nyerere well. Cordially known as Mwalimu, which means Teacher in Kiswahili, he led by example; his humility equaled by his commitment to the well-being of the poorest of the poor, yet without ignoring the rights of others. And he asked all to make sacrifices for our collective well-being. As he put it, "It can be done. Play your part." His dedication and identification with the masses, and his passion for fairness, were evident throughout his tenure as the nation's leader. When he became president, he worked and lived with them in the villages, slept in their huts, and ate their food. He spent days, and weeks, working with them in the rural areas in all parts of the country. He mingled with the peasants so well that you wouldn't even know who the leader was in the group, let alone be able to identify him as president of a country if you didn't know how he looked like. I know this because I worked as a news reporter in Tanzania. No other African leader lived the way he did, and worked in the rural areas as much as he did, clearing and tilling the land for hours with ordinary peasants. He was one of them and, they said, "He's one of us." Not a detached, arrogant leader and intellectual who felt it was beneath him to soil his hands like the poor, illiterate peasants did. I also know how humble he was, because of what I witnessed years before I even became a national news reporter, first at the *Standard*, next at the Ministry of Information and Broadcasting as an information officer, and then at the *Daily News*.

I remember Nyerere when he was campaigning for independence. It was in the late 1950s when I first saw him. He had already been to the United States, and even appeared on American television with Eleanor Roosevelt in 1956 when he was interviewed by Mike Wallace, a prominent American television journalist and interviewer who was still on the air in 2002 and beyond, although in his eighties. Nyerere went to the United States to present our case for independence at the United Nations where he appeared more than once in the late fifties, and before American audiences including academic gatherings such as the one at Wellesley College in Massachusetts in 1960 where he participated in a symposium and delivered a lecture, "Africa and the World."

I was just a little boy then, under ten, when he came to our home district in the late fifties more than once. I first saw him around 1958. He was about 36 years old. But in spite of my age - I was born on 4 October 1949 - what I saw then remains vivid in my memory as if it happened only yesterday. I was a pupil at Kyimbila Primary School, about two miles from Tukuyu. Founded by the German colonial rulers and named Neu Langenburg, Tukuyu was our district headquarters for Rungwe District. The town was destroyed by an earthquake in 1919 but was rebuilt. It had been the district headquarters since the German colonial rulers built it when they first came to the area in the early 1890s. When the British took over Tanganyika - then known as German East Africa which included Rwanda and Burundi as one colony - after the Germans lost World War I, they continued the tradition and kept the town (whose name was changed from Neu Langenburg to Tukuyu) as the headquarters of Rungwe District headed by a British District Commissioner, simply known as DC, who lived there.

Nyerere came to Tukuyu one afternoon and our head teacher, who also happened to be a relative of mine, led us on a trip from our school to Tukuyu to listen to him. As life was then, and as it still is today across Africa for most people including children, we walked the two miles to Tukuyu to hear him speak; a man who, we were told, was our leader and who was going to be president of Tanganyika in only about three years, replacing the British governor.

I was then too young to understand the complexities of politics and political campaigning all of which to us at that age seemed to be expressed in esoteric terms. Yet we were old enough to understand what Nyerere was saying in general; a message delivered in his usual simple style everybody, including children my age, was able to understand. And he knew there were children at the rally. He saw us.

He arrived in an open Land Rover, standing in the back, waving at the crowd. The people were just as jubilant. He stepped out of the Land Rover and walked to the football (soccer) field to address the mass rally. He wore a simple short-sleeved light-green shirt and a pair of long trousers (pants), and started speaking, using a megaphone.

It was a cloudy afternoon and, after he spoke for only a few minutes, it started raining. The leading local politician of the Tanganyika African National Union (TANU), Mr. Mwambenja, a formidable personality and relentless campaigner for independence, who welcomed Nyerere at the rally tried to hold an umbrella over him. But he refused to accept it and continued to speak. He even joked about himself implying that he was a non-entity, an insignificant personality, and said something to the effect that the colonialists and other detractors were now, with all that rain saying, "Just let him get soaked and washed away." The subtle message in this self-deprecating humor was that he was not going to fade into oblivion and give up the struggle for independence. And it kept on raining. But the rain did not dampen his spirits. We also stayed as almost everybody else did, impressed by his humility and simplicity despite his status as the most prominent and acknowledged leader of Tanganyika, besides the British governor Sir Edward Twining who was later succeeded by Sir Richard Turnbull, the last governor. He got soaked in the rain just like the rest of us and continued to speak until he finished addressing the rally.

It was such humility, devotion and simplicity, which remained the hallmark of his life and leadership. And it was evident even among some members of his family. I attended school with his eldest son, Andrew, at Tambaza High School, the former H.H. The Aga Khan High School which had been exclusively for students of Asian origin, mostly Indian and Pakistani, almost all of whom were Tanzanians. There were also some Arab students. And there were only a few of us, black students. We were among the first to integrate the school as mandated by the government under Nyerere. In fact, Mwalimu himself had experienced racial discrimination, what we in East Africa - and elsewhere including southern Africa - also call color bar. As Colin Legum states in a book he edited with Tanzanian Professor Geoffrey Mmari, *Mwalimu: The Influence of Nyerere:*

> I was privileged to meet Nyerere while he was still a young teacher in short trousers at the very beginning of his political career, and to engage in private conversations with him since the early 1950s. My very first encounter in 1953 taught me something about his calm authority in the face of racism in colonial Tanganyika. I had arranged a meeting with four leaders of the nascent nationalist movement at the Old Africa Hotel in Dar es Salaam. We sat at a table on the pavement and ordered five beers, but before we could lift our glasses an African waiter rushed up and whipped away all the glasses except mine. I rose to protest to the white manager, but Nyerere restrained me. 'I am glad it happened,' he said, 'now you can go and tell your friend Sir Edward Twining [the governor at the time] how things are in this country.' His manner was light and amusing, with no hint of anger.[14]

Simple, yet profound. For, beneath the surface lay a steely character with a deep passion for justice across the color line and an uncompromising commitment to the egalitarian ideals he espoused and implemented throughout his political career, favoring none. He sent his son to a local school - with the sons of peasants and workers - when he could have sent him abroad, as was customary among most leaders across the continent. They either sent their children to exclusively private and expensive schools within their own countries, or flew them overseas, and still do.

All this was in keeping with his commitment to social equality for all Tanzanians. He said we are not going to build a society based on privilege; we are going to narrow the gap between the haves and the have-nots, and abolish classes which accentuate cleavages and define some human beings as better than others. At our high school, many people knew that President Nyerere's eldest son was one of the students. Yet he got no special favors. He was treated just like the rest of us, and we saw him as just another student like us.

And he saw himself that way, and acted that way. You wouldn't even know he was the president's son because of the way he behaved and carried himself, just as an ordinary student, and the way the rest of us treated him. We lived in the same hostel, most of whose students were Tanzanians of Asian origin; ate the same food at the same table, and worked on the farm together, tilling the land, as true sons of a nation of peasants and workers. Our school in Dar es Salaam had a farm, near Muhimbili National Hospital, where we were required to work to instill egalitarian values in our minds. We walked to the farm, about two miles round trip, carrying hoes and sickles and other agricultural implements; a strong reminder that we were no better than ordinary peasants and workers simply because we had acquired some education and were destined to become part of the nation's elite. And Nyerere's son also walked around the city with fellow students and other friends, just like the rest of us, when many people would probably have expected him as the president's son to ride in a Mercedes Benz. But that was not the kind of society based on class and privilege President Nyerere was trying to build. And to his son's credit, he was just as humble and friendly with everybody.

Our school was also fully integrated. We lived in the same hostel with Asian and Arab students. We also had African, Asian and European teachers, most of them Tanzanian citizens. Other schools across Tanzania were also fully integrated - student and faculty. At our school, students came from all parts of the country and from many different tribes. We were not encouraged to attend school - except at the primary school level - in our home districts, which were usually inhabited by members of our own tribes. We were, in fact, assigned to schools and jobs after graduation far away from our tribal homelands in order to live and work with members of other tribes. It was a deliberate effort by the government to break down barriers between members of different tribes and races in order to achieve national unity. And it worked. This was probably Nyerere's biggest achievement - the creation of a cohesive political entity unique on a continent rife with ethnic tensions and torn by conflict caused and fueled by ethno-regional rivalries in the struggle for power and for the nation's resources. Our schools were a microcosm of what Tanzania became: a united, integrated, peaceful and stable nation.

It was also when I was in high school at Tambaza that I first got hired in June 1969 as a reporter by the *Standard*, which became the *Daily News* the following year. I started working full-time in 1971 after I finished high school the previous year. Our managing editor was Brendon Grimshaw, a British, and the news and deputy editor was David Martin, also British, who also worked for the London *Observer* for many years after he left Tanzania. David Martin also worked for the BBC and even covered the Angolan civil war. I remember listening to him in a live report from Angola on the CBC (Canadian Broadcasting Corporation) radio when I lived in Detroit, Michigan, USA, in the seventies. President Nyerere was our editor-in-chief. But he never served in an executive capacity at the *Daily News*. As an overall guardian of this publicly owned institution - the paper, the *Standard*, was renamed *Daily News* in 1970 when it was nationalized - he gave us the freedom to say what we wanted to say and even encouraged us to criticize the government and its policies. And he meant what he said. We wrote what we wanted to write without any fear of retribution or censorship. Others also testify to that. As Philip Ochieng', probably Kenya's best known journalist and political commentator who was attracted to Tanzania by Nyerere's leadership and policies and joined our editorial staff at the *Daily News*, stated in a tribute to Mwalimu, "There Was Real Freedom in

Mwalimu's Day," in *The East   African*:

I never really covered Mwalimu Nyerere. By the time I got to Tanzania to work for *The Standard Tanzania*, I had been an editorial pontiff in Nairobi's *Sunday Nation* for upwards of two years. And that was what I continued to do in Dar-es-Salaam....

Working for the president, between September 1970 and January 1973, was probably the most enjoyable period of my entire journalistic career. There were at least two reasons for this. The first was that ours was a community of ideas. The second, contrary to what was constantly claimed here in Nairobi and by the Western press, was that the Dar-es-Salaam newspapers enjoyed a high level of freedom to publish. This reflected the fact that Tanzania enjoyed an unprecedented freedom of speech. But it was never licentious freedom of the kind with which Nairobi's alternative press assails our eyes every morning.

Following the Arusha Declaration of 1967, Julius Kambarage Nyerere had, early in 1970, nationalised *The Tanganyika Standard* from Lonhro and rechristened it *The Standard Tanzania* (sic) as the official print organ of the government. *The Nationalist* and its Kiswahili sister *Uhuru* already existed as the organs of the ruling Tanganyika African National Union (TANU), with Ben Mkapa as its editor. Brought in from London as Managing Editor of *The Standard* was a tough-talking South African woman of Asian origin called Frene Ginwala. Ginwala, who is now the Speaker of the South African Parliament in Cape Town, was a woman of strong left-wing convictions. She very soon collected around men and women from the international community with equally strong socialist views.

This was the context in which I left Nairobi for Dar-es-Salaam, invited by Ginwala. Mwalimu Nyerere acted as our - non-executive - Editor-in-Chief. And yet every Friday I published an opinion column highly critical of his system.

I waxed critical especially of the recent nationalised commercial and industrial houses: the corruption that was beginning to invade them and their umbrella organisations, the ineptitude, the apparent absence of development ideas. Yet never once did Ginwala or myself receive a telephone call from or a summons to Ikulu - State House - complaining about anything we had written. Of course, there were many murmurs in the corridors of power against us. They accused us of being a bunch of communists, though we never were. But they dared not call a press conference to attack us. Nyerere simply would not have allowed them to do so....

Kambarage Nyerere remained one of Africa's quintessential men of the 20th century. His personal probity was unequalled...(as was) his refusal to use his immense power to enrich himself or his family.

It was his intellectual strength and moral fiber that enabled him, when he saw that his (socialist) experiment could not succeed, to admit openly that his life career had been a failure. When he nationalised *The Tanganyika Standard*, he gave us a charter, which expressly challenged its news editors to criticise all social failings by whomever they are committed. I had never been and would never be freer than when I worked in Dar.... This freedom of the press...was only a mirror-reflection of the much more important freedom of ideas throughout the country. Though Nyerere believed more than 100 per cent in Ujamaa, he never tried to force it down anybody's throat. Nor did he ever issue *The Standard*, *The Nationalist* or the latter's Swahili daily and weekly counterparts *Uhuru* and *Mzalendo*, with any instruction to print only Nyerereist ideas or to slant news in favour of that ideology and its exponents.

If that had been the case, Tanzania's amazing pluralism of ideas at that time would not have reached the world. Yet it did reach the world, attracting into that country hundreds of intellectuals from all over the world. The University of Dar-es-Salaam at Ubungo was Africa's, perhaps the world's, intellectual Mecca. Dar-es-Salaam harboured all the radical liberation movements in Africa, Latin America, the Middle East, Ireland, South-East Asia, even the United States. It was a crossroads of such celebrated freedom fighters as Agostinho Neto, Samora Machel, Marcelino dos Santos, Jorge Rebello, Janet Mondlane, Yoweri Museveni, Sam Nujoma, Thabo Mbeki, Oliver Tambo, Gora Ebrahim, Amilcar Cabral, Angela Davis and others, changing ideas with us, often hotly.... There were intellectuals - both native and alien - who expressed ideas so far to the right that they bordered on fascism. Others expressed ideas so far to the left that again they bordered on fascism.... For these were not uniform minds.... The humdinger, however, was that all these ideas were expressed freely and printed in the party and government newspapers with little attempt at editorial slanting and chicanery....

Until his death, Nyerere, who was humble, self-effacing and selfless, continued to serve humanity on many capacities - particularly his promotion of mutual South-South assistance to reduce dependence on Western alms and his attempt to bring about order in Burundi.

An intellectual of immense stature, a man of great personal integrity, a paragon of humanism, Julius Kambarage Nyerere will be hard to replace in Tanzania, in Africa and on the globe. I was privileged to know and work with such a man. That is why, as I mourn, I ask, with Marcus Antonius, whence cometh such another?[15]

Members of the entire editorial staff were fully aware of the kind of freedom we had to criticize the government, although we worked for a government-owned newspaper. But the government owned it on behalf of the people, *wananchi*. Therefore we were free to criticize leaders and policies and express our views across the spectrum without being censured. President Nyerere established that as a policy. Our editors, first Sammy Mdee who later became President Nyerere's press secretary, and next Ben Mkapa who was elected president of Tanzania in 1995 and won a second five year-term in 2000, did not violate this policy which was adopted after the newspaper was nationalized. They sometimes even invited reporters to write and contribute to editorials. Self-criticism was also routine. Every morning before we went out on assignments, we had a post-mortem of the paper presided over by the editor, dissecting the stories we wrote the previous day.

Such was the camaraderie, the ambience and egalitarian disposition, and freedom, we enjoyed at our newspaper; the largest English daily in Tanzania and one of the three largest and most influential in East Africa.

Although we were independent and wrote whatever we wanted to write, we were also at the center of a maelstrom because of the ideological ferment that the country was undergoing during that period in its quest for socialist transformation in pursuit of the egalitarian ideals of Ujamaa (which means familyhood in Kiswahili) espoused by Nyerere: a political theorist and philosopher, scholar and politician, without an equal on the continent in terms of intellectual prowess and pursuits among leaders with the exception of President Leopold Sedar Senghor of Senegal, a poet-philosopher - "I feel, therefore I am," he mused, reminiscent of Rene Descartes, "I think, therefore I am"; and Dr. Kwame Nkrumah, president of Ghana and revolutionary thinker and theoretician.

But Nkrumah was overthrown in February 1966 in a CIA-engineered coup, before Nyerere enunciated his socialist ideology in the Arusha Declaration almost exactly one year later in February 1967 after the Ghana coup. So, with Nkrumah gone - he died in April 1972, six years after he was overthrown - only Nyerere and

Senghor remained on the scene as the leading political thinkers on the continent. I remember when Nkrumah died. I was at work on that day at the *Daily News* when the bulletin on his death came in on the telex in the evening in our editorial office. One of the first persons to express profound shock was Karim Essack, about whom more later, but Dr. Nkrumah's death equally affected the rest of us who read the news bulletin that evening. The other reporters were gone by then.

Although Nkrumah's death left on the scene two towering intellectual presidents, Nyerere and Senghor, it was Nyerere who was the far more influential between the two on the continent and in the international arena. Senghor was also seen as a white man in black skin. But his unabashed Francophilia did not diminish his stature as an intellectual, especially among his admirers, and even among some of his critics who saw him as a black Frenchman who should have been born white and brought up in France. In 1980, he stepped down as president of Senegal and went to live in France where he died in December 2001 at the age of 95. He was one African leader - and there were many others - who was not admired by many reporters on our editorial staff, anymore than Dr. Hastings Kamuzu Banda, the president of Malawi, was. I didn't know any on our staff who admired Banda.

Our newspaper, like the country itself, attracted not only reporters and revolutionary thinkers from different parts of Africa and beyond but also reporters of different ideological interests within Tanzania itself. There was, for instance, Karim Essack - a Tanzanian of Asian (Indian) origin - who was a leftist revolutionary and, like the rest of us on our editorial staff who were not leftist although some were, also an uncompromising foe of apartheid and other oppressive regimes. He also wrote a book about Dr. Eduardo Mondlane and the liberation struggle in Mozambique and maintained, until his death in 1997, close ties with revolutionaries and radical thinkers around the world including many in Latin America. As the socialist-oriented International Emergency Committee (IEC) - founded to defend the life of Dr. Abimael Guzman, a Peruvian Marxist philosophy professor and leader of the revolutionary group Shining Path, captured and imprisoned in Peru in 1992 - stated in October 1997 in its eulogy, "In Memory of Karim Essack":

The IEC coordinating committee was saddened to learn that Karim Essack died this summer. He was a Tanzanian anti-imperialist who, for several decades, actively supported national liberation movements across the world. Karim Essack was a friend of the Peruvian people and a supporter of the People's War in Peru who dedicated some of his writings to Dr. Guzman and other PCP fighters. He was a signatory to the IEC Call and helped propagate the campaign in Africa. He will be missed.[16]

Karim Essack was just one of the reporters of Asian descent on our staff, which was fully integrated: black African being in the majority; Asian, mostly of Indian and Pakistani origin; Arab; and British. This also reflected Nyerere's ideals. As Tanzania's president and editor-in-chief of our newspaper, he would not have tolerated an editorial team that was exclusivist and intentionally did not reflect the racial and ethnic composition of our society - although, for practical purposes, not every tribe could have been represented on our staff or any anywhere else in the country. But the bedrock principle on which our society was built under Nyerere was that no one should be discriminated against. And he meant what he said. Few countries in the world can match Tanzania's record of inclusion. And it is not uncommon to hear people from other countries who have lived in Tanzania say, "There is no racism and tribalism in Tanzania"; "Tanzania is the only country in Africa that has conquered tribalism," as Keith Richburg says in his book *Out of America: A Black Man Confronts Africa*;[17] "There is very little tribalism - and racism - in Tanzania"; "Tribalism and racism are not major problems in Tanzania." The last statement is closest to reality.

And in keeping with Tanzania's policy of welcoming refugees and promoting Pan-African solidarity as enunciated by Nyerere, members of our editorial staff from other African countries were not only guaranteed equal rights and accorded full protection like the rest of us, but also career advancement like everywhere else in Tanzania. So were other non-citizens from outside Africa. In fact, in the 1970 general elections, people from other African countries who were not citizens of Tanzania were allowed to vote. President Nyerere allowed that as one of the ways of promoting African unity. And it is possible some of them even voted against him. But his gesture of goodwill was highly appreciated and resonated far beyond our national borders.

At our newspaper, some of the foreign reporters who held responsible positions included Tommy Sithole, sports editor, who returned to Zimbabwe and became managing editor of the state-owned *Zimbabwe Herald* after his country won independence under the leadership of Robert Mugabe, himself of scholarly bent like Nyerere, although not of the same intellectual stature and influence as a Pan-African leader. There was also Philip Ochieng', a Kenyan, who wrote a weekly column, "The Way I See It." He also served as a sub-editor, one among several, including Felix Kaiza, Paschal Shija, Robert Rweyemamu, Uli Mwambulukutu, Abdallah Ngororo, Kassim Mpenda, Jenerali Ulimwengu, Emmanuel Bulugu, and a few others. The news editor was Nsubisi Mwakipunda. Two senior reporters, Reginald Mhango - originally from Malawi - who later in 2002 became managing editor of the *Guardian,* one of Tanzania's leading daily newspapers, and Kusai Khamisa, also served as acting news editors in Mwakipunda's absence. All these were Tanzanians. Philip Ochieng' eventually went back to Kenya - after further studies in Germany - and served as editor of the government-owned *Kenya Times* before returning to the *Daily Nation*, Nairobi, where he worked before he joined our editorial staff at the *Standard*, later *Daily News*, in Dar es Salaam. He also wrote a book, *I Accuse the Press: An Insider's View of the Media and Politics in Africa.*[18]

We also had sub-editors from South Africa, Nigeria, and Britain. The Nigerian sub-editor came from Biafra and fled his country during the civil war and was one of the many Eastern Nigerians, mostly Igbos, who sought asylum in Tanzania after the Eastern Region seceded from the Nigerian Federation. They included judges and professors, many other professionals and others who came to live in Tanzania during that critical period. And many remained in Tanzania after the war. It was Nyerere who extended such hospitality to them after Tanzania became the first country to recognize Biafra. And in Dar es Salaam even today, there is a place called Biafra Grounds where mass rallies are held. There are also many Nigerian doctors and other professionals in Tanzania. They would not have been able to live and work in Tanzania in such large numbers had it not been for Tanzania's track record of hospitality initiated by Nyerere way back in the sixties soon after Tanganyika won independence from Britain on December 9, 1961. And his Pan-African commitment and achievements were internationally acknowledged, despite his failed socialist policies. As Professor Harvey Glickman who made a study tour of Tanzania stated in his article, "Tanzania: From Disillusionment to Guarded Optimism," in *Current History: A Journal of Contemporary World Affairs*:

Tanzania's profile, in the life and career of President Julius Nyerere, was poor, earnest, caring, and honest - at least until 1985, when Nyerere formally stepped aside in a peaceful constitutional transition (which is extremely rare in Africa). Tanzania's government was stable while other African governments succumbed to coups and civil wars. The country conducted consecutive national elections at regular five-year intervals. Other one-party states ignored mass participation; Nyerere's Tanzania devised a system of constituency primaries under the party umbrella, controlled at the center, but offering a voice for localism. Other African governments extolled the virtues of Pan-Africanism; Nyerere engineered the union of his own country and an offshore neighbor. Other African governments denounced white racist governments on the continent; Tanzania took action, cutting off relations with Britain over the issue of African rule in Rhodesia in 1965 (the first country to do so), and offering shelter to the liberation parties and guerrilla forces of southern Africa.

While most African governments rejected the secession of Biafra from Nigeria in 1967, Tanzania recognized Biafra's short-lived government on moral grounds (and was the first to recognize the secessionist region), arguing it was an act of self-defence against ethnic pogroms. While other African countries merely denounced Idi Amin in Uganda in the 1970s, Tanzania's army defeated him in battle in 1979 and drove him from the country.[19]

And Nyerere's policy of good neighborliness and Pan-African solidarity was also clearly evident at our newspaper which had an exchange program with neighboring Zambia, and whose president, Dr. Kenneth Kaunda was Nyerere's ideological compatriot. A reporter from the *Times of Zambia*, Francis Kasoma, joined our editorial staff while our news editor Nsubisi Mwakipunda went to Zambia to work at the *Times*. Kasoma covered some of the most important political events in the country just as we did. It didn't matter he and a number of other reporters were not Tanzanians. After working at the *Daily News* for quite some time, Kasoma returned to Zambia and years later became professor and head of the mass communications department at the

University of Zambia. He also wrote some books including *The Press and Multiparty Politics in Africa.*[20] Another member of our editorial staff who also wrote a book was deputy editor Hadji Konde, one of the most renowned Tanzanian journalists with vast experience in the profession. He wrote *Press Freedom in Tanzania.*[21] His work was preceded only by Karim Essack's among those written by newsmen who worked at the *Daily News*, Dar es Salaam, Tanzania.

Another reporter on our editorial staff, Clement Ndulute, also became an author with the publication of his book, *The Poetry of Shaaban Robert,*[22] published in 1994 by the Dar es Salaam University Press. It is a translation of the works of Tanzania's eminent poet from Kiswahili into English. Ndulute went on to pursue further education and became a lecturer in literature at the University of Dar es Salaam, Tanzania, and later an associate professor of African literature at Mississippi Valley State University in the United States. Another member of our editorial staff who became a professor is Issa Kaboko Musoke. He attended Michigan State University in the United States during the seventies when I was also a student in the same state. He returned to Tanzania and joined the academic staff at the University of Dar es Salaam teaching sociology. He also taught in Botswana for some time.

Yet another reporter from the *Daily News* who also attended school in Michigan around the same time I did, was Deogratias Michael Masakilija. Both of us were sponsored by the Pan-African Congress-USA, an organization based in Detroit and founded by a group of African-Americans in that city to strengthen ties between Black America and Africa and promote African unity. Their Pan-African philosophy was based on the teachings of Kwame Nkrumah and Julius Nyerere who were the ideological mentors of the organization. They even had the pictures of the two leaders on the wall in their conference hall, together with those of Ahmed Sekou Toure, Malcolm X and Patrice Lumumba. These were the five leaders they admired the most and whose writings they studied for ideological guidance and inspiration.

Tanzania's national dress, the dark suit with a collar-less jacket worn by President Nyerere and other Tanzanian leaders, was the official attire of the male members of the organization. Some of the members of the organization went to live or work in Tanzania, while others simply visited the country, one of their favorites, together with Ghana. And a number of others attended the Sixth Pan-African Congress, under the stewardship of President Julius Nyerere, held at the University of Dar es Salaam in Nkrumah Hall in 1974. It was the first one held on African soil. The last one, the Fifth Pan-African Congress, was held in Manchester, England, in 1945, and was attended by a number of future African leaders including Kwame Nkrumah, Jomo Kenyatta, and Nnamdi Azikiwe. It galvanized the African independence movement.

Amadou Taal from the Gambia who became a high government official under President Dawda Jawara and one of Gambia's leading economists. He held the following high-profile posts consecutively: Principal Planner in the Ministry of Economic Planning and Industrial Development; Permanent Secretary on the Ministry of Agriculture; and finally Permanent Secretary in the Ministry of Local Government and Lands. And throughout his tenure, he represented the Gambia at international conferences in many countries including Tanzania. He served his country in high capacity until President Jawara was overthrown in a military coup in July 1994, and later became one of the main leaders of the opposition United Democratic Party (UDP). He was not sponsored by the Pan-African Congress-USA but was supported by the organization.

Another student who was sponsored by the Pan-African Congress-USA but did not attended Wayne State University and entered public life when he returned home was Kwabena Dompre from Ghana. He was the third student to be sponsored by the organization - after Kojo Yankah, and Olu Williams from Sierra Leone - and went to Western Michigan University. After he returned to Ghana, he entered politics and worked for President Hilla Limann, and later became a lawyer in Ghana and in the United   States.

My other schoolmates at Wayne State University who went into public life, but who were not sponsored by the Pan-African Congress-USA, included Raphael Munavu who became a professor at Nairobi University and then vice-chancellor of Moi University after he returned to Kenya. Although an academic, his position as vice-chancellor of one of Kenya's universities made him a leading educational authority and a public figure. Another graduate of Wayne State University who was in a similar position but who went to school there long before I did was Dr. Philemon Msuya from Tanzania, assistant dean of the Muhimbili Medical School in Dar es salaam headed by Dr. Nhonoli when I was a reporter at the *Daily News*. I once interviewed him and wrote a feature article about the school in our newspaper; that's how I learned that he was a graduate of Wayne State University Medical School, the largest in the United States.

My interview with Dr. Msuya had to do with high-level manpower and how we would meet our country's needs in the medical field. The projections by the Tanzanian government that we would have enough doctors by 1985 did not correspond to reality; a point I underscored in my article. Wayne State University also had ties to Tanzania in other ways. Tanzania's junior minister of health and the first female cabinet member, Lucy Lameck, also attended Wayne State University. And there were two professors from Tanzania, Mark Kiluma and Mayowera, who taught Kiswahili at Wayne State University when I was a student there in the seventies. And the head of the linguistics department, Professor Sorensen, lived in Tanzania - what was then Tanganyika - for 25 years, and first went there before I was born. He was, all those years, a Catholic priest in Morogoro where I also lived when I was under five years old.

Besides the two Tanzanians teaching Kiswahili, other African professors at Wayne State University included Mxolisi Ntlabati from South Africa. An associate of Nelson Mandela and others who ended up in the dock in the Rivonia Trial, he would have been one of them had he not fled the country via Tanganyika and gone to the United States for further studies. Tragically, he was killed in 1979 by the same apartheid regime he fled from, after he left Detroit, Michigan, and returned to South Africa and was banished to a remote part of Ciskei, one of the homelands, where the only job he could find was teaching and which severely limited his career opportunities in a deliberate effort by the white racist government to destroy him. He died at the hands of the authorities. Another fellow African student at Wayne State University, Emmanuel Sendezera from Malawi, also ended up in South Africa as a physics professor at Witwatersrand University and at another university in Kwazulu/Natal Province. He and John Muhanji from Kenya were the only two black PhD students in physics at Wayne State University in the seventies. They were also among the few students from East Africa on campus besides me.

Wayne State University also had students from many other African countries. And our organization on campus, the Organization of African Students (OAS) of which I was president, had a monthly publication called *Ngurumo*, which was also the name of a Swahili newspaper in Tanzania. The students, most of whom came from West Africa, chose the name because they were attracted by its literal meaning, Thunder. And probably just as many said they liked the name because it reminded them of Nkrumah, an embodiment of Pan-Africanism, which our organization also embraced as a unifying ideology. My association with this publication was the last I would have as a journalist. After I left Wayne State University, my life veered in another direction in terms of academic pursuits and career advancement. Years later, I ended up writing books, mostly academic works.

While Musoke and I never returned to journalism after finishing our studies in Michigan, Masakilija did. After he returned to Tanzania, he not only continued to work as a journalist but went on to pursue other interests as well in the private sector. And one of our colleagues on the editorial staff at the *Daily News*, Abdallah Ngororo, who joined the government and became permanent secretary - head of the ministry's civil service - at different ministries under President Benjamin Mkapa, our former editor, died in 2002.

And I came up way down the road as an author with my first book published in 1999, 27 years after I left the *Daily News*. And unlike the works of my colleagues all of which dealt with the press, except Ndulute's about poetry, mine was about economics, entitled, *Economic Development in Africa*,[23] which also came to be used as a college textbook mainly for graduate (post-graduate) studies in colleges and universities in the United States, Canada, Britain, Australia, South Africa and other countries, as have a number of other books I have written including *The Modern African State: Quest for Transformation*,[24] and *Africa and the West*.[25] Although they are mostly found in university libraries around the world, and in a number of public libraries, they are also intended for members of the general public. I never intended to write them exclusively for the academic community. And I have taken the same approach in writing this book.

In *Economic Development in Africa*, I do acknowledge that our socialist policies failed, as President Nyerere himself admitted when he stepped down in November 1985 as much as he did on other occasions in the following years. But I also do know that Nyerere's economic policies were *not* - total failure. We had significant achievements in a number of areas. As I state on Amazon.com in my review of a book by George Ayittey, A Ghanaian professor of economics at The American University, *Africa in Chaos*:

Ayittey has written an excellent book. In fact, I'm just as critical of Africa's despotic and kleptocratic regimes in all the books I have written. But I don't entirely agree with his assessment of Kwame Nkrumah, Julius Nyerere, and Kenneth Kaunda.

He says his focus is not on the leadership qualities of any of the African leaders but on their policies. It is true that socialism failed to fuel economic growth. But an objective evaluation of what Nkrumah, Nyerere, and Kaunda did, shows that they had some success in a number of areas. Yet, Ayittey has almost nothing good to say about them in his book, *Africa in Chaos*. In fact, these are the three leaders of whom he's most critical in his book, devoting several pages to them more than any other African leader.

Under Nkrumah, Ghana had the highest per capita income in sub-Saharan Africa. It was Nkrumah who laid the foundation for modern-day Ghana. He built the infrastructure that has sustained and fuelled Ghana's economic development through the years. It is true that there were also many failures under Nkrumah, and after he was gone; for example, institutional decay and crumbling infrastructure. But who built those institutions and the infrastructure?

Nkrumah built schools, hospitals, roads, factories, dams and bridges, railways and harbours. Tens of thousands of people in Ghana who are lawyers, doctors, engineers, nurses, teachers, accountants, agriculturalists, scientists and others wouldn't be what they are today had it not been for the educational opportunities provided by Nkrumah.

Ayittey talks about quality, saying that what mattered during Nkrumah's reign was quantity, not quality. What's the quality of the Ghanaian elite, including Ayittey himself, educated under Nkrumah? Are they not as good as anybody else? What was the quality of education at the University of Ghana, Legon? Did it admit and train students of mediocre mental caliber? Did it have inferior academic programs? And an inferior faculty? Were more people dying in Ghanaian hospitals than they were being saved? Did the schools, hospitals, factories, roads and other infrastructure Nkrumah built do more harm than good? Would Ghana have been better off without them like Zaire under Mobutu?

In Tanzania, Nyerere also built schools, hospitals, clinics, factories, roads and railways, dams and bridges, hydroelectric power plants and other infrastructure. Although his policy of Ujamaa (meaning familyhood in Kiswahili) was not very successful, it did enable the country to bring the people together and closer to each other in order to provide them with vital social services. The people had easier access to schools, clinics, clean water and other services provided by the government, than they otherwise would have been, because they lived closer to each other; which would have been impossible had they been spread too thin across the country, living miles and miles apart.

Also under Nyerere, education was free, from primary school all the way to the university level. Medical services were also free, in spite of the fact that Tanzania is one of the poorest countries in the world. Still, under Nyerere, it was able to afford all that. Everybody had equal opportunity. Under his leadership, Tanzania also made quantum leaps in education. It had the highest literacy rate in Africa, and one of the highest in the world, higher than India's, which has one of the largest numbers of educated people and the third largest number of scientists after the United States and the former Soviet Union.

One of the biggest achievements under Nyerere was in the area of adult education. Tanzania, on a scale unprecedented anywhere else in the world, launched a massive adult education campaign to teach millions of people how to read and write. Within only a few years, almost the entire adult population of Tanzania - rural peasants, urban workers and others - became literate. Almost everybody in Tanzania, besides children not yet in school, was able to read and write. And the University of Dar es Salaam in Tanzania became one of the most renowned academic institutions in the world, in less than ten years, with an outstanding faculty including some of the best and internationally acclaimed scholars from many countries.

Provision of vital services even to some of the most remote parts of the country - far removed from urban and social centers - was not uncommon although the services were, I must admit, curtailed through the years because of economic problems. Yet, all that was achieved under Nyerere who sincerely believed, and made sure, that everybody had equal access to the nation's resources. I know all this because I am a

Tanzanian myself, born and brought up in Tanzania, and was one of the beneficiaries of Nyerere's egalitarian policies.

Tanzania has come a long way, and still has a long way to go. But give credit where credit is due, in spite of failures in a number of areas, and which must be acknowledged by all of us. I even admit that in my books. But also look at where we were before: At independence in 1961, Tanganyika (before uniting with Zanzibar in 1964 to form Tanzania) had only 120 university graduates, including two lawyers who had to draft and negotiate more than 150 international treaties for the young nation and handle other legal matters for the country. With 120 university graduates, Tanganyika was, of course, better off than the former Belgian Congo which had only 16 at independence in 1960, and Nyasaland (now Malawi) with only 34 at independence in 1964. Still, that was nowhere close to what Tanganyika would have been had the British tried to develop the colony; which was never their intention. None of the 120 university graduates got their degrees in Tanganyika. There was no university in the country. The British never built one, and never intended to build one. Tanganyika built one after independence, and it became internationally renowned as an excellent academic institution in less than a decade.

The 120 university graduates Tanganyika had at independence was nothing in terms of manpower for a country; not even for a province or region. As Julius Nyerere said not long before he died:

'We took over a country with 85 percent of its adults illiterate. The British ruled us for 43 years. When they left, there were two trained engineers and 12 doctors. When I stepped down there was 91 percent literacy and nearly every child was in school. We trained thousands of engineers, doctors, and teachers.'

Nyerere stepped down in 1985. And all that was achieved within 24 years since independence. No mean achievement.[26]

The cornerstone of his economic policy for Tanzania's development was Ujamaa. And it was supported by the majority of Tanzanians, even if grudgingly by a significant number of them. But even some of the skeptics wanted to give it a chance. And when it failed, even Nyerere's harshest critics admitted that he meant well; which explains his enormous popularity across the country after he stepped down, although the economy virtually came to a grinding halt especially during the last several years of his presidency. He remained as popular as he was through the decades since independence, and was even admired by some of his most ardent critics. As Jonathan Power, who was highly critical of Nyerere's policies and one party-rule, stated in his article, "Lament for Independent Africa's Greatest   Leader":

Tanzania in East Africa has long been one of the 25 poorest countries in the world. But there was a time when it was described, in terms of its political influence, as one of the top 25. It punched far above its weight. That formidable achievement was the work of one man, now lying close to death in a London Hospital....

His extraordinary intelligence, verbal and literary originality... and apparent commitment to non-violence made him not just an icon in his own country but of a large part of the activist sixties' generation in the white world who, not all persuaded of the heroic virtues of Fidel Castro and Che Guevara, desperately looked for a more sympatheitc role model.

Measured against most of his peers, Jomo Kenyatta of Kenya, Kwame Nkrumah of Ghana, Ahmed Sekou Toure of Guinea, he towered above them. On the intellectual plane only the rather remote president of Senegal, the great poet and author of Negritude, Leopold Senghor, came close to him.

Not only was Nyerere financially open, modest and honest, he was uncorrupted by fame or position. He remained throughout his life, self-effacing and unpretentious. Above all, he inspired his own people to resist the tugs of tribalism and to pull together as one people. To this day Tanzania remains one of the very few African countries that has not experienced serious tribal division. Its continuously fraught relationship with the Arab-dominated off-shore island of Zanzibar is another matter.

Later, discarding his earlier more pacifist convictions, he was to become the eminence rise of the southern African liberation movements in Angola, Zimbabwe, Namibia and South Africa extending a wide open embrace to their operations. For this his country paid a heavy price, in material terms, but also because Nyerere's role as interlocutor with the West demanded enormous amounts of time and energy that often led him to neglect his domestic responsibilities....

Nyerere was not an egomaniac who banged the table and surrounded himself only with sycophants. He was simply the self-assured headmaster that he had been since his teaching days....

Tanzania remains one of the very poorest countries in the world.... Whereas a once equally poor nearby country, Botswana, has progressed rapidly to the point where it is barely recognizable as the impoverished backwater it was only thirty years ago, Tanzania remains mired in the rut of underdevelopment and only recently, since Nyerere voluntarily retired in 1985, has begun to make up for lost time.

For most of Nyerere's long period in office his country was in economic difficulties. Inherited poverty, appalling weather, world recessions, crazed neighbours and war in southern Africa were all parts of the problem, but in the end there was not a good excuse for such continuous failures....

Nyerere's Christian socialist ideology dreamed of new ways of organizing society when there were hardly the rudiments of modern structures.... His biggest mistake of all was what he called 'ujamaa' - a kind of African, Israeli kibbutz-inspired collectivisation....

Later Nyerere was to admit that even in his home village (Butiama), which he often liked to visit, ujamaa had not really taken hold. In the end he was forced to put ujamaa on a back burner, but the damage had been done.

Many of us will mourn Julius Nyerere when he is gone. He was, without any doubt, second only to Nelson Mandela, the most inspiring African leader of his generation.[27]

Although most Tanzanians - and millions of other Africans - were indeed inspired by Nyerere, there were many who disagreed with him and did not like his policies, especially socialism and one-party rule. And like the general population, our editorial staff at the *Daily News* was not a monolithic whole. Many reporters professed to be socialist or supported Tanzania's socialist policies. But some were clearly at the other end of the ideological spectrum, including a number of those who claimed to be socialist and strong supporters of Nyerere's ujamaa policies. This dichotomy or ambivalence is probably best explained by Nyerere's sincerity and enormous popularity among the masses. Reporters were part of the elite. So, going against the president who was the embodiment of the wishes and aspirations of the poor peasants and workers, and who articulated their sentiments, would have been "treacherous" and "unpatriotic," some of them felt; in spite of the fact that he encouraged us to be critical and freely express our views.

Yet few people - anywhere across the country - wanted to be seen as uncaring, betraying the masses. Therefore for some on our editorial staff, it was self-censorship, to identify themselves with the poor peasants and workers who constituted the vast majority of the population and the backbone of our economy. They were the nation. Many people including reporters found it hard to criticize Nyerere. His sincerity, humility, and deep concern for the masses confounded even some of his most persistent critics, as did his disarming and startling candor. And even after he stepped down from the presidency, he did not hesitate to criticize his successor whenever he felt such criticism was warranted. And he was blunt about it, and applauded for his honesty and deep concern for the well-being of the nation. Even newsmen, known for their distrust of politicians, applauded   him:

Former Tanzanian president Julius Nyerere on Tuesday (March 13, 1995) accused the government of President Ali Hassan Mwinyi of corruption and violating the constitution and urged Tanzanians to vote differently in the next elections.

Addressing a gathering of local and foreign journalists at the Kilimanjaro International Hotel here (in Dar es Salaam), Nyerere also accused Mwinyi's administration of condoning religious differences and tribalism.

'This would not only lead to the collapse of the now-sensitive 30-year-old union between the twin-islands of Zanzibar and Pemba and Tanzania mainland, but would also plunge the country into chaos,' Nyerere warned and urged Tanzanians to ensure that they voted for 'a president able to correct the situation and put the country on the right track.'

Nyerere, who ruled Tanzania for 24 years after independence from British colonial rule in 1961, described Tanzania as a country 'stinking with corruption.'

'Corruption in Tanzania has no bounds. Every country I visit they talk about corruption in Tanzania. Tanzania is stinking with corruption,' Nyerere told journalists gathered at the Tanzania Press Club.

Referring to a tax fraud in the country that recently led to aid suspension by donor countries and organisations, Nyerere declared: 'This was one quality of corruption. Any government that works for the wealthy does not collect tax, it chooses to harass small-time dealers,' Nyerere charged.

Nyerere, affectionately referred to as 'Mwalimu (Teacher) and Father of the Nation' by Tanzanians, said he was speaking of qualities required of a future president to avoid plunging the country into total collapse.

Comparing Tanzania to 'a house that has just been completed,' Nyerere said 'the country has been hit by a tremor, developing cracks which must be filled,' and said the cracks were 'the political union between Zanzibar and the mainland, corruption, religious tensions, tribalism, the constitutional crisis and lack of rule of law.'

In an apparent reference to President Mwinyi himself, Nyerere told the journalists that Tanzania needed a leader who will defend and promote the national constitution. 'It can't be a person that gets advice from his wife, and tomorrow we see some decision has been made. You can't have such a guy. You won't know what his wife will advise him,' Nyerere said amid applause from more than 100 journalists attending the gathering.

Tanzania goes to the polls next October (1995) in the first multi-party presidential and parliamentary elections since the country attained independence 34 years ago.[28]

Much as Nyerere was revered, he remained humble until his last days. His humility and genuine compassion for the masses was probably the most prominent quality of his long political career spanning almost half a century. I particularly remember one incident in 1972 when another reporter, Stanley Kamana, and I were assigned to cover the president. More than 30 years later, Kamana was still a journalist and one of the leading veterans in the profession in the country, together with my other former colleagues at the *Daily News*, including Kassim Mpenda who became director of Radio Tanzania, Dar es Salaam (RTD), and later Tanzania's director of Information Services at the ministry of information and broadcasting, as he still was at this writing in 2002. So was Charles Kizigha who was still at the *Daily News*, an enduring phenomenon at the paper for three decades after I left the editorial staff; Reginald Mhango, a senior reporter for 30 years who was appointed editor of the *Guardian*, Tanzania, in 2002; and Jenerali Ulimwengu, one of the two lawyers who were reporters on our editorial staff, who became chairman and publisher, Habari Corporation, responsible for the publication of several newspapers in Kiswahili. When my colleagues and I were together at the *Daily News* 30 years ago, covering the president with Stanley Kamana on that day was one of the main assignments I was given, besides covering parliament which I did many times, only a few months before I left for the United States to pursue further studies.

President Nyerere addressed a mass rally in Dar es Salaam where he criticized the authorities of the Coast Region (Mkoa wa Pwani, in Kiswahili) for ordering the demolition of stands owned by hawkers on a major street, Ilala, which feeds into Pugu Road that goes all the way to the national airport. Foreign dignitaries from a number of countries were coming to Dar es Salaam in only a few days to attend a major conference. But the regional officials, including Regional Commissioner Mustafa Songambele who was also at the rally, did not want these dignitaries to see the peddlers and their stands on this major route they were going to take on their way into the city from the airport. They felt ashamed and did not want to "humiliate" and "embarrass" our country. The hawkers and their stands were, in fact, more than any eyesore, according to these officials. Such a spectacle could not be reconciled with our determination to maintain national dignity in spite of all the poverty we had and still have in Tanzania. That was the twisted logic of these leaders.

In his public address, President Nyerere asked about the peddlers: "What have they done wrong? What do you want them to do without income? What are you going to give them instead, once you demolish the stands? That's the only means they have to earn a living." Some stands had already been demolished, but the rest were not, after Nyerere's speech.

What happened then reminds me of what happened in 1998 when American President Bill Clinton visited Ghana and other African countries. Many government officials in Accra, Ghana's capital, did not want Clinton and his entourage to see the open sewage in the capital. President Jerry Rawlings ordered them to leave everything as it was so that the Americans should "see the way we live." Just covering it up won't solve the problem. Once the Americans are gone, the raw sewage will still be there.

Nyerere, for whom Rawlings had profound respect, had the same attitude. Impressing foreigners was not part of his personality. His biggest concern was the well-being of the poor, the downtrodden, the oppressed. With or without stands on Ilala Street, the visiting dignitaries would probably not even have noticed any difference, any way, and would not have been impressed either way. Nyerere's response to the callous indifference of the Coast Region government officials is an enduring memory I have always cherished. And it should be a lesson for other African leaders who claim that they care about their people while they are busy doing exactly the opposite.

Another memorable but tragic occasion during my career as a reporter in Tanzania was when I covered the country's first vice president, Sheikh Abeid Karume, who was also president of Zanzibar. Our constitution allowed that because Zanzibar was an autonomous - not a sovereign - entity within the union. And it still, although there have been some changes stipulating that the country shall have only one vice president, not two as before (one from the isles and the other from the mainland), and that contenders for the presidency and vice presidency can come from anywhere in the union without any restrictions except those prescribed by law. The changes took place after multiparty democracy was introduced in the early 1990s.

I covered Karume in 1972 not long after I returned to Dar es Salaam from Zanzibar where I had been sent with another reporter, Juma Penza, to cover the eighth anniversary of the Zanzibar revolution of January 1964. A senior reporter at the *Daily News*, Penza later became an information officer of Tanzania's ruling party (CCM), and still held that post in the 1990s and probably beyond. We were in Zanzibar for several days. Karume came to Dar es Salaam after we got back from Zanzibar and gave a speech at the Police Officers' Mess in Msasani, an area on the outskirts of the capital where President Nyerere also lived in a simple house, away from his official residence, Ikulu (State House).

Speaking in Kiswahili, Karume told the officers to examine their inner selves in order to conduct themselves in an exemplary manner when performing their duties. That was his last speech in Dar es Salaam. He returned to Zanzibar and, not long afterwards, was assassinated on April 7 in a hail of bullets. He was reportedly shot eight times at close range. Coincidentally or not, he had also been in office for eight years as first vice president of Tanzania. The number of times he was shot may have been deliberately calculated to symbolize the number of years he had been in office - one bullet for each year - if indeed he was hit eight times.

Abdulrahman Mohammed Babu, a Zanzibari from Pemba Island and senior cabinet member in the union government and one of the most prominent Tanzanian leaders, was accused by the Zanzibari authorities of masterminding the assassination and detained on the mainland in connection with the murder. But

President Nyerere refused to send him back to Zanzibar where he probably would have been executed, as Kassim Hanga was, under a judicial system that had little regard for justice and individual rights, let alone for those accused of killing the country's first vice president. As an autonomous entity, Zanzibar also had its own judicial system whose dispensation of justice differed from what we had on the mainland in many fundamental respects.

That was the first assassination of a Tanzanian leader since independence, preceded by Tom Mboya's in neighboring Kenya only three years before in July 1969. Aboud Jumbe succeeded Karume and became Zanzibar's president and Tanzania's first vice president under Nyerere, but resigned in 1984. Rashidi Kawawa, a veteran politician since independence who together with Nyerere and Oscar Kambona constituted a trio and the most influential political team in Tanzania until Kambona went into self-imposed exile in Britain in July 1967, was the country's second vice president. President Nyerere continued to lead Tanzania until November 1985 when he voluntarily stepped down after being in office for 24 years since independence from Britain on December 9, 1961. It was a long political career, marked by successes and failures.

A lot has been said about the failure of his economic policies. But little has been said about his achievements. As he told the World Bank in 1998: "We took over a country with 85 percent of its adults illiterate. The British ruled us for 43 years. When they left, there were two trained engineers and 12 doctors. When I stepped down there was 91 percent literacy and nearly every child was in school. We trained thousands of engineers, doctors and teachers."[29]

He was painfully aware of our long, tortuous journey since independence, being one of the few university graduates himself when he assumed stewardship of the nation. He was, in fact, the first African from Tanganyika to obtain a master's degree in 1952 at Edinburgh University in Scotland where he studied economics, history, and philosophy. We had very few trained people and had to rely on expatriates in most fields. But because of his excellent leadership, we were able to achieve a lot in only a few years.

I, myself, wouldn't be what I am today had it not been for his leadership. And you wouldn't be reading this book or any of the others I have written. And the reason is simple: I would not have been able to go to school. Under his leadership, education was free for everybody, unlike today. Medical service was also free, again unlike today. Even transportation for us to go to boarding school, to any part of the country, was free, paid for by the government; which means by the peasants and workers of Tanzania, with their tax money. We all had equal opportunity to be the best we could be. Few countries can claim that, and mean it. Tanzania did that, because of Nyerere.

But none of this would have been possible had the country not been united. There was a strong possibility back in the sixties and even in the seventies that our country could have fallen apart or been plunged into chaos, fractured along tribal and regional and even religious lines, if we had poor leadership; especially under the multiparty system which capitalizes on greed and partisan interests as has happened in Tanzania since the introduction of multiparty politics, although it doesn't have to be that way if the parties involved transcend sectarianism and ethno-regional loyalties. As Nyerere said many years after his retirement:

> I really think that I ran the most successful single-party system on the continent. You might not even call it a party. It was a single, huge nationalist movement....I don't believe that our country would be where it is now if we had a multiplicity of parties, which would have become tribal and caused us a lot of problems. But when you govern for such a long time, unless you are gods, you become corrupt and bureaucratic.... So I started calling for a multiparty system.[30]

Neighboring Kenya faced the same problem, regional fragmentation, when one of the political parties, the Kenya African Democratic Union (KADU) led by Ronald Ngala - a former teacher and prominent politician in the Coast Province - pursued a regionalist agenda which could have split the country along ethno-regional lines. Or it could have weakened the central government so much that national leaders would not have been able to exercise any power over the regions. His agenda was also supported by many other Kenyans who were not members of KADU, especially those from smaller tribes. And there is still strong interest in *majimboism* (regionalism) even today in Kenya, mainly because of the political dominance of the ruling party, the Kenya African National Union (KANU), which seems to be destined to rule perpetually. *Majimbo*, a Kiswahili word, means regions or provinces; *jimbo* being its singular form.

But Jomo Kenyatta succeeded in establishing a unitary state under a strong central government to keep the country united like Nyerere did in Tanganyika, later Tanzania. The difference is that Kenya's ruling party, KANU, was dominated by the Kikuyu, Kenyatta's tribe and the country's biggest; while in Tanganyika, the ruling Tanganyika African National Union (TANU) was pluralistic. No single tribe became dominant; another great achievement by Nyerere.

Yet, Ngala's quest for regional autonomy in Kenya seems to have been vindicated by President Kenyatta himself because of his dictatorial instincts. He was highly sensitive to criticism and neutralized his opponents quickly. That is what he did to his vice president, Oginga Odinga, who resigned and went on to form the opposition party, the Kenya People's Union (KPU), based on egalitarian ideals like Nyerere's to pursue policies which would benefit the masses, not just the elite like KANU's under Kenyatta did. Odinga accused Kenyatta's government of ignoring and exploiting *wananchi*, the people, and was neutralized, with Kenyatta claiming, "I have been kind for too long."[31]

Ronald Ngala also had a taste of Kenyatta's bile in parliament one day in a very distasteful way. As Mundia Kamau stated in his article, "A Nation in Distress," in Kenya's *Mashada Daily*:

> Jomo Kenyatta was not a democrat at all. He was the exemplification and personification of the African 'Big Man,' a ruthless dictator. Jomo Kenyatta carried on where the British left off, continuing with the plunder of public resources, and theft of public land. He mastered the art of oppression the African way, by ruthlessly exploiting the ignorance, biases, and prejudices of most Africans, a trend that still sadly persists....
>
> An example of Kenyatta's ruthless intolerance comes out in Koigi wa Wamwere's autobiography when he states how Kenyatta once drew his gun in parliament intending to shoot the late Ronald Ngala for criticising his government, and was only restrained by then Speaker, Humphrey Slade. The myth that Kenyatta was a democrat and professional must be dispensed with immediately, if we truly hope to solve the problems of this country. The only essential difference between Kenyatta and his successor Moi, is that Kenyatta was more widely travelled and more eloquent in English.[32]

Kenyatta may have been wrong in silencing Ronald Ngala and his opposition party, KADU, the way he did in parliament by threatening to shoot the opposition leader. Yet, the threat to national unity posed by extensive autonomy (*majimboism*, derived from majimbo) as advocated by Ngala and his party KADU, and by the multiparty system, cannot be ignored if such devolution of power is not implemented within prescribed limits and specifically designated areas of authority; and if multiparty democracy is allowed to thrive on ethno-regional loyalties and partisan interests at the expense of the nation. But this was not a major problem in Tanzania under Nyerere, although he decentralized power under a unitary state, something rarely done - if at all - in most highly centralized states across the continent.

Tragically, tribalism is beginning to gain a foothold in Tanzania, with tribal organizations emerging on the scene, tolerated or sanctioned by the state by invoking pluralism. And appeal to tribal and regional sentiments has become a feature of national politics since multiparty democracy was introduced in the early nineties. The resurgence of this ugly phenomenon was underscored by former Vice President Joseph Sinde Warioba, also a distinguished jurist, in a speech in Dar es Salaam in March 2001. President Benjamin Mkapa himself was fully aware of these sectarian threats and won his second term with a promise to keep the country united, transcending ethinc, regional, racial and religious differences.

The introduction of multiparty politics, which has exacerbated the situation prompted many people to re-evaluate the transition from one-partyism to multipartyism. Many Tanzanians are probably having second thoughts about the wisdom of the decision by the national leaders who made this fundamental change against what was generally perceived to be popular will. When the people across the country were asked in the early nineties whether or not Tanzania should adopt the multiparty system, it was reported that the majority of those who participated in the survey were opposed to the change. This may be one of the reasons - besides poor organization, lack of direction, and personal rivalries - why opposition parties have not been able to win significant support in Tanzania; prompting one prominent opposition leader who rejoined the ruling party, CCM, in 2002 to say that CCM will rule Tanzania for the next 500 years. As the old saying goes, if you can't beat them, join them. A number of other opposition leaders and members have taken this pragmatic approach, which may also help to maintain national unity and stability.

Although I am in favor of multiparty democracy if it works well, I sometimes also have had strong reservations about the functional utility of the multiparty system in the African context because of its divisive tendencies and potential for catastrophe. To contend otherwise, given Africa's experience in many cases, is rank dishonesty or sheer naiveté. In most cases, the multiparty system tends to fuel tribal and regional rivalries. But the one-party system itself is not above reproach when it discriminates against some groups and individuals as has been the case in most African countries - in Kenya under Kenyatta and Moi, favoring members of their tribes, the Kikuyu and the Kalenjin, respectively; Malawi under Banda whose government was dominated by the Chewa; Ivory Coast which was a *de facto* one-party state under Felix Houphouet-Boigny and Henri Bedie who favored members of their Baoule tribe; Togo under Gnassingbe Eyadema favoring members of his northern tribe, the Kabye, who also constituted 70 percent of the national army, to name only a few.

However, the multiparty system, more than the one-party system, can promote democracy in Africa if the people vote across tribal and regional lines to advance a common agenda. Yet, few African countries can honestly claim to have a majority of such voters who have transcended ethno-regional loyalties; a strong case for federalism and a limited number of parties as prescribed by law. Their interests are highly partisan. And they are not based on policy differences, bringing together members of different tribes and social and economic classes to pursue common interests. Their interests are defined by tribal and regional identities more than anything else.

The multiparty system is strongly advocated as a safeguard against corruption and dictatorship. It can, indeed, serve as a watchdog for the underdog to expose corruption, ensure transparency, and end dictatorship in African countries; but only if the parties don't, however surreptitiously, appeal to their regional constituencies to win elections. So, limit the number of political parties to broaden their base across the nation. Have three parties at the most, or may be even two. And this will, in fact, strengthen the opposition because, more often than not, governments thrive on divided opposition, making it easy for incumbents to win elections by fair means or foul. Therefore the opposition should be the first to support limiting the number of political parties, since this will help government opponents to mobilize forces into a cohesive bloc even if it is based on a coalition of interests, as is the case in politics in general. Politics is based on compromise. But dominant political parties which are in power in African countries will probably be the last to support limiting the number of political parties, since this will help unite their opponents; unless a limited number of political parties is going to benefit them somehow, for example, by co-opting the opposition, thus reducing it to nothing.

The argument for a limited number of political parties is validated by experience. There are very few truly national parties in Africa. And if we can't form such parties which attract substantial numbers of people from all the tribes across the country as TANU - and even CCM - did under Nyerere and his successors, without lopsided membership, then only the one-party system can claim to be truly national; but only if it also embraces members of all tribes, is liberalized, and decentralized to curb autocratic instincts.

Under Nyerere, I remember when students openly questioned, without fear of retribution, the merits of the one-party system. For example, at Tambaza High School in Dar es Salaam, we had such free discussion - risky, and even deadly, in most African countries - in class conducted by our headmaster, Mr. Lila (pronounced as Lee-la), a highly articulate man with profound insight into political theory and mass participatory politics. He had thorough command of the subject and explained Nyerere's ideology well. And he supported it, yet was open to criticism; which was very encouraging and reassuring to the students. We were not muzzled.

We also knew the kind of opportunities we had. There were Asian (mostly Indian and Pakistani), Arab, and African students in my class. Yet, despite the fact that Tanzania was under a black majority government, the Asian and Arab students knew they had equal opportunity just like the rest of their fellow countrymen because of the kind of leadership and moral vision provided by Nyerere. He led by example. Many students of different tribes and races went on to lead successful lives in different areas because of the equal opportunities provided by Nyerere. That was not the case in most African countries, including neighboring Kenya, where discrimination was rampant as it still is today.

In his cabinet since independence - and even before in 1960 when Tanganyika worn self-government with Julius Nyerere as chief minister but still under colonial rule - he had members of all races, including women; for example, Derek Bryceson, an Englishman, who came to Tanganyika in 1951; Amir H. Jamal, an Indian; Abdulrahman Mohammed Babu, an Arab; Salim Ahmed Salim, also an Arab; Lucy Lameck, the first female cabinet member appointed as junior minister of health, and one of Tanzania's most prominent leaders. These are only a few examples.

There were many others - across the racial spectrum - in high government positions including the diplomatic service. In fact, Salim Ahmed Salim, former Tanzania's permanent representative to the United Nations, was recalled by Nyerere and given a succession of senior cabinet posts through the years. He once served as defence minister, minister of foreign affairs, and as prime minister. He then went on to become secretary-general of the Organization of African Unity (OAU) in Addis Ababa, Ethiopia. He served for 15 years from 1986 to 2001; an unprecedented term, longer than any of his predecessors did, and was the last OAU secretary-general before the organization was transformed into the African Union (AU) at the last OAU meeting in June 2001 in Lusaka, Zambia. But the actual transition was a gradual process, and the AU did not start functioning until later, after being formally launched in Durban, South Africa, in July 2002 under the chairmanship of South African President Thabo Mbeki.

When Salim Ahmed Salim was Tanzania's ambassador to the UN, he was almost elected UN secretary-general and won the support of the majority of the members in the General Assembly. But the big powers had their own agendas and preferences and blocked his election. The United States did not want him at the helm because of Tanzania's relentless support of the People's

Republic of China through the years to get the world's most populous nation admitted into the UN, with Ambassador Salim being one of the strongest advocates even when he served in a neutral capacity as president of the UN General Assembly - he was still Tanzania's ambassador. And the Soviet Union did not want him because the Russians felt that he was too independent and would not bend to their wishes. And it is possible he could even be elected president of Tanzania one day. Following the death of Tanzania's Vice President Omar Ali Juma in July 2001, it was reported that Salim Ahmed Salim was the favorite of the political heavyweights in the country's ruling party, CCM, to succeed him but did not become vice president because he turned down the post. Others claimed that because of his high international profile, he would have overshadowed President Benjamin Mkapa, and therefore turned down or was not given the post. Whatever the case, he remained a formidable political personality and had a chance to be elected president in the future.

There is evidence everywhere across Tanzania showing that Nyerere built a truly pluralistic society with equal opportunity for all. My classmates are some of the beneficiaries, regardless of their tribal and racial identities. For example, one of them, Mohamed Othman Chande of Arab extraction, once served as a senior prosecution attorney and chief prosecutor at the International Criminal Tribunal for Rwanda (ICTR) established by the UN in Arusha, Tanzania. He earned his law degree at the University of Dar es Salaam, one of the best law schools in Africa, and the first to be established in East Africa. After working at the UN court in Tanzania, he was assigned to East Timor where he was appointed general prosecutor - UN's chief prosecutor - to help the young southeast Asian nation establish its judicial system under UN auspices.

And there are countless other Tanzanians, of all races and tribes, who have reached the pinnacle of success through the years at home and abroad because of the foundation laid by Nyerere that has sustained Tanzania as a peaceful, stable country, with opportunity for all. And he did that with humility and simplicity, which characterized his political career more than any other leader on the continent.

After Nyerere voluntarily stepped down as president of

Tanzania in November 1985, it was with a simple bicycle that he returned to his home village of Butiama in northern Tanzania near the southeastern shores of Lake Victoria, to live and work on the farm; and eat simple breakfast of porridge with the children from poor families in the area. He did it every morning. As James Mpinga wrote in *The East African*:

> There is little to show that Butiama, the birthplace of Julius Nyerere, raised one of Africa's greatest sons. Mud huts surround the Catholic Church where Nyerere used to pray, and both the church and the mud huts tell a story. From the mud huts came the children who knew exactly when Mwalimu would have his breakfast, and dutifully came to share it with him every morning, and in the church their parents shared a common faith and prayer.
>
> 'At first it was bread and butter for both Mwalimu and the kids. Soon I couldn't cope with the increasing numbers of children joining him for breakfast, so I downgraded it to porridge and *kande* (a boiled mixture of maize off the cob and pulses),' recalls Mwalimu's former housekeeper, Dorothy Musoga, 74, now living in retirement in Mwanza in a house built for her by Mwalimu....
>
> She was worried...about the future of his family and what she called Mwalimu's 'other children' who loved to share his breakfast. 'With Mwalimu dead, free breakfast for poor villagers will become a thing of the past,' Dorothy reflected.... The poverty of their parents remains, as does the lack of infrastructure at Butiama, which Mwalimu didn't want to transform into an edifice to be envied....
>
> On Saturday, October 23 (1999), when Mwalimu was buried, Butiama may well have started to slip back into oblivion, to become what it once was, an unknown village in the middle of nowhere.... The process may, indeed, have started earlier, with Mwalimu's own house...(which) bears marks of his self-denial. Children fetch water from a public standpipe and their mothers wash clothes in the open. The house itself could do with a fresh coat of paint.... Judging from the relatively wealthier homestead of the chief (nearby), Mwalimu was no more than a peasant....
>
> When I later visited the compound of Mwitongo, where Mwalimu was buried not far from the graves of his parents, only a few insiders and the late Nyerere's close family members had remained, among them his former press secretary Sammy Mdee....
>
> When Chairman Mao was asked what he thought about the French Revolution, a century and a half after it had taken place, he retorted: 'It's too early to say.'

Few in Tanzania can give a better answer about the impact of Nyerere's death. For the poor children of Butiama, however, the days of free breakfast with their beloved grandpa are gone. It is hard to imagine what will follow.[33]

It is indeed hard to imagine what will follow, in a world where there are few such men and women. Nyerere embodied the best that man can achieve in the service of fellow men, but which few are willing to do. He was no saint, in the religious sense, but may deserve to be called Saint Julius because of his selfless devotion to the poor in the tradition of saints. He sacrificed so much, yet got so little in return, and did not expect or want anything in return. He just did his job, what he knew had to be done, for his people and others, no matter what the cost. He was the least paid head of state, earning $500 per month, yet one of the most revered. And, instead of living in magnificent splendor, and in the president's official residence, the State House (Ikulu, as we call it), he chose to live a humble life in a simple house on the outskirts of the capital in an area called Msasani.

He did not even have a pension to live on when he retired, until parliament hastily voted for one to help sustain him. As *Newsweek* stated soon after he died: "The world has lost a man of principle."[34] Unlike most leaders, including religious leaders, he practiced what he preached. And he admitted his mistakes, a rare quality among leaders, almost all of whom equate such admission with weakness. Yet it's probably the most important quality of leadership on which everything else depends.

Perhaps it is worth remembering that even some of his ardent critics acknowledged his contributions and paid him lasting tribute. Probably no other African scholar kept up a lively debate on the merits of Nyerere's policies as Ali Mazrui did; although he never questioned his commitment and integrity, and powerful intellect, and remained friendly with him until Mwalimu's final days, despite differences between the two. In a tribute to Mwalimu and on the special bonds between the two, Professor Mazrui had a lot to say in his article in *Voices*, Africa Resource Center, entitled, "Nyerere and I":

In global terms, he was one of the giants of the 20th Century....

While his vision did outpace his victories, and his profundity outweigh his performance, he did bestride this narrow world like an African colossus....

As personalities, what did Julius and I have in common? He was a politician who was sometimes a scholar. I was a scholar who was sometimes a politician.... Nyerere and I were trying to build bridges between Africa and great minds of Western civilisation.... With his concept of Ujamaa, Nyerere also attempted to build bridges between indigenous African thought and modern political ideas....

'The two top Swahili-speaking intellectuals of the second half of the 20th Century are Julius Nyerere and Ali Mazrui.' That is how I was introduced to an Africanist audience in 1986 when I was on a lecture-tour of the United States to promote my television series: The Africans: A Triple Heritage (BBC-PBS). I regarded the tribute as one of the best compliments I had ever been paid. In reality, Mwalimu Nyerere was much more eloquent as Swahili orator than I although Kiswahili was my mother tongue and not his.

In the month of Nyerere's death (October 1999), the comparison between Mwalimu and I took a sadder form. A number of organisations in South Africa had united to celebrate Africa's Human Rights Day on October 22. Long before he was admitted to hospital, they had invited him to be their high-profile banquet speaker.

When Nyerere was incapacitated with illness, and seemed to be terminally ill, the South Africans turned to Ali Mazrui as his replacement. I was again flattered to have been regarded as Nyerere's replacement. However, the notice was too short, and I was not able to accept the South African invitation.

It is one of the ironies of my life that I have known the early presidents of Uganda and Tanzania far better than I have known the presidents of Kenya (my country). Over the years, Julius Nyerere and I met many times. (Ugandan President) Milton Obote was one of the formative influences of my early life, in spite of our tumultuous relationship....

Let me also refer to Walter Rodney. He was a Guyanese scholar who taught at the University of Dar es Salaam and became one of the most eloquent voices of the left on the campus in Tanzania. When Walter Rodney returned to Guyana, he was assassinated.

Chedi Jagan, on being elected President of Guyana, created a special chair in honour of Walter Rodney. Eventually I was offered the chair and became its first incumbent. My inaugural lecture was on the following topic: 'Comparative Leadership: Walter Rodney, Julius K. Nyerere and Martin Luther King Jr.'

After delivering the lecture, I subsequently met Nyerere one evening in Pennsylvania, USA. I gave him my Walter Rodney lecture. He read it overnight and commented on it the next morning at breakfast. He promised to send me a proper critique on my Rodney lecture on his return to Dar es Salaam. He never lived long enough to send me the critique.

Nyerere's policies of Ujamaa amounted to a case of Heroic Failure. They were heroic because Tanzania was one of the few African countries, which attempted to find its own route to development instead of borrowing the ideologies of the West. But it was a failure because the economic experiment did not deliver the goods of development.

On the other hand, Nyerere's policies of nation-building amount to a case of Unsung Heroism. With wise and strong leadership, and with brilliant policies of cultural integration, he took one of the poorest countries in the world and made it a proud leader in African affairs and an active member of the global community.

Julius Nyerere was my Mwalimu too. It was a privilege to learn so much from so great a man.[35]

A man of high integrity and an enormous and astonishing intellect, he was one of the most exalted, yet extremely humble. He was, indeed, a man of the people. Such is the mark of true genius, a rare breed among men. As former American President Jimmy Carter said: "Julius Nyerere should be remembered as one of the greatest leaders of this century."[36] It is a fitting tribute, although somewhat of an understatement. The world has, in fact, produced only a few such men and women in a span of centuries. And he had few peers on the African continent who could equal his stature; a point underscored by Ali Mazrui in another tribute to Nyerere at Cornell University, although he disagreed with him on a number of fundamental issues. He last saw Nyerere when both were among the main speakers in different forums during the inauguration of Nigerian President Olusegun Obasanjo in May 1999. As he stated in his lecture at Cornell, also published in Kenya's *Daily Nation*:

Most Western judges of Julius Nyerere have concentrated on his economic policies and their failures. Ujamaa and villagisation have been seen as forces of economic retardation, which kept Tanzania backward for at least another decade.

Not enough commentators have paid attention to Nyerere's

achievements in nation-building. He gave Tanzania a sense of national consciousness and a spirit of national purpose. One of the poorest countries in the world found itself one of the major actors on the world scene. Nyerere's policies of making Kiswahili the national language of Tanzania deepened this sense of Tanzania's national consciousness and cultural pride....

Above all, Nyerere as president was a combination of deep intellect and high integrity. Leopold Senghor's intellect was as deep as Nyerere's, but was Senghor's integrity as high as Nyerere's? Nelson Mandela's integrity was probably higher than Nyerere's, but was Mandela's intellect as deep as Nyerere's?

Some East African politicians might have been more intelligent than Nyerere. Others might have been more ethical than Nyerere. But Julius K. Nyerere was in a class by himself in the combination of ethical standards and intellectual power. In the combination of high thinking and high ethics, no other East African politician was in the same league.

He and I deeply disagreed on the merits of Ujamaa. He and I once disagreed on East African federation. I thought his socialist policies harmed East African integration. He and I disagreed on the Nigerian civil war. He and I disagreed on the issue of Zanzibar. I thought Zanzibar was forced into a marriage, which was not of its own choosing.

And yet Nyerere and I were committed to the proposition that patriotic Africans could disagree and still be equally patriotic. I saw him in Abuja in Nigeria, just before the inauguration of President Olusegun Obasanjo late in May 1999. Julius Nyerere and I gossiped in Kiswahili. He looked well - deceptively well, considering his illness.

He and I were keynote speakers at a workshop to inaugurate Nigeria to a new era of democracy in 1999. We were voices from East Africa at a major West African event. We were voices of Pan-Africanism on the eve of the new millennium. Nyerere's voice was one of the most eloquent voices of the 20th Century. It was a privilege for me to stand side-by-side with such a person to mark a momentous event in no less a country than our beloved Nigeria.[37]

A man whom Mazrui also once hailed as "the most original thinker in English-speaking Africa," a tribute he also paid to Senghor with regard to Francophone Africa,[38] Nyerere will always remain an inspiration to millions, including some of his critics.

Mazrui, himself a leading critic of Nyerere's policies yet an admirer of Nyerere's intellect and integrity, drew fire through the years from some of the most vociferous defenders of Nyerere and his policies. They included the late Dr. Walter Rodney from Guyana who taught at the University of Dar es Salaam when I was a reporter at the *Daily News*; other professors and students at the university as well as a number of Tanzanians including some reporters at the *Daily News* and *The Nationalist* in Dar es Salaam. To many of them, his criticism of Tanzania's egalitarian policies in a nation of por peasants and workers amounted to a case of Tanzanphobia by one of Africa's leading academics, and probably the most well-known in international circles besides his nemesis Wole Soyinka. I also disagreed with Mazrui on a number of issues, although I did not have the visceral hatred for him that was obvious among some of his leftist critics, of which I wasn't one. I was simply a nationalist and Pan-Africanist, neither to the right nor to the left, as I still am today, although I have sympathized with some leftist causes more than I have with those on the right, if at all.

When I was a student at Tambaza High School in standard 14 (Form VI) in 1970, I remember reading in one of Tanzania's two major daily newspapers, *The Nationalist*, a letter to the editor - Ben Mkapa, later my editor at the *Daily News*, and president of Tanzania (1995 - 2005) - from Professor Ali Mazrui. It was a passionate defence of his patriotism in response to his critics who felt that he was highly critical of Tanzania's policies out of sheer spite and hatred, and not out of genuine commitment to the well-being of the country. He responded by saying that he loved Tanzania, and that Tanzania meant a lot to him. He went on say that he spent part of his childhood in Tanzania, in what was then Zanzibar, and partly attended school in Tanzania (then Tanganyika) when he was growing up. He said he went to school in Moshi, in Kilimanjaro Region in northeastern Tanzania, and that Tanzania will always be important to him. The letter may have elicited some sympathy for him from some of the readers, but many of his critics were probably impressed by none of this.

Some of them were brutally frank in their assessment of the renowned Kenyan professor. I remember talking to Philip Ochieng' - a Kenyan himself - one day in 1972 when we worked together at the *Daily News*, and asking him what he thought about Ali Mazrui. I brought up the subject, and knowing Philip's strong political views, I wanted to hear what he had to say about it. A fiery Marxist, yet who years later was appointed editor of the capitalist government-owned *Kenya Times* under President Daniel arap Moi after he returned to Kenya, he dismissed Mazrui as a very dangerous academic. No capital offense, but criticism of government, the kind Mazrui was known for even if just as a scholar engaged in objective evaluation and analaysis of ideas, has sent people to the gallows in many African countries. Others have been summarily executed, shot on the spot, or simply "disappeared." As Mazrui himself says, he almost got killed by Idi Amin in Uganda for criticizing him. I remember reading an article Mazrui wrote after he fled Uganda and when Amin was busy expelling Asians, including Ugandan citizens who just happened to be of Asian origin. It was entitled, "When Spain Expelled the Moors," and incurred the wrath of the dictator, obviously after someone read it to him and told him what Mazrui meant by that. Amin had only a standard two - second grade - education and could hardly read or write. Mazrui taught at Makerere University in Kampala, Uganda.

But such blunt assessment of pro-capitalist academics like Mazrui and others was not unusual in socialist-oriented Tanzania among leftists like Philip Ochieng'. Nor was criticism of the West. Although I myself was a strong admirer of Nyerere and other African leaders such as Nkrumah because of their egalitarian policies and Pan-African commitment, and was not enamored of the West, I was sometimes criticized by some of my colleagues on the editorial staff at the *Daily News* for wearing a necktie. One day, Philip, who always wore a short-sleeved shirt or a dashiki, lifted my tie and said, half-jokingly, "Godfrey, you're tied to the West," as he shook it.

That was ridiculous. I was tied to the West as much as he was when he enjoyed drinks imported from the West and wore Western clothes, minus tie; and as much as he enjoyed Western music. Philip loved humming Western tunes, including "Guantanamera," one of his favorites he often whistled in our editorial office, punctuating the tune with the song's name. The name Philip itself tied him to the West - not just to the Biblical homeland - just as much, and like mine, of course. So did President Nyerere's first name, Julius!

Just remember Mobutu, with his full African name and

indigenization policy of "Authenticity," complete with a leopard-skin hat, and a traditional cane he carried and so common among African chiefs and other traditional rulers as a symbol of authority. In 1971, he ordered all names in the country changed to African names. He also "indigenized" the economy by raiding national coffers for himself and giving property - seized from foreigners - to his cronies and family members, who had also amassed wealth by stealing from the masses. Now, contrast that with Patrice Lumumba who wore Western suits and necktie. Who was more tied to the West? Leopold Senghor espoused Negritude - about which Wole Soyinka said "a tiger does not have to proclaim its tigritude" - yet he was unabashedly Francophile, and proud to be a "black Frenchman." Dr. Milton Obote wore Western suits and a necktie, besides African safari suits also worn by Dr. Kenneth Kaunda who stopped wearing Western suits and replaced them with what came to be popularly known as Kaunda style. Was Obote tied to the West? What about Robert Mugabe and Samora Machel, admirers of Chairman Mao, and Marxist firebrands until they they were tempered by harsh economic realities, who also wore Western suits and neckties? Were they tied to the West? During the land crisis in Zimbabwe in the late 1990s and beyond, Mugabe showed the whole world how much he was tied to the West!

But that is the twisted logic of some leftists, although many of their counterparts are Westerners and wear Western suits and neckties, just like the politburo members in the former Soviet Union and her satellites, as well as ordinary citizens in those countries, did. It is ironic that many people in Third World countries are highly critical of the industrialized West - and for good reasons in many cases, although sometimes out of sheer spite - yet they want to live like Westerners, admire the Western life style, and ape the consumption proclivities of the West.

Philip Ochieng', one of Africa's most prominent journalists and Kenya's best known, remained an unrepentant Marxist, despite the collapse of communism and renunciation of Marxism-Leninism as a state ideology by almost all the countries which had adopted it, except North Korea, ruled by Stalinist hardliners, and Cuba under the internationalist Castro.

But we agreed on one thing: Nyerere was a great leader.

And he was not just Tanzania's, but Africa's leader. He first wanted to unite East African countries, but failed to do so. Yet that was not his fault. Some of his critics blamed him for this. They include Ali Mazrui who blamed Nyerere's - hence Tanzania's - policies for the failure of the proposed federation. But that is not why the three East African countries of Kenya, Uganda, and Tanganyika did not unite. They did not unite because of nationalism; which is also the main reason why regional integration in Africa has failed, to answer one of the questions Mazrui raised in his memorial lecture at Cornell University in October 1999, in which he paid tribute to President Julius Nyerere.

Nationalism triumphed over Pan-Africanism in the East African context because Kenya and Uganda did not want to surrender their sovereignties to a macro-national state in which they would be submerged. Only Nyerere, among the three East African leaders, was ready to do so. Nyerere even offered to delay Tanganyika's independence so that the three East African countries could attain sovereign status on the same day and unite under one government. And among the three, Kenya was the least enthusiastic.

At a meeting in Nairobi, Kenya, in June 1963, the three East African leaders - Kenyatta, Nyerere, and Obote - signed a declaration of intent to form a federation before the end of the year. Many people were excited about this, and songs were composed heralding the dawn of a new era. I remember a song in Kiswahili which was often played in the early and mid-1960s on the radio in Tanganyika and Kenya, called "Shirikisho la Afrika ya Mashariki,"which means the Federation of East Africa. It was sung by one of Kenya's and East Africa's most popular musicians and guitarists, Peter Tsotsi, originally from Northern Rhodesia, which is Zambia today. Others sang the same song. Other famous musicians and guitar players in Kenya included Daudi Kabaka, originally from Uganda, and Fadhili Williams. But the federation was never consummated, in spite of all the optimism we had.

It was expected that the president of the East African Federation - Federal Republic of East Africa or whatever - would be Jomo Kenyatta, in deference to Mzee, the Grand Old Man; and Julius Nyerere would be vice president. But Kenya also wanted the foreign minister of the East African federation to be a Kenyan, probably Tom Mboya. Uganda would therefore have been frozen out of all the three top positions; hardly a basis for unity. And, obviously, the extortionate demands by Kenya were deliberately intended to frustrate Nyerere's - and to a smaller degree, Obote's - efforts to unite the three East African countries. Therefore Kenyan leaders would, perhaps, have agreed to unite with Uganda and Tanganyika only if they were going to dominate the federation.

Kenya also did not want to lose its dominant position as the most developed and industrialized country in East Africa. During British colonial rule, Nairobi was virtually the capital of East Africa. It was the headquarters of the East African Common Services Organisation (EACSO) - railways and harbors, posts and telecommunications, airways, currency board, research facilities and much more. It was also the largest and most developed city in East Africa. And of all the East African countries, Kenya had the largest number of European settlers, about 70,000 and mostly British including members of the British aristocracy. They invested heavily in Kenya and tried to develop its economy because they saw it as an outpost of Britain which one day would become an independent state under white rule like South Africa, Australia and New Zealand; a dream white settlers in Rhodesia, now Zimbabwe, also tried to pursue. That is why Lord Delamere, Kenya's first governor, called it "White Man's Country."

Had Kenya agreed to unite with Uganda and Tanganyika to form a federation, it would have to be an equal among equals; would have been required to contribute a bigger share to the federal budget because of its relatively strong economy; and would have to make other sacrifices - in terms of revenue sharing and removing tariffs to import more goods from Uganda and Tanganyika - in order to help the two weaker economies catch up. And this was just too much for the Kenyan leadership. Kenya, not East Africa, came first, because of nationalism.

Uganda was also a major problem. Dr. Milton Obote wanted to form the federation probably as much as Nyerere did, and even spoke out against the dissolution of the Central African Federation of Rhodesia (Northern Rhodesia and Southern Rhodesia) and Nyasaland. He was the only African leader to do so. He believed that had the Central African Federation (which was formed in 1953 and dissolved in 1963) emerged from colonial rule as a single entity, it would have been a powerful African supra-nation and a major step towards continental unity.

But Uganda had serious internal problems because of strong opposition to the national government led by Obote. The strongest opposition came from the Buganda kingdom, vistually a state within a state, whose leaders were determined to reclaim its original glory as an independent nation, as it was before the advent of colonial rule like the Ashanti in Ghana. Other traditional strongholds in Uganda were also opposed to central authority. If all these kingdoms - Buganda, Ankole, Bunyoro, and the princedom of Busoga as well as other traditional centers of authority such as the Teso and the Acholi - were not ready to surrender power to the national government in Kampala; then one would certainly not have expected them to do so to an even more distant authority at the federal level of the three East African countries.

In terms of national integration, Uganda faced the toughest problem among all the three countries. Nyerere himself conceded that much, despite his unflinching determination to unite all the countries in the region, a goal he pursued until his death. Many Ugandan leaders also invoked the constitution saying it did not allow them to surrender their country's sovereignty to any other authority; a provision that was included to appease the Buganda kingdom and others opposed to any further diminution of their authority. The national government itself was more than enough for them. Yet, if the Ugandan leaders were serious about federation, they could have changed the constitution and included a provision requiring Uganda to renounce her sovereign status in favor of union as the Ghanaian constitution of March 1960 did, committing Ghana to full or partial renunciation of her sovereignty to achieve African unity.

Regarding Tanzania's socialist policies as an obstacle to federation, we need not look further to see that it was in fact Kenya, not Tanzania, which was an anomaly among the three countries, and therefore the main obstacle to federation. Both Nyerere and Obote were socialist-oriented even far back then, in 1963, before they proclaimed their socialist policies, while Kenyatta was not. Therefore it was Kenya's capitalist policies, which wrecked the proposed federation, as Nyerere and Obote moved closer ideologically, and in terms of policy formulation, eventually promulgating socialist policies. Tanzania issued the Arusha Declaration in February 1967, and Uganda the Common Man's Charter in October 1969. But even they failed to unite, without Kenya, in spite of their common socialist policies and one-party states. Kenya also became a one-party state in 1969 following the banning of the opposition Kenya People's Union (KPU) led by former vice president Oginga Odinga.

The three countries even had a common market, a common currency, and common services - including posts and telecommunications, railways and harbors, the East African Airways (EAA), and research institutes - inherited from the British and which would have formed a solid foundation for a federal state. Still, they failed to unite, because of nationalism.

There was also the Nyerere factor, a potent factor, especially among Kenyans who wanted to dominate the federation but who also feared that the charismatic and highly influential Tanganyikan leader would emerge as the dominant political figure on the scene and become president of the East African Federation; a dreadful prospect for nationalist-minded Kenyans. There was also, among the national leaders of Kenya and Uganda, fear of losing power and status to a higher authority at the federal level. For example, not all the cabinet members in the three national governments would have become cabinet members in the federal government, or even ambassadors. This was one of the strongest disincentives to consummation of the union, and all professions by them in different forums - including diplomatic conclaves - in support of East African unity was no more than empty rhetoric. But in fairness, we must also admit that there were some people in the government of Tanganyika who felt the same way as their counterparts did in Kenya and Uganda. There was, however, one fundamental difference. Tanganyika under Nyerere was committed to federation. Kenya and Uganda were not.

Another reason why the three East African countries did not form a federation was the unwillingness among Kenyan and Ugandan leaders to lose platforms in international forums where their countries would no longer be sovereign entities. They would cease to exist. Thus, instead of having three East African governments, each speaking for its own country at the United Nations, the World Bank and other international organizations and institutions, there would - under federation - be only one government; which was unthinkable.

That is why the federation was never formed. And none of those factors had anything to do with Tanganyika, the strongest proponent of East African integration, for which Nyerere was prepared to sacrifice so much, including Tanganyika's status as a separate entity. Even if Tanganyika and Uganda had chosen the capitalist path, capitalist Kenya would still not have united with them. And Uganda would have continued to rationalize her opposition to such a union on constitutional grounds. Obote supported the unification of the three East African countries, unlike most of his colleagues in Uganda. But when in 1964 the Ugandan government and parliament invoked the constitution to justify their opposition to federation, with Kenya already opposed to such a merger, it became obvious that the union could not be formed even under the best of circumstances: similar political and economic systems - neither Tanzania nor Uganda had gone socialist then, and Tanzania did not become a *de jure* one-party state until 1965. And the constitutional argument advanced by Uganda was not a very clever one, as we showed earlier. Constitutions can be amended and even abrogated.

The failure of the three East African countries to unite was one of the Nyerere's biggest disappointments; a point he underscored in an interview with James McKinley of *The New York Times* in his home village of Butiama in August 1996, more than 30 years after that abortive attempt, and 11 years after he voluntarily stepped down from the presidency. Looking back on his political career, he said his greatest failure was that although he managed to form a union with Zanzibar in 1964 to create Tanzania, he never succeeded in persuading neighboring countries to form a larger entity, a move, he said, that would have made the region a powerhouse.[39] Yet, he succeeded in uniting a country of almost 130 different tribes into a cohesive and stable nation unparalleled on the African continent. And in another unprecedented move, he not only succeeded in uniting two independent countries, but in forming the only union in the history of post-colonial Africa, and which has survived for almost 40 years.

His unsurpassed skills in nation-building were clearly evident, not only across tribal but also racial lines, creating a political entity that is virtually indistinguishable from an organic whole. In terms of racial harmony, Tanzania is one of the very few countries in Africa to have achieved that. And it is probably the only one where non-black candidates - of European, Asian, and Arab descent - never lost elections to black candidates in predominantly black constituencies. There was, for example, Derek Bryceson, a Tanzanian of British descent who always won elections against black candidates to represent Kilosa District in parliament. He was also the only white elected official on the entire continent representing an overwhelmingly black district in parliament, and held a number of cabinet posts under President Nyerere for many years, mostly as minister of agriculture. When he died in a British hospital in 1980, his body was flown back to Tanzania for burial after a state funeral. Thousands of people went to the airport to receive the body, and thousands more lined the streets of Dar es Salaam to pay their last respects as the vehicle carrying his body in a convoy of cars passed by. He was one of the most popular and respected leaders of Tanzania.

Amir H. Jamal, of Indian descent, was another very popular and highly respected leader and technocrat who represented Morogoro District in parliament and, like Bryceson, never lost an election against black candidates in a predominantly black constituency. He also held several senior cabinet posts - finance; commerce and industries; development and economic planning, and others including ambassadorial - for many years since independence. He also served as chairman of the Board of Governors of the International Monetary Fund (IMF) when he was Tanzania's minister of economic planning. Both Bryceson and Jamal were also veterans of the independence struggle. And there were many others - white, Asian, Arab - in different leadership positions and other posts working together with indigenous Africans, as they still do today including some cabinet members.

None of this would have been possible had it not been for President Julius Nyerere or another leader of such high caliber capable of uniting members of different tribes and races into a cohesive entity. And he inspired those who followed in his footsteps, President Ali Hassan Mwinyi and President Benjamin Mkapa, to pursue the same policies of tolerance, harmony, and peaceful co-existence; although after his death, agitation for greater autonomy - euphemism for independence in this context - in Zanzibar gained momentum, and ethnoregional rivalries and racial hostilities began to surface on an unprecedented scale. But he still left behind a stable nation, relatively speaking, and continues to inspire millions of Tanzanians to close ranks and maintain national unity.

In the pantheon of African leaders, he is one of those who continue to inspire millions across the continent. And his Pan-African commitment was no mere rhetoric, unlike that of most of his colleagues. He meant what he said, and did it. For example, the liberation struggle in southern Africa would probably have taken a different turn had it not been for his commitment and sacrifice. And tens of thousands of refugees from other African countries were given citizenship through the decades when he was president. In the early eighties alone, almost 100,000 people, mostly from Rwanda and Burundi, became Tanzanian citizens. And he extended his hospitality to others who were equally embraced with open arms. Tens of thousands of refugees from Mozambique during the liberation war in the Portugues colony also became citizens of Tanzania because of Nyerere's magnanimous policies.

And he continued to make sacrifices for fellow Africans across the continent until his last days; his relentless effort to help resolve the conflict in Burundi being only one example. When Dr. Kenneth Kaunda was jailed by President Frederick Chiluba for allegedly plotting to overthrow him, Nyerere intervened and helped get him out of jail. When Olusegun Obasanjo was imprisoned by Nigerian military dictator Sani Abacha, Nyerere worked relentlessly to help free him. After he was freed, Obasanjo said Nyerere was the first person outside Nigeria to call him, and told him he was sorry he did not work hard enough to help get him out of prison; testament to his humility. At Nyerere's funeral in Dar es Salaam, President Obasanjo nearly whispered as he recalled how Nyerere worked hard to free him from prison where he was serving a life sentence - reduced to 15 years - for allegedly trying to overthrow the government of military dictator Sani Abacha: "He was the first non-Nigerian who called me when I was freed, and he told me he was afraid he hadn't done enough."[40]

His death will never be forgotten by many people, including me. Nyerere's death will remain memorable to me in another respect, although this is only coincidental. He entered Edinburgh University in Scotland in October 1949 where he earned a master's degree in economics and history. That was the same year, and the same month, in which I was born in Kigoma in western Tanganyika under British colonial rule. And he died almost exactly 50 years later, on October 14, 1999, 10 days after my 50th birthday on October 4th. That is not the best way to remember one's birthday, yet, because of this, I will never forget when he died. He was mourned around the world, by the most humble and the most exalted; true testament to his greatness as a selfless leader who put the people first, including those groaning under apartheid and other oppressive regimes, black and white. Without his commitment and sacrifice, Tanzania would probably not have survived as a stable and united country.

And that pretty much sums up what ails Africa today: lack of good leadership more than anything else. It is lack of effective, dedicated leadership, which led to the destruction of Somalia as a nation, the first African country to "disappear" from the map. It is also lack of good leadership, which explains why other African countries dissolved in anarchy, torn by civil wars: Rwanda, Burundi, Congo-Kinshasa, Congo-Brazzaville, Liberia, and Sierra Leone. That is also why other forms of civil strife in different parts of the continent have become a prominent feature of the political landscape and national life. One can't help but wonder what would have happened in all these countries if they had leaders of Nyerere's and Mandela's caliber, genuinely committed to the well-being of their people, instead of being only interested in how much they are going to steal from them, and how they are going to oppress them and favor members of their tribes and sell their countries to outsiders. As Nyerere said in Accra, Ghana, where he was invited to participate in celebrations marking the 40th anniversary of Ghana's independence in March 1997:

We must not allow the future of Africa to be determined by those outside Africa. This is 1997 not 1887 - three years away from the 21st century. We must determine our own destiny. We've got to empower ourselves through unity to determine the fate of our continent...

Today we have African leaders who have simply looted their countries and their countries have gone to the dogs. We don't need those men...but we do need leadership. We need government that works and we need a hard-core of people who are willing to work hard and contribute to their country's welfare.[41]

It is a fitting tribute that Africans from different countries across the continent and other people elsewhere decided to institute a continental award known as the Nyerere Prize for Ethics, proposed by the Independent Commission on the Third Millennium for Africa based in Cotonou, Benin. The award will go to leaders who have demonstrated outstanding ethical conduct, in honor of the late Julius Nyerere because of his exemplary leadership, which earned him the title, "The Conscience of Africa." Supporters of the project include African governments, the United Nations, and other different organizations and institutions.

But, commendable as the project is, who is really going to get this award? Who deserves it on this beleaguered continent of brutal autocrats and kleptocrats, who don't mind bleeding their people to death in more than one way? It is a continent mangled, crippled, and bled by the very same leaders who are going to claim the award "in the name of the people." As Nyerere himself said not long before he died: "Africa is in a mess."

The award may, indeed, have been established in vain; hardly a fitting tribute to a man who died trying to bring peace to one of the most embattled parts of our continent, the Great Lakes region of East-central Africa, and elsewhere.

Although he is gone, his ideals will always be with us. And they will continue to inspire us in our quest for peace and stability, justice and equality, for which he lived and died. It is ideals, which can be achieved through unity, without which no country can survive, let alone thrive. But they will remain unattainable ideals if the building blocks for African unity are fragmented by ethnic conflicts and other forms of civil strife.

Many countries have been pulverized from within, and several others continue to sustain crippling blows because of their inability or unwillingness to address one vital issue: There can be no peace without stability, and no stability without justice and equality for all. And that entails, not only guaranteeing freedom of expression as a fundamental democratic right, but equal participation in the political process and in policy formulation and implementation on consensus basis at all levels of government. It also requires equitable redistribution of wealth to all regions and groups in order to contain and defuse ethnic and regional tensions and rivalries. Most of these are caused by discrimination; hardly a basis for unity. Fortunately, we were able to avoid these problems in Tanzania because of Nyerere's leadership.

Growing up in Tanganyika in the fifties and sixties was a memorable experience for me. I was born under colonial rule 12 years before independence. I grew up not only in an independent but a united republic. When Tanganyika won independence from Britain on December 9, 1961, I was 12 years old and did not have the slightest idea of what was going to happen in only two years. Even grown-ups involved or interested in politics did not have any idea that we would be living in a new country within so short a time. On April 26, 1964, Tanganyika united with Zanzibar. The new country was called the Union of Tanganyika and Zanzibar until October 29 the same year when it was renamed the United Republic of Tanzania.

It has been one long journey since then, and we still have a long way to go towards unity across the continent. But achieving this noble objective entails, first and foremost, conflict resolution in Africa. It is a goal Nyerere was trying to achieve when his life came to an end, an end, which also marked the beginning of a new era towards the end of the twentieth century. As he said in Accra, Ghana, on March 6, 1997, in a speech celebrating Ghana's 40th independence anniversary, his generation fought for independence. It is now for this generation to unite Africa. His speech was entitled, "Africa Must Unite":

Forty years ago the people of Ghana celebrated the raising of the flag of their independence for the first time. Throughout Africa people celebrated - in solidarity with Ghana but also for themselves. For the liberation of Africa was a single struggle with many fronts. Ghana's independence from colonial rule in 1957 was recognised for what it was: the beginning of the end of colonialism for the whole of Africa. For centuries we had been oppressed and humiliated as Africans. We were hunted and enslaved as Africans, as we were colonized as Africans.

The humiliation of Africans became the glorification of others. So we felt our African-ness. We knew that we were one people, and that we had one destiny regardless of the artificial boundaries, which the colonialists had invented. Since we were humiliated as Africans we had to be liberated as Africans.

So forty years ago we recognised your independence as the first triumph in Africa's struggle for freedom and dignity. It was the first success of our demand to be accorded the international respect, which is accorded free peoples. Ghana was the beginning, our first liberated zone. Thirty-seven years later in 1994 - we celebrated our final triumph when apartheid was crushed and Nelson Mandela was installed as the president of South Africa. Africa's long struggle for freedom was over.

But Ghana was more than just the beginning. Ghana inspired and deliberately spearheaded the independence struggle for the rest of Africa.

I was a student at Edinburgh University when Kwame Nkrumah was released from prison to be Leader of Government Business in his first elected government. The deportment of the Gold Coast students changed. The way they carried themselves up - they way they talked to us and others, the way they looked at the world at large, changed overnight. They even looked different. They were not arrogant, they were not overbearing, they were not aloof, but they were proud. Already they felt free and they exuded that quiet pride of self-confidence of freedom without which humanity is incomplete.

And so eight years later when the Gold Coast became independent, Kwame Nkrumah invited us, the leaders of the various liberation movements in Africa, to come and celebrate with you. I was among the many invited. Then Nkrumah made a famous declaration, that Ghana's independence was meangingless unless the whole of Africa was liberated from colonial rule. Kwame Nkrumah went into action almost immediately.

In the following year he called the liberation movements to Ghana to discuss a common strategy for the liberation of the continent from colonialism. In preparation for the African Peoples' Conference, those of us in East and Central Africa met in Mwanza, Tanganyika, to discuss our possible contribution to the forthcoming conference. That conference lit the liberation torch throughout colonial Africa.

Kwame Nkrumah was your leader, but he was our leader too: For he was an African leader. People are not gods. Even the best have their faults, and the faults of the great can be very big. So Kwame Nkrumah had his faults. But he was great in a purely positive sense. He was a visionary. He thought big, but he thought big for Ghana and its people and for Africa and its people. He had a great dream for Africa and its people. He had the well-being of our people at heart. He was no looter. He did not have a Swiss bank account. He died poor. Shakespeare wrote that the evil that men do lives after them, but the good is often interred with their bones.

Five years later, in May 1963, thirty-two independent African states met in Addis Ababa, founded the Organisation of African Unity (OAU), and established the liberation committee of the new organisation, charging it with the duty of coordinating the liberation struggle in those parts of Africa still under colonial rule.

The following year, 1964, the OAU met in Cairo. That Cairo summit is remembered mainly for the declaration of the heads of state of independent Africa to respect the borders inherited from colonialism. The principle of non-interference in the internal affairs of member states of the OAU had been enshrined in the charter itself; respect for the borders inherited from colonialism comes from the Cairo Declaration of 1964 (the resolution was Nyerere's idea and he introduced it at the Cairo summit). In 1965, the OAU met in Accra. That summit is not well remembered as the founding summit in 1963, or the Cairo summit of 1964.

The fact that Kwame Nkrumah did not last long as head of state of Ghana after that summit may have contributed to the comparative obscurity of that important summit. But I want to suggest that the reason why we do not talk much about that summit is probably psychological: it was a failure. That failure still haunts us today.

The founding fathers of the OAU had set themselves two major objectives: the total liberation of our continent from colonialism and settler minorities, and the unity of Africa. The first objective was expressed through the immediate establishment of the Liberation Committee by the founding summit. The second objective was expressed in the name of the organisation - it is the Organisation of African Unity.

Critics could say that the charter itself, with its great emphasis on the sovereign independence of each member state, combined with the Cairo Declaration on the sanctity of the inherited borders, makes it look like the 'Organisation of African Disunity.' But that would be carrying criticism too far and ignoring the objective reasons which led to the principles of non-interference in the Cairo Declaration.

What the founding fathers - certainly a hard-core of them - had in mind was genuine desire to move Africa towards greater unity. We loathed the balkanization of the continent into small non-viable states, most of which had borders, which did not make ethnic or geographical sense. The Cairo Declaration was prompted by a profound realisation of the absurdity of those borders.

It was quite clear that some adventurers would try to change those borders by force of arms. Indeed, it was already happening. Ethiopia and Somalia were at war over inherited borders. Kwame Nkrumah was opposed to balkanization as much as he was opposed to colonialism in Africa. To him and to a number of us, the two -

balkanization and colonization - were twins. Genuine liberation of Africa had to attack both twins. A struggle against colonialism must go hand in hand with a struggle against the balkanization of Africa.

Kwame Nkrumah was the great crusader for African unity. He wanted the Accra summit of 1965 to establish a union government for the whole of independent Africa. But we failed. The one minor reason is that Kwame, like all great believers, underestimated the degree of suspicion and animosity, which his crusading passion had created among a substantial number of his fellow heads of state. The major reason was linked to the first: already too many of us had a vested interest in keeping Africa divided.

Prior to independence of Tanganyika, I had been advocating that East African countries should federate and then achieve independence as a single political unit. I had said publicly that I was willing to delay Tanganyika's independence in order to enable all three-mainland countries to achieve their independence together as a single federated state. I made the suggestion because of my fear, proved correct by later events, that it would be very difficult to unite our countries if we let them achieve independence separately.

Once you multiply national anthems, national flags and national passports, seats at the United Nations, and individuals entitled to 21-gun salute, not to speak of a host of ministers, prime ministers, and envoys, you will have a whole army of powerful people with vested interests in keeping Africa balkanized. That was what Nkrumah encountered in 1965.

After the failure to establish the union government at the Accra summit of 1965, I heard one head of state express with relief that he was happy to be returning home to his country still head of state. To this day I cannot tell whether he was serious or joking. But he may well have been serious, because Kwame Nkrumah was very serious and the fear of a number of us to lose our precious status was quite palpable.

But I never believed that the 1965 Accra summit would have established a union government for Africa. When I say that we failed, that is not what I mean, for that clearly was an unrealistic objective for a single summit. What I mean is that we did not even discuss a mechanism for pursuing the objective of a politically united Africa. We had a Liberation Committee already. We should have at least had a Unity Committee or undertaken to establish one. We did not. And after Kwame Nkrumah was removed from the African political scene nobody took up the challenge again.

So my remaining remarks have a confession and a plea. The confession is that we of the first generation leaders of independent Africa have not pursued the objective of African unity with the vigour, commitment and sincerity that it deserves. Yet that does not mean that unity is now irrelevant.

Does the experience of the last three or four decades of Africa's independence dispel the need for African unity? With our success in the liberation struggle, Africa today has 53 independent states, 21 more than those, which met in Addis Ababa in May 1963. If numbers were horses, Africa would be riding high! Africa would be the strongest continent in the world, for it occupies more seats in the UN General Assembly than any other continent. Yet the reality is that ours is the poorest and weakest continent in the world. And our weakness is pathetic. Unity will not end our weakness, but until we unite, we cannot even begin to end that weakness.

So this is my plea to the new generation of African leaders and African people: Work for unity with firm conviction that without unity there is no future for Africa. That is, of course, assuming that we still want to have a place under the sun.

I reject the glorification of the nation-state, which we have inherited from colonialism, and the artificial nations we are trying to forge from that inheritance. We are all Africans trying very hard to be Ghanaians or Tanzanians. Fortunately for Africa we have not been completely successful. The outside world hardly recognises our Ghanaian-ness or Tanzanian-ness. What the outside world recognises about us is our African-ness.

Hitler was a German, Mussolini was an Italian, Franco was a Spaniard, Salazaar was a Portuguese, Stalin was a Russian or a Georgian. Nobody expected Churchill to be ashamed of Hitler. He was probably ashamed of Chamberlain. Nobody expected Charles de Gaulle to be ashamed of Hitler. He was probably ashamed of the complicity of Vichy. It is Germans, and Italians and Spaniards and Portuguese who feel uneasy about those dictators in their respective countries.

Not so in Africa. Idi Amin was in Uganda, but of Africa, Jean Bokassa was in Central Africa, but of Africa. Some of the dictators are still active in their respective countries, but they are all of Africa. They are all Africans, and all are perceived by the outside world as Africans. When I travel outside Africa the description of me as former president of Tanzania is a fleeting affair. It does not stick. Apart from the ignorant who sometimes asked me whether Tanzania was Johannesburg, even to those who knew better, what stuck in the minds of my hosts was the fact of my African-ness. So I had to answer questions about the atrocities of the Amins and the Bokassas of Africa.

Mrs. Gandhi did not have to answer questions about the

atrocities of Asia. Nor does Fidel Castro have to answer about the atrocities of the Somozas of Latin America. But when I travel or meet foreigners, I have to answer questions about Somalia, Liberia, Rwanda, Burundi and Zaire, as in the past I used to answer questions about Mozambique, Angola, Zimbabwe, Namibia or South Africa.

And the way I was perceived is the way most of my fellow heads of state were perceived. And that is the way you are all being perceived. So accepting the fact that we are Africans gives you a much more worthwhile challenge than the current desperate attempts to fossilize Africa into the wounds inflicted upon it by the vultures of imperialism....

Reject the return to the tribe. There is richness of culture out there, which we must do everything we can to preserve and share. But it is utter madness to think that if these artificial, non-viable states, which we are trying to create, are broken up into tribal components and we turn those into nation-states, we might save ourselves.

That kind of political and social atavism spells catastrophe for Africa. It would be the end of any kind of genuine development for Africa. It would fossilize Africa into a worse state than the one in which we are. The future of Africa, the modernization of Africa that has a place in the 21st century is linked up with its decolonization and detribalization. Tribal atavism would be giving up any hope for Africa. And of all the sins that Africa can commit, the sin of despair would be the most unforgivable.

Reject the nonsense of dividing African people into Anglophones, Francophones and Lusophones. This attempt to divide our people according to the language of their former colonial masters must be rejected with the firmness and utter contempt that it richly deserves. The natural owners of those wonderful languages are busy building a united Europe. But Europe is strong, even without unity. It has less need for unity and strength that comes from unity than Africa....

The second phase of the liberation of Africa is going to be much harder than the first. But it can be done. It must done. Empower Africa through unity, and Africa shall be free, strong and prosperous....

A new generation of self-respecting Africans should spit in the face of anybody who suggests that our continent should remain divided and fossilized....in order to satisfy the national pride of our former colonial masters.

Africa must unite! This was the title of one of Kwame Nkrumah's books. That call is more urgent today than ever before. Together, we the people of Africa will be incomparably stronger internationally than we are now with our multiplicity of non-viable states. The needs of our separate countries can be, and are being, ignored by the rich and powerful. The result is that Africa is marginalised when international decisions affecting our vital interests are made.

Unity will not make us rich, but it can make it difficult for Africa and the African people to be disregarded and humiliated. And it will therefore increase the effectiveness of the decisions we make and try to implement for our development.

My generation led Africa to political freedom. The current generation of leaders and the people of Africa must pick up the flickering torch of African freedom, refuel it with their enthusiasm and determination, and carry it forward.[42]

His death was indeed a significant event in the history of Africa. It marked the end of an era in which African countries won independence, and in which the African founding fathers left an indelible mark on the young nations they helped to nurture during the post-colonial period. In spite of the failures they had in a number of areas, especially in the economic arena, they will always be remembered as the leaders who not only led our countries to independence but who also helped end white minority rule in southern Africa by supporting liberation movements waging guerrilla warfare against the racist regimes in the region. This concerted effort culminated in the collapse of apartheid in the citadel of white supremacy and the last bastion of white minority rule on the continent, and whose demise was witnessed by Nyerere when he attended the inauguration of Nelson Mandela as the first democratically elected president of South Africa. The struggle for African liberation had finally come to an end. It was a struggle to which Nyerere dedicated his life. And he will always be remembered for that. Always.

APPENDIX I

Julius Nyerere
On the Boycott of South Africa
In A Letter to the Editor
Africa-South, October-December 1959

ON JUNE 26, 1959, Julius Nyerere was the principal speaker - along with Father Trevor Huddleston - at a meeting in London, which launched the Boycott South Africa Movement. It was re-named the Anti-Apartheid Movement in 1960.

That was at a time when most African leaders were only concerned about the independence struggle and problems in their own countries. Tanganyika itself was then not yet independent. But Nyerere still felt that it was necessary for the people of Tanganyika and others to get involved in the struggle for the liberation of South Africa from apartheid. An injustice to one is an injustice to all because humanity is one. As he stated in his letter to the editor of *Africa-South*, October-December 1959:

When I was a schoolboy, a friend of mine took me to the tailor one day and had me measured for a pair of shorts. We were great friends. His was mine and mine was his. He knew I needed a pair of shorts very badly. A few days later I got my pair of shorts, well made, fitting perfectly. I was proud of myself and proud of my friend. But it was not long before I discovered how my friend had obtained the money with which he had bought that pair of shorts for me. I returned it to him immediately. I could not disapprove of the manner in which the money had been obtained and still enjoy what the money had bought for   me.

It is this same principle, which makes me now support the boycotting of South African goods. We in Africa hate the policies of the South African Government. We abhor the semi-slave conditions under which our brothers and sisters in South Africa live, work and produce the goods we buy. We pass resolutions against the hideous system and keep hoping that the United Nations and the governments of the whole world will one day put pressure on the South African Government to treat its non-European peoples as human beings.

But these resolutions and prayers to the United Nations are not enough in themselves. Governments and democratic organisations grind very slowly. Individuals do not have to. The question then is what an individual can do to influence the South African Government towards a human treatment of its non-white citizens.

Can we honestly condemn a system and at the same time employ it to produce goods, which we buy, and then enjoy with a clear conscience? Surely the customers of a business do more to keep it going than its shareholders. We who buy South African goods do more to support the system than the Nationalist Government or Nationalist industrialists.

Each one of us can remove his individual prop to the South African system by refusing to buy South African goods. There are millions of people in the world who support the South African Government in this way, and who can remove their support by the boycott. I feel it is only in this way that we can give meaning to our abhorrence of the system, and give encouragement to sympathetic governments of the world to act.

It is most fitting that Jamaica, that island which has solved its racial problems so well, should have taken the action it has in support of the boycott. It is equally fitting that the Trade Union Congress of Ghana should immediately have given its support. I was personally happy to participate in a meeting in London where the boycott was launched. Already the authors of apartheid are beginning to feel the sharp effect of the boycott. But they cannot feel it fully until every person in the whole world who disapproves of the South African system withdraws his support of it by withdrawing his contribution to its upkeep.

I must emphasise that the boycott is really *a withdrawing of support*, which each one of us gives to the racialists in South Africa by buying their goods. There is a very real sense in which we are part of the system we despise, because we patronise it, pay its running expenses.

We are not being called upon to make much of a sacrifice.

We are not being called upon to go hungry and court imprisonment. That is the lot of our brothers and sisters inside South Africa. We are being asked to substitute other goods for South African goods, however much of a sacrifice this may mean to our suffering brethren in South Africa itself. We are not being called upon to support or not to support the oppressed in South Africa. We are being called upon to stop supporting those who oppress them.

The issue is as simple as that. Let every man and woman who disapproves of the South African system search his or her conscience, and decide to support or not to support the racialists of South Africa.

Source:

ANC Documents, African National Congress (ANC), South Africa. See also *Voices*, Africa Resource Center, On the Boycott of South Africa, by Julius Nyerere, then president of the Tanganyika African National Union (TANU), in a letter to the editor of *Africa-South*, October-December 1959.

The principle enunciated here by Nyerere, and which he upheld throughout his life, was also reflected in his conduct whe he was a student at St. Mary's Secondary School, Tabora. He was appointed a prefect, overseeing other students. Because of his status, he and the other prefects were entitled to double rations. Nyerere objected to that, saying all the students were equally entitled to the same amount of food. The double rations were dropped, and there was no more double-dipping for prefects, at least not as an   entitlement.

APPENDIX II

Julius Nyerere: Reflections

YOU WANTED me to reflect. I told you I had very little time to reflect. I am not an engineer (reference to the vice-chancellor of the University of Dar es Salaam who identified himself as an engineer in his introductory remarks) and therefore what I am going to say might sound messy, unstructured and possibly irrelevant to what you intend to do; but I thought that if by reflecting, you wanted me to go back and relive the political life that I have lived for the last 30, 40 years, that I cannot do. And in any case, in spite of the fact that it's useful to go back in history, what you are talking about is what might be of use to Africa in the 21st century. History's important, obviously, but I think we should concentrate and see what might be of use to our continent in the coming century.

What I want to do is share with you some thoughts on two issues concerning Africa. One, an obvious one; when I speak, you will realise how obvious it is. Another one, less obvious, and I'll spend a little more time on the less obvious one, because I think this will put Africa in what is going to be Africa's context in the 21st century. And the new leadership of Africa will have to concern itself with the situation in which it finds itself in the world tomorrow - in the world of the 21st century. And the Africa I'm going to be talking about, is Africa south of the Sahara, sub-Saharan Africa. I'll explain later the reason why I chose to concentrate on Africa south of the Sahara. It is because of the point I want to emphasise.

It appears today that in the world tomorrow, there are going to be three centers of power: some, political power; some, economic power, but three centers of real power in the world. One center is the United States of America and Canada; what you call North America. That is going to be a huge economic power, and probably for a long time the only military power, but a huge economic power. The other one is going to be Western Europe, another huge economic power. I think Europe is choosing deliberately not to be a military power. I think they deliberately want to leave that to the United States. The other one is Japan. Japan is in a different category but it is better to say Japan, because the power of Japan is quite clear, the economic power of Japan is obvious.

The three powers are going to affect the countries near them. I was speaking in South Africa recently and I referred to Mexico. A former president of Mexico, I think it must have been after the revolution in 1935, no, after the revolution; a former president of Mexico is reported to have complained about his country or lamented about his country. "Poor Mexico," said the president, "so far from God yet so near the United States." He was complaining about the disadvantages of being a neighbour of a giant. Today, Mexico has decided not simply to suffer the disadvantages of being so close to the United States. And the United States itself has realised the importance of trying to accommodate Mexico. In the past there were huge attempts by the United States to prevent people from moving from Mexico *into* the United States; people seeking work, seeking jobs. So you had police, a border very well policed in order to prevent Mexicans who *seek*, who *look* for jobs, to *move* into the United States. The United States discovered that it was not working. It *can't* work. There is a kind of economic osmosis where whatever you do, if you are rich, you are attractive to the poor. They will come, they'll even *risk* their own lives in order to come. So the United States tried very hard to prevent Mexicans going into the United States; they've given up, and the result was NAFTA. It is in the interest of the United States to try and create jobs in Mexico because, if you don't, the Mexicans will simply come, to the United States; so they're doing that.

Europe, Western Europe, is very wealthy. It has two Mexicos. One is Eastern Europe. If you want to prevent those Eastern Europeans to come to Western Europe, you jolly will have to create jobs in *Eastern* Europe, and Western Europe is actually *doing* that. They are *doing* that. They'll help Eastern Europe to develop. The whole of Western Europe will be doing it, the Germans are doing it. The Germans basically started first of all with the East Germans but they are spending lots of money also helping the other countries of Eastern Europe to develop, including unfortunately, or *fortunately* for them, including Russia. Because they realise, Europeans realise including the Germans, if you don't help *Russia* to develop, one of these days you are going to be in trouble. So it is in the interest of Western Europe, to help Eastern Europe including Russia. They are pouring a lot of money in that part of the world, in that part of Europe, to try and help it to develop.

I said Western Europe has two Mexicos. I have mentioned one. I'll jump the other. I jump Europe's second Mexico. I'll go to Asia. I'll go to Japan. Japan - a wealthy island, *very* wealthy indeed, but an *island*. I don't think they're very keen on the unemployed of Asia to go to Japan. They'd rather help them where they are, and Japan is spending a lot of money in Asia, to help create jobs *in* Asia, prevent those Asians dreaming about going to Japan to look for jobs. In any case, Japan is too small, they can't find wealth there. But apart from what Japan is doing, of course Asia *is* Asia; Asia has *China!* Asia has *India*, and the small countries of Asia are not very small. The population of Indonesia is twice the population of Nigeria, your biggest. So Asia is virtually in a category, of the Third World countries, of the Southern countries; Asia is almost in a category of its own. It is developing as a power, and Europe knows it, and the United States knows it. And in spite of the *huge* Atlantic, now they are talking about the Atlantic *Rim*. That is in recognition of the importance of Asia.

I go back to Europe. Europe has a second Mexico. And Europe's second Mexico is North Africa. North Africa is to Europe what Mexico is to the United States. North Africans who have no jobs will not go to Nigeria; they'll be thinking of Europe or the Middle East, because of the imperatives of geography and history and religion and language. North Africa is part of Europe and the Middle East.

Nasser was a great leader and a great *African* leader. I got on extremely well with him. Once he sent me a minister, and I had a long discussion with his minister at the State House here, and in the course of the discussion, the minister says to me, "Mr. President, this is my first visit to Africa." North Africa, because of the pull of the Mediterranean, and I say, history and culture, and religion, North Africa is pulled towards the North. When North

Africans look for jobs, they go to Western Europe and southern Western Europe, or they go to the Middle East. And Europe has a specific policy for North Africa, specific policy for North Africa. It's not only about development; it's also about security. Because of you don't do something about North Africa, they'll come.

Africa, south of the Sahara, is different; *totally* different. If you have no jobs here in Tanzania, where do you go? The Japanese have no fear that you people will flock to Japan. The North Americans have no fear that you people will flock to North America. Not even from West Africa. The Atlantic, the Atlantic as an ocean, like the Mediterranean, it has its own logic. But links North America and Western Europe, not North America and West Africa.

Africa south of the Sahara is isolated. That is the first point I want to make. South of the Sahara is totally isolated in terms of that configuration of developing power in the world in the 21st century - on its own. There is no centre of power in whose self-interest it's important to develop Africa, *no* centre. Not North America, not Japan, not Western Europe. There's no self-interest to bother about Africa south of the Sahara. Africa south of the Sahara is on its own. *Na sijambo baya.* Those of you who don't know Kiswahili, I just whispered, "Not necessarily bad."

That's the first thing I wanted to say about Africa south of the Sahara. African leadership, the coming African leadership, will have to bear that in mind. You are on your own, Mr. Vice President. You mentioned, you know, in the past, there was some Cold War competition in Africa and some Africans may have exploited it. I never did. I never succeeded in exploiting the Cold War in Africa. We suffered, we suffered through the Cold War. Look at Africa south of the Sahara. I'll be talking about it later. Southern Africa, I mean, look at southern Africa; devastated because of the combination of the Cold War and apartheid. Devastated part of Africa. It could have been *very* different. But the Cold War is gone, thank God. But thank God the Cold War is gone, the chances of the Mobutus also is gone.

So that's the first thing I wanted to say about Africa south of the Sahara. Africa south of the Sahara in those terms is isolated. That is the point I said was not obvious and I had to explain it in terms in which I have tried to explain it. The other one, the second point I want to raise is completely obvious. Africa has 53 nation-states, most of them in Africa south of the Sahara. If numbers were power, Africa would be the most powerful continent on earth. It is the weakest; so it's obvious numbers are not power.

So the second point about Africa, and again I am talking about Africa south of the Sahara; it is fragmented, fragmented. From the very beginning of independence 40 years ago, we were against that idea, that the continent is so fragmented. We called it the Balkanisation of Africa. Today, I think the Balkans are talking about the Africanisation of Europe. Africa's states are too many, too small, some make no logic, whether political logic or ethnic logic or anything. They are non-viable. It is not a confession.

The OAU was founded in 1963. In 1964 we went to Cairo to hold, in a sense, our first summit after the inaugural summit. I was responsible for moving that resolution that Africa must accept the borders, which we inherited from colonialism; accept them as they are. That resolution was passed by the organisation (OAU) with two reservations: one from Morocco, another from Somalia. Let me say why I moved that resolution. In 1960, just before this country became independent, I think I was then chief minister; I received a delegation of Masai elders from Kenya, led by an American missionary. And they came to persuade me to let the Masai invoke something called the Anglo-Masai Agreement so that that section of the Masai in Kenya should become part of Tanganyika; so that when Tanganyika becomes independent, it includes part of Masai, from Kenya. I suspected the American missionary was responsible for that idea. I don't remember that I was particularly polite to him. Kenyatta was then in detention, and here somebody comes to me, that we should break up Kenya and make part of Kenya part of Tanganyika. But why shouldn't Kenyatta demand that the Masai part of Tanganyika should become Masai of Kenya? It's the same logic. That was in 1960.

In 1961 we became independent. In 1962, early 1962, I resigned as prime minister and then a few weeks later I received Dr. Banda. *Mungu amuweke mahali pema* (May God rest his soul in peace). I received Dr. Banda. We had just, FRELIMO had just been established itself here and we were now in the process of starting the armed struggle. So Banda comes to me with a big old book, with lots and lots of maps in it, and tells me, "Mwalimu, what is this, what is Mozambique? There is no such thing as Mozambique." I said, "What do you mean there is no such thing as Mozambique?" So he showed me this map, and he said: "That part is part of Nyasaland (it was still Nyasaland at that time). That part is part of Southern Rhodesia, that part is Swaziland, and this part, which is the northern part, Makonde part, that is *your* part." So Banda disposed of Mozambique just like that. I ridiculed the idea, and Banda never liked anybody to ridicule his ideas. So he left and went to Lisbon to talk to Salazar about this wonderful idea. I don't know what Salazar told him. That was '62.

In '63 we go to Addis Ababa for the inauguration of the OAU, and Ethiopia and Somalia are at war over the Ogaden. We had to send a special delegation to bring the president of Somalia to attend that inaugural summit, because the two countries were at *war*. Why? Because Somalia wanted the Ogaden, a *whole* province of Ethiopia, saying, "That is part of Somalia." And Ethiopia was quietly, the Emperor quietly saying to us that "the whole of Somalia is part of Ethiopia." So those three, the delegation of the Masai, led by the American missionary; Banda's old book of maps; and the Ogaden, caused me to move that resolution, in Cairo 1964. And I say, the resolution was accepted, two countries with reservations, and one was Somalia because Somalia wanted the Ogaden; Somalia wanted northern Kenya; Somalia wanted Djibouti.

Throw away all our ideas about socialism. Throw them away, give them to the Americans, give them to the Japanese, give them, so that they can, I don't know, they can do whatever they like with them. *Embrace* capitalism, fine! But you *have* to be self-reliant. You here in Tanzania don't dream that if you privatise every blessed thing, including the prison, then foreign investors will come rushing. No! No! Your are dreaming! *Hawaji*! They won't come! (*hawaji*!). You just try it. There is more to privatise in Eastern Europe than here. Norman Manley, the Prime Minister of Jamaica, in those days the vogue was nationalisation, not privatisation. In those days the vogue was *nationalisation*. So Norman Manley was asked as Jamaica was moving towards independence: "Mr. Prime Minister, are you going to nationalise the economy?" His answer was: "You can't nationalise *nothing*."

You people here are busy privatising not *nothing*, we did

build something, we built *something* to privatise. But quite frankly, for the appetite of Europe, and the appetite of North America, this is privatising nothing. The people with a really good appetite will go to Eastern Europe, they'll go to Russia, they'll not come rushing to Tanzania! Your blessed National Bank of Commerce, it's a branch of some major bank somewhere, and in Tanzania you say, "It's so big we must divide it into pieces," which is *nonsense.*

Africa south of the Sahara is isolated. Therefore, to develop, it will have to depend upon its own resources basically. Internal resources, nationally; and Africa will have to depend upon Africa. The leadership of the future will have to devise, try to carry out policies of *maximum* national self-reliance and *maximum* collective self-reliance. They have no other choice. *Hamna*! (You don't have it!) And this, this need to organise collective self-reliance is what moves me to the second part. The small countries in Africa must move towards either unity or co-operation, unity of Africa. The leadership of the future, of the 21st century, should have less respect, less respect for this thing called "national sovereignty." I'm not saying take up arms and destroy the state, no! This idea that we must *preserve* the Tanganyika, then *preserve* the Kenya as they *are*, is nonsensical! The nation-states we in Africa, have inherited from Europe. They are the builders of the nation-states par excellence. For centuries they fought wars! The history of Europe, the history of the *building* of Europe is a history of war. And sometimes their wars when they get hotter although they're European wars, they call them *world wars*. And we all get involved. We fight even in Tanganyika here, we *fought* here, one world war.

These Europeans, powerful, where little Belgium is more powerful than the whole of Africa south of the Sahara put together; these *powerful* European states are moving towards unity, and you people are talking about the atavism of the tribe, this is nonsense! I am telling *you* people. How can anybody think of the tribe as the unity of the future? *Hakuna!* (There's nothing!). Europe now, you can take it almost as God-given, Europe is not going to fight with Europe anymore. The Europeans are not going to take up arms against Europeans. They are moving towards unity - even the little, the little countries of the Balkans which are breaking up, Yugoslavia breaking up, but they are breaking up at the same time the building up is taking place. They break up and say we want to come into the *bigger* unity. So there's a *building* movement, there's a *building* of Europe. These countries which have old, old sovereignties, countries of hundreds of years old; they are forgetting this, they are *moving* towards unity. And you people, you think Tanzania is sacred? What is Tanzania!

You *have* to move towards unity. If these powerful countries see that they have no future in the nation-states - *ninyi mnafikiri mna future katika nini*? (what future do you think you have?). So, if we can't *move*, if our leadership, our future leadership cannot move us to bigger nation-states, which I *hope* they are going to try; we tried and failed. I tried and failed. One of my biggest failures was actually that. I tried in East Africa and failed. But don't give up because we, the first leadership, failed, no! *Unajaribu tena*! (You try again!). We failed, but the idea is a good idea. That these countries should come together. Don't leave Rwanda and Burundi on their own. *Hawawezi kusurvive* (They cannot survive). They can't. They're locked up into a form of prejudice. If we can't move towards bigger nation-states, at least let's move towards greater co-operation. This is beginning to happen. And the new leadership in Africa should encourage it.

I want to say only one or two things about what is happening in southern Africa. Please accept the logic of coming together. South Africa, small; South Africa is very small. Their per capita income now is, I think $2,000 a year or something around that. Compared with Tanzanians, of course, it is very big, but it's poor. If South Africa begins to tackle the problems of the legacy of apartheid, they have no money! But compared with the rest of us, they are rich. And so, in southern Africa, there, there is also a kind of osmosis, also an economic osmosis. South Africa's neighbours send their job seekers *into* South Africa. And South Africa will simply have to accept the logic of that, that they are big, they are attractive. They attract the unemployed from Mozambique, and from Lesotho and from the rest. They have to accept that fact of life. It's a problem, but they have to accept it.

South Africa, and I am talking about post-apartheid South Africa. Post-apartheid South Africa has the most developed and the most dynamic private sector on the continent. It is white, so what? So forget it is white. It is South African, dynamic, highly

developed. If the investors of South Africa begin a new form of
trekking, you *have* to accept it. It will be ridiculous, absolutely
ridiculous, for Africans to go out seeking investment from North
America, from Japan, from Europe, from Russia, and then, when
these investors come from South Africa to invest in your own
country, you say, "a! a! These fellows now want to take over our
economy" - this is nonsense. You can't have it both ways. You
want foreign investors or you don't want foreign investors. Now,
the most available foreign investors for you are those from South
Africa.

And let me tell you, when Europe think in terms of
investing, they *might* go to South Africa. When North America
think in terms of investing, they *might* go to South Africa. Even
Asia, if they want to invest, the first country they may think of in
Africa *may* be South Africa. So, if *your* South Africa is going to be
your engine of development, accept the reality, accept the reality.
Don't accept this sovereignty, South Africa will reduce your
sovereignty. What sovereignty do you have? Many of these debt-
ridden countries in Africa now have no soverignty, they've lost it.
Imekwenda (It's gone). *Iko mikononi mwa IMF na World Bank*
(It's in the hands of the IMF and the World Bank). *Unafikiri kuna
sovereignty gani?* (What kind of sovereignty do you think there
is?). So, southern Africa has an opportunity, southern Africa, the
SADC group, *because* of South Africa.

Because South Africa now is no longer a destabiliser of the
region, but a partner in development, southern Africa has a
tremendous opportunity. But you need leadership, because if you
get proper leadership there, within the next 10, 15 years, that
region is going to be the ASEAN (Association of South-East Asian
Nations) of Africa. And it is possible. But forget the protection of
your sovereignties. I believe the South Africans will be sensitive
enough to know that if they are not careful, there is going to be this
resentment of big brother, but that big brother, frankly, is not very
big.

West Africa. Another bloc is developing there, but that
depends very much upon Nigeria my brother (looking at the
Nigerian High Commissioner - Ambassador), very much so.
Without Nigeria, the future of West Africa is a problem. West
Africa is more balkanised than Eastern Africa. More balkanised,

tiny little states. The leadership will have to come from Nigeria. It came from Nigeria in Liberia; it has come from Nigeria in the case of Sierra Leone; it will have to come from Nigeria in galvanising ECOWAS. But the military in Nigeria must allow the Nigerians to exercise that vitality in freedom. And it is my hope that they will do it.

I told you I was going to ramble and it was going to be messy, but thank you very much.

Source:
Mwalimu Nyerere Memorial Site: Written Speeches, South Centre, Geneva, Switzerland, 2001.

This is an abridged version of Nyerere's speech at the conference at the University of Dar es Salaam, Tanzania. The transcription of the non-written speech came from Mrs. Magombe of the Nyerere Foundation, Dar es Salaam.

Translation of Kiswahili words, phrases and sentences in Nyerere's speech into English in the preceding text, done by the author, Godfrey Mwakikagile.

APPENDIX III

Address by President Benjamin Mkapa
of the United Republic of Tanzania
at the state funeral for Mwalimu Julius Kambarage
Nyerere
National Stadium, Dar es Salaam, Tanzania
Thursday, 21st October, 1999

Your Excellencies
Heads of State and Government;
Your Royal Highnesses;
Honourable Ministers and
Ministers of Parliament;
Representatives of Foreign Governments;
Members of the Diplomatic Corps;
My Fellow Citizens;
Ladies and Gentlemen.

This is the saddest day in the history of our country. It marks a life ceased and a service ended. But, let me first thank the doctors, nurses and staff that day and night struggled to save the life of our beloved Founding Father of the United Republic of Tanzania, Mwalimu Julius Kambarage Nyerere.

I thank everyone who stood by us, and helped us, and all those that sent messages of support and encouragement during Mwalimu's illness, and condolences on his demise.

I thank British Prime Minister Tony Blair and Her Majesty's Government for being so helpful and supportive throughout the illness and death of Mwalimu Nyerere.

I thank most sincerely all of you, the leaders and other distinguished people from Africa and beyond that are here to support and comfort us. We really appreciate your coming.

I ask everyone who helped us and the bereaved family to accept the gratitude of the family, the gratitude of my Government, and the gratitude of the entire people of Tanzania to whom Mwalimu has always been, and will always be, much more than a Founding Father.

To you, the people of the United Republic of Tanzania, I am also very grateful. On 26th September I addressed the Nation, explaining the illness of Mwalimu Nyerere and asking everyone to pray for his recovery. Across the country, across all religious faiths, prayers were said, day and night. Now that he is no more we have all joined hands across the country, regardless of tribe, faith, gender or race to mourn his passing away in unity, solidarity, peace and tranquility just like Mwalimu taught us. We have learnt well, and this is clearly a good beginning for life after Mwalimu.

Since he passed away I have received hundreds of messages of condolences from all corners of the continent and the world sent Kings and Queens, Presidents and Prime Ministers, leaders of international and regional organisations, political and civil society leaders, and yes, from ordinary citizens of the world. They are unanimous in their description of Mwalimu as a person, as a national leader, as an African statesman and as an international personality.

I cannot read all the messages to you. But on behalf of our continent I will read part of the message sent by the OAU Chairman, President Abdelaziz Bouteflika of Algeria. He refers to Mwalimu as:

"The peerless leader who devoted his life to the service of his country and continent, the tireless defender of just causes and worthy architect of the conquest by African peoples of   their rightful place among nations of the world."

On behalf of the international community I will quote the United Nations Secretary General Kofi Annan. Of Mwalimu he says: "He set an example in Africa by voluntarily renouncing power and handing over to his successor through an orderly constitutional process."

Mwalimu is one of the leaders of developing countries who challenged and critiqued the economic prescriptions of financial institutions such as the World Bank and the International Monetary Fund in the early 1980's when he was still President, and afterwards as Chairman of the South Commission. I believe

Mwalimu had an influence in changing the perspectives of these institutions and making them more responsive to our points of view. For that reason, on behalf of international financial institutions, I will read the full message of the President of the World Bank, Mr. James D. Wlofensohn. He said:

"For the men and women who have served the great cause of development in the world, one of the lights of our lives went out today. Mr. Julius Nyerere was one of the founding fathers of modern Africa. He was also one of the few world leaders whose high ideals, moral integrity, and personal modesty inspired people right around the globe.

While world economists were debating the importance of capital output ratios, President Nyerere was saying that nothing was more important for people than being able to read and write and have access to clean water.

He gave his compatriots a sense of hope and achievement early in their life as a country. And he gave them a sense of nation with few parallels in Africa and the world - bound by a common language (Kiswahili) and a history almost entirely free of internal divisions and conflict. His political ideals, his deep religious convictions, his equally deep religious tolerance, and his belief that people of all ethnic and regional origins should have equal access to knowledge and material opportunities have marked his country - and Africa - forever.

He was a leader in the liberation of Southern Africa. He looked after hundreds of thousands of refugees forced to live in western Tanzania by political turmoil in central Africa. And he left office peacefully at an age when he could certainly have continued. He was known as 'Mwalimu' (or 'Teacher') - which was his first profession. Many of us still regard ourselves as his students, and we feel very honoured to have known and worked with him in his life.

To the people of Tanzania - and his wider family across Africa and around the world - I want to say how much we share your sadness at his passing. However, the example he set and the ideals he represented will remain a source of inspiration and comfort for all of us. That is a legacy which even President Nyerere - modest as he was - would have been proud of."

There are very, very many in this country who, like me, consider ourselves lucky that our lives were touched by Mwalimu. I for one have no hesitation to say, with pride, that I learnt politics at the hands of a true master; a man who proved that politics does not have to be, as conventionally portrayed, a dirty game; an upright man, a man who would stand for what is right and just though the heavens fell.

Here was a man who friends, comrades and his fellow countrymen loved deeply, and whose political foes respected highly. A man of outstanding integrity, imbued with an intense love for his fellow human beings across the lines of geography, race, colour, and   gender.

Mwalimu was averse to empty phrases, averse to the development of a personality cult. His humility and disdain for flattery is legendary. But the people of this country, other Africans, developed and developing countries, have all recognised Mwalimu's contribution to Tanzania, to Africa and to the world, awarding him over the years with medals, awards, honorary degrees from Africa, East and West Europe, Asia, and the Americas.

In his 77 years of mortal life, Mwalimu did much for our nation, for the African continent, and for the world. He made us free and contributed to the freedom of others beyond our borders. Like Nkrumah he believed the indignity of one African was the indignity of all Africans; and that as long as there was an African country under colonial domination, the freedom of one African country was meaningless. He mobilised our national will, spirit and resources for the total liberation of Africa.

His life-long philosophy rested on the premise that all human beings are created equal and deserve equal freedom, justice, respect and dignity. He believed in, and practised, that principle in whose advocacy he was both passionate and inspiring. He built a united nation with a vision of equality and respect across racial, religious, tribal, and gender divides. Until this day, the union between Tanganyika and Zanzibar remains an enduring example of African unity. We shall defend and strengthen this union with all our might.

His commitment to unity within the country, and African unity, had an almost missionary zeal. To him the imperative of unity, solidarity, and co-operation between poor and weak countries in pursuit of greater democracy ond a global scale, and the sovereign equality of nations, was paramount. We are not less human just because we are poor, he consistently told his political and economic interlocutors.

His view of freedom was all encompassing. It was not restricted to political independence, but extended to a vision of a totally liberated human being - in political, economic, social and cultural terms.

One of the nicknames Tanzanians gave Mwalimu as President was "Musa" (Moses). Like Moses in the Holy Books, he had given us freedom and was leading the People of Tanzania through the desert to the promised land of prosperity. We believe the new century and millennium will indeed witness a more prosperous Tanzania. But, alas, like Moses of the Holy Books, Mwalimu's life was cut short before we reached the new century of   promise.

A man of faith, a devout person, he had tremendous respect for all faiths. Love begets love, trust begets trust, respect begets respect, he taught us. Mwalimu, as a result, was loved, trusted and respected by all tribes, all races, all religions and all regions of Tanzania.

Mwalimu was extremely sensitive to the downtrodden, the weak, the disabled, the powerless. He was acutely sensitive to the plight of refugees and displaced persons. Under his leadership Tanzania was not only peaceful, thereby not generating refugees, but he made Tanzania home to everyone seeking political and personal refuge.

A few months before he died he visited refugee camps in western Tanzania and talked to the Burundi refugees there, giving them hope that his role as an international facilitator for rhe Burundi peace process would soon restore peace in their country so they could go back to their homes. His perseverance in peace efforts, regardless of the many disappointments along the way, never ceased to amaze me and others.

I talked to him a few days before he was admitted to the St. Thomas Hospital in London, and even at that stage of his illness he was impatient to return to Tanzania to carry on with his facilitation of the Burundi peace process. I had to plead to dissuade him. A peacemaker, he was a universal man, God's gift to mankind. The gift we can give him in return is to quickly finalise the Burundi peace process, and facilitate the voluntary and peaceful repatriation of those who had reason to flee for their lives.

Mwalimu was a teacher in many ways. He had an unquenchable thirst for knowledge, and an unending desire to impart knowledge to others. A man of great patience, a great listener, he was always willing to weigh and consider a wide array of opinion. A voracious reader of books, what helped to persuade him to accept a bigger house, in his own words spoken light-heartedly, was because he had run out of room for books in his former house.

A man of great vision, he had exceptional intellect and wit. A man of ideas, a creative thinker, he was always challenged by new ideas, fascinated by the search for truth, for reality, for science and history.

UNICEF, in their message on his death, described Mwalimu as: "A slender, diminutive figure of irresistbly infectious chuckle, with a mind so sharp as to cut to the heart of every argument, but a tongue so kind as to soothe the soul of every adversary."

It has been said that the true measure of humanity is the care one has for the weaker members of society. On this score, on account of his intense spirituality, Mwalimu distinguished himself as a veritable human being. His concern, perhaps even obsession, with removing inequalities in society, and in the world is legendary.

His disdain for affluence amid poverty had a spiritual aura and was deeply imbedded in his heart and mind. Mwalimu saw himself as a man with a mission, and refused the distraction that the accumulation of earthly riches would bring in his life. My Fellow Citizens, this is a sad occasion. But I am sure if Mwalimu could speak to us now, he would be exhorting us to pick up his mantle and carry on the struggle against poverty, against injustice, against bigotry. He would exhort us, as he always did in his life time, to cherish and protect the union between Tanganyika and Zanzibar. He would ask us to be on guard against any divisive tendencies. He would urge us to move much more quickly to integrate African economies, and promote African unity. He would appeal for collective South-South self-reliance.

So sad as we are, this must also be a celebration of the life of an outstanding man - an extraordinary man who more than any other devoted his whole life and being to the service of others, within and beyond Tanzania. A man of chiefly heritage who abolished privilege. A man who is the embodiment of good leadership, leadership as service to others. A man who is the example of public service for the public good. We all know, and the world knows, that unlike many post-independence African leaders, he did not use public office for personal enrichment. What Mwalimu has is what the people of this country have willingly given him.

Today all Tanzanians weep for Mwalimu, a man in whom all kinds of people saw a saviour. A man who believed in giving everyone an education, so that everyone can have a chance in life. There are many in this country today who hold important positions in government and society who will never forget Mwalimu for giving them the key to their present status - the key of education. A man who two years ago at his 75th birthday grieved that "we are wasting too much life" on account of the many children and adults who die of preventable and curable diseases, or lack of proper nutrition.

As the funeral cortege passed the hundreds of thousands of people lining the streets of Dar es Salaam the echo of the cry "Mkombozi umetuacha," meaning "Saviour you have left us," was everywhere. He was so much to everyone; a pillar of what Tanzania is today, a repository of wisdom, counsel and guidance. He has left us, but we shall not let slip his legacy. We shall safeguard his achievements and hold high the torch of struggle and freedom he has bequeathed us.

I have been privileged to lead the cortege procession of this unique man and leader through the streets of Dar es Salaam. I was overcome by the ubiquitous outpouring of grief and sense of loss. But I was encouraged by the words and hand-written placards that vowed to protect the freedom, unity, solidarity, tolerance, and principles Mwalimu taught us all his life.

And I want to assure everyone within and without Tanzania that my Government will ensure that the legacy of Mwalimu never dies. We will do all within out power:

* To maintain national unity, concord and harmony;

* To prosecute the war on poverty with even greater zeal and ensure the fruits of that war are shared as widely and equitably as possible among the downtrodden; and

* To defend the union between Tanganyika and Zanzibar which he founded together with another of our beloved founding leader, the late Sheikh Abeid Aman Karume.

Let us not forget, my dear brothers ans sisters, that the presence among us of so many leaders from our sub-region and the African continent, from Europe and the Americas and from Asia is testimony to the stature in the world that Mwalimu earned for his pursuit of the legacy he has left us. Their presence here, therefore, is not only in honour of Mwalimu but also an exhortation to us to be worthy inheritors of Mwalimu's legacy. We must stay the course. My Fellow Citizens, there is no doubt that Mwalimu was richly blessed by the Almighty God. He used those talents as his Maker wanted him to. And as he stands before God at the end of his life's ministry, I am sure he can say with confidence: Lord, I used everything you gave me, not for personal gain or comfort, but for the freedom, dignity and well-being of the people you put under my charge, and those well beyond Tanzania's borders and shores.

Our world is composed of givers and takers. The takers may eat better, but the givers sleep better. In death, as in life, Mwalimu sleeps better. For his entire life was a life of giving, not taking.

We thank Almighty God most profoundly for the life and service of Mwalimu Julius Kambarage Nyerere.

And we whose lives were touched by him join in a chorus of prayer:

"May Almighty God rest his soul in eternal peace."

Thank you.

APPENDIX IV

David Martin on Mwalimu Julius Kambarage Nyerere

"WE, the people of Tanganyika, would like to light a candle and put it on top of Mount Kilimanjaro which would shine beyond our borders giving hope where there was despair, love where there was hate and dignity where before there was only humiliation... We cannot, unlike other countries, send rockets to the moon. But we can send rockets of love and hope to all our fellow [humans] wherever they may be."

That statement, over two years before Tanganyika's independence, was made by Julius Kambarage Nyerere to the Legislative Assembly in October 1959. It expressed the essence of his beliefs: hope, love and dignity.

While those in the developed world walked, his brisk and sprightly stride implied, as he repeatedly said, that Africa had to run to catch up. ("We must run while others walk"). Once political freedom was attained, unity and development, coupled with hard work, were essential pre-requisites in nation building.

Nyerere was the champion of the liberation of southern Africa becoming the first chairman of the Frontline states. In Tanzania, Africa and the world he was regarded almost with awe.

Such reaction was contrary to that which Nyerere wanted. He was above all a simple man combining this with formidable discipline. Once a chain-smoker, he simply stopped when he became involved in politics and he rarely drank imbibing only an occasional glass of "Samora" as he called the Portuguese wine the Mozambican leader had introduced him to. His wife, he once said in a statement, was simply Mrs. Nyerere and not "the First Lady."

Apart from his simplicity and piercing intellect, one of Nyerere's most endearing traits was his honesty. Today it is no longer fashionable among journalists - and much of the public - to take politicians at their word or even imagine in advance what those words might be.

Yet if you applied obvious logic, Nyerere was highly predictable. Once I said on the BBC that the Tanzanian president would take the extreme step of leaving the Commonwealth if British prime Minister Edward Heath resumed arms supplies to South Africa. Some days later Nyerere asked me how I knew that was his decision. To this day I have never been sure whether he was flattered or not at being told he was that obvious.

Early in his presidency he decided he wanted to be like everyone else and have a home to go to after the office. But he had no money. So he called in his commercial bank manager and asked for a loan. It is said, before giving the loan, that the white banker jokingly observed that African presidents in those days of coup d'etats were not a very good risk. Nyerere later nationalised the bank but kept up his payments.

When he retired as Tanzania's first president in 1985, he gave the Msasani house he had built to the state. He waived all the payments he had made leaving the state with the balance. Somewhat to his chagrin, the state paid off the mortgage and gave him the house back; including all the upkeep costs that went with it.

Whenever he could, Nyerere went back to his village. There he had a farm - of sorts. Olusegun Obasanjo, then a farmer and now Nigeria's president, once observed that although Nyerere had more tractors than he did, the Tanzanian president would never be a commercial farmer.

To the end Nyerere retained his simplicity. He was concerned that his enforced stay in London (for leukemia treatment at St. Thomas Hospital) was costing his people money they could ill afford. After his death his body was flown home in the simple and aged plane in which successive Tanzanian presidents had flown many thousands of miles. The plane was simply diverted through London after a routine service in Holland.

Soon after independence, Nyerere resigned as Tanganyika's prime minister to forge unity within his party, offered to delay his country's independence for the sake of unity with Kenya and Uganda, merged Tanganyika and Zanzibar in the union now known as Tanzania. He was deeply committed to the unity of East Africa and the rest of Africa, a reality that ironically may now come to pass after his death.

For his countrymen and women he was an inspirational leader. He rarely relaxed and when he did it was usually to play *bao* (an indigenous game similar to chess) with the elders. He was an avid reader who believed in hard work whether it was behind the portals of State House, building bricks for an ujamaa village at Chamwino near Dododma where he moved the country's capital, or marching with blistered feet to Mwanza at the head of his people.

He evolved a uniquely African electoral system for his people in the days when Tanzania was a one-party state well before pluralism became the buzzword. Two candidates from the ruling party ran against each other. They had to both speak in Swahili from their shared platform so use of the local language by one did not disadvantage the other, and they could not make promises that they would do such and such if elected.

Reference to the other candidate's gender, religion, race or tribe was forbidden, the aspirants had to travel together at all times and even eat from the same plate in case of poisoning. In the country's first post-independence election the electorate voted out two ministers, seven junior ministers and over 60 backbench members of parliament.

It was an outcome that would have stunned western political parties and while some aspects of this unique electoral system may have been undesirable, it is a sad reflection on the developed nations that they forced its entire abandonment in 1995 in favour of the "western model of democracy."

Nyerere's distinctive grey hair atop a slight but athletic body always stood out from the crowd. When he was in his seventies, young security officers had to run to keep up with him and the sound of his mercurial voice, raised and then whispered, was still resonant and haunting.

I arrived in Dar es Salaam in early 1964, just four years after Nyerere's speech to the Legislative Assembly (in October 1959). Nyerere, I had been told in London by my interviewers in that strangely confiding way many whites have when talking to other whites, was "almost one of us." A liberal, a catholic and so on.

How right - and how wrong - they were.

I was fascinated by the man who was to become my informal professor teaching me the meaning of principles and non-racialism. Nyerere, as his record testifies, recognised the equality of all human beings irrespective of race, ethnicity, gender and religion.

He greatly admired the late American president, Jack kennedy, and was the second visitor to the Oval Office during Kennedy's tenure in the White House. Kennedy, the subsequent American analysis showed, tried to set his African visitor at ease before realising that Nyerere was more at ease than he was.

It was a year after my arrival in Dar es Salaam that I met Nyerere for an interview and when I did so it was strictly on his own terms.

The West Germans had just given him an ultimatum; if he allowed the East Germans to open a consulate in Dar es Salaam they would withdraw their support for his fledgling air force. His response was immediate. The West German ambassador was shown the door and the Canadians took over. Now Nyerere wanted the story in the British media.

I learned two things about the man from that meeting. The first was that he was a master media manager, a quality some other contemporary leaders could well emulate. He spoke to journalists on his terms when he had something to say. Interminable lectures and harangues were not his style.

The second point was that you gave Nyerere ultimatums at your own peril. His logic was disarming; his determination both forceful and occasionally somewhat chilling.

At another meeting I recall commenting on the number of African countries who were not paying their dues to the Organisation of African Unity Liberation Committee. He looked at me thoughtfully chewing the inner corner of his cheek in the characteristic way he had when concentrating.

Having made his decision, he passed across a file swearing me to secrecy as to its details. It contained Tanzania's budget for that year for the liberation movements fighting colonialism and minority rule in Angola, Guinea Bissau, Mozambique, Zimbabwe, Namibia, South Africa and the Comoro Islands.

I was astounded by just how much Tanzanians were paying; a sum well beyond the country's publicised contribution.

The vast amount that one of the continent's poorest countries materially - and morally - contributed to the liberation of Africa should shame those who are more materialistically inclined.

Therein, in the view of many non-Tanzanians, lies Nyerere's greatest contribution. All of the countries of the continent - with the exception of Spanish Sahara (Western Sahara) - are now fully independent. When Nyerere had spoken to the (Tanganyika) Legislative Assembly in 1959 only nine countries were independent; today the number is 53.

All of southern Africa's liberation movements at one time had their headquarters in Dar es Salaam. Nyerere, along with Hastings Banda of Malawi and Kwame Nkrumah of Ghana, were the only three leaders to recognise the Zimbabwe African National Union (ZANU) when it was formed in 1963 and Herbert Chitepo (its leader) was Tanzania's Director of Public Prosecutions.

In the days of the heady 1960s through to the somewhat calmer 1980s, Tanzania was to be the crossroads of Africa. Almost everyone who was anyone visited Dar es Salaam during those years to meet Nyerere and the leaders of southern Africa's liberation movements.

The Chinese Premier Chou en Lai spoke of Africa being "ripe for revolution." Others came with their own agendas such as Marshall Tito, Olof Palme, Robert Kennedy, Henry Kissinger, Che Guevara, Malcolm X and sporting legends such as Arthur Ashe (and Muhammed Ali).

From Africa there were leaders such as Gamal Nasser of Egypt, Emperor Haile Selassie of Ethiopia whose subsequent death (in 1975) Nyerere tried to prevent, William Tubman of Liberia and a host of others.

There is a saying in Africa, which holds that every time an old man dies a library burns down. Nyerere was such a library and regrettably much of his knowledge has gone to his grave with him. Curiously, after strongly opposing his memoirs, he spoke of them to his closest staff near the end.

Revisionist historians will judge the man and his times in their own way. Some will even claim to be his "official" biographer. Few will have the historical memory and knowledge to rebut their contentions. It remains incumbent on those who were involved with him to record his side of the story.

Almost all Tanzanians hold him in special esteem. They are stunned by his death, gathering in silent groups beneath the official photograhph which in Swahili proclaims him Baba wa Taifa meaning Father of the Nation. To Tanzanians he remains, Mwalimu, the teacher, the title they gave him.

Tanzanians, despite the conspicuous pride they retain in their country's role in the liberation of southern Africa, have several very different reasons to remember the man who shaped their lives.

One of the most lasting legacies is the union of the sovereign states of Tanganyika and Zanzibar into the single country now called Tanzania. Not everyone, including many mainland Tanzanians, look on the union through the same rose-tinted spectacles they once wore; for, it has been fraught with difficulties.

But were it not for that union, and particularly the potential protection the mainland military offered, the former Arab rulers - the second largest minority in Africa behind the whites of South Africa - may have tried to re-seize power from the African majority.

Ujamaa, the concept of togetherness often erroneously referred to as African socialism, is another of Nyerere's enduring legacies. There can be no doubt of the logic of bringing scattered communities together into centres where goods and services can reach them. Nyerere had the vision to do this but the implementation of others was found wanting.

Another legacy, in some people's view now sadly confined to history, was the Arusha Declaration and the leadership code which sought to stem the earliest manifestation of corruption.

Yet another, in the days when the World Bank regarded investment in education and health as non-productive, was his determination to provide basic social services for his people.

But domestically Nyerere's most enduring legacy must be Tanzania's unity and stability. From over 120 ethnic groups, Nyerere forged a united nation bonded by a single language, Swahili. The pride of nationhood is palpable: never more so than when Tanzanians drove the dictator Idi Amin out of Uganda.

Such unity is unique in eastern and southern Africa. And in a curious sense Tanzania was to be a poor classroom for me as it did not prepare me for the mysteries and miseries of ethnic political strife elsewhere in Africa and Europe.

Nyerere was born at Butiama, a village near Musoma on the shores of Lake Victoria in April 1922. He was the son of Chief Nyerere Burito of the Wazanaki and his mother was to exert a considerable influence on his life.

He attended primary school at Musoma and secondary at Tabora. He spent two years at Makerere University in Uganda before returning to Tabora as a teacher. In 1949, he enrolled at Edinburgh University in Scotland completing a Master of Arts degree three years later.

A spell of teaching followed at Pugu near Dar es Salaam. But politics were beckoning and in 1954 he became a founder member of the Tanganyika African National Union (TANU) and its first president.

Faced with a choice between teaching and politics, he chose the uncertainty of the latter. There were to be difficult days for his young wife, Maria. In July 1957, Nyerere was nominated to the Tanganyika Legislative Council (LEGCO) but resigned in December that year in protest at Britain's delaying independence.

In Tanganyika's first elections in 1958, he was elected to parliament and he was returned unopposed in the 1960 general election. He formed the first Tanganyika Council of Ministers and became the first chief minister. In May 1961, he became prime minister, resigning six weeks after independence to bridge the potential gap between the government and the party (TANU).

Tanganyika became independent on 9 December 1961 and a year later when the country became a republic, Nyerere, elected by over 96 per cent of the voters, became its first president.

For the next 24 years Nyerere was to fill the African and international stage like a colossus. When he met the astute American Secretary of State Henry Kissinger for the first time in Dar es Salaam in 1976, the two men began a mental verbal fencing match of David and Goliath proportions.

One began a quote from Shakespeare (some of whose works Nyerere translated into Swahili setting them in an African context) or a Greek philosopher and the other would end the quotation. Then Nyerere quoted an American author. Kissinger laughed: Nyerere knew Kissinger had written the words.

Neither man trusted the other. Kissinger wanted the negotiations (over Rhodesia, now Zimbabwe, and southern Africa) kept secret. Nyerere, understanding the Americans' duplicity, took the opposite view and as Africa correspondent of the London Sunday newspaper, *The Observer*, I was to become the focal point of the Tanzanians' strategic leaks. That year the newspaper led the front page on an unprecedented 13 occasions on Africa. All the leaks, as Kissinger knew, came from Nyerere. One political fox had temporarily outwitted the other.

Nyerere was both forthright and disarming. He did not tolerate fools and when a conversation had run its course the Tanzanian leader left his guest in no doubt that the meeting was over.

When he told his mother in 1985 that he had decided to retire as president her response, which he gleefully repeated, was "Julius, you are a silly boy." His decision to step down as president only added to the high regard in which he was held. Nevertheless, from that day until his death, Nyerere remained the first among equals. His endorsement was to be a vital component for any contemporary Tanzanian politician for, in truth, he never ceased to be Tanzania's leader.

In the 1995 election he formally endorsed Ben Mkapa, a former newspaper editor and foreign minister, as his choice for Tanzania's third president. One of those he had opposed observed that the "constitution" made it impossible for him to become president. By the "constitution" he said he meant Nyerere and not a written document.

In that election Nyerere refused for the only time in his life to vote for the official party's candidate in his home constituency alleging the nominee was corrupt. He mobilised the youth wing against the candidate and personally voted for the opposition who won. But in the presidential race his vote went to Mkapa.

Some would regard such an action as akin to heresy or, at best, anarchistic. Yet it was a measure of the man's firm principles that he could not bring himself to vote for someone he regarded as morally delinquent.

Another reason to remember Nyerere is the way in which he stood up to the international donors and said "No" when he believed that the course they proposed was not in his people's best interests. One wishes that today there were more leaders with his courage and mettle.

Nyerere was a charmingly forthright and visionary leader, the most forward looking politician Africa has yet seen. He also had his share of warts. But it is the man's vision and purpose, which will live on. Tanzania, which in some ways will be a more difficult place to rule without him, Africa and the world is a very much poorer place today.

Source:
David Martin, "Mwalimu Julius Kambarage Nyerere: Obituary," Southern African Research and Documentation Centre (SARDC).

David Martin, former news editor and deputy managing editor of the *Standard*, renamed *Daily News*, Dar es Salaam, Tanzania, was a founder-director of the Southern African Research and Documentation Centre (SARDC) of which Julius Nyerere was patron. He lived in Tanzania for 10 years from 1964 to 1974 and frequently talked with Nyerere through the decades, a period of 35 years, until Nyerere's last days.

APPENDIX V

Tributes to Mwalimu Julius Kambarage Nyerere From Around the World

MESSAGES PAYING TRIBUTE to Mwalimu Julius Nyerere began coming into the BBC almost from the moment the death of Tanzania's former president was announced; with numerous references made to his honesty, humility, and vision. The messages were posted on BBC News Online.

A man of the people, Julius Nyerere chose to be admitted into a common man's hospital, St Thomas, in London, for treatment of leukemia, instead of seeking treatment at a hospital for the rich and powerful - aristocrats, high government officials, and other "important" people. It is in that common man's hospital that Nyerere died on October 14, 1999. It is therefore appropriate to conclude this study with the words of ordinary people Nyerere identified with, more than anybody else, as a fitting tribute to a leader who was one of the giants of the 20th century, and one of the few in a span of centuries; and about whom millions of ordinary people simply said, "He was one of us."

Christian Sorenson, Denmark:

A true humanist, a great communicator and unifier. An African of the highest intellect. He made mistakes, but who doesn't? I admire him..

Bobana Badisang, Botswana:

In the desert wastelands of Botswana Mwalimu was an icon, a motivator and mentor. Farewell Mwalimu. Dusk has approached too soon.

Chris Chilufya Kalyamba, Zambia:

A great loss to, not only the people of Tanzania, but the whole of Africa and whole world. A champion of peace and a true Pan-Africanist. May his soul rest in peace.

Moses Rotich, South Africa:

We have lost a leader who tried his best to unite the people of Africa and the region of Great Lakes. He also showed an example to African leaders that it is good to retire and yet play very important political roles. His contribution will be hard to replace.

Gideon Kalokola, Tanzania:

It is very sad that Tanzania and indeed Africa has lost a statesman, a great son of Africa, a father of our nation....I can not think of a suitable expression, which can exhaustively describe Mwalimu Julius Kambarage Nyerere. Mwalimu Nyerere will be remembered for his dedication to serve his people by educating them and showing the way. We will always cherish all the qualities he had during his lifetime.

Kaunda Matoke, Kenya:

I grew up listening to you. The more I listened to you, the more I wanted to be you. I will always miss you Mzee. Thanks for instilling Africanism in me.

Nancy Kula, The Netherlands:

Being one of the first African presidents to willingly step down from power, I hope your high standard will be emulated by many more. We shall sorely miss your advice to Africa. Rest in peace, Mwalimu.

Nduwuisi A. Akandu, Nigeria:

Dr. Nyerere's regime was kind to my tribe (Igbos) during the Nigeria/Biafra civil war. May his soul rest in peace.

Rachel Mukwaya, Uganda:

Your relentless involvement in the struggle to liberate Uganda from dictatorial regimes will never be forgotten.

Julien Bucyabahiga, Rwanda:

He was the man of the Great Lakes Region. The death has taken him at the moment when we all needed his solutions to African problems.

K. Gebret Sadik, Canada:

He was one of the best leaders to Africa and to Tanzanians that we as Africans lost in the worst crisis in African time. Let God accept him in His heaven.

Lusako, USA:

The world has lost a true hero. May God rest his sould in eternal peace.

Dr, Bamidele A. Ojo, Nigeria/USA:

As the Executive Director of the Council for African

Affairs as well as a Nigerian and an Africanist who has been greatly influenced by Nyerere's dedication to Africa in particular, we are going to miss this great son of Africa. One remembers the greatness and the inspirations that pour from his ideas and his vision. There is only one such unique African leader alive now, Nelson Mandela; and we have lost Nyerere as he joins others like him, Kwame Nkrumah and Senghor.

Amandi Esonwanne, Nigerian in Canada:

The death of Mwalimu Nyerere is indeed a blow to Africa. He stands out as an example of what a people's leader should be. At a time that other African leaders were embezzling their country's wealth, Nyerere stood above all that and remained his people's teacher. His policy of Ujamaa may have had some shortcomings but his intention was altruistic. He ranks with people like Mandela in the annals of African history. It will be a good thing if present leaders of the continent would emulate these two great leaders.

Gift Sikaundi, Zambia:

Nyerere, you were a source of hope to the Central African region. Nobody can replace you. May your soul rest in peace.

Kobina Harleston, Sierra Leone:

A great man has passed that we Africans are proud of. I wish I could say the same for 95 percent of our African leaders who, without a doubt, love their sweethearts more than they love their countries. God I pray you bring him back for we are running short of Prophets.

Mshenga Abdy Nasseb, from Zanzibar, Tanzania:

It was such a big shock for us. I believe that this pain will be in our hearts for centuries. Losing Mwalimu Nyerere is a very big loss not only for Tanzania itself, but this is a big loss for Africa. May God put his soul in peace.

Debesay Tesfagaber, Eritrea:

It is with great sorrow that I have learned of the loss of one of the most outstanding African leaders. He was a great teacher and inspiration to many Africans including Eritreans on the principles of freedom, hard work and self-reliance. May his soul rest in peace.

Mungai Mutonya, Kenya:

Mwalimu is not dead and Mwalimu will never die. His

influence on politics, African identity, Pan-Africanism will live on for ages. A salute to you Mwalimu, your dream will carry on. As you join Nkrumah, Lumumba, Biko, Sankara, Nasser, Kenyatta in the land of our ancestors, rejoice for we the children of Africa will carry on with NYEREREISM. Accept my regards for your very positive contribution to African linguisitics. Sleep well Mwalimu - Lala salama Mwalimu. Africa loves you Mwalimu. A true African son, statesman, philosopher.

Matthieu w. Yangambi, Democratic Congolese in USA:

Dr. Nyerere is truly a big loss for the entire Africa. Africans need to see him as a highly political role model to follow, a model of love, service and compassion. May he repose in peace around the Almighty. I will pray for his soul.

Judith Busingye, Uganda:

Nyerere was a true Pan-African, a man who cared for all Africans and always tried to find ways and means to protect them. May his soul rest in peace.

Dr. Victor A. Obajuluwa, Gary, Indiana, USA:

It is a pity that while Africa continues to lose the few heroes she has, the satanic military are the faces we see like recurring decimals on the African political scene. May his humble and gentle soul rest in Peace.

Althea Campbell, Jamaica:

Tanzania has lost a great son; Africa, a great influential figure, and the world a great human being. Sleep well my friend.

Conrad Msoma, Tanzania:

Dr. Nyerere was one of the greatest leaders post-colonial Africa has ever produced. He will be remembered for his vision and determination. He was able to unite this nation, a task which we should all accomplish as respect for him.

Kenneth Gibussa, Tanzania:

Dr. Julius Kambarage Nyerere means so much to me, Tanzanians as well as for all Africa. I can't find words to describe his character. He is truly "the man of the people," and will remain the father of the nation. He was not only the leader of Tanzania but also Africa in general. Though he left us, we are sure that one day we will be together with him. We Tanzanians promise to follow your footsteps forever. Peace and unity will prevail. Amen.

O. Oduwole, Nigeria:

Adieu! Mwalimu, the great African patriot.

Beatrice A. Hamza, New York, USA:

A great Pan-African giant has fallen! This is a loss not only to those who knew him, but to generations of Africans who continue to benefit from his legacies. As a co-founder of the OAU, as a champion for the entrenchment of democracy in Africa, for his efforts to free Africa from colonialism and apartheid, he has earned the title "father of Africa"! May God grant him eternal rest!

Alemayehu Daba, United States:

Credit for the current democracy, peace and stability in Tanzania goes to the late President Nyerere. Tanzania is one of the few African countries exercising the democratic political process. We Africans have to learn from Nyerere's legacy. History is always a fair judge. Let him rest in peace.

Efosa Aruede, Nigeria:

Our dear Mwalimu is gone at 77 years and may his gentle soul rest in perfect peace. While there is a tendency to highlight the economic difficulties, which his rule foisted on Tanzania, it is pertinent to point out that he pointed the country in the right direction in many other respects. Tanzania was spared the consumer society, which characterised many post-independence African states thereby drastically reducing social problems. The simple and ascetic lifestyle of Mwalimu was always a reference point for Tanzanians. It is hoped that despite the embracing of market economics by the present rulers of Tanzania, they will not jettison all that is noble and edifying in the teachings of Mwalimu. While I wish our teacher, Nyerere, a peaceful rest, I also wish all Tanzanians and indeed all Africans and humanity a more positive and responsible social direction as envisaged by Mwalimu.

Mziwakhe John Tsabedze, Swaziland:

We Africans are victims of many tragedies, most of them unfortunately self-inflicted. Dr. Julius Nyerere, Mwalimu, remained as a shining inspiration to many of us. An inspiration that reminded us that we can rid our continent of all these tragedies. He helped us defeat apartheid. He taught us integrity, he taught us to serve our fellow citizens, he taught us to know that the measure of a leader is not how many Mercedes Benz cars he has or how many wives he has. He taught us that a leader can relinquish power and still remain influential. He taught us to listen to one another. He brought respect to the continent that, more often than not, fails to respect the rights of its people. Mwalimu will be missed but not forgotten. Be at peace Mwalimu with yourself, you have done more than was expected of you for Africa.

George Mwale, Malawi:

He was indeed a great man who set a very good but rare example of voluntarily stepping down to pave way for younger leaders. May his soul rest in eternal peace.

Frank Mathew, Tanzania:

It is difficult to believe that the father of our nation is dead. Left are the memories of the good things he did to his nation and the world at large during his life time. Tanzanians will always remember him. May God rest your soul in peace. Amen!

Primus Dias Nkwera, Tanzania:

We will never forget what you did for our country and the rest of Africa. People of your type occur once in a century... Rest in peace and help us from wherever you are now!

Hansel Ramanthal, India/USA:

My condolences go out to all Tanzanians, both at home and away. For myself, having spent most of my formative years in Tanzania, I got to see the influence that Baba wa Taifa (Father of the Nation) Nyerere had on everyone. His guidance was well respected and honoured by Tanzanians. He showed true leadership when he stepped down to make way for Ali Hassan Mwinyi. This was a single act of mature leadership and it is something rarely seen in many of the world's governments especially in Africa and Asia. I can say this much that his presence will be well missed and our prayers are with the family and nation at this time.

Ted Andemichael, USA:

Nyerere was one of the very few leaders who worked for Africa to be self-dependent. There is a lot to be learned from him.

Joshua Lichakala, Malawi:

Mwalimu, you made Tanzania a great neighbour to Malawi. Your efforts to unite the turbulent continent of Africa will be greatly missed.

Ephrem Hunde, Ethiopia:

My heartfelt condolence to all Tanzanians and fellow Africans who mourn Nyerere. We lost a great son of Africa.

Shekania Bisanda, United Kingdom:

I find it difficult to find the best words that explain him well. However, as one of the most influential statemen history has ever produced on the continent, his name will live above all others. He remains a fallen hero of his generation.

Ngahyoma, Tanzania:

Tanzania will not be the same again. However, the strong foundations of unity and love in Tanzania will live forever.

Henry O, USA:

The world has lost a true giant; the conscience of Africa.

Bjorg Evjen Olsen, Norway:

There are many Norwegians here who are saddened by the news of the death of Mwalimu J.K. Nyerere. He was very respected and loved.

George Were, Sudan:

Mwalimu Julius Kambarage Nyerere has gone down this day as a true and admirable citizen of the world. If he erred, that was only because he was human - not because he meant any harm to humanity. Yes, "mzee" was wise, honest and, I strongly believe, abhorred corruption. Did you come too early or too late for Africa? Where shall we get a replacement for this modern-time Colossus? Now we must create one out of his ideals. Is there any greater honour? To Tanzania, I mourn with you with all my heart.

James Mhagama, Tanzania:

Nyerere our brave man, you won so many battles and you fought for so many... May God retain the great wall of peace, which you built for us, stone by stone.

Gracian Tukula, Malawi:

The loss of Mwalimu Julius Nyerere goes beyond the borders of Tanzania. The story of today's freedom in the region cannot be complete without the mention of Mwalimu. He set standards his contemporaries could not match, standards, which the present generation of leaders is struggling to emulate. He deserves a peaceful rest.

Michael Mbagu, USA:

We Africans have lost one of the best figures at the turn of the century. Let us be strong in this time of grief and sorrow. Be strong and follow his steps.

I.O. Mensa-Bonsu, Switzerland:

If tears are an expression of extreme grief and sorrow, then let the tears flow in all corners of Africa, for, with the death of Mwalimu, Africa has lost its shining star.

Noel Servigon, Philippines:

As a teacher of social and political thought, I included his ujamaa ideology in my course syllabus to enrich our class discussions and provoke students to explore other ideologies.

Gebre Gebremariam, USA/Ethiopia:

It is a sad moment for Africa. It would be a proper tribute to Nyerere if some of the African leaders who are clinging to power for so long by manipulating the poltical systems of their countries could borrow a page from Nyerere's life and opt for a smooth transition of power.

Sindou Diarrasouba, USA:

Man of dignity, courage and honesty, Nyerere was an example for Africa, especially for African heads of state who stick to power, are afraid of democracy, and only care about themselves.

Evelyn Mukasa, Belgium:

Africa has lost a father. We thank you for the work you have done for us and the generations to come. The best tribute Africans and especially the leaders have to give Mwalimu is to emulate his example and to work hard for African Unity. Then the work he began would be accomplished. May the Lord bless his soul and he rest in everlasting peace. Amen.

Sigombe Paul, Uganda:

Africa and the free world will miss you Mwalimu. Humble, intelligent, and always ready to fight for freedom of the black man. Rest in peace.

Dr. J.K. Lonyangapuo, Kenya:

What a great loss to Africa as a whole. Mwalimu Nyerere must be remembered by all, and in fact the current African leaders need to complete the work started by him. They must seek ways to bring peace in the Democratic Republic of Congo and many other volatile countries.

Zakariya Suleyman, Australia:

There is no doubt that Dr. Julius Nyerere is one of the most influential leaders of this century. He was certainly the most respected in Africa. Many Africans see him as the advocate of democracy, decency and the rule of law in Africa. I wish to send my condolences to his family, friends and all Tanzanians and acknowledge that Dr. Nyerere will be remembered by many and emulated by many.

Joy Clancy, Netherlands:

The world is a poorer place today. My heart-felt sympathy to the people of Tanzania and the family of Mwalimu. If only more world leaders would demonstrate his compassion, humility and the wisdom to admit when they get things wrong.

O. Mongi and E. Mosha, Tanzania:

Mwalimu J.K. Nyerere, it is hard to accept the truth that you are gone. You will always be remembered for your guidance, honesty, dedication, and wisdom. Tanzania enjoyed peace, freedom of religion and national unity throughout because of you. Father, may God rest you in Peace.

Aida Kiangi, Tanzania:

May his soul rest in peace. In his greatness, he was humble. Africa will not forget him.

Tony Janes, UK:

Mwalimu will be greatly missed as a true world leader. His legacy is the unity and peace of Tanzania in a troubled continent.

Alex Maira, Tanzania:

To me Mwalimu was more than a father but also God's messenger of his days. I won't forget free education, free water supply services, electricity, and the like. I won't forget the peace we are enjoying this moment, unity among Tanzanians, sense of humility, which was given to us through his wisdom, love and co-operation - all these are the result of his leadership.

Tobias Mufuruki, Tanzania:

It is a big loss for Tanzania, Africa and the world that Mwalimu has left us! His wisdom and contribution towards the liberation of Africa as a whole will be remembered forever. With great sorrow I say "Kwaheri Mwalimu!" May God rest his soul in eternal peace!

Abdallah Liguo, Tanzania:

We have to believe that he is dead, but his spirit and his thoughts are still with us. May the great teacher's soul rest in peace.

Allan Shoo, Tanzanian:

I never looked at Nyerere as a president, but as a great teacher. This is very sad to me. I hope that Tanzanian leaders will follow his leadership. And I am sure God will rest his soul in geatest peace.

Said H.S. Al Dhahry, Sultanate of Oman:

Mwalimu Nyerere was the most honest, dedicated, and charismatic African leader. I and my family share Tanzania's grief and send our condolences to his family.

Carole Andrew, South Africa:

Hamba Kahle (Farewell) Julius Nyerere. A towering African philosopher and politician. A man of rare integrity. Would that there were more like him!

Esther Kasalu-Coffin, Cote D'Ivoire:

Rest in Peace. You led Tanzania with dignity, and when the time came you stepped down and gave way to others who had new ideas in the running of your country. I hope other leaders in Africa will emulate you, instead of holding on to the myth of life leadership. Africa needs more Nyereres. If there is magic on how to do this effectively on the other side, please send us some. Africa badly needs it.

Shadrack Mziray, Tanzania:

We believe that you are the one that led us to where we are. You are the father of our nation. For many, many years to come, your name shall be remembered because you were "a god of small people."

Makundi Emmanuel, University of Bergen, Norway:

He was a Great Philosopher. The Tanzanian government should consider establishing a Nyerere memorial centre in Tanzania to honour his greatness.

Ishmael Iekwape, Botswana:

Not only Tanzania has lost, Africa as a whole has lost. He played a vital role in the liberation of the people of Africa and the world at large. May his soul rest in peace.

Joshua Odeny, Kenya:

Other East African leaders should take opportunity of his death to reflect on their own popularity and performance. He was still popular 14 years since he left power because he led by example, he preached Ujamaa and practised it. In other words, "he preached water and drank water." He remains the most honest leader East Africa has ever produced. God bless Africa with another Nyerere. His type is all we ever needed.

Mike Bess, UK:

Mwalimu was a great man, ahead of his time, a visionary whose vision for Africa is accepted as the norm today, but whose vision of rural Africa was not right for the time. He had the confidence in his people and himself to hand over leadership to a new generation - something his brothers in most other African countries have never had. He was a great man, the father not only of Tanzania but of much of post-colonial Africa. He will be missed.

Abel, Kenya:

This is truly a patriot Africa has lost.... His non-corruption stand should serve as a good example to many leaders... His is an honourable exit....

Anne Lydia Sekandi, Uganda:

When someone you've known all your life dies, it sure is a tragedy. Mwalimu Nyerere is as close to the people of Uganda as to the people of Tanzania. He has been one of the fathers of the liberation of our nation. Truly, he was a great man, and should be recognised by friend and foe, even as we go into the (next) millennium.

Habte Asfaha, USA:

I extend my heartfelt condolences to the people of Tanzania at the loss of this great man, Dr. Nyerere, the Teacher and the leader. I feel the loss is also shared by all Africans, for, Dr. Nyerere was one of the few early founders of Africa.

E. Kinyangi, Kenya:

The death of Mwalimu Nyerere is indeed saddening especially to all of us who saw him as a man with a vision of a united and peaceful continent of Africa. We share this grief with our brothers and sisters in Tanzania and hope to build upon his vision in securing unity and peace in this region. May God rest his soul in eternal peace.

Yusufu-Shaft Kayima, Uganda-Sweden:

Africa has lost a geat leader! A leader who left power without force. He will always be remembered as "The Father of Africa." May Dr. Nyerere rest in peace.

Ronald Goredema, Zimbabwe:

Long live Mwalimu the great teacher. Your great works are your immortality. Thank you for teaching African leaders that there is life after power.

Source:

BBC News: Africa: E-mails Tell of Nyerere's Honesty and Humility, Thursday, October 14, 1999.

BBC News: Talking Point: Your Tributes to Julius Nyerere, Friday, October 15, 1999.

CHAPTER NOTES

Introduction

1. Ali A. Mazrui, "Nyerere and I," in *Voices*, Africa Resource Center, October 1999: Professor Ali Mazrui writes a memorial tribute on the special bonds between him and the late Mwalimu Julius Nyerere, one of Africa's few great statesmen. As he wrote in conclusion: "Julius Nyerere was my Mwalimu too. It was a privilege to learn so much from so great a man."

Chapter One

1. Ahmadu Bello, quoted by Odumegwu Ojukwu in his speech to the Organization of African Unity (OAU), seeking recognition of the secessionist region of Eastern Nigeria as the independent Republic of Biafra, in Addis Ababa, Ethiopia, August 5, 1968, in Colin Legum and John Drysdale, *Africa Contemporary Record: Annual Survey and Documents 1968 - 1969* (London: Africa Research Ltd., 1969), p. 670.

2. Northern Nigerian delegation to the Ad Hoc Conference on the Nigerian Constitution, Lagos, Nigeria, September 1966, in *Africa Contemporary Record*, ibid.

3. Odumegwu Ojukwu, ibid., p. 652.

4. Obafemi Awolowo, *Path to Nigerian Freedom* (London: Faber & Faber, 1947), chap.5. See also George Padmore, *Pan-Africanism or Communism?: The Coming Struggle for Africa* (London: Dennis Dobson, 1956), p. 276.

5. Kenneth Kaunda, quoted in *Africa Contemporary Record*, op. cit., p. 245. See also Kenneth Kaunda, in *Times of Zambia*, Lusaka, Zambia, February 1968.

6. Obafemi Awolowo, *Path to Nigerian Freedom*, op. cit.

7. Julius Nyerere, quoted by James C. McKinley Jr., "Many Failures, and One Big Success," in the *International Herald Tribune*, September 2, 1996, p. 2.

8. Ibid.

9. Julius Nyerere, quoted in *Sunday Independent*, Johannesburg, South Africa, October 17, 1999; and by R.W. Johnson, "Nyerere: A Flawed Hero," in *The National Interest*, Washington, D.C., No. 60, Summer 2000, p. 73.

On Tanzania's achievements under his leadership despite many failures, see Nyerere in R.W. Johnson, "Nyerere: A Flawed Hero," ibid. As Johnson stated: "Until the end Nyerere was proud about how well he had served Tanzanians. As he told the World Bank: 'We took over a country with 85 percent of its adults illiterate. The British ruled us for 43 years. When they left, there were two trained engineers and 12 doctors. When I stepped down there was 91 percent literacy and nearly every child was in school.

We trained thousands of engineers, doctors and teachers.'"

10. Nyerere, in his radio broadcast to the nation on the seventh anniversary of Tanzania's independence, Radio Tanzania, Dar es Salaam (RTD), December 9, 1968, quoted in *Africa Contemporary Record*, op. cit., pp. 216 - 217. See also full text of the speech released in Kiswahili, and translated into English, by the Tanzania Ministry of Information and Broadcasting, Dar es Salaam, Tanzania, December 10, 1968.

11. Nicephore D. Soglo, "Benin's Election Was A Victory for Democracy and the People," in *The Washington Post*, reprinted in the *International Herald Tribune*, August 24 - 25, 1996, p. 6.

12. Godfrey Mwakikagile, *Military Coups in West Africa since the Sixties* (Huntington, New York: Nova Science Publishers, Inc., 2001), pp. 7 - 13. See also, pp. 211 - 232.

13. Crawford Young, "The Impossible Necessity of Nigeria: A Struggle for Nationhood," in *Foreign Affairs*, November/December 1996, p. 142. See also, Wole Soyinka, *The Open Sore of A Continent: A Personal Narrative of the Nigerian Crisis* (New York: Oxford University Press, 1996).

14. Wole Soyinka, *The Open Sore of A Continent*, op. cit., p. 8; George B.N. Ayittey, *Africa in Chaos* (New York: St. Martin's Press, 1998), p. 171.

15. Soyinka, ibid. See also, "Soyinka at SOAS (Schoo of Oriental and African Studies, University of London), in *Africa Analysis: Fortnightly Bulletin of Financial and Political Trends*, London, No. 259, 1 November, 1996, p. 5.

16. Ibid.

17. Crawford Young, "The Impossible Necessity of Nigeria: A Struggle for Nationhood," in *Foreign Affairs*, op. cit., p. 143.

18. Sekou Toure, quoted in *West Africa*, July 22, 1961, p. 799. See also Julius Nyerere, "One-Party Rule," in *Spreahead*, Dar es Salaam, Tanganyika, November 1961; Nyerere, "The Role of African Trade Unions," in *Labour*, Accra, Ghana, June 1961; Gwendolen M. Carter, editor, *African One-Party States* (Ithaca, New York: Cornell University Press, 1962); Thomas Hodgkin, *African Political Parties* (Baltimore, Maryland: Penguin Books, 1961); Immanuel Wallerstein, *Africa: The Politics of Independence* (New York: Random House, 1961); Herbert J. Spiro, *Politics in*

Africa: Prospects South of the Sahara (Englewood Cliffs, New Jersey: Prentice-Hall,   1962).

See also, in his analysis of the creation of a new nation, David Apter, *The Gold Coast in Transition* (Princeton, New Jersey: Princeton University Press, 1955). And for a distinction between "mobilization" and "consociational" regimes, see David Apter, *The Political Kingdom of Uganda* (Princeton, New Jersey: Princeton University Press, 1961). See also Thomas Hodgkin, "A Note on the Language of African Nationalism," in *African Affairs*, Carbondale, Illinois, No. 1, 1961, pp. 22 - 40.

For a general comparison between Africa and other developing regions of the world, see Gabriel Almond and James S. Coleman, *The Politics of the Developing Areas* (Princeton, New Jersey: Princeton University Press, 1960); Rupert Emerson, *From Empire to Nation* (Cambridge, Massachusetts: Harvard University Press, 1960); Vera Micheles Dean, *Builders of Emerging Nations* (New York: Holt, Rinehart and Winston, 1961); Max F. Millikan and Donald L.M. Blackmer, editors, *The Emerging Nations* (Boston: Little, Brown & Co., 1961); John H. Kautsky, editor, *Political Change in Underdeveloped Countries* (New York: John Wiley & Sons, 1962); Barbara Ward, *The Rich Nations and the Poor Nations* (New York: W.W. Norton & Co., 1962).

19. Sekou Toure, in *La Lutte du Parti Democratique de Guinee pour l'Emancipation Africaine* (Conakry, Guinea: Imprimerie National, 1959), pp. 58, and 149; translated in Sekou Toure, "African Emancipation," in Paul E. Sigmund, Jr., editor, *The Ideologies of the Developing Nations* (New York: Frederick A. Praeger, 1963), pp. 154 - 169.

For an opposing view on the one-party system, see Nnamdi Azikiwe, "Parliament and Parties," and "Parliamentary Democracy," in Nnamdi Azikiwe, *Zik: A Selection from Speeches of Nnamdi Azikiwe* (New York: Cambridge University Press, 1961); Obafemi Awolowo, "A Critique of One-Party Systems," in *Awo: The Autobiography of Chief Obafemi Awolowo* (New York: Cambridge University Press, 1961); James S. Wunsch and Dele Olowu, editors, *The Failure of the Centralized State: Institutions and Self-Governance in Africa* (Boulder, Colorado: West View Press, 1996).

20. Robert S. Greenberger, "Africa Ascendant: New

Leaders Replace Yesteryear's 'Big Men,' and Tanzania Benefits,"
in *The Wall Street Journal*, December 10, 1996, pp. A1, and A5.

21. Thomas Sowell, *Race and Culture: A World View* (New
York: Basic Books, 1994).

22. Godfrey Mwakikagile, *Africa and the West*
(Huntington, New York: Nova Science Publishers, Inc., 2000).

23. Harold Cruse, *The Crisis of the Negro Intellectual*
(New York: William Morrow, 1967).

24. Harold Cruse, *Rebellion or Revolution?* (New York:
William Morrow, 1968), pp. 240 - 241. See also, Cornel West,
Race Matters (Boston, Massachusetts: Beacon Press, 1993);
Andrew Hacker, *Two Nations: Black and White, Hostile, Unequal*
(New York: Ballantine, 1992).

25. Bailey Wyat, a former slave, quoted by Hugh Pearson,
"The Birth of the New South," in *The Wall Street Journal*, June 24,
1996.

26. Ali A. Mazrui, *Towards A Pax Africana* (London:
Weidenfeld & Nicolson, 1967), p. 97.

27. Kwame Nkrumah, *Ghana: The Autobiography of
Kwame Nkrumah* (New York: Thomas Nelson and Sons, 1957).
See also Julius Nyerere, "The Rational Choice," in Andrew
Caulson, editor, *African Socialism in Practice* (Nottingham: Russel
Press, 1979), pp. 19 - 26; "False Starts: Capitalist and Socialist," in
Richard Sandbrook, *The Politics of Africa's Economic Recovery*
(Cambridge: Cambridge University Press, 1993), chap. 2; Nigel
Dower, "Is the Idea of Development Eurocentric?," in Richard
Auty and John Toye, editors, *Challenging the Orthodoxies* (New
York: St. Martin's Press, 1996), pp. 85 - 102.

The asymmetrical relationship between African countries
and the former colonial powers and other industrialized nations,
which is inherently exploitative, is analogous to the situation in the
United States where African-Americans (black Americans),
constituting a virtual colony within, are at the mercy of white
Americans because of racism, an in-built component of the
American political socio-economic system; an argument rejected
by black American conservatives such as Thomas Sowell, and
others, without any empirical evidence.

See, for example, Thomas Sowell, *Race and Economics*
(New York: Longman, 1975), and *Markets and Minorities* (New

York: Basic Books, 1981), in which he dismisses the significance of racism in the American context, contending that it is overcome by market forces in a capitalist economy because of the nature of the system which is driven by competition in the quest for profit.

This is a very myopic view, and deeply flawed analysis, which ignores the racist practices of many white business owners and employers who simply refuse to patronize or hire blacks even if it means losing them as customers or as prospective and highly productive employees. They don't need blacks because most of their customers and employees are white in a predominantly white nation. Otherwise there would have been no need for civil rights laws to open up opportunities for blacks and try to level the playing field, if market forces by themselves were enough to eliminate or effectively contain racism. They had not done that in 300 years, a simple historical fact black conservatives, for some inexplicable reason, fail to grasp.

Whites also view with apprehension the fact that they are going to be a minority within a few decades; which partly explains their siege mentality, hence their belief that they are being overwhelmed - swamped - by hordes of non-whites who must be ketp at bay. Therefore they must help only their own kind in terms of employment, housing and whatever else; nothing but feeble attempts to justify racism.

28. Tom Mboya, in *Transition*, Kampala, Uganda, Vol. 3, No. 8, March 1963, p. 17. See also Tom Mboya, *Challenge of Nationhood* (London: Heinemann, 1970); Julius Nyerere, *Freedom and Socialism: A Selection from Writings and Speeches 1965 - 1967* (Dar es Salaam, Tanzania: Oxford University Press, 1968).

29. Nnamdi Azikiwe, *Zik: A Selection from the Speeches of Nnamdi Azikiwe* (Cambridge: Cambridge University Press, 1961), p. 102.

30. Charity Ngilu, speaking in Bokoli village, Bungoma, Kenya, January 8, 2000. Quoted by Kenyan Professor Kivutha Kibwana, "Ethnic Politics: Curse or Blessing," Nairobi, Kenya, July 2001. As Kibwana states in his paper:

"I cannot resist joining debate with both Kwendo Opanga (The tribal card in the succession game plan) and Murungi Kiraitu (Gema and the politics of tribal solidarity). The question both writers were addressing is: Is it the tribe or the political party which matters in Kenya's politics and society?....

Kwendo Opanga bluntly concluded his piece by stating that he rather a political party told him what to do and not his tribe through a proxy political party. Kiraitu on the other hand concluded that tribal alliances have a key role in Kenya's politics.

If we organize politics through tribes, are we not conceding either poverty of ideas and issues or opting for a deliberate strategy of concealing our political vision or ideology? Or are we saying political parties will always be eclipsed by tribe? Should we then search for a new vehicle for our African democracy? Is President Yoweri Museveni's no-party system one of the viable alternatives? Or should we go back to the one-party model?

I think two dangerous trends are emerging in Kenya currently. We are entrenching the ethnic principle to such an extent that we shall have to live with it for many decades to come. Do we want to? All sectors of the elite including the media elite are popularizing ethnic politics. Secondly, those who attempt to shift Kenya's politics to the plane of issue politics are not encouraged and are often villified. It would therefore seem to me that a conspiracy to banish issue politics is afoot.

Interestingly, however, GEMA is not one tribe. If one can bring several tribes together through GEMA, why not do so through broad issues and a party?....

Tribal alliances are another form of trying to recreate new political parties. Frankly, Kenya needs about three or even two political parties i.e. a conservative party, a liberal party and a radical party. We have to work on reducing the 40 or so registered political parties into two or three.

If we organize on the basis of tribal alliances, we could easily encounter a stalemate if one alliance does not put together most tribes together (sic). We would be fanning secession fires. What do tribes that lose do? How are the expectations of their people to be satisfied?

Where an ethnic group comes into power after mobilizing on ethnic basis, it must satisfy its ethnic following. Can it do so and equally satisfy all other ethnic groupings?....

My personal dream - and I agree with Kwendo Opanga - is that Kenyans should develop parties of issues. We must venture beyond tribe."

The question is, how is that going to be done, in the midst of such intense ethnoregional loyalties, not only in Kenya but in other African countries as well? People talk about issues, yet mobilize forces on ethnic basis.

See also one of my books in which I address the subject, suggesting, among other things, formation of coalition governments, and reduction of the number of political parties to two or three to broaden the base of support that cuts across ethnoregional lines. With only two or three parties allowed, members of different tribes - including enemies - will have to work together as members of the only political parties they can join in the country. After all, when we talk about a multi-party system for functional purposes, we are really talking about a two-party system, *not* a system of 5, 10, 20, or 40 parties. That's nothing but chaos. And it is used to justify dictatorship or military intervention in government. Even third parties don't win elections; it's extremely rare. When was the last time the Liberal Party won a general election in Britain? Just remember that.

See Godfrey Mwakikagile, *Ethnic Politics in Kenya and Nigeria* (Huntington, New York: Nova Science Publishers, Inc., 2001).

See also, "Kenyan MPs Seeks End to Political Parties," in "BBC News: Africa," 7 December, 2000:

"A Kenyan opposition legislator has moved a motion in parliament seeking the abolishment of political parties and the creation of a partyless state.

Social Democratic Party (SDP) member for Juja, Stephen Ndicho, wants all political party activities in the country to be suspended for at least 10 years to curb tribalism.

Kenya, which has 47 (sic) tribes, ended its single party rule in 1991 and has since held two multi-party general elections.

Mr. Ndicho insisted that his motion did not advocate for a return to a single party political system but seeks to provide a stopgap measure in the country's politics to heal tribal and political divisons.

'Since the advent of multi-partism in this country in 1991, tribalism has really taken a tall order on this country,' Mr. Ndicho told the BBC. 'Every tribe in Kenya seems to be owning a political party,' he said, adding that 'if this trend continues, you can imagine Kenya will be a disintegrated country.'

The member said Kenya should borrow a leaf from Uganda where President Museveni banned political parties when he took power in 1986 in order to restore stability in a country that had been ravaged by war.

Mr. Ndicho said there was political enmity among Kenya's different party members, adding that during the 1992 and 1997 general elections, results showed that voting was done along tribal or regional lines."

Chapter Two

1. Julius K. Nyerere, in a speech delivered to the Second Pan-African Seminar, World Assembly of Youth, Dar es Salaam, Tanganyika, August 1961, in *WAY* (World Assemby of Youth) *Forum*, No. 40, September 1961; reprinted in Paul E. Sigmund, Jr., editor, *The Ideologies of the Developing Nations* (New York: Frederick A. Praeger, 1963), pp. 205, 208, and 209. See also *Tanganyika Standard*, Dar es Salaam, Tanganyika, August and September 1961.

2. Godfrey Mwakikagile, *Africa after Independence: Realities of Nationhood* (Atlanta, Georgia: Protea Publishing, 2002).

3. John Reader, *Africa: A Biography of the Continent* (New York: Alfred A. Knopf, 1998), pp. 659, 660, and 662.

4. Ibid., p. 662; Catherine Hoskyns, *The Congo since Independence: January 1960 - December 1961* (Oxford: Oxford University Press, 1965), p. 308; M. Meredith, *The First Dance of Freedom* (London: Hamish Hamilton, 1984), p. 150. See also Patrice Lumumba, *Congo: My Country* (London, 1962).

5. Quoted in Madeleine G. Kalb, *The Congo Cables: The Cold War in Africa: From Eisenhower to Kennedy* (New York: Macmillan, 1982), p. 27; J. Reader, *Africa: A Biography of the Continent*, op. cit., p. 659.

6. Adam Hochschild, *King Leopold's Ghost: A Story of Greed, Terror, and Heroism in Colonial Africa* (New York: Houghton Mifflin Co., 1998), pp. 301 - 302; Sean Kelly, *America's Tyrant: The CIA and Mobutu of Zaire* (Washington, D.C.: American University Press, 1993), pp. 57 - 60, 71, and 178.

7. Ibid. See also John Ranelagh, *The Agency: The Rise and Decline of the CIA* (New York: Simon & Schuster, 1986), p. 342; John Stockwell, *In Search of Enemies* (New York: W.W. Norton, 1978), p. 105; Report from the US Senate investigation, headed by Democratic Senator Frank Church of Idaho, into CIA covert activities against foreign leaders and governments, *Alleged Assassination Plots Involving Foreign Leaders: An Interim Report of the Select Committee to Study (US) Governmental Operations*

with Respect to Intelligence Activities, Washington, D.C., November 20, 1975.

8. Ludo de Witte, *The Assassination of Lumumba* (New York: Verso, 1999).

9. Allen Dulles, quoted by Kevin Whitelaw, "A Killing in Congo: Lumumba's Death...," in *U.S. News & World Report*, July 24, 2000, p. 63.

10. "A Killing in Congo," in *U.S. News & World Report*, ibid.; Ludo de Witte, *The Assassination of Lumumba*, op. cit. See also (US) National Security Archive: "It is possible to kill a man with bare hands, but very few are skillful enough to do it well," reads a declassified 1954 CIA "Study of Assassination" on covert activities in Guatemala. And "persons who are morally squeamish" make bad assassins. This and other CIA documents can be seen at www.gwu.edu/-nsarchiv. Choose Electronic Briefing Books, and click on "CIA and Assassinations."

11. Zaire, in *1997 Almanac: Information Please* (Boston: Houghton Mifflin Co., 1996), p. 295.

12. Government of Tanganyika, in a message to UN Secretary-General U Thant, on the assassination of President Sylvanus Olympio of Togo, in *Tanganyika Standard*, Dar es Salaam, Tanganyika, January 26, 1963; quoted by Ali A. Mazrui, *Towards A Pax Africana* (London: Weidenfeld & Nicolson, 1967), p. 123.

13. Ronald Ngala, in *Uganda Argus*, Kampala, Uganda, April 25, 1964; A.A. Mazrui, *Towards A Pax Africana*, op.cit., p. 270.

14. Julius Nyerere, "The Honour of Africa," address to the Tanzania National Assembly, December 14, 1965, before Tanzania broke off diplomatic relations with Britain the following day, the first African country to do so (followed by Ghana under Nkrumah), in J.K. Nyerere, *Freedom and Socialism: A Selection from Writings and Speeches 1965 - 1967* (Dar es Salaam, Tanzania: Oxford University Press, 1968), pp. 123 - 124.

15. *Sunday Times*, Johannesburg, October 3, 1999; R.W. Johnson, "Nyerere: A Flawed Hero," in *The National Interest*, No. 60, Washington, D.C., Summer 2000, p. 76.

16. *The Mercury*, Durban, South Africa, October 5, 1999; R.W. Johnson, "Nyerere: A Flawed Hero," ibid., pp. 67 - 68.

17. Julius Nyerere, quoted in *Sunday Times*, London, October 3, 1999; R.W. Johnson, "Nyerere: A Flawed Hero," ibid., p. 73. See also, "Farewell to the Father of Tanzania," in the *Mail and Guardian*, Johannesburg, October 15, 1999; "Julius Nyerere of Tanzania Dies; Preached African Socialism to the World," in *The New York Times*, October 15, 1999, p. B10; "Former Tanzanian President Julius Nyerere Dies at 77; African leader Led Independence Movement and Worked to Unify Nation, Continent," in *The Washington Post*, October 15, 1999, p. B-06; "Julius Nyerere: Former President of Tanzania Led Country to Independence," in the *Los Angeles Times*, October 15, 1999, p. 30.

18. Hackman Owusu-Agyemang, "Tribute to Dr. Julius Nyerere: Death Has Robbed Africa of A Leading Light," in *The Independent*, Accra, Ghana, October 27, 1999. See also "Tanzania Mourns Its 'Teacher'; Nyerere Remembered as A Leader Who Unified the Nation, " in *The Washington Post*, October 22, 1999, p. A-25.

Chapter Three

1. Arthur Wille, "Maryknoll and Politics in Tanzania," Maryknoll Fathers & Brothers Africa Region, 2002.

2. Kwame Nkrumah, *Ghana: The Autobiography of Kwame Nkrumah* (New York: Nelson & Sons, 1957).

3. Julius Nyerere, in an interview with Ikaweba Bunting, "The Heart of Africa: Interview with Julius Nyerere on Anti-Colonialism," in *New Internationalist*, Issue 309, January-February 1999.

4. Ibid.

5. Nyerere, quoted by Arthur Wille, "Maryknoll and Politics in Tanzania," op. cit.

6. Arthur Wille, ibid.

7. Ibid.

8. Julius Nyerere, "Africa's Place in the World," Wellesley College *Symposium on Africa* (Wellesley, Massachusetts, 1960), p. 15; cited by Ali A. Mazrui, *Towards A Pax Africana* (London: Weidenfeld & Nicolson, 1967), p. 14. As Nyerere stated at the symposium: "One need not go into the history of colonization, but that colonization had one significant result. A sentiment was created on the African continent - a sentiment of oneness."

See also: Colin Legum and Geoffrey Mmari, editors, *Mwalimu: The Influence of Nyerere* (Trenton, New Jersey: Africa World Press, 1995); Shirley Graham DuBois, *Julius K. Nyerere: Teacher of Africa* (Julian Messner); Bert Thomas, *The Struggle for Liberation: From DuBois to Nyerere* (Desomd a Reid Enterprises, 1982); John Charles Hatch, *Two African Statesmen: Kaunda of Zambia and Nyerere of Tanzania* (London: Secker & Warburg, 1976).

Chapter Four

1. Issa Shivji, cited by Ronald Aminzade, "The Politics of Race and Nation: Citizenship and Africanization in Tanganyika," Department of Sociology, University of Minnesota, December 2, 1998. See also Issa Shivji, *Class Struggles in Tanzania* (New York: Monthly Review Press, 1976); Issa Shivji, *Tanzania: The Silent Class Struggle* (Lund: Zenit, 1971); and the East Africana Collection, University of Dar es Salaam Library, Dar es Salaam, Tanzania.

2. Julius Nyerere, in *Tanganyika National Assembly Debates* (Hansard), Official Report, Thirty-Sixth Session (Fifth Meeting), October 17 - 18, 1961, p. 335; R. Aminzade, "The Politics of Race and Nation: Citizenship and Africanization in Tanganyika," op. cit.

3. Julius Nyerere, quoted by Judith Listowel, *The Making of Tanganyika* (New York: London House and Maxwell, 1965), p. 401. See also James Clagett Taylor, *The Political Development of Tanganyika* (Stanford: Stanford University Press, 1963), pp. 133 - 134.

4. Julius Nyerere, in *Tanganyika National Assembly Debates*, op. cit., p. 333. See also *Tanganyika Standard*, Dar es Salaam, Tanganyika, October 1961.

5. Mtaki, in *Tanganyika National Assembly Debates*, ibid., pp. 310 - 313.

6. Christopher Kasanga Tumbo, ibid., pp. 313 - 317.

7. Michael Kamaliza, ibid., p. 364.

8. John Mwakangale, ibid., pp. 329 - 330.

9. Krishna, ibid., p. 326.

10. Julius Nyerere, cited by Ronald Aminzade, "The Politics of Race and Nation: Citizenship and Africanization in Tanganyika," op. cit.

11. Julius Nyerere, in *Tanganyika National Assembly Debates*, op. cit., pp. 333 - 334.

12. Wambura, ibid.

See also, Julius K. Nyerere, *Freedom and Unity* (Dar es salaam, Tanzania: Oxford University Press, 1966); Colin Legum and Geoffrey Mmari, editors, *Mwalimu: The Influence of Nyerere* (Trenton, New Jersey: Africa World Press, 1995); M. H. Kaniki, editor, *Tanzania Under Colonial Rule* (Nairobi, Kenya: Longman, 1980); John Charles Hatch, *Two African Statesmen: Kaunda of Zambia and Nyerere of Tanzania* (London: Secker & Warburg, 1976); W.E. Smith, *Nyerere of Tanzania* (Nairobi, Kenya: TransAfrica Publishers, 1974).

Chapter Five

1. Colin Legum, *Pan-Africanism: A Short Political Guide* (New York: Frederick A. Praeger, 1965), see texts of declarations of the Ghana-Guinea union, and the Ghana-Guinea-Mali union, appendices 6 and 12.

2. Haroub Othman, "The Union with Zanzibar," in Colin Legum and Geoffrey Mmari, editors, *Mwalimu: The Influence of Nyerere* (Trenton, New Jersey: Africa World Press, 1995), p. 173.

3. Frank Carlucci, quoted by Haroub Othman, "The Union with Zanzibar," ibid.

4. Haroub Othman, ibid., pp. 173 - 174.

5. Benjamin Mkapa, in his national broadcast on Radio Tanzania, Dar es Salaam (RTD), announcing the death of Julius Nyerere, quoted by the Associated Press (AP), October 14, 1999.

6. Benjamin Mkapa, quoted in "Tanzania: IRIN Focus on the Union," October 28, 1999.

7. Ali A. Mazrui, "Nyerere and I," in *Voices*, Africa Resource Center, 1999.

8. Julius Nyerere, in *The New York Times*, December 19, 1961; Ali A. Mazrui, *Towards A Pax Africana* (London: Weidenfeld & Nicolson, 1967), p. 77.

9. Julius K. Nyerere, "Nationalism and Pan-Africanism," in *WAY Forum*, No. 40, September 1961; and in Paul E. Sigmund, Jr., editor, *The Ideologies of the Developing Nations* (New York: Frederick A. Praeger, 1963), pp. 208, and 209.

10. Julius K. Nyerere, "Policy on Foreign Affairs," in J.K. Nyerere, *Freedom and Socialism: A Selection from Writings and Speeches 1965 - 1967* (Dar es Salaam, Tanzania: Oxford University Press, 1968), p. 369.

11. Ann Talbot, "Nyerere's Legacy of Poverty and Repression in Zanzibar," in "World Socialist Web Site: WSWS: News & Analysis: Africa," International Committee of the Fourth Internationale (ICFI), London, November 15, 2000.

12. Abdulrahman Babu, "The 1964 Revolution: Lumpen or Vanguard?", in Abdul Sheriff and Ed Ferguson, editors, *Zanzibar Under Colonial Rule* (Athens, Ohio: Ohio University Press, 1991).

See also, A. M. Babu, *African Socialism or Socialist Africa* (Dar es Salaam, Tanzania: Tanzania Publishing House, 1981).

13. Jorge Castaneda, *Companero: The Life and Death of Che Guevara* (New York: Alfred A. Knopf, 1997), pp. 326 - 327, and 328.

14. Gamal Nkrumah, "The Legacy of A Great African," in *Al-Ahram Weekly*, Issue No. 452, Cairo, Egypt, 21 - 27 October 1999.

15. Jim Lobe, "Tanzania: Restiveness in Zanzibar," in *Foreign Policy Focus: Self-Determination*, 2 May 2001.

16. Averill Harriman, "Telegram from the Embassy in Nigeria to the Department of State/1/," Lagos, Nigeria, March 25, 1964, 7 p.m., in US Diplomatic Archives: Nigeria (1964 - 1968), *Foreign Relations of the United States 1964 - 1968, Vol. XXIV Africa*, US Department of State, Washington, D.C. Source: Johnson Library, National Security File, International Meetings and Travel File, Africa, Box 31, Harriman's Trip, 3/64. Confidential; Priority; Passed to the White House.

17. Averill Harriman, in *Foreign Relations of the United States 1964 - 1968*, op. cit.; Kevin kelly, "How Communism Affected US Policy in East Africa," in *The East African*, Nairobi, Kenya, December 6, 1999.

18. US State Department document, February 7, 1964, in *Foreign Relations of the United States 1964 - 1968*, op. cit.

19. Julius Nyerere, in the *East African Standard*, Nairobi, Kenya, February 13, 1964; Ali A. Mazrui, *Towards A Pax Africana*, op. cit., p. 153.

20. Ronald Aminzade, "The Politics of Race and Nation: Citizenship and Africanization in Tanganyika," Department of Sociology, University of Minnesota, December 2, 1998. See also *Tanganyika Standard*, Dar es Salaam, Tanganyika, January 22, 1964; *Tanganyika Standard*, January 23, 1964, on the mutiny.

On the incendiary debate on Africanization in the preceding years, which led up to the mutiny in January 1964, see also, *Mwafrika*, Dar es Salaam, Tanganyika, October 4, 1960, a newspaper published in Kiswahili. The Minister of Labour Derek Bryceson, a British who settled in Tanganyika in 1951, said in parliament that Tanganyikans of Asian and European origin should also be considered as Africans, and defined as such; to which leaders of the opposition African National Congress (ANC) responded: "The meaning of Tanganyikans is Africans with black skins."

See also Tanganyika Council Debates (LEGCO - Legislative Council - Debates), speech of Bhoke Munanka, October 13, 1960: "Africanisation means Africanisation, it does not in any way suggest localisation (to include local Asian and European Tanganyikans and other non-blacks together with African Tanganyikans)"; *Ngurumo*, Dar es Salaam, Tanganyika, 3 - 4 November 1960, another Kiswahili newspaper containing reports on the heated debate on Africanization, and definition of "Africans."

Besides Zuberi Mtemvu, leader of the opposition African National Congress (ANC) and others in parliament, another ardent and uncompromising advocate of rapid Africnization was Christopher Kasanga Tumbo, former trade union leader and member of parliament who resigned from his position as high commissioner (ambassador) to Britain and returned to Tanganyika in August 1962 to form the People's Democratic Party (PDP). The PDP's leading and founding members included several ANC activists, and the party advocated racial policies on citizenship, Africanization, and on minorities - Asians, Europeans, Arabs and other non-blacks - contrary to what TANU said, and objected to clauses of the new republican constitution, "which made the president a virtual dictator." See *Tanganyika Standard*, Dar es Salaam, Tanganyika, January 9, 1963.

21. In early January 1963, the PDP leaders met to discuss plans to merge with the ANC. See *Tanganyika Standard*, Dar es Salaam, Tanganyika, January 4, 1963; *Tanganyika Standard*, January 18, 1963, in which it was reported that the opposition parties, including AMNUT (All-Muslim National Union of Tanganyika), demanded a referendum on the one-party system.

See also Julius Nyerere, in a letter to all the cabinet members and their ministries, January 7, 1964, against Africanization: "The nation must use the entire reservoir of skill and experience.... The skin in which this skill is encased is completely irrelevant.... This means that discrimination in civil service employment as regards recruitment, training, and promotion must be brought to an end immediately.... We cannot allow the growth of first and second-class citizenship. Africanization is dead." In the *Tanganyika Standard*, Dar es salaam, Tanganyika, January 8, 1964.

Trade union leaders objected vehemently to this directive from President Nyerere. Teendwa Washington, leader of the Local Government Union, accused Nyerere of taking Tanganyika "back to the colonial days." See *Tanganyika Standard*, Dar es Salaam, Tanganyika, January 9, 1964.

Almost exactly two weeks later, on January 20, after Nyerere issued his policy directive against Africanization, the army mutinied over this very policy, demanding higher salaries and the replacement of British army officers by black ones in pursuit of full Africanization of the armed forces.

21. US State Department background paper, February 7, 1964, in *Foreign Relations of the United States 1964 - 1968*, op. cit.

22. Ulric Haynes, in a National Security Councuil memo, June 8, 1966, in *Foreign Relations of the United States 1964 - 1968*, op. cit.

23. Julius Nyerere, "Principles and Development," in J.K. Nyerere, *Freedom and Socialism: A Selection from Writings and Speeches 1965 - 1967* (Dar es Salaam, Tanzania: Oxford University Press, 1968), pp. 202 - 203.

24. Julius Nyerere, "Rhodesia in the Context of Southern Africa," in *Foreign Affairs*, New York, April 1966; J.K. Nyerere, *Freedom and Socialism*, op. cit., pp. 143, 154 - 155, and 156.

25. J.K. Nyerere, on the Warsaw Pact invasion of Czechoslovakia, August 1968.

26. J.K. Nyerere, "Policy on Foreign Affairs," in Nyerere, *Freedom and Socialism*, op. cit., pp. 370, and 371.

27. J.K. Nyerere, ibid., p. 203.

28. Ibid., p. 202.

29. Samir Amin, "The First Babu Memorial Lecture," London, September 22, 1997. See also Abdulrahman Mohammed Babu, "A New Europe: Consequences for Tanzania," in the *Review of African Political Economy*, Vol. 18, No. 50, Spring 1991, pp. 75 - 78. Mohamed Suliman and A.M. Babu, "Face to face with A.M. Babu," in the *Review of Aprican Political Economy*, vol. 22, No. 66, December 1995, pp. 596 - 598.

30. Ali A. Mazrui, in "Africa's Mwalimu: Ali Mazrui Pays Tribute to Julius Nyerere," in *Washington Magazine*, Washington, D.C., Vol. 12, No. 4, Fall 1999; Ali A. Mazrui, "Mwalimu Rise to Power," in the *Daily Nation*, Nairobi, Kenya, October 17, 1999; Ali A. Mazrui, "Nyerere and I," in *Voices*, Africa Resource Centre, October 1999.

31. Julius K. Nyerere, in an interview with M.A. Novicki and B. Boorstein, in *Africa Report*, November 30, 1985, p. 10. See also Pal Ahluwalia and Abebe Zegeye, "Multiparty Democracy in Tanzania: Crises in the Union," in *Africa Security Review*, Vol. 10, No. 3, 2001; Martin Bailey, "Union of Tanganyika and Zanzibar: A Study in Political Integration" (Syracuse, New York: Syracuse University, June 1973).

32. Julius Nyerere, during the 40th anniversary of Ghana's independence, Accra, Ghana, March 1997.

33. Julius Nyerere, quoted by Austin Ejiet, "Kwa heri, Mtukufu Rais Julius K. Nyerere," in *The Monitor*, Kampala, Uganda, October 17, 1999. See also A. Ejiet, Ibid.:

"Three things sum up Mwalimu Julius Nyerere for me. Sometime in the mid-sixties (sic) a Swiss bank wrote offering to keep his money in a secret-coded account at extremely generous interest rates.... But far from jumping at the offer, the president published the letter in the national newspapers with the memorable declaration that he had no money to hide and that the little that he had could only be banked in Tanzania where it belonged....This action underscored the president's faith in his country and spoke volumes about the extent of his sincerity.

Shortly after this, a type of precious stone was unearthed in Tanzania. The country's parliament unanimously resolved to name this gem the 'Nyeretrite' in recognition of his stature as a statesman locally as well as internationally. The president thanked his countrymen for their kind consideration but politely declined the honour. Instead he proposed that the stone be named the 'Tanzanite.' Tanzania, he aruged, was more important than individuals.

Just one more. Mwalimu Julius Nyerere paid a visit to Ghana shortly after his retirement in 1985 and reportedly berated the leadership of that country for the shabby way in which the republic's founder, Kwame Nkrumah, had been treated."

34. Julius K. Nyerere, in "The Heart of Africa: Interview with Julius Nyerere on Anti-Colonialism," in *New Internationalist*, Issue 309, January-February 1999.

The interviewer was Ikaweba Bunting, an African-American who had lived in Tanzania for 25 years when he interviewed Nyerere. As he stated:

"In recognition of Nyerere's passing, I present his last great interview. The first issue of *The Internationalist* in 1970 had as its cover story an interview with President Julius Nyerere of Tanzania, then at the very centre of the new movement for world development. Three decades on, Nyerere is, Mandela aside, Africa's most respected elder statesperson, still active in attempts to resolve the current conflicts in Burundi and DR Congo. No one is better placed to look back on the anti-colonial century....

It has been my privilege to be associated with Mwalimu Nyerere for the past 25 years. During a visit to Harlem, New York, in the late 1960s Mwalimu extended an invitation to Africans in the Diaspora to come to Tanzania and participate in building a socialist African state. I came over through a new organization called the Pan-African Skills project and have lived in Tanzania ever since, for a quarter of the century.

Nyerere's Tanzania was a magnet for anti-colonial activists and thinkers from all over the world. Uganda's President Yoweri Museveni, for instance, was deeply influenced by his time as a student at the University of Dar es Salaam. Museveni belonged to a study group led by the Guyanan Walter Rodney, who wrote his seminal book *How Europe Underdeveloped Africa* while he was a professor there.

The University of Dar es Salaam became the centre for the guerrilla-intellectuals and activists of African liberation movements. FRELIMO of Mozambique, the ANC and PAC of South Africa, ZANU and ZAPU of Zimbabwe, the MPLA of Angola and SWAPO of Namibia all had offices and training camps in Tanzania. The country also gave safe haven to US civil-rights activists, Black Panther Party-members and Vietnam War resisters.

It was an exciting place to be. Under a head of state who valued equal rights, justice and development more than pomp and power of office, Tanzania was at the heart of the anti-colonial struggle.

Over the years I have often been able to sit with Mwalimu and reflect on Africa's struggle for self-determination and development. Now, in December 1998, prompted by the *New Internationalist* special issue on the Radical Twentieth Century, Mwalimu Nyerere and I sat down over two days at his home in Butiama, Tanzania, and reflected on his role over the past 50 years as an activist and statesperson in the anti-colonial cause."

Nyerere's awakening started early when he was a student at Makerere University College, Kampala, Uganda, which was then and for many years the most renowned institution of higher learning in colonial Africa, attracting students from all parts of the continent. As he stated in the same interview:

"At Makerere in 1943 I started something called the Tanganyika African Welfare Association. Its main purpose was not political or anti-colonial. We wanted to improve the lives of Africans. But inside us something was happening.

I wrote an essay in 1944 called The Freedom of Women. I must be honest and say I was influenced by John Stuart Mill, who had written about the subjugation of women. My father had 22 wives and I knew how hard they had to work and what they went through as women. Here in this essay I was moving towards the idea of freedom theoretically. But I was still in the mindset of improving the lives and welfare of Africans: I went to Tabora to start teaching.

Then came Indian independence. The significance of India's independence movement was that it shook the British empire. When Gandhi succeeded I think it made the British lose the will to cling to empire. But it was events in Ghana in 1949 that fundamentally changed my attitude. When Kwame Nkrumah was released from prison this produced a transformation.... First India in 1947, then Ghana in 1949.... Under the influence of these events, while at university in Britain, I made up my mind to be a full-time political activist when I went back."

Nyerere was 27 years old in 1949, and 21 when he founded the Tanganyika African Welfare Association at Makerere University College in 1943.

Chapter Six

1. Alburto-Joaquim Chipande, "Massacre of Mueda," in Eduardo Mondlane, *The Struggle for Mozambique* (Middlesex: Penguin Books, Ltd., 1969), p. 117. See also Thomas H. Henriksen, *Revolution and Counterrevolution* (London: Greenwood Press, 1983), p. 19.

2. Richard Gibson, *African Liberation Movements: Contemporary Struggles Against White Minority Rule* (New York: Ocford University Press, 1972), p. 277.

3. Eduardo Mondlane, in his report on his tour of Mozambique, cited on this web site: www.palgrave.com/pdfs/0333920015.pdf. See also Eduardo Mondlane, *The Struggle for Mozambique*, op. cit.

4. Ibid.

5. www.palgrave.com/pdfs/0333920015.pdf.

6. Thomas Byrne, ibid.

7. Ibid.

8. Thomas H. Henriksen, *Mozambique: A History* (Southampton: Camelot Press, 1978), p. 172.

9. Philemon Sarungi, in "Remains of Fallen Heroes to be Returned," in *Daily News*, Dar es Salaam, Tanzania, July 12, 2002.

10. Mwelwa C. Musambachime, Permanent Mission of the Republic of Zambia to the United Nations, "Memorial to Mwalimu Nyerere on his 80th Birthday," April 15, 2002.

See also Barbara Cornwall, *The Bush Rebels: A Personal Account of Black Revolt in Africa* (New York: Henry Holt & Co., 1972); Luis B. Serapiao, *Mozambique in the Twentieth Century: From Colonialism to Independence* (Maryland: University Press of America, 1979); M.D.D. Newitt, *A History of Mozambique* (Bloomington, Indiana: Indiana University Press, 1995).

Chapter Seven

1. Richard Coggins, "Rhodesian UDI and the British Government 1964 - 1970," Queen's College, Oxford University, Oxford, United Kingdom. See also, "Rhodesian Crisis: Legal Issues: Constitution Test Case Appeal," in *Africa Research Bulletin, Vol. V, 1968*, p. 957 et seq.; "Constitutional Proposals: Constitutional Commission Reports," in *Africa Research Bulletin*, ibid., p. 1046 et seq.; Colin Legum and John Drysdale, *Africa Contemporary Record: Annual Survey and Documents 1968 - 1969* (London: Africa Research Ltd., 1969), pp. 689 - 711; *The Economist*, October 12, 1968.

2. Ken Flower, *Serving Secretly: Rhodesia's CIO Chief on Record* (Galago: 1989).

3. Akwasi A. Afrifa, *The Ghana Coup* (London: Cass, 1967); A.K. Ocran, *A Myth is Broken: An Account of the Ghana Coup D'etat of 24th February 1966* (London: Longmans, 1968).

4. Colin Legum, "Witness Seminar on Rhodesian UDI: Commentary by Colin Legum," Public Record, Kew, 6 September 2000.

5. Ibid. See also, *Africa Contemporary Record*, op. cit., pp. 370 - 383.

6. *Africa Contempoary Record*, ibid., p. 220.

7. S.A. Melville, ibid., p. 291.

8. P.W. Botha, ibid.

9. *Africa Research Bulletin, Vol. V*, p. 937 et seq.; "Rhodesian Crisis: Legal Issues," in *Africa Contemporary Record*, ibid., pp. 689 - 690. See also, Claire Palley, "No Majority Rule Before 1999," in *The Guardian*, London, November 14, 1968; "We Want Our Country!" in *Time*, November 5, 1965: "They were black...more than 6,000 of them....'Mambokadzi tinoda nyika yehu!' roared the black Rhodesians who had come to greet Harold Wilson last week. 'Your Majesty the Queen, we want our country!'"

10. Julius K. Nyerere, "The Honour of Africa," in J.K. Nyerere, *Freedom and Socialism: A Selection from Writings and Speeches 1965 - 1967* (Dar es Salaam, Tanzania: Oxford

University Press, 1968), pp. 115 - 133; *The Nationalist*, Dar es salaam, Tanzania, December 15, 1968; *Standard*, Dar es Salaam, Tanzania, December 15, 1968.

11. Reuben Kamanga, quoted in *Africa Contemporary Record*, op. cit., p. 372. See also *The Times of Zambia*, Lusaka, Zambia, March 1966.

12. Ian Smith, quoted in *Africa Contemporary Record*, ibid., p. 372.

13. Privy Council, ibid.

14. Julius K. Nyerere, "Rhodesia in the Context of Southern Africa," in *Foreign Affairs*, Council on Foreign Relations, New York, April 1966; J.K. Nyerere, *Freedom and Socialism*, op. cit., pp. 143 - 156.

See also Paul Redfern, "How Nyerere Tried to Stop Britain Arming South Africa in the '70s," in *The East African*, Nairobi, Kenya, February 19, 2001.

15. John Kamau, "Anti-Mugabe Sanctions Hypocritical," in the *Daily Nation*, Nairobi, Kenya, February 22, 2002.

16. Reginald Mhango, "Mugabe: Teaching White Rhodesians A Final Lesson or Two," in *The Guardian*, Dar es Salaam, Tanzania, March 15, 2002.

President Benjamin Mkapa of Tanzania was one of Mugabe's staunchest allies and one of his biggest supporters during and after the controversial March 2002 presidential election in Zimbabwe.

17. George Shire, "The Struggle for Our Land: Britain is Interfering in Zimbabwe in Support of Corporate Power and A Wealthy White Minority," in *The Guardian*, London, January 24, 2002.

Chapter Eight

1. Mallam Muhammadu Maude Gyari, quoted in Colin Legum and John Drysdale, *Africa Contemporary Record: Annual Survey and Documents 1968 - 1969* (London: Africa Research Ltd., 1969), p. 664.

2. Julius K. Nyerere on why Tanzania recognized Biafra, published by the Government of Tanzania, Dar es Salaam, Tanzania, April 13, 1968, and issued by the Ministry of Information and Broadcasting, Dar es Salaam; also published in *The Nationalist*, and the *Standard*, Dar es Salaam, Tanzania, April 13, 1968.

3. Julius K. Nyerere, "Why We Recognised Biafra," in *The Observer*, London, April 28, 1968.

4. George Ayittey, *Africa in Chaos* (New York: St. Martin's Press, 1998), pp. 170 - 171; *New African*, April 1994, p. 8.

5. Ken Saro Wiwa, in one of his last interviews, in the *Guardian*, Lagos, Nigeria, October 31, 1995. See also the Niger Delta Congress on the campaign for minority rights, and for some of Ken Saro Wiwa's statements.

6. Christopher Clapham, "Rethinking African States," in *Africa Security Review*, Vol. 10, No. 3, 2001. See also Sam G. Amoo, "The Challenge of Ethnicity and Conflicts in Africa: The Need for A New Paradigm," United Nations Development Programme (UNDP), New York, January 1997.

7. Odumegwu Ojukwu, quoted in "Biafra: Thirty Years On," in BBC News: Africa, London, January 13, 2000.

8. Ojukwu, on remembering Biafra and the civil war, in an interview with *USAfrica*, Houston, Texas, August-September 1999.

9. Ojukwu, in an interview with Paul Odili, "Ojukwu at 68 on State of the Nation: Why We Can't Have Peace Now," in the *Vanguard*, Lagos, Nigeria, November 4, 2001.

10. Ibid.

11. Sam G. Amoo, "The Challenge of Ethnicity and Conflicts in Africa: The Need for A New Paradigm," United

Nations Development Programme (UNDP), New York, January 1997.

See also Christopher Clapham, professor of politics and international relations, Lancaster University, UK, "Rethinking African States," in *Africa Security Review*, Vol. 10, No. 3, 2001; Francis M. Deng, editor, *Sovereignty as Responsibility: Conflict Management in Africa* (Washington, D.C.: The Brookings Institution, 1996); Francis M. Deng and I. William Zartman, editors, *Conflict Resolution in Africa* (Washington, D.C.: The Brookings Institution, 1991); Alexander A. Madiebo, *The Nigerian Revolution and the Biafran War* (Enugu, Nigeria: Fourth Dimension Publishers, 1980); John De St. Jorre, *The Nigerian Civil War* (London: Hodder and Stoughton, 1972).

See also Chukwuemeka Odumegwu Ojukwu, *Biafra: Selected Speeches and Random Thoughts*:

"It is worthwhile mentioning here that following the abduction and massacre of the Supreme Commander (General J.T.U. Aguiyi Ironsi), the intention of (Yakubu) Gowon and his fellow Northerners was to secede. Gowon, in fact, personally told me over the phone - and the conversation was duly recorded - that the North wanted to secede. Much as the idea shocked me at the time, I told him that if that would lead to peace, they could go ahead....

A speech had been prepared for him, announcing secession of the North.... There is evidence that the British High commissioner in Lagos, after expounding to Gowon the opportunities now offered to him and the Northern people for the domination of Nigeria, also assured Gowon of the British government's pledge to give him support to maintain that domination. As a result, the speech as finally delivered by Gowon bore traces of very hasty amendment and edition which did not conceal the real underlining reason for the mutiny (of July 1966 in which Ironsi was overthrown and assassinated by Northern Nigerian soldiers) - and that the basis of unity in Nigeria did not exist."

Ojukwu's claim that Northern Nigerians wanted to secede in July 1966 after Nigeria's first military of head of state, General Ironsi, an Igbo, was assassinated by Northern army officers, and that Gowon was not supposed to be the next military head of state, is supported by others including Ojukwu's nemesis and former military later civilian head of state Olusegun Obasanjo, who also - as a senior army commander - perpetrated some of the worst atrocities against the Igbos during the civil war (1967 - 1970). As he states in his book, *My Command*:

"The coup planners (of july 29, 1966) were unwilling to hand over to Brigadier Ogundipe (a Yoruba like Obasanjo himself), who was then the Chief of Staff, Supreme Headquarters, and the highest ranking officer in the absence of the Supreme Commander (General Aguiyi Ironsi who had been assassinated). They slighted him also because in their eyes (as Northerners) he was somebody who 'did not belong' (as a Southerner). Ogundipe realized that he could not effectively command the Army... He realized he would not be able to control the chaotic and confusing situation and arrest the imminent break-off of the North. He was made quietly and gracefully to exchange, with Lieutenant-Colonel Gowon, the post he should have assumed for the peaceful job of the Nigerian High Commissioner (Ambassador) in London. At that time, Lieutenant-Colonel Gowon was (at 33) the most senior Army officer of Northern origin...."

See also Wole Soyinka who, although a Yoruba, once supported Biafra and was imprisoned for his political activism. As he says about the massacre of the Igbos in 1966 which forced them to withdraw from the feferation, in his prison diaries published in 1972 as a book, *The Man Died*:

"The ATROCITIES were so public even in the South (Lagos, the federal capital and territory in Yorubaland in southwestern Nigeria)... Executions and torture (of the Igbos)...were common daylight occurrences known to Yakubu Gowon (then already military head of state). As for the events in the North - let us simply sum it up and say that ATROCITIES did take place on a scale so vast and so thorough, and so well-organized that it was variously referred to as the Major Massacres - as distinct from the May rehearsals, genocide, and sometimes only as disturbances and - this gem is by Ukpabi Asika - a state of anomie!"

See also Brigadier Victor Banjo, speaking with Wole Soyinka in Enugu in 1967, in *The Man Died:*

"The Igbo were not a danger to anyone. The May and July

murders (in 1966) had sapped their capacity to make any serious trouble. What explanations did you people have to keep you so silent in the face of those damnable days of September and October (1966)?

What happened to all you people in the West (you Yorubas)? Otegbeye and all those people who are never off the pages of the newspapers. Not a word of condemnation from anyone. No protest to Gowon (then head of state), not even a student demonstration, not one act of solidarity with the victims. How did the rest of the country expect them (Igbos) not to feel cut off?"

On May 30, 1967, the Igbos and other Eastern Nigerians finally severed ties with the rest of the federation and declared independence as the Republic of Biafra. The ensuing war cost them at least 1 million lives, some say up to 2 million.

Chapter Nine

1. Idi Amin, on Radio Uganda, Kampala, Uganda, January 25, 1971; *Uganda Argus*, Kampala, Uganda, January 26, 1971. See also *The Nationalist*, and the *Standard*, Dar es Salaam, Tanzania, January 26, 1971; *Daily Nation*, and *The East African Standard*, Nairobi, Kenya, January 26, 1971.

2. Linda de Hoyos, "Idi Amin: London Stooge Against Sudan," in the *Executive Intelligence Review*, June 9, 1995, pp. 52 - 53. See also George Ivan Smith, *Ghosts of Kampala: The Rise and Fall of Idi Amin* (New York: HarperCollins, 1980).

3. Milton Obote, quoted in *Executive Intelligence Review*, ibid.

4. Ali A. Mazrui, "Nyerere and I," in *Voices*, Africa Resource Center, October 1999.

5. Henry Kyemba, quoted by Wairagala Wakabi, "Idi Amin Just Won't Go Away," in *The Black World Today*, Maryland, USA, April 30, 1999. See also Henry Kyemba, *State of Blood: The Inside Story of Idi Amin* (New York: Putnam, 1977).

6. Brigadier Moses Ali, quoted by Wairagala Wakabi, "Idi Amin Just Won't Go Away," ibid.

7. Edward Heath's remarks to Obote, Nyerere, and Kaunda, during the Commonwealth conference in Singapore, January 1971, quoted in "The Making of Idi Amin," in *New African*, London, February 2001.

8. *The Daily Express*, London, January 1971.

9. *The Daily Telegraph*, London, January 1971.

10. *The Times*, London, January 1971.

11. Quoted in *New African*, op. cit.

12. Pat Hutton and Jonathan Bloch, "The Making of Idi Amin," People's News Service, 1979; *New African*, ibid. British gvernment documents, declassified at the end of the 1990s under the 30-year rule, verify earlier accounts by journalists Pat Hutton and Jonathan Bloch which said the coup by Idi Amin against Dr. Milton Obote was engineered by outside powers - Britain, Israel, and the United States. Sky News, the London-based satellite TV channel, also quoted from one of the British documents in which

the Foreign Office in London had said, "Amin was reliable."

13. *The Economist*, August 1972. See also Ralph Uwechue, editor, *Africa Today* (London: Africa Books Ltd., 1996), pp. 1554 - 1557; Jeffrey T. Strate, *Post-Military Coup Strategy in Uganda: Amin's Early Attempts to Consolidate Political Support in Africa* (1973); Phares Mutibwa, *Uganda since Independence: A Story of Unfulfilled Hopes* (Lawrenceville, New Jersey: Africa World Press, 1992).

14. Bernard Rwehururu, in "Fighting for Amin: A Career Soldier Recalls His Thankless Task," in *The East African African*, Nairobi, Kenya, April 8, 2002. Colonel Bernard Rwehururu's *Cross to the Gun*, was first published by *The Monitor*, Kampala, showing - in a series of articles - a professional army being humiliated and defeated by young boys in the Tanzanian army, the Tanzania People's Defence Forces, popularly known as TPDF. Tanzania committed 50,000 troops to combat, led by a general. See also Colonel Bernard Rwehururu, "Defeated by Small Boys," in *The East African*, Nairobi, Kenya, April 15, 2002:

"After less than a week of fighting, some of the troops of the First Infantry Regiment who had replaced us at the front line started arriving at our barracks with their equipment, but did not give any reasons for their abrupt withdrawal from the battlefield. A few days later, Abdallatif himself arrived with the rest of his men, abandoning Sanje to the advancing enemy. When confronted in the Mess, he said, without batting an eyelid, that the fighting was 'too heavy'....

The Libyan infantrymen... were dispatched to Masaka barracks, while their Air Force counterparts were left at the Air Base in Entebbe.... They joined the forces waiting for the enemy in Kalisizo. Sure enough, no sooner had they arrived in Kalisizo, than the enemy descended upon the area in force. Our troops suffered heavy casualties, but nothing like the Libyans, who of course failed to understand the orders to withdraw, which were issued in Swahili.

The following morning, trooping into Masaka barracks after the fall of Kalisizo, they were a sad sight. It was pitiful to watch those who were lucky to escape without injuries unloading their wounded and dead colleagues off their small trucks. The rate at which we were losing ground was alarming. After the swift fall of Kalisizo, I had no doubt the enemy woild soon be on the outskirts of Masaka. I called an impromptu meeting to discuss our next course of action. Lieutenant.Colonel Abdallatif and his sub-commanders were invited to attend the meeting, which was basically held to decide whether to defend Masaka until reinforcements arrived from Kampala, or to abandon the town to the enemy. It was agreed to defend the town and the different units were duly allocated their roles. Suicide Regiment was to defend an area that covered Mutukula Road, Mbarara Road and Bukakata-Nyendo Road. The regiment was also charged with blocking the hill that housed the television mast. Other troops from the First Infantry Brigade and Chui Regiment under the command of Major Zziwa were assigned to the second defence axis - Buwala, Kitovu and the road to Bukakata, facing a large tea estate behind Kitovu hill. Before we could move to our assigned areas, mortar and rocket fire started landing in our barracks, forcing us to rush up the slopes of Boma Hill near the hospital and prison....

Bitter divisions had cropped up within the rank and file. Most senior officers, especially those of Sudanese and Congolese origin, plus a few from West Nile, had abandoned all pretence of patriotism... Another problem was that most units felt that it was Suicide Regiment who had sparked off the war by attacking Tanzania. The general feeling was that the defence of Masaka and indeed the rest of the country was Suicide's responsibility. Sure enough, a few days after we had divided up the defence of Masaka, Chui Regiment and the First Infantry Brigade deserted their assigned areas and went off to Lukaya, 40 kilometres away.

Information about Chui's desertion seems to have quickly got to the enemy, for before we could make fresh arrangements to defend Masaka from that side, the enemy attacked through Kitovu, Nyendo and the pineapple farm, all of which were behind our backs, before descending on Masaka in force. We knew that we were outnumbered.... We marched out of Masaka.... From the hill, we watched our beautiful Masaka being mercilessly set upon in an orgy of destruction....

After the fall of Masaka, news items on Radio Tanzania in Luganda, English, Lugbara and Kakwa began hitting the Ugandan airwaves, seriously denting the morale of the soldiers. Among the senior officers, especially at the Army General Headquarters, there was total panic. Most, immediately began looking for ways of bringing the war to an immediate end.... The senior officers, led by Sule, decided to depose Amin. With Amin out of the way, they reasoned, they could enter into negotiations with both the Tanzanian government and the hundreds of Ugandan exiles who had joined them. This information was passed on to the frontline. We were ordered to prepare white flags to raise in case the mission was successful. Arrangements were made for the senior officers to meet Amin...and brief him about what already turned into a very fluid situation. Though Amin agreed to meet the officers, he was suspicious of their intentions and the motive of the meeting. Word had spread that there was a general loss of morale among the fighting forces and that a section of the Army High command would rather throw him out of office and negotiate with the invaders than die fighting or go into exile. Amin sensed that the night meeting could end in a gunfight leading to a coup. He therefore took preemptive steps... (and) did not come out of his heavily fortified bedroom.... (After) Gore arrived... accompanied by a platoon of paratroopers... Amin came out of his room....

Amin called for more loyalty and commitment from his officers. He told them that he appreciated the fact that the enemy's propaganda machine had dealt a major blow to the morale of the soldiers, but urged them to go back to work. It was during that same meeting that it was declared a crime to listen to Radio Tanzania....

At the same time, it was easy to run away, for there was no organisation among the fighters. No one in the high command seemed to be bothered by the rate at which soldiers were abandoning their sectors and nothing was done to stop the mass desertion...

The fall of Masaka clearly had the effect on the troops on both sides. While the Tanzanians' morale was higher than ever, ours hit an all-time low. We were simply in total disarray. The ease with which our troops on the Masaka-Kampala axis fell prey to the enemy was testimony to this....

The enemy forces positioned in Bukomansimbi decided to outflank us, attacking at six in the morning and engaging us in a bitter fight that lasted till six in the evening... Two Tanzanian soldiers had been captured.... We interrogated the captives only to discover that one of them, who identified himself as Wasiwasi, was a 15-year-old schoolboy... Having seen the type of soldiers we were fighting, the morale of my soldiers rose. There was a feeling that if we could not throw such small boys off Ugandan soil, we would at least not allow Sembabule to fall to schoolchildren. As a commander, I was happy, but the parent in me was horrified. I could not imagine my son, Paul, who was then only 12, carrying a gun and attacking a band of trained, battle-hardened soldiers like the group under my command. I could not imagine an army full of children winning a war against us....

While we continued to hold Sembabule, the enemy forces operating along the Masaka-Kampala axis relentlessly continued their advance towards the capital. It was then that real mobilisation of troops for the defence of Kampala began. Even among the foreign legions that had long become our national army, the word being passed was that the enemy had to be repulsed....

Sule's death was the turning point... The minute the news trickled down to the troops, the entire command and organisational structure in Lukaya simply fizzled out. Foot soldiers and officers alike abandoned their locations and fled, making the enemy's advance to Kampala a cakewalk. Suicide Regiment now lost all communication with other fighting forces. We were left with no option but to dig in and continue defending our location in Sembabule.

On the afternoon of April 11, 1979, I gave one of my platoons orders to engage a company of Tanzanian soldiers who were reported to have pitched camp at the nearby sub-county headquarters. I was, however, forced to put my plans off when a warrant officer II called Constantine approached me and advised me not to send out any soldiers before listening to the five o'clock news bulletin on Radio Uganda.

The waiting was tense. We smoked continuously. At five o'clock, we gathered around the radio. A voice I first heard in 1965 was speaking - the deep, unmistakable voice of Major-General David Oyite Ojok.

Amin had been overthrown."

15. Julius Nyerere, quoted by Peter Jennings, ABC Evening News, New York, November 1978. See also *Daily News*, Dar es salaam, Tanzania, November 1978.

16. Ali Mazrui, "Mwalimu's Rise to Power," in the *Daily Nation*, Nairobi, Kenya, October 17, 1999; A. Mazrui, "Nyerere and I," in *Voices*, Africa Resource Center, October 1999; "Africa's Mwalimu: Ali Mazrui Pays Tribute to Julius Nyerere," in *Worldview Magazine*, Washington, D.C., Vol. 12, No. 4, Fall 1999.

17. Julius Nyerere, quoted by Michael T. Kaufman, "Julius Nyerere of Tanzania Dies; Preached African Socialism to the World," in *The New York Times*, p. B1, October 15, 1999.

18. Julius Nyerere, in his introduction to *Yoweri Museveni: What is Africa's Problem?* (Minneapolis: University of Minnesota Press, 2001).

19. Ibid.

20. James Kahigirizi, quoted by Brian Barron, "Idi Amin's Legacy of Terror," on BBC News: Africa, July 27, 1999.

21. Henry Kyemba, "Reign of Terror: Amin's Unorthodox Methods," in *New Vision*, Kampala, Uganda, April 11, 1999.

22. Alfred Wasike, "Kampala to Host 14 Heads of State," in *New Vision*, Kampala, Uganda, March 8, 2002.

See also Mahmood Mamdani, *Imperialism and Fascism in Uganda* (Lawrenceville, New Jersey: Africa World Press, 1986); Dan Barnett and Ray Wooding, *Uganda Holocaust* (Grand Rapids, Michigan: Zondervan Publishing House, 1980); David Gwyn, *Idi Amin: Death Light of Africa* (New York: Little Brown & co., 1977); Festo Kivengere, *I Love Idi Amin: The Story of Triumph Under Fire in the Midst of Suffering and Persecution in Uganda* (Marshall, Morgan and Scott).

I met and talked to Festo Kivengere, an Anglican minister, in the summer of 1977 in Grand Rapids, Michigan, USA, when he spoke at a Christian Reformed Church in the city during his tour of the United States, recounting the horrors under Idi Amin's regime. Members of the congregation were shocked when they heard him describe the atrocities - sometimes in graphic detail - perpetrated by Amin (including canniblaism) and his henchmen. As a minister, hardly anyone who heard him speak doubted his testimony. I doubt any did.

As a Tanzanian living in Grand Rapids during that time, where I had also attended Aquinas College, and as a former news reporter in Tanzania who was there when Amin's forces invaded our country more than once in 1972; I had no reason to question Kivengere's credibility or the veracity of his testimony. I already knew of the atrocities he described, when I was still a reporter at the *Daily News* in Dar es Salaam, Tanzania, and only helped confirm what he told his American audience. Unfortunately, a number of African students in Grand Rapids admired Amin for needling the white man who had oppressed blacks for so long, while totally ignoring Amin's brutalities to the point of denial. Fortunately, none of them attended Kivengere's lecture.

Chapter Ten

1. John Marcum, quoted by William Blum, "Angola 1975 to 1980s: The Great Powers Poker Game," in W. Blum, *Killing Hope: U.S. Military and CIA Interventions since World War II* (Monroe, Maine: Common Courage Press, 1995).

2. "Hearings Before the House Select Committee on Intelligence (The Pike Committee)" published in *CIA: The Pike Report* (Nottingham, England, 1977), p. 199. See also Angola in *The New York Times*, September 25, 1975; *The New York Times*, December 19, 1975.

3. William Blum, *Killing Hope: U.S. Military and CIA Interventions since World War II*, op. cit.; *The Guardian*, London, August 15, 1986; *The Times*, London, August 4, 1986, p. 10.

4. Wayne S. Smith, "Dateline Havana: Myopic Diplomacy," in *Foreign Policy*, Washington, D.C., Fall 1982, p. 170.

5. Gerald Bender, in "Hearings Before the Subcommittee on Africa of the House Committee on International Relations," May 25, 1978, p. 7.

6. W. Blum, *Killing Hope: U.S. Military and CIA Interventions since World War II*, op. cit.

7. *The New York Times*, January 17, 1993, p. 5.

8. Henry A. Kissinger, *Years of Renewal* (New York: Simon & Schuster, 2000).

9. Piero Gleijeses, quoted by Andrew Buncombe, "CIA Angola Lies Exposed 25 Years Later: CIA 'Ran Covert Missions' to Stop Communist Coup," in *The Independent*, London, April 5, 2001; Anthony Boadle, "U.S. Lied About Cuban Role in Angola - Historian," Reuters, April 1, 2002; Piero Gleijeses, *Conflicting Missions: Havana, Washington and Africa, 1959 - 1976* (Charlotte, North Carolina: University of North Carolina Press, 2002).

10. Nathaniel Davis, quoted by Andrew Buncombe, "CIA Angila Lies Exposed 25 Years Later," op. cit.

11. Piero Gleijeses, quoted by Anthony Boadle, "U.S. Lied About Cuban Role - Historian," op. cit.

12. Robert Hultslander, CIA station chief in Angola from

August to November 1975, quoted by Andrew Buncombe, "CIA Angola Lies Exposed 25 Years Later," op. cit.

13. A. Hultslander, quoted by Jim Lobe, "Cuba Followed U.S. into Angola, Secret Papers Reveal," in *Imagen*, May 1, 2002.

14. James Schlesinger, ibid.

15. Julius K. Nyerere, "America and Southern Africa," in *Foreign Affairs*, Vol. 55, No. 4, July 1977, pp. 671 - 684.

Chapter Eleven

1. Kwame Nkrumah, *Africa Must Unite* (New York: Frederick A. Praeger, 1963).

2. Ibid., pp. 214 - 215; Ali A. Mazrui, *Towards A Pax Africana* (London: Weidenfeld & Nicolson, 1967), p. 70.

3. Julius Nyerere, quoted by Ali A. Mazrui, ibid., p. 71; cited by Richard Cox, *Pan-Africanism in Practice: An East African Study* (London: Oxford University Press, 1964), p. 77.

4. Basil Davidson, *Black Star: A View of the Life and Times of Kwame Nkrumah* (London: Allen Lane, 1973); cited by Geoffrey Mmari, "The Legacy of Nyerere," in Colin Legum and Geoffrey Mmari, editors, *Mwalimu: The Influence of Nyerere* (Trenton, New Jersey: Africa World Press, 1995), pp. 179 - 180.

5. Julius K. Nyerere, "Relations with the West," in J. K. Nyerere, *Freedom and Socialism: A Selection from Writings and Speeches 1965 - 1967* (Dar es Salaam, Tanzania: Oxford University Press, 1968), p. 50.

6. Jaramogi Oginga Odinga, *Not Yet Uhuru: An Autobiography* (London: Heinemann, 1967); Geoffrey Mmari, ibid., p. 175.

7. Julius Nyerere, in "The Heart of Africa: Interview with Julius Nyerere on Anti-Colonialism," in *New Internationalist*, Issue 309, January-February 1999.

8. Ahmed Ben Bella, cited by Jorge G. Castaneda, *Companero: The Life and Death of Che Guevara* (New York: Alfred A. Knopf, 1997), p. 279.

9. Ben Bella, in an interview with Jorge G. Castaneda, Geneva, Switzerland, November 4, 1995, ibid., p. 277.

10. Julius K. Nyerere, "A United States of Africa," in *The Journal of Modern African Studies*, Vol. I, No. 1, March 1963.

11. Nyerere, at the OAU summit, Cairo, Egypt, July 1964, quoted by Colin Legum, "The Goal of an Egalitarian Society," in Colin Legum and Geoffrey Mmari, editors, *Mwalimu: The Influence of Nyerere*, op. cit., p. 191.

12. Ali A. Mazrui, "Nkrumahism and the Triple Heritage: Out of the Shadows," Third Lecture, Aggrey-Fraser-Guggisberg

Memorial Lectures, University of Ghana, Legon, Accra, 2002.

13. Ibid.

14. Kwame Nkrumah, *Africa Must Unite*, revised edition, op. cit.

15. Nelson Mandela, *Long Walk to Freedom: The Autobiography of Nelson Mandela* (New York: Little, Brown & Co., 1994).

16. Kwame Nkrumah, *Dark Days in Ghana* (London: Zed Books, 1968).

Chapter Twelve

1. Julius K. Nyerere, quoted by Michael T. Kaufman, "Julius Nyerere of Tanzania Dies; Preached African Socialism to the World, " in *The New York Times*, October 15, 1999, p. B1.

2. Nyerere in an interview in December 1998 with the *New Internationalist*, January-February 1999.

3. Oginga Odinga, *Not Yet Uhuru* (London: Longmans, 1967).

4. Kenneth Kaunda, *Zambia Shall Be Free* (London: Heinemann, 1962).

5. Kaunda, quoted in Colin Legum and John Drysdale, *Africa Contemporary Record: Annual Survey and Documents 1968 - 1969* (London: Africa Research Ltd., 1969), p. 250. See also *Times of Zambia*, Lusaka, Zambia, September 1968.

6. Nyerere, quoted in *Africa Contemporary Record*, ibid., p. 220.

7. Nyerere, in an address to the Tanganyika Legislative Council (LEGCO), Dar es Salaam, Tanganyika, October 22, 1959.

8. David Martin, "A Candle on Kilimanjaro," in *Southern African Features*, December 21, 2001.

9. Nelson Mandela, *Long Walk to Freedom: The Autobiography of Nelson Mandela* (New York: Little Brown & Co., 1995).

10. Yoweri Museveni, in Elizabeth Kanyogonya, editor, *Yoweri K. Museveni: What Is Africa's Problem?: Foreword by Mwalimu Julius K. Nyerere* (Minneapolis: University of Minnesota Press, 2000); Museveni, cited by Lara Santoro, "West Cheers Uganda's One-Man Show," in *The Christian Science Monitor*, March 2, 1999; Peter Graff, "Ex-Leninist Leads Uganda to Prosperity: Single-Party Rule Troubles Free-Market Admirers," in *The Boston Globe*, December 7, 1997, p. A44:

"Museveni is a guerrilla leader who spent much of his life in exile in socialist Tanzania and received his education at the University of Dar es Salaam, then a hotbed of post-colonial leftist radicalism. At the time, Tanzania's patriarch, Julius Nyerere, was a hero to most students for implementing the policy of 'ujamaa'

(African socialism)... Museveni still considers himself a disciple of Nyerere."

See also Museveni, in Godfrey Mwakikagile, *Economic Development in Africa* (Commack, New York: Nova Science Publishers, Inc., 1999), p. 142.

11. Che Guevara, *Congo Diaries.*

12. P. W. Botha, in *Africa Contemporary Record*, op.cit., p. 291.

13. Walter Rodney, *How Europe Underdeveloped Africa* (Dar es Salaam, Tanzania: Tanzania Publishing House, 1972).

14. Colin Legum, "The Goal of an Egalitarian Society," in Colin Legum and Geoffrey Mmari, editors, *Mwalimu: The Influence of Nyerere* (Trenton, New Jersey: Africa World Press, 1995), p. 187.

15. Philip Ochieng', "There Was Real Freedom in Mwalimu's Day," in *The East African*, Nairobi, Kenya, October 20, 1999.

16. "In Memory of Karim Essack," the International Emergency Committee (IEC) to Defend the Life of Dr. Abimael Guzman, London, October 1997.

17. Keith B. Richburg, *Out of America: A Black Man Confronts Africa* (New York: Basic Books, 1998).

18. Philip Ochieng', *I Accuse the Press: An Insider's View of the Media and Politics in Africa* (Initiatives Press: ACT Press).

19. Harvey Glickman, "Tanzania: From Disillusionment to Guarded Optimism," in *Current History: A Journal of Contemporary World Affairs*, May 1997, p. 217.

20. Francis Kasoma, *The Press and Multiparty Politics in Africa* (University of Tampere); F.P.Kasoma, *Communication Policies in Botswana, Lesotho, and Swaziland* (University of Tampere); F.P. Kasoma, *Communication Policies in Zambia* (Tempereen Yliopisto); F.P. Kasoma, *The Press in Zambia: The Development, Role, and Control of National Newspapers in Zambia 1906 - 1983* (Multimedia Publications).

21. Hadji Konde, *Press Freedom in Tanzania* (Nairobi, Kenya: Eastern Africa Publications).

22. Clement Ndulute, *The Poetry of Shaaban Robert* (Dar es Salaam, Tanzania: University of Dar es Salaam Press, 1994).

23. Godfrey Mwakikagile, *Economic Development in*

Africa (Commack, New York: Nova Science Publishers, Inc., 1999).

24. Godfrey Mwakikagile, *The Modern African State: Quest for Transformation* (Huntington, New York: Nova Science Publishers, Inc., 2001).

25. Godfrey Mwakikagile, *Africa and the West* (Huntington, New York: Nova Science Publishers, Inc., 2000).

26. Godfrey Mwakikagile, book review of George B.N. Ayittey, *Africa in Chaos* (New York: St. Martin's Press, 1998), on Amazon.com, December 2001.

27. Jonathan Power, TFF Jonathan Power Columns, "Lament for Independent Africa's Greatest Leader," London, October 6, 1999.

28. Julius Nyerere, in "Julius Nyerere Press Conference," Dar es Salaam, AFP, 14 March 1995.

29. Nyerere, remarks to the World Bank, quoted in the *Sunday Times*, October 3, 1999.

30. Nyerere, in the *Sunday Independent*, Johannesburg, October 17, 1999.

31. Jomo Kenyatta, quoted in *Africa Contemporary Record*, op. cit., p. 157. See also *Kenya Weekly News*, Nairobi, Kenya, June 21, 1968:

"How will KPU contest the elections if it is not allowed to be organised on a country-wide basis like KANU?... In its brief, but turbulent history, Kenya has had numerous political parties, which in many cases died a natural death. Let KPU follow them into the grave if the Wananchi do not support its programme after a fair and full hearing of its case...." See also, same quotation, in *Africa Contemporary Record*, ibid.

32. Mundia Kamau, "A Nation in Distress," in *Mashada Daily*, Nairobi, Kenya, November 13, 1999.

33. James Mpinga, "With Mwalimu Gone, Free Bread for Butiama Children Goes Too," in *The East African*, Nairobi, Kenya, November 3, 1999.

34. "Newsweek," October 1999.

35. Ali A. Mazrui, "Nyerere and I," in *Voices*, Africa Resource Center, October 1999.

36. Jimmy Carter, on Nyerere's death, quoted in "Tanzania: Former President Julius Nyerere Dies at 77," in *UN Wire*, New

York, October 15, 1999.

37. Ali A. Mazrui, "Mwalimu's Rise to Power," in *Daily Nation*, Nairobi, Kenya, October 17, 1999; "Africa's Mwalimu: Ali Mazrui Pays Tribute to Julius Nyerere," in *Worldview Magazine*, Washington, D.C., Vol. 12, No. 4, Fall 1999.

38. Ali A. Mazrui, *On Heroes and Uhuru-Worship: Essays: Independent Africa* (London: Longmans, 1967).

39. Nyerere, in an interview with James McKinley, "Tanzania's Nyerere Looks back: Many Failures, and One Big Success - Bringing A Nation to Life," in *International Herald Tribune*, September 2, 1996. See also Godfrey Mwakikagile, *Economic Development in Africa*, op. cit., p. 62. As Nyerere stated:

"I felt that these little countries in Africa were really too small, they would not be viable - the Tanganyikas, the Rwandas, the Burundis, the Kenyas. My ambition in East Africa was really never to build a Tanganyika. I wanted an East African federation. So what did I succeed in doing? My success is building a nation out of this collection of tribes."

40. Olusegun Obasanjo, at Nyerere's funeral, Dar es Salaam, Tanzania, quoted by Susan Linnee, "Tanzanian Leader's Funeral Marks End of Era," Associated Press (AP), October 22, 1999.

41. "Look Beyond Mobutu, Nyerere Tells Zaireans," in Features Africa Network, Africa Online, March 12, 1997.

42. Julius K. Nyerere, "Africa Must Unite," his speech in Accra, Ghana, March 6, 1997, marking Ghana's 40th independence anniversary; edited excerpts published by New Africa International Network (NAIN): Debate: www.nain.unitedafricastar.com/html/africa.htm. See also *Daily Graphic*, Accra, Ghana, March 1997; *Daily News*, Dar es salaam, Tanzania, March 1997.

ABOUT THE AUTHOR

GODFREY MWAKIKAGILE, from Tanzania, is the author of a number of books including *Economic Development in Africa*; Africa *and the West*; *The Modern African State: Quest for Transformation*; *Ethnic Politics in Kenya and Nigeria*; *Military Coups in West Africa since the Sixties*.

His forthcoming books include *Africa after Independence: Realities of Nationhood*; *Civil Wars in Rwanda and Burundi: Conflict Resolution in Africa*; *The Angolan Civil War: Its Cold War Origins and Ethnic Dimensions*; *Quest for Peace and Stability in Africa: Are Colonial Boundaries Outmoded? Africa since the Sixties: Algeria to Zimbabwe: A Political History*; *Black Conservatives*; *Conservatives and Black America*; *Resistance to Racial Equality: Options for Black America*.

He specializes in African affairs, international and race relations.

Index

African unity, African union, one-party system, one-party states, independence, economic development, modernization, national unity, Mau Mau, tribalism, nationalism, Pan-Africanism, Pan-African Congress-USA, Wayne State University, Detroit, Grand Rapids, Michigan, David Mabunda, Ahmadu Bello, Ojukwu, Azikiwe, Awolowo, Organization of African Unity, OAU, Nyerere, Nkrumah, multiparty system, democracy, national development, multiparty politics, consensus building, devolution, regionalism, regional integration, federation, confederation, alliances, multiparty democracy, Mkapa, Colin Legum, Mazrui, Hackman Owusu-Agyemang, John Kufuor, Adam Hochschild, Ronald Aminzade, Haroub Othman, George Shire, Reginald Mhango, Ann Talbot, Jorge Castaneda, Gamal Nkrumah, Samir Amin, Ikaweba Bunting, Salim Ahmed Salim, Sam Amoo, Tanzania, Angola, Mozambique, South Africa, Ghana, Nigeria, Uganda, Zimbabwe, Amin, Obote, Biafra, Katanga, Tshombe, Albert Kalonji, Lumumba, Joseph Okito, Kasavubu, Maurice Mpolo, Mobutu, Buganda, Mutesa, Kabaka, Zambia, Barotse Province, Barotseland, nation building, national disintegration, Berlin Conference, Nicephore Soglo, Benin, Dahomey, Rwanda, Burundi, Hutu, Tutsi, Sierra Leone, Liberia, Somalia, Foday Sankoh, Kenya, Banda, Kanyama Chiume, Yatuta Chisiza, Hubert Maga, Igbos, Hausa-Fulani, Hausa, Fulani, Balewa, Obasanjo, Shagari, Gowon, Babangida, Abacha, Soyinka, Kambona, Kawawa, Abiola, Yoruba, Congo, Congo-Brazzaville, Laurent Kabila, Joseph Kabila, King Leopold II, Christopher Mtikila, Chama Cha Mapinduzi, CCM, Tanganyika African National Union, TANU, KANU, KADU, Afro-Shirazi Party, Sudan, Sekou Toure, Guinea, Kenyatta, indoctrination, ideology, Malcolm X, Thomas Sowell, Harold Cruse, Alexander Hamilton, Philadelphia convention, Articles of Confederation, unitary state, Arthur Creech Jones, ujamaa, African socialism, Modibo Keita, Mali, Arusha Declaration, Common Man's Charter, Uganda People's Congress, central planning, socialism, capitalism, communism, decentralization, Soviet Union, Soviets, Peter the Great, colonialism, Mboya, Europe, Charity Ngilu, Moi, United States, CIA, China, Eisenhower, Laurence Devlin, John Reader, Sidney Gottlieb, France, Rhodesia, South Africa, Belgium, Ludo de Witte, Allen Dulles, Mandela, Olympio, Togo, Eyadema, Algeria, Felix Houphouet-Boigny, Henry Konan Bedie, Nicholas Grunitzky, OAU, Tanganyika, Egypt, Zanzibar, Ronald Ngala, Castro, Cuba, Mwinyi, North Korea, UDI, Namibia, Ian Smith, apartheid, African National Congress, Mugabe, Evariste Kimba, Tshombe, Akintola, Ironsi, Ho Chin Mihn, Franklin Williams, Gowon, Germany, West Germany, East Germany, Canada, Jews, Middle East, Libya, Nasser, Kaunda, Britain, Samora Machel, Masie Nguema, Equatorial Guinea, Bokassa, Central African Republic, Ethiopia, Oromo, Haile Selassie, Somalia, Mengistu, Guinea-Bissau, Niger, Mali, Chad, Upper Volta, Savimbi, Ansumane Mane, Muammar al-Qaddafi, Shona, Ndebele, Kenya, RENAMO, FRELIMO, MPLA, UNITA, FNLA, Habre, Russia, AIDS, Revolutionary United Front, Charles Taylor, Eritrea, Lissouba, Sassou-Nguesso, Senegal, Casamance Province, Comoros, Museveni, Lord's Resistance Army, East African Community, ECOWAS, SADC, Ben Bella, Lloyd George, Woodrow Wilson, Edward Twining, Zanaki, Butiama, Musoma, Eleanor Roosevelt, Sukuma, Johann Fichte, Hitler, Isa Shivji, Mtemvu, Amir H. Jamal, Christopher Kasanga Tumbo, Mtaki, Kamaliza, Mwakangale, Wambura, Okello, Lyndon B. Johnson, Frank Carlucci, Kennedy, Hanga, Civic United Front, Cold War, World War I, World War II, slavery, racism, West Germany, East Germany, capitalism, communism, socialism, federation, confederation, Karume, Babu, Umma Party, Ann Talbot, Marxism, Trotskytes, Marxist-Leninists, Che Guevara, Castro, Vietnam, Iron Curtain, Harriman, Dean Rusk, Wachuku, Zanzibar revolution, mutiny, United States, Portugal, Warsaw Pact, Czechoslovakia, Gulf States, Oman, Liberia, Mondlane, Pan-Africanist Congress, Sobukwe, ZANU ZAPU, Neto, Savimbi, Holden Roberto, Makonde, Chipande, Mueda, Simango, Kavandame, MANU, UDENAMO, Marcelino dos Santos, UNAMU, Nyasaland, Malawi, TPDF, Gwambe, Nkomo, Sithole, Mahluza, Bowles, Santos, Chagonga, Milinga, Thomas Byrne, Mmole, Philemon Sarungi, Musambachime, Botswana, Richard Coggins, Realpolitik,

Malaysia, Aden, South Arabia, Ken Flower, Afrifa, Harold Wilson, P.W. Botha, NIBMAR, Muzorewa, David Owen, Andrew Young, Chirau, Patriotic Front, Joseph Garba, Chiluba, John Kamau, Morgan Tsvangirai, Getrude Mongella, Seychelles, Joseph Kabila, Gabon, Ivory Coast, Oliver Lyttelton, George Ayittey, Shagari, Niger Delta, Ogoni, Ijaw, Ken Saro-Wiwa, Christopher Clepham, Jos, Kano, Aburi, BBC, Israel, Singapore, Kagera, Israelis, Kyemba, Edward Heath, Amin, Mossad, M16, Nimeiri, Jack Anderson, Bernard Rwehururu, Kakwa, John Marcum, Soviet Union, Soviets, Kissinger, Donald Rickard, William Colby, Wayne Smith, Havana, Gerald Bender, Thomas Byrne, Gulf Oil, William Blum, Reagan, Piero Gleijeses, Nathaniel Davis, James Schlesinger, Basil Davidson, Oginga Odinga, Jerry Rawlings, Modibo Keita, Group of Six, East African federation, Kigoma, Leopoldville, Elisabethville, Stanleyville, Simba rebellion, Pierre Mulele, Kwilu rebellion, Njenga Njoroge, Kenya People's Union, KANU, Alice Lenshina, Kapwepwe, Kaunda, Lumpa Church, Harry Nkumbula, Sixth Pan-African Congress, Nkumbula, Maluniko Mundia, Reuben Kamanga, Ginwala, Mbeki, Chissano, Tanganyika Legislative Council, LEGCO, David Martin, Olof Palme, Samora Machel, Nujoma, Pablo Ribalta, Soumialot, Rodney, Claude Ake, Okwudiba Nnoli, Mahmood Mamdani, Shamuyarira, Chikerema, C.L.R. James, Padmore, Ngugi wa Thiong'o, Ayi Kwei Armah, Stokely Carmichael, Angela Davis, Black Panther Party, Jesse Jackson, Andrew Young, Philip Ochieng', Senghor, Karim Essack, Keith Richburg, Harvey Glickman, Jonathan Power, Warioba, Bryceson, Lucy Lameck, Omar Ali Juma, James Mpinga, Sammy Mdee, Jimmy Carter, EACSO, Lord Delamere, Ashanti, Bunyoro, Ankole, Busoga, Teso, Acholi, Arusha Declaration, Common Man's Charter, East African Airways, International Monetary Fund, World Bank, secession, separatists, irredentist movements

Printed in the United States
42394LVS00003B/9